UNAUTHORIZED ENTRY:
THE TRUTH ABOUT NAZI WAR CRIMINALS IN CANADA,
1946–1956

UNAUTHORIZED ENTRY

The Truth about Nazi War Criminals in Canada, 1946–1956

Howard Margolian

UNIVERSITY OF TORONTO PRESS
Toronto Buffalo London

© University of Toronto Press Incorporated 2000
Toronto Buffalo London

Printed in Canada

ISBN 0-8020-4277-5

Printed on acid-free paper

Canadian Cataloguing in Publication Data

Margolian, Howard
   Unauthorized entry : the truth about Nazi war criminals in Canada, 1946–1956

   Includes bibliographical references and index.
   ISBN 0-8020-4277-5

   1. War criminals – Canada.   2. War criminals – Germany.   3. Nazis – Canada.
   4. Refugees – Government policy – Canada.   5. Refugees – Europe.
   6. Canada – Emigration and immigration – Government policy – History –
   20th century.   I. Title.

   D803.M365 2000   325'.24'097109045   C99-932542-6

University of Toronto Press acknowledges the financial assistance to its publishing program of the Canada Council for the Arts and the Ontario Arts Council.

University of Toronto Press acknowledges the financial support for its publishing activities of the Government of Canada through the Book Publishing Industry Development Program (BPIDP).

Canadä

Contents

Acknowledgments

The research for this book spanned two continents, more than a dozen archives, and took a year to complete. Everywhere I went, my task was made easier by knowledgeable and enlightened archivists. While it is perhaps unfair to single out individuals, I must thank those people whose contributions were indispensable. As always, the staff at the National Archives in Ottawa offered expert advice, efficient service, and a pleasant environment in which to work. Isabelle Tessier, John Armstrong, and Ernie Fraser conducted their Access to Information reviews with all due speed, diligence, and fairness. Patricia Birkett allowed me to review a portion of the unprocessed papers of the Canadian Council of Churches. Myron Momryk provided helpful suggestions for researching the immigration to Canada of members of the 14th SS Division 'Galicia,' while Larry McNally did the same for the German scientists and technicians. All are public servants of the highest competence and integrity.

My research also benefited from the generosity of a number of private individuals. Vera Yuzyk gave me permission to review the papers of her late father, Senator Paul Yuzyk. David Matas granted me access to his submissions to the Deschenes Commission of Inquiry on War Criminals. Leah Toombs, court reporter with the Ontario Provincial Court (General Division) in Windsor, assembled the documents and rulings in the Grujicic case and sent them to me. Julian Hendy, of Yorkshire, United Kingdom, supplied me with key documents on Brigadier Fitzroy Maclean's screening commission. Christopher Amerasinghe, with whom it was my privilege to work while we were members of

Canada's war crimes prosecution unit, allowed me to probe his excellent memory for information about the Rauca case. All have my deepest gratitude.

I consider myself fortunate that *Unauthorized Entry* was read at the manuscript stage by Angelika Sauer and Reg Whitaker. As experts in the fields of immigration history and security policy, respectively, they provided invaluable comments that helped me to evaluate the evidence, clarify points of interpretation, and sharpen my arguments. The result is a much improved book. Of course, I am solely responsible for any errors.

Once again, it has been a pleasure to work with everyone at the University of Toronto Press. I am particularly grateful to Gerry Hallowell for taking a chance on the controversial subject of war criminals in Canada. I must also thank Barbara Tessman, whose editing has transformed a sow's ear of a manuscript into a silk purse of a book.

Finally, I owe more to my wife Randy than I can ever hope to put into words. She is my inspiration, my conscience, my soulmate. For these reasons, and many more, this book is hers.

UNAUTHORIZED ENTRY:
THE TRUTH ABOUT NAZI WAR CRIMINALS IN CANADA,
1946–1956

Introduction

Answers to the question of how Nazi war criminals gained admission to Canada remain elusive. What little Canadians know about the issue comes from one seriously flawed royal commission report[1] and from the dollops of misinformation that war crimes advocacy groups periodically dish out. The best that can be said about these sources is that they are one-sided; at their worst, they are pandering polemics. In the absence of any objective public discussion, it is little wonder that Canadians have long regarded their government's handling of the war crimes issue with suspicion and anger.

Unauthorized Entry is sure to make some people angry, too, though not for the same reasons. Readers expecting a familiar tale of government duplicity and incompetence will not find it here. In the first decade after the Second World War, nearly 1.5 million people emigrated to Canada. Almost two-thirds of them came from war-ravaged Europe.[2] Included in this mass of immigrants, according to the best estimates, were about 2,000 Nazi war criminals and collaborators,[3] or just over one-eighth of 1 per cent of the total number of new Canadians. Approximately three-quarters of these undesirables arrived here disguised as refugees. Yet the ratio of war criminals to refugees is almost as insignificant. Of the more than 150,000 European refugees who were admitted to Canada between 1946 and 1951,[4] only 1 per cent were suspected Nazi war criminals.

Canada's record at screening immigrants for war criminal or collaborationist backgrounds, while not unblemished, still redounds overwhelmingly to the country's credit. Between 1947 and 1956, approximately 15,000 would-be newcomers were denied Canadian visas because of their prior Nazi affiliations.[5] This means that out of a total of 17,000 of Hitler's former henchmen who tried to settle in Canada after the war, 88 per cent were rejected. By any standards of measurement, then, Canada was successful at preventing the large-scale influx of its most despicable wartime enemies.

Was the postwar screening of immigrants perfect? Of course not.[6] In the space of a few years after 1945, immigration to Canada, which over the previous decade and a half had been drastically curtailed, increased tenfold.[7] To deal with such a profound change in policy, new visa-issuing offices had to be opened, new regulations had to be written, and new procedures had to be formulated. Indeed, an entire immigration-screening system had to be developed almost from scratch. Like all new systems, the one created to deal with the mass of postwar immigrants had flaws. As was to be expected, it was only with time and experience that the flaws were detected and remedies devised.

The bureaucrats who designed the system of immigration screening and supervised its operation were similarly imperfect. Many held the social and political prejudices of the first half of the twentieth century. As a consequence, they sometimes allowed ethnic preferences or an excessive fear of communism to cloud their judgment.[8] Moreover, most had only the vaguest understanding of the inner workings of the Nazi machine. Accordingly, they were hard pressed to fashion immediately effective measures for detecting and weeding out war criminals. On the other hand, several had served in the Canadian armed forces during the two great wars of this century, and all were aware of the heinous crimes perpetrated by the enemy they had so recently fought and defeated.[9] Perhaps most importantly, some of the bureaucrats had previously administered Canada's wartime security apparatus, and thus were already sensitive to the dangers of Nazi infiltration.

How were two thousand Nazi war criminals and collaborators able to gain admission to Canada? That is the question *Unauthorized Entry* seeks to answer. To do so, it will be necessary to examine the postwar immigration-screening system in depth, to identify its strengths and weaknesses, and to understand the intentions behind it. It will also be necessary to assess the power and influence of the immigration lobby. Finally, in light of allegations that some ex-Nazis were smuggled into

Canada in secret Cold War operations, the role of western intelligence agencies will have to be addressed as well.

To truly understand the problem, however, one must go back to the days immediately following the termination of hostilities in Europe, to the unprecedented refugee crisis that confronted the western Allies. It was this crisis that provided Nazi war criminals and collaborators with the opportunity to escape justice and to seek new lives elsewhere. It was this crisis that led Canada to open its doors to mass immigration. And it was this crisis that determined the early character and effectiveness of Canada's immigration-screening system. It is with the postwar refugee crisis, then, that this book begins.

CHAPTER ONE

Escape

On 7 May 1945, at Allied military headquarters, German representatives signed the articles of their country's surrender. With a few strokes of a pen, the most destructive conflict in European history was ended. There was little time for celebration, however. The liberation of Europe from Nazi tyranny revealed a continent on the brink of social and economic collapse. Six years of war had reduced many cities to rubble, while the ebb and flow of battle had rendered large tracts of rural land uninhabitable. Amid the squalor of bombed-out buildings and unburied corpses, urban residents eked out a miserable existence, their ranks swollen by hungry and homeless people from the countryside. All that stood in the way of famine, disease, and civil unrest was the distribution of emergency aid by Allied military forces.

Jeopardizing the Allies' early relief efforts was a refugee crisis of unprecedented magnitude. According to some estimates, as many as twenty million Europeans were displaced by the Second World War. At least eight million were from the enemy side. Known as *Volksdeutsche*, ethnic Germans from eastern Europe had fled or been driven westward in the wake of Hitler's defeat. Despised by their former compatriots and barely tolerated by the western Allies, the Volksdeutsche roamed the roads of devastated Germany in search of food and shelter.[1]

Allied refugees posed an even greater problem. Comprising the nationals of every German-occupied country in Europe, their number exceeded eleven million. Some were recently liberated concentration-camp inmates. Others were the slave labourers who had kept Hitler's war machine running. There were also political detainees, resistance fighters, prisoners of war (POWs), and ordinary civilians. Regardless of how they got there, most of the refugees were concentrated in Germany, although sizeable contingents had found their way into Austria and Italy. Hungry, exhausted, and desperate, these unfortunate victims of war choked the roads, crowded relief distribution centres, and in general were an obstacle to the restoration of orderly conditions.[2]

Repatriation of refugees had been provided for in the inter-Allied agreements reached at Yalta. Though actuated by very different priorities, each party to the February 1945 accord was determined to fulfil its repatriation obligations. Worried that the predominantly eastern European refugees might coalesce into an anti-communist emigré community, the Soviets forcibly withdrew them from their zone of occupation. At the same time, Moscow demanded their return from the American, British, and French zones. Loath to assume the burden of caring for so many displaced persons, the western Allies complied. As a result, more than fifteen million eastern Europeans and Soviet citizens were repatriated during the summer and autumn of 1945. By the onset of winter, less than two million still remained in the West.[3]

The easing of Europe's refugee crisis in the space of a few months constituted the last great achievement of the wartime Anglo-American-Soviet alliance. The accomplishment was all the more remarkable in view of the chaos that reigned during the immediate postwar period. In the western zones of Allied-occupied Germany, a veritable hodge-podge of military and civilian organizations vied for control over refugee affairs. As was to be expected, the hundreds of thousands of enemy prisoners of war were the responsibility of the various occupation forces. Almost a million displaced civilians, on the other hand, had been entrusted to the care and supervision of the Intergovernmental Committee on Refugees (IGCR).[4] Established before the war to deal with the plight of persecuted Jews, IGCR had neither the mandate nor the means to undertake repatriation.[5] As for the remaining million or so civilian refugees, they came under the jurisdiction of a newer, relatively untried organization. Inaugurated in November 1943 with high hopes and much fanfare, the United Nations Relief and Rehabilitation Administration (UNRRA), unlike IGCR, had been envisioned primarily as a repatriation agency.[6]

Over the course of its mandate, UNRRA returned an additional one million displaced Europeans to their homes. Yet its tenure was marred by controversy. Most of the agency's problems were of its own making. For example, questionable staffing practices and poor management led to numerous cases of corruption and black marketeering. Its attention often diverted by scandal, UNRRA became increasingly ineffective. Things got so bad, in fact, that the agency was compelled to turn over many of its operations to Allied military forces.[7]

More damaging to UNRRA's credibility than either scandal or ineptitude was its blundering intrusion into the Cold War. After the initial wave of repatriation had subsided, those eastern European refugees who were left behind began to voice fears about returning home. To some degree, their fears were justified. Allied assurances of safe passage were in stark contrast to the brutal repression enveloping Soviet-dominated eastern Europe. However, it was also the case that the refugees' fears were being manipulated by people who had a clear conflict of interest. Using operatives within the refugee camps, certain anti-Soviet nationalist groups, some of which included known Nazi collaborators, wildly exaggerated the dangers of repatriation and relentlessly agitated against it.[8]

Caught between its mandate and its sympathy for the plight of the refugees, UNRRA acted in characteristic fashion: it did nothing. Emboldened by the agency's paralysis, the nationalists intensified their inflammatory rhetoric. The result was a hardening of anti-repatriation feeling among the refugees. Indeed, after 1945 most displaced eastern Europeans would not return to their native lands except by force. Not surprisingly, then, UNRRA's abdication of its responsibilities contributed greatly to the breakdown of the Yalta consensus on repatriation.[9]

To be fair, UNRRA was not alone in its drift away from mandatory repatriation. By 1946, the agency's stance was being publicly supported by western governments. Angered by the Soviets' refusal to permit free elections in eastern Europe, the United States became the first of the western Allies to repudiate Yalta's refugee provisions. In December 1945, the Americans announced the end of compulsory repatriation from their zone of occupation. Henceforth, the U.S. government declared, only Red Army soldiers would be obliged to return home. Britain quickly followed suit. Reluctant to confront the Soviets over what was seen in London as a marginal issue, the British nevertheless adopted Washington's line on repatriation.[10]

It was within the context of the breakdown of the Yalta consensus that problems first arose regarding Nazi war criminals and collaborators. While many of Hitler's erstwhile auxiliaries had been returned to their home countries during the first wave of repatriation, many others had not. Reliable estimates placed the number of collaborators who had originally found sanctuary in the Allied zones as high as several hundred thousand.[11] Of these, some – like the thirty thousand or so Cossacks who had been mobilized by the German Army – were caught in German uniform and therefore easily marked for repatriation.[12] Most collaborators, however, had disguised themselves as innocent refugees. Their uniforms and identity papers long discarded, their arrogant swagger replaced by a weary shuffle, these camouflaged Nazis were not easy to ferret out.

The western Allies knew that significant numbers of Nazi collaborators were hiding in the refugee camps. Their position was that such individuals should not be granted asylum, but rather ought to be surrendered to their countries of origin.[13] The problem was how best to distinguish between fugitive collaborators and legitimate refugees. On this point, there was substantial disagreement. The Soviet Union and its satellites wanted a say in determining which of their nationals were to be classified as collaborators. Fearing intimidation by Soviet-bloc repatriation officers, western countries wanted the decision to remain with UNRRA.[14]

It was not long before the simmering repatriation controversy boiled over. At a meeting of the United Nations' (UN) General Assembly in February 1946, the Soviet and Yugoslav delegations accused the western Allies of deliberately harbouring thousands of Hitler's former henchmen.[15] There is little question that these charges were politically motivated. After all, the refusal of so many of their citizens to be repatriated was a source of acute embarrassment to Soviet-bloc countries. What better way to divert attention from the real source of the problem than by portraying all who refused to return home as war criminals or collaborators?[16]

Notwithstanding the Soviets' less than noble motives, there was some truth to their allegations. With memories of the war still fresh, the presence of even a few ex-Nazis in the refugee camps would have been intolerable. Facing a public relations disaster, London and Washington had no choice but to instruct their UN delegations to negotiate with their Soviet-bloc counterparts.

After several weeks of diplomatic wrangling, a deal was worked out. It was agreed that anyone proven to have collaborated with the Nazis or to have committed war crimes would be considered ineligible for UNRRA assistance and would be liable to expulsion from the refugee camps. To sort out who was eligible and who was not, Allied military authorities were authorized to begin screening operations in the camps immediately, with rescreening to be conducted periodically. In the event that war criminals or collaborators were identified during these operations, it was further agreed that they would be handed over to their countries of origin.[17]

Crafted in the Byzantine environment of the UN, the deal was probably the best that could be expected. Soviet-bloc countries received assurances that any of their nationals proven to have given aid and comfort to the enemy would be returned to face justice. They were also granted permission to circulate lists of those of their nationals whom they suspected of having been collaborators.[18] In return, the western Allies retained the exclusive right to define what constituted collaboration. Hereafter, no refugees would be repatriated against their will unless there was compelling evidence that they had assisted the Nazis.[19]

While the compromise worked out at the UN dealt primarily with war criminals and collaborators, the eligibility criteria applied in the field were far more comprehensive. Enemy nationals, for example, were also considered ineligible for UNRRA assistance. This meant that a refugee found to be of Austrian, Bulgarian, German, Hungarian, Italian, or Romanian nationality could be evicted from the camps. Similarly, Volksdeutsche, regardless of whether they had been citizens of enemy or Allied countries, were subject to the rules governing enemy nationals – that is, they were ineligible for UNRRA assistance and could be expelled from the camps. Finally, non-Germans who had served in the German armed forces were also deemed to be ineligible.[20]

The process for determining eligibility comprised both civil and military investigations. Civil investigations were carried out by UNRRA and included, among other things, verification of a refugee's declared nationality. Military investigations were carried out by Allied military authorities and involved inquiries into a refugee's wartime activities. In the case of a refugee who was believed to have been a member of the German armed forces, military authorities began the screening, followed by UNRRA. In the case of a refugee who declared himself to have been a civilian throughout the war, the order of investigation was reversed.[21]

The aim of Allied military screening was to determine whether a refugee had been a collaborator, had perpetrated war crimes, had volunteered for service in the German armed forces, or was a Volksdeutsch. Toward that end, he or she was required to complete a questionnaire. Three pages in length, the questionnaire was designed to provide a complete history of the refugee's activities over the previous decade. Among the details sought were the number, nature, and duration of the applicant's memberships in youth, political, or military organizations, how and when he or she had arrived in Germany, and whether he or she was of ethnic German origin.[22] Taken by themselves, truthful answers to these questions would not have revealed whether the individual had committed war crimes. They would, however, have given some indication as to whether he or she had been a collaborator.

Upon completion of the questionnaire, the investigating military authorities checked it for accuracy against available sources. If the refugee passed these checks, a certificate was issued to that effect. He or she then had to present the certificate to representatives of UNRRA's Care and Eligibility Department, whose job it was to investigate refugees from the civil point of view. The first step in UNRRA's civil investigation also involved the completion of questionnaire.[23] While there was some overlap between this form and that used by military authorities, the UNRRA questionnaire focused primarily on refugees' nationality at birth and on any subsequent changes in their national status.[24] Obviously, its aim was to determine whether refugees were of enemy nationality.

Once the civil questionnaire had been completed, it was sent for review to a UNRRA screening panel. That body usually consisted of the director and assistant director of the camp of which the refugee was an inmate. It was their job to put him or her into one of three categories – eligible for UNRRA assistance, ineligible, or questionable.

The panel's conclusions were then forwarded to a regional UNRRA screening board. Like the panel, the screening board comprised the agency's civilian personnel, but it could, on request, include a military security officer. The regional board checked over the questionnaire and reviewed any supporting documents. Refugees who were classified as questionable would be interviewed at this time.[25]

After the regional board completed its inquiries, its findings and recommendations were sent to the appropriate military authorities. If the refugee were claiming that he had been a civilian during the war, he would, at this point, be subjected to military investigation. If he were an admitted former member of the German armed forces, Allied military authorities, having completed their investigation, would merely review the results of UNRRA's civil inquiries. In either case, the final decision as to the eligibility of the refugee rested with Allied military authorities.[26]

With its extensive background checks and built-in redundancies, the joint UNRRA-military system of refugee screening looked good on paper. In practice, however, it failed to live up to expectations. Some of the system's shortcomings can be traced to human frailty. Distracted by the monumental tasks of European relief and reconstruction, military authorities were often less than thorough in their conduct of screening operations.[27] The integrity of the screening process could also be undermined by corrupt or hostile UNRRA staff. Anecdotal and documentary evidence suggests that known Nazi sympathizers were occasionally able to procure jobs in the administration of refugee camps.[28] While the extent of such infiltration is unknown, it would have installed dubious individuals in positions from which they could sabotage screening operations.

Beyond the human factor, the main problem confronting UNRRA and Allied investigators was the paucity of reliable corroborating sources. In carrying out its investigations, UNRRA's ability to verify the information provided was contingent upon the nationality of the refugee in question. For example, if an individual were trying to conceal German or Austrian nationality, records confirming his or her true heritage would be extant and accessible. This was also the case if a person were trying to hide Volksdeutsch origins.[29] On the other hand, if the individual were of Bulgarian, Hungarian, Italian, or Romanian nationality, there was a good chance of escaping detection. Italian civil records were notoriously unreliable,[30] while those of the Soviet bloc were off limits.

Allied military authorities were as handicapped as their UNRRA counterparts by the paucity of corroborating documentation. Of the four criteria that military security officers were obliged to investigate, only two lent themselves to independent verification. Voluntary service in the German armed forces could be checked against captured German military records. Similarly, Volksdeutsch origins could be checked against captured German civil records. However, there were few effective means of determining whether an individual from eastern Europe or the Soviet Union had committed war crimes or collaborated with the enemy. Soviet-bloc countries generally did not grant access to their captured German records.[31] The only alternative was the UN's database of the names of suspected war criminals and collaborators. Impressive as the UN lists were in terms of sheer volume, their emphasis on German suspects rendered them almost useless as a source of allegations against other European nationals.[32]

The shortcomings of UNRRA-military screening were confirmed by an Allied fact-finding team. Known as the Special Refugee Commission (SRC), the British-sponsored team was originally intended as a kind of roving eligibility board. Its mandate was expanded, however, in the wake of a new controversy.[33] Specifically, SRC was ordered to look into allegations that British military authorities in Italy were harbouring Yugoslav collaborators.[34] Toward that end, the team was authorized to rescreen all displaced Yugoslavs in Allied custody. Armed with far-reaching investigative powers, SRC began its work late in January 1947.[35]

There was little chance that SRC would attempt a whitewash. For one thing, the British government had acknowledged that screening of the Yugoslavs had been less than thorough, and was publicly committed to making amends.[36] Secondly, the man selected to head the commission was eminently qualified for the job. As Britain's liaison to Marshal Tito during the war, Brigadier Fitzroy Maclean had witnessed first-hand some of the atrocities perpetrated in German-occupied Yugoslavia. In the process, he had developed an almost visceral hatred of Yugoslav collaborators.[37]

With the zealous Maclean at the helm, SRC demonstrated a commitment to screening rarely exhibited by Allied military authorities. Informed by both a detailed knowledge of events in wartime Yugoslavia and a healthy scepticism, the British investigators subjected the refugees' stories to intense scrutiny. Maclean's wartime contacts proved to be of great benefit in this regard. Owing to the brigadier's personal relationship with Tito, he was provided with ready access to Yugoslav records. The results of the mission were predictable. Of the hundreds of Yugoslavs who were rescreened, scores were determined to have collaborated with the Nazis and were removed from the refugee camps.[38]

The success of SRC demonstrated what could be accomplished with vigorous screening and access to reliable corroborating sources. Yet it also raised a disturbing question. If so many Nazi collaborators in Italy had initially evaded detection, how many more might have done so in Germany and Austria? The question was not hypothetical. By the time of the expiration of UNRRA's mandate, about 800,000 refugees still remained in the western zones of Germany. To be sure, almost 180,000 were Jews. But the remainder, totalling more than 600,000, were Balts, Poles, Ukrainians, and Yugoslavs. Further complicating matters, an undetermined number of the non-Jewish refugees were actually Volksdeutsche who were concealing their German origins.[39] The incidence of collaboration among all of these groups was known to have been significant.[40] With the exception of the Volksdeutsche, however, proving it would have been extremely difficult.[41] Thus, even after the repeated screening operations conducted by UNRRA and Allied military authorities, it must be reckoned that tens of thousands of Nazi war criminals and collaborators continued to find sanctuary in the refugee camps.

Concurrent with the end of the Maclean mission, the presence of former Nazis in the camps ceased to be UNRRA's concern.[42] Scheduled for closure at the end of June 1947, the beleaguered agency had already relinquished day-to-day operations to its replacement.[43] Designated the International Refugee Organization (IRO), the new body had a mandate very different from that of its predecessor. In recognition of the collapse of the Yalta consensus, the UN had abandoned the policy of compulsory repatriation. Resettlement was now the preferred option.

Accordingly, IRO's primary task was to find homes for those refugees who could not or would not return to their native lands.[44]

The new refugee organization was formally inaugurated on 1 July 1947. In keeping with IRO's mandate as a resettlement agency, its eligibility requirements were somewhat less stringent than those of UNRRA. For example, with the exception of Germans, enemy nationals were no longer ineligible for assistance. If an enemy national could prove he had retained civilian status during the war, he might be granted access to the refugee camps. Similarly, service in the German armed forces did not automatically render an enemy national ineligible. In such cases, the determining factor was whether his military service had been performed voluntarily or under duress. If a refugee could prove he had been conscripted by the Germans, he might be considered eligible for IRO assistance.[45]

Another factor that resulted in the easing of eligibility requirements was the end of mandatory repatriation. According to IRO's governing constitution, refugees could not be forced to return home unless the conditions that had compelled them to leave no longer prevailed. If refugees were able to demonstrate that they were still in danger of being persecuted because of their race, religion, nationality, or political opinions, they were entitled to remain under IRO care.[46] With the Iron Curtain descending over eastern Europe, it would not have taken much to convince IRO officials of the dangers of repatriation.

IRO's eligibility criteria reflected two fundamental changes in international opinion on the refugee question. First, they signified the West's desire to help resettle people who were seen more as Cold War exiles than as Second World War refugees. Second, they were indicative of the uneasiness with which many had come to regard UNRRA eligibility criteria. The basis for denying assistance to refugees, it was felt, should be individual behaviour, not an immutable characteristic like nationality or ethnic background. The one exception was the continued ineligibility of German nationals. In the case of the Germans, however, IRO's hard line seemed to be based more on common sense than on any residual wartime prejudice. After all, persons who had a record of German citizenship and residence going back prior to 1945 could not reasonably claim to be refugees in their own country.[47]

IRO's unforgiving policy toward German nationals was relaxed only slightly for their ethnic German brethren. Volksdeutsche, it will be remembered, had been ineligible for UNRRA assistance. Under the new organization's rules, most remained ineligible.[48] Indeed, the only group of ethnic Germans whom IRO would initially consider helping were the Mennonites from the southern USSR.

The disqualification of most Volksdeutsche from IRO (and UNRRA) assistance was based on the perception that their communities had served as Nazi fifth columns during the war. This perception had some basis in fact. Throughout eastern Europe and the Soviet Union, ethnic Germans had been mobilized for Hitler's war effort in substantial numbers. Though many were simply drafted into the German armed forces, many others volunteered to serve. Some found their way into auxiliary police units that have been linked to the most horrific atrocities of the war. In recognition of their stalwart service, many of these same Volksdeutsche were rewarded with German citizenship before the termination of hostilities.[49]

Judging by their rates of naturalization and service in the German armed forces, the Mennonites appear to have had a greater affinity for the Third Reich than other Volksdeutsche. Nonetheless, IRO made an exception for them. There were two reasons. First, the Mennonites had experienced years of religious persecution at the hands of Soviet authorities. Second, they claimed, convincingly, that their service to the Nazis had been rendered under duress.

Persecution by the Soviets was a powerful argument, but sympathy for the Mennonites evaporated with the emergence of contradictory evidence about their wartime activities. In the course of screening them for eligibility, IRO discovered that their claims of duress had been greatly exaggerated. Many Mennonites, it turned out, had been willing servants of the Nazi regime. As a result, IRO tightened up its eligibility criteria for Volksdeutsche. Thereafter, Mennonites could still apply for IRO assistance, but the onus would be on them to prove that their German naturalization had been involuntary or their service in the German armed forces conscripted.[50]

If IRO was more lenient than UNRRA on the question of enemy nationality, it was actually stricter in its treatment of Nazi war criminals and collaborators. War criminals were, by definition, considered ineligible for the organization's assistance. Included in IRO's definition were persons who had aided the enemy in the persecution of Allied civilians. Also ineligible were collaborators, even when there was no evidence that they had personally ordered or participated in atrocities. For example, the holding of cabinet or other senior positions in a Nazi puppet government was considered by IRO to be prima facie evidence of collaboration. Furthermore, leaders of political movements that had been hostile to Allied governments during the war, even if they had not collaborated with the enemy, were also deemed to be ineligible.[51]

One group of Nazi collaborators that attracted considerable attention from IRO eligibility officers were former members of the military wing of the SS, known as the Waffen-SS. As German casualties mounted, the Nazi regime had been forced to seek front-line reinforcements from among the indigenous populations of the occupied territories. People who had demonstrated some measure of support for the Nazis by their prior service in German auxiliary police units, for example, became the target of SS recruitment drives.[52] Though the response varied from country to country, by the end of the war Waffen-SS units had been raised in virtually every corner of Hitler's empire.

In northwestern Europe, the Germans were able to form three SS divisions and two SS brigades. They had even more success in southeastern Europe, raising two divisions in Hungary, one in Ukraine, two in Russia, one in Albania, and two in Yugoslavia. Yet nothing compared with the response in the Baltic states. Despite its tiny population, Estonia provided an entire SS division to German forces in the East. With two SS divisions of its own in the field, Latvia's contribution to the German war effort paralleled that of its Baltic neighbour.[53]

Contemporary documents reveal that IRO was fully aware of the extent of SS membership in Estonia and Latvia.[54] They further reveal that the organization was particularly strict in applying its eligibility criteria to the Baltic SS. Like all former members of the German armed forces, Waffen-SS veterans were considered ineligible for IRO assistance unless they could prove they had been conscripted. In the case of Baltic SS men, the dates on which the Germans were believed to have initiated mass conscription were used to determine eligibility.[55] Anyone who had enlisted prior to such a cut-off date was considered to have been a volunteer and was automatically classified as ineligible. An individual whose SS service had commenced after that date might be considered for IRO assistance, but the onus was on him to prove he had been conscripted.[56]

Owing to ambiguities and omissions in the German enlistment forms, proving conscription was often extremely difficult. IRO did nothing to ease the evidentiary burden. On the contrary, its eligibility criteria all but precluded the possibility that former members of the Baltic Waffen-SS had been conscripted. According to the instructions issued to IRO eligibility officers, service in Baltic SS units was to be considered voluntary even when it had resulted from a general mobilization. In such cases, recruits had been given a choice from among labour duty, auxiliary police service, or enlistment in the Waffen-SS. But some form of service had been mandatory. Nevertheless, if an individual who was called up in a general mobilization had opted to join the Waffen-SS, under IRO rules that still constituted voluntary service and rendered him ineligible for admission to the refugee camps.[57]

The process for determining eligibility for IRO assistance was patterned after UNRRA-military screening procedures. Prior to being granted admission to one of the IRO-administered camps, a refugee had to fill out a questionnaire. Four to seven pages in length in its various incarnations, the CM/1 form was a composite of the questionnaires previously used by UNRRA and Allied military investigators. Among the details sought were a refugee's nationality, the number, nature, and duration of his or her political, paramilitary, or social associations over the previous twelve years, and his or her residence and employment history for the same period, including any military service. Supporting documents and testimonials were to be itemized on the form as well.[58]

After completing the questionnaire, the applicant handed it in to one of the refugee intake centres. The information contained in the CM/1 was then verified against available sources by IRO and, depending on the zone in which the centre was located, by either British or American military intelligence.[59] Assuming these checks revealed nothing untoward, the refugee would be granted an interview with an IRO eligibility officer. Only if the officer were satisfied with his or her answers would the refugee be admitted to the camp.[60] In cases where individuals were declared ineligible, they could appeal to one of thirty-two regional review boards. Of course, since the review boards went over the same evidence as had been developed by the IRO field officer, there was little chance that a negative decision would be overturned.[61]

In screening applicants for war criminal or collaborationist backgrounds, IRO checked their names against a list of suspects compiled from various sources, including the UN and western intelligence agencies. Captured German military and civil records were also consulted. If an individual were found to be ineligible, his or her name was placed on an IRO blacklist, which was regularly updated and circulated to all refugee intake centres.[62] Even if a war criminal or collaborator managed to evade detection and was mistakenly admitted to a refugee camp, he or she was not necessarily in the clear. In addition to serving as panels of appeal, IRO's regional review boards conducted periodic screenings.[63] Anyone found on re-examination not to meet the criteria for IRO assistance was subject to immediate eviction from the refugee camp.[64]

With the introduction of standardized questionnaires and mandatory interviews as well as the circulation of a blacklist, IRO had made significant improvements over the screening procedures of UNRRA. Yet problems remained. Like the operations conducted by its predecessor, those of IRO were sometimes compromised by corruption or fraud on the part of its officers in the field.[65] Indeed, owing to IRO's mandate as a resettlement agency, the temptation to circumvent or waive eligibility requirements was much greater than it had been in UNRRA days.[66] Furthermore, IRO proved to be no more successful than its predecessor in preventing Nazi sympathizers from infiltrating its eligibility boards.[67]

Apart from human weakness and sabotage, the main problem with IRO screening was that which had hampered UNRRA – namely, the paucity of reliable corroborating documentation. To be sure, service in the German armed forces could be checked against captured German military records. Similarly, German citizenship or ethnic origin could be checked against captured German civil records. It must be reiterated, however, that most of the refugees under the IRO's care were from eastern Europe or the Soviet Union. Thus, the German records available in the West were often of little value in piecing together their wartime activities.[68] IRO did check the names of refugees against a composite list of Nazi war criminals and collaborators, but, as has already been noted, the list's heavy emphasis on German suspects rendered this an exercise in futility.

When it came to culling Nazi war criminals and collaborators from the refugee camps, IRO's record was mixed.[69] On the positive side of the ledger, the organization was fairly effective at rooting out ethnic Germans who were trying to pass themselves off as nationals of other European countries.[70] The stringency with which IRO enforced the prohibition against Waffen-SS volunteers suggests that this category, too, would have been reduced from UNRRA levels. On the other hand, the organization's inability to conduct proper checks behind the Iron Curtain meant that collaborators from eastern Europe and the Soviet Union often would have evaded detection. Their number cannot be determined with any degree of precision, of course. Still, it must have been significant. Even if one accepts the most conservative estimate, that only 10 per cent of the people in the German-occupied eastern territories had collaborated during the war, this would mean that at least sixty thousand ex-Nazis continued to find sanctuary in the refugee camps in Germany.

Despite the failure of IRO and its predecessors to prevent Nazi war criminals and collaborators from contaminating the European refugee pool, there was no immediate danger to Canada. While sympathetic to the plight of the refugees, the Canadian government was slow to put out the welcome mat. Indeed, apart from some token measures, Canada's contribution to solving the postwar refugee crisis was initially limited to providing money for international relief efforts.[71] As one former Department of External Affairs bureaucrat described the Canadian position, 'sharing the finances was one thing; sharing the refugees was another.'[72] Informed primarily by economic considerations, Ottawa's ambivalence translated into the maintenance of a restrictive immigration policy. More than a year would pass before this ambivalence was overcome. The story of the easing of Canada's immigration restrictions, and its implications for the admission of Nazi war criminals and collaborators, is the subject of the following chapters.

CHAPTER TWO

Fortress Canada

'Canada is a country of immigrants' is one of the more hackneyed phrases in our national discourse. Yet, like most clichés, there is some truth in it. Between 1867 and 1914, Canada's population doubled, rising from four to eight million.[1] Much of this increase was the result of immigration. Determined to fill the young nation's vast uninhabited spaces, particularly the Prairies, Ottawa used publicity campaigns and financial inducements to attract more than two and a half million immigrants from the United States, Britain, and continental Europe. Scuttled by the outbreak of the First World War, the policy of nation-building by immigration would be resumed following the end of hostilities.[2]

To be sure, the era of 'open door' immigration prior to the Great War was marked by periods of diminished access. Like all nations built on a foundation of colonists, Canada manifested a certain ambivalence toward each group of newcomers. At times, this ambivalence was informed by nativist fears of what immigration might mean for the ethnic make-up of the country. More often, public perceptions of immigration and immigrants were influenced by economic considerations. When the economy was doing well, immigration was seen as desirable, even necessary to sustain growth. When the economy slumped, Canadians tended to regard immigrants as a drain on both jobs and social welfare.[3]

Perhaps at no time in Canadian history were immigration levels so closely linked to economic conditions as during the interwar years. With the country in the grip of a recession in 1918–19, wartime restrictions on immigration continued to be enforced. As stability and prosperity returned, the restrictions were gradually lifted. While it never attained earlier levels, immigration to Canada rose steadily during the 1920s, reaching an interwar high of almost 163,000 in 1929.[4] Then, with the onset of the Great Depression, the doors were slammed shut once more.

Unable to stem the rising tide of bankruptcies and unemployment, in March 1931 the Conservative government of Prime Minister R.B. Bennett brought in draconian new immigration regulations. Enacted as PC 695, the regulations amounted to a virtual ban on immigration. The only people exempted were British or American nationals with the means to support themselves, close relatives of Canadian residents who were in a position to care for them, foreigners who had served in the Canadian armed forces during the First World War, and farmers with sufficient finances to start up their own homesteads. Anyone falling outside of these narrow categories had only one recourse – applying to cabinet for a waiver of the regulations.[5] In the unforgiving political climate of the Depression, however, non-exempt visa-seekers were unlikely to get a sympathetic hearing around the cabinet table.

The impact of the new regulations on the flow of immigrants was immediate and devastating. Within a year of the enactment of PC 695, immigration to Canada plummeted from almost 90,000 to less than 26,000.[6] Two decades would pass before it again reached pre-Depression levels.[7] The number of new Canadians declined steadily during the 1930s, reaching a peacetime low of 16,000 in 1939. The outbreak of war in Europe brought further reductions. Continuing its decline during the early years of the Second World War, immigration to Canada bottomed out in 1942, when a paltry 7,500 newcomers were admitted.[8]

Notwithstanding its exemption for immigrants from the United States and Britain, the 'means test' that was the cornerstone of PC 695 effectively barred most American and British nationals from admission to Canada. This is borne out by some comparative statistics. By 1945, immigration from Britain had fallen off to one-fifth of what it had been in 1929. The impact of the regulations on the flow of immigrants from south of the border was even more pronounced, amounting to a reduction of seven-eighths. But their most deleterious effect was on European immigration. From its peak of more than 60,000 in 1929, the number of immigrants from Europe dropped to less than 6,000 in the space of a decade. When supplemented by wartime restrictions on the admission of persons from German-occupied territories,[9] PC 695 barred the door almost completely to prospective European settlers. Not surprisingly, then, less than 150 European nationals were able to obtain Canadian visas during the last year of the war.[10]

It was not until the collapse of the Nazi regime and the end of the war in Europe that pressure for the resumption of immigration to Canada resumed. Displaced by the war and seeing no future for themselves amid the continent's ruin and turmoil, many European refugees began to seek opportunities for settlement elsewhere. Those fortunate enough to have family in Canada asked them for assistance in this regard. The refugees' relatives, in turn, applied to cabinet to have the regulations waived in their particular cases.[11] At first, the number of such requests was manageable. By the autumn of 1945, however, hundreds of applications on behalf of European refugees were pouring into Ottawa.[12]

Despite mounting pressure both at home and from abroad, the Liberal government of Prime Minister Mackenzie King was reluctant to relax Canada's long-standing immigration restrictions. Regardless of how plaintive the appeal or deserving the case, applications from would-be immigrants or their Canadian sponsors almost invariably were rejected.[13] In keeping with tradition, the government's hard line appears to have been informed primarily by economic considerations. The prevailing view was expressed by Minister of Mines and Resources James A. Glen, who recommended in September 1945 that PC 695 be kept in place 'until the country is well advanced toward normal conditions and its immigrant absorption possibilities ... [have been] accurately determined.'[14] Glen's recommendation was given official sanction a few weeks later, when cabinet decided to maintain the status quo in immigration policy, at least for the foreseeable future.[15]

So pervasive was anti-immigration feeling in official Ottawa that only one large-scale waiver of PC 695 was granted during the early postwar period. In that case, the government was compelled to act because the status of a group of resident aliens required clarification. Between 1939 and 1945, Canada had admitted some 3,500 European refugees on a temporary non-immigrant basis. These unfortunate victims of war included civilian internees, many of them German Jews who had been brought over from Britain; European refugees of various nationalities; and a small number of Jews who had been transported to Canada from Portugal and Spain. Shortly after the end of hostilities in Europe, about 60 per cent of them applied for landed-immigrant status. Forced to choose between settlement or repatriation, cabinet approved the aliens' permanent admission in the autumn of 1945.[16]

Frustrated by what they regarded as Ottawa's heavy-handed enforcement of the immigration regulations, Canadians with relatives in Europe's refugee camps stepped up their efforts at family reunification. Their direct contacts with the government having been rebuffed, they tried a different approach. Flexing their new-found political muscle, Canadians of central and eastern European extraction urged their representative associations to press Ottawa for the admission of their beleaguered relatives. Unable to ignore the pro-immigration agitation emanating from the grassroots, the various ethnic associations took up the plight of the refugees with individual members of Parliament. Across Canada, but particularly in constituencies with large central and eastern European populations, MPs of all parties began to pressure the government for a relaxation of PC 695.[17]

The political process involved in effecting changes to the immigration regulations was slow and unpredictable. As a consequence, some of the larger ethnic associations considered lobbying the government directly. But that approach was precluded by the anti-immigration sentiment still prevalent among cabinet ministers and senior bureaucrats. Instead, the only direct action in which the associations engaged was to seek Ottawa's permission to supply food, clothing, and medicine to the refugees. In contrast to the pro-immigration clamour, such overtures were welcomed by a government that was looking for an easy way to fulfil its moral obligations. Yet what was an end in itself for the government was but the means to an end for the immigration lobby. Once they had set up shop as overseas relief agencies, the ethnic associations found themselves in a much stronger position to press for the extension of their humanitarian efforts into the realm of immigration.[18]

The leaders of the various ethnic associations realized that if their lobbying efforts were to be successful, they would need help. Accordingly, they enlisted the aid of their old allies, the Canadian railway companies. Both around the turn of the century and then again during the 1920s, the railways had been an important intermediary between the various immigration lobby groups and the government. As the primary mode of mass inland transportation, the railways had been essential partners in earlier settlement programs. Of course, the relationship had been beneficial to the railways as well. Whether it was from the proceeds of land sales to immigrants heading out west or from the fares they charged for the transport of each newcomer, the railways had always profited from their partnership with the immigration lobby. Moribund since the mid-1930s, the railways' colonization departments welcomed the opportunity to re-establish contacts that had proven so lucrative in the past.[19]

Bringing the railway companies on side was important. Though war and depression had forced some lines into bankruptcy and others into co-ownership with Ottawa, the railways retained considerable political clout. Slowly but surely, other segments of the business community followed their lead in supporting a more open immigration policy. First it was the turn of small independent manufacturers. Having lost many of their skilled workers to the war effort, these firms lobbied for the admission of limited numbers of refugee specialists.[20] Soon, major corporations, most notably from the agricultural, forestry, and mining sectors, were adding their voices to the pro-immigration chorus. Unlike the smaller firms, the interest of the corporations lay in the procurement of cheap labour in substantial numbers.[21]

To be sure, there were limits to the ability of big business to effect changes to Canada's immigration policy. Yet the corporations were not without influence. For example, by enlisting the aid of its allies in Parliament, the business community was able to reactivate the Senate's long-dormant Standing Committee on Immigration and Labour. The committee did not have the power to set priorities, but it could review the existing immigration regulations. The result of the senators' work was a report that was highly critical of the restrictive immigration policy of a succession of governments.[22] Perhaps more importantly, the committee's hearings provided immigration advocates with a platform from which they could build public support.[23]

With the forging of alliances between the ethnic associations and big business, the immigration lobby was emerging as a powerful force in postwar Canadian politics. Some senior civil servants watched this development with trepidation. Perhaps the most compelling expression of the bureaucracy's concern was that articulated by Norman A. Robertson. At the time the ranking bureaucrat at the Department of External Affairs, Robertson predicted in a February 1946 memorandum that 'the demands upon Canada to make further contributions to the solution of this [refugee] problem will probably increase in the near future.' Citing the growing resistance to repatriation, he estimated that there were several hundred thousand persons from eastern Europe for whom new homes would have to be found. In addition, Robertson warned, untold numbers of Volksdeutsche would also want to settle elsewhere. While reluctant to reopen the issue of Canada's long-term immigration priorities, Robertson admitted that the growing pressure both at home and from abroad had made some change in policy imperative.

Robertson offered two recommendations for governmental action. First, he suggested that Canada provide for the immediate admission of a small number of European refugees drawn from one of the categories – close relatives – already deemed admissible under PC 695. Though a mere drop in the bucket, such an initiative would have the dual effect of enhancing Canada's international reputation while at the same time appeasing some of the pro-immigration forces at home. Second, he advised that an interdepartmental committee be established to study a range of possible Canadian responses to the European refugee crisis.[24]

Incisive in its analysis and yet cautious in its counsel, Robertson's memorandum found favour among cabinet ministers and his fellow bureaucrats alike. Indeed, less than a month after its circulation, cabinet established an interdepartmental committee with the mandate to advise the government on immigration matters. The committee spent the next several weeks reviewing policy options with respect to the problem of the European refugees. After careful study, it came up with recommendations that signalled the first postwar departure from Canada's restrictive immigration policy.

In keeping with Robertson's suggestions, the committee advised that PC 695 be amended to allow for the admission of refugees who had close relatives in Canada. There was one proviso. Refugees were to be considered for admission only if their Canadian relatives were able and willing to pay for both their transportation from abroad and their shelter and maintenance upon arrival. Aware of the pressure being exerted

by the immigration lobby, the committee went beyond Robertson's proposals, suggesting that the intake of refugees be expanded to include
persons whose shelter and maintenance could be guaranteed by ethnic,
religious, or other representative associations. As for the future, the
committee was more circumspect. Unable to agree on a long-term
course of action, its members confined themselves to recommending
further study of those aspects of a more open immigration policy
that were likely to be controversial – namely, its impact on employment levels, the social safety net, and the ethnic composition of the
country.[25]

In practical terms, the committee's report amounted to little more
than a tentative first step in the liberalization of Canada's immigration
policy. It in no way heralded a return to the expansive policies of the
1920s, much less to the 'open door' of the late nineteenth and early
twentieth centuries. In fact, the changes advocated by the committee
were relatively minor. For example, while European refugees with family in Canada would be eligible to apply for Canadian visas under the
revised regulations, whether or not they were admitted would still
depend on their ability to support themselves upon arrival. The same
was true for refugees without Canadian relatives. In order for unat-
tached individuals to be granted landed-immigrant status, their maintenance and shelter would have to be guaranteed by the ethnic, religious,
or benevolent association that was sponsoring them. In short, admissibility would still be determined by the economic circumstances of each
prospective immigrant. Having extended PC 695's means test to the
refugees, the committee's proposed amendments clearly were not
intended to bring about a dramatic upsurge in European immigration to
Canada.[26]

Besides being rather modest, the committee's recommendations
were not particularly original. On the contrary, the proposal to relax the
immigration regulations for refugees with close relatives in Canada
was almost a carbon copy of Britain's 'Distressed Relatives Scheme.'
Conceived by the British government in the autumn of 1945, the program was intended to facilitate the reunification of husbands, wives,
and dependent children and to provide some familial care for orphans
and the elderly. To achieve these limited objectives, the British Foreign
Office had instructed its passport-control officers to issue visas to oth-

erwise inadmissible European refugees, provided, of course, that they had offers of maintenance and shelter from close relatives in the United Kingdom. Though slightly more restrictive, the Canadian proposal mirrored the British program in its essentials.[27]

Notwithstanding the incremental nature of the changes proposed by the interdepartmental committee, official Ottawa wrestled with them for weeks. Indeed, it was not until the end of May 1946 that they were finally accepted by cabinet. Consistent with Robertson's recommendations, PC 695 was amended to extend admissibility to the parents, unmarried children, siblings, or orphaned nephews and nieces of any Canadian resident who was prepared to receive and care for them.[28] Since European refugees were intended to be the primary beneficiaries of the change in policy, the regulations were further amended so that persons who no longer held passports from their countries of origin could still apply for Canadian visas. Henceforth, any travel document that established the bearer's identity would be sufficient to obtain a visa.[29] Since all refugees who were under the care of the International Refugee Organization (IRO) were automatically issued something called the Certificate of Identity, later renamed the London Travel Document (LTD), the lack of a national passport would pose no impediment to their entry into Canada. Even refugees ineligible for IRO assistance could be considered for admission, provided they were able to obtain a Temporary Travel Document (TTD) from Allied military authorities.[30]

If cabinet ministers were of the view that the immigration lobby would be placated by the close relatives scheme, they were mistaken. Far from easing the pressure on the government, the relaxation of Canada's immigration regulations had the effect of galvanizing both prospective immigrants and the individuals or groups who were working on their behalf.[31] Robertson's prediction was proving to be accurate. In the first few months after the enactment of the amended regulations, the Canadian military mission in Berlin reported that the number of immigration applications it was processing had more than doubled.[32] Close relatives submitted the bulk of these applications, but an increasing number of inquiries were coming from ethnic, religious, and non-denominational relief organizations.[33] Several attempts were made to dissuade the growing throng of visa seekers, but to no avail. Even published warnings about the restrictive nature of Canadian immigration policy seemed to have little effect.[34]

Remarkably, in view of the persistence of the immigration lobby, another seven months would pass before Canada's immigration regulations were further relaxed.[35] Two factors account for the delay. First, there was a severe shortage of transatlantic shipping. The few vessels that were available, moreover, had been earmarked for the repatriation of Canadian servicemen and their dependants.[36] Second, there were no Canadian immigrant-examination facilities on the European continent.[37] Canada's military mission in Berlin was doing its best to cope, but it was not equipped to deal with the increasing number of applicants.[38] In any event, owing to restrictions on travel within Allied-occupied Germany, few refugees were able to make use of the mission. Thus, most applications had to first go through Immigration Branch in Ottawa before being forwarded to Berlin.[39]

There was another reason why Canada was slow to relax its restrictive immigration policy in the early postwar period – bureaucratic inertia. In part, officialdom's sluggishness can be traced to the institutional disarray wrought by the Great Depression and the Second World War. With the downsizing of the Department of Immigration and Colonization to a branch of the Department of Mines and Resources in 1936, some of its responsibilities had been transferred to other government departments.[40] The resulting fragmentation of the immigration bureaucracy brought about confusion, turf wars, and, for a time, paralysis.[41] But the real problem may have been the inability of the bureaucrats to overcome their ambivalence toward immigration. On the one hand, most tended toward the view that a more populous country would, in the long run, be a more prosperous one.[42] On the other hand, their careers had spanned depression and war. The trauma of these cataclysmic events could not have helped but make them more cynical, less tolerant, and inordinately protective of the country they served. In light of the deprivation and hardship visited on so many of their fellow Canadians, it became easier for senior officials to harden their hearts to the plight of the European refugees.[43]

In the years immediately following the Second World War, Canadian immigration policy was crafted and implemented by ten men. Six were born in central Canada, one was from the West Coast,[44] one hailed from the Maritimes, and two were transplanted Britons. Their average age in 1945 was forty-six years old, meaning they had reached adulthood long before the onset of the Depression or the outbreak of the Second World War. They were well-educated, with nine having university degrees, including two with doctorates. All but two were lifelong civil servants. One was a career military officer. Six had served in the armed forces in either the First or the Second World War. Four of the bureaucrats had also recently been involved in the enforcement of Canada's wartime security measures.

The Ottawa mandarin who had the greatest influence on Canada's immigration policy during the early postwar period was Norman Robertson. A Rhodes scholar in economics who had bounced around academia during the 1920s, Robertson joined the civil service in 1928 as a third secretary at the Department of External Affairs. He was a rising star at External over the next decade, impressing his superiors with his deft handling of several key issues, most notably Ottawa's delicate trade and tariff negotiations with Britain and the United States. Notwithstanding his youth, Robertson was appointed acting undersecretary of state for external affairs after the sudden death of the venerable O.D. Skelton in January 1941.[45] Vaulted into the position of the most senior bureaucrat at External, he took over a vast array of responsibilities, including the protection of Canada's interests within the wartime Anglo-American alliance.

Robertson held the post of undersecretary throughout the remainder of the war and during the early postwar period. Late in the summer of 1946, he was dispatched to London as Canada's high commissioner.[46] He functioned in that capacity until 1949, when he was brought back from overseas to serve as clerk to the Privy Council and secretary to the cabinet.[47]

Robertson's views on immigration were decidedly liberal. This was not evident in his February 1946 memorandum, but his subsequent advocacy of a more open immigration policy leaves little doubt as to his true feelings.[48] Conversely, Robertson was uncomfortable with the nationality-based eligibility criteria (he regarded them as discriminatory) that were being applied by international relief agencies like the United Nations Relief and Rehabilitation Administration (UNRRA) and IRO. Indeed, his primary concern seems to have been to prevent

Canada from falling into the same trap. Ethnic preferences, he believed, would allow the country's immigration policy to be manipulated by national, religious, and political lobby groups, thereby dooming it to endless controversy and divisiveness.[49]

To be sure, there were limits to Robertson's liberalism. This was particularly true where Canada's domestic security was concerned. Even before the outbreak of the Second World War, he had shown no qualms about using the power of the state to block German and Italian consular officials from disseminating Nazi propaganda. As a member of the government's Committee on the Treatment of Aliens and Alien Property, he supported its recommendation, submitted to cabinet the same day Britain declared war on Germany, that several hundred German nationals and Canadians of ethnic German origin be arrested and interned. Though troubled by the subsequent relocation of Japanese Canadians from Canada's West Coast, Robertson ultimately went along with that policy. Later in the war, at his request, the National Research Council (NRC) established a cryptographic unit whose task it was to intercept and decode the wireless traffic being sent from and received by Vichy France's legation in Ottawa.[50]

Another External Affairs bureaucrat who helped to chart the course of Canada's immigration policy during the early postwar period was Hugh L. Keenleyside. A PhD in history who had managed to garner a succession of two-year teaching appointments during the 1920s, Keenleyside, like Robertson, joined External in 1928 as a third secretary. Though his rise was not as meteoric as Robertson's, Keenleyside moved up the ranks steadily over the next decade. His big break occurred in 1939, when, as organizer of the successful royal tour of Canada, he came to the attention of Prime Minister King. Subsequently assigned as an advisor to a number of wartime committees, he helped to craft government policy in the areas of national defence, scientific development, the exploitation of the Canadian North, and economic relations between Canada and the United States. His most controversial appointment was to the Committee on Orientals in British Columbia, whose mandate it was to advise the government on what to do with Japanese Canadians in the event of war with Japan.

After Robertson was named undersecretary of state for external affairs, Keenleyside was promoted to assistant undersecretary, a post he held for the next three years. He returned to the field in 1944, first as ambassador to Mexico and later as part of Canada's delegation to the first session of the UN General Assembly.[51] With the European refugee crisis assuming ever greater domestic importance, he was appointed deputy minister of mines and resources early in 1947.[52]

Keenleyside represented the same progressive External Affairs tradition as Robertson.[53] Indeed, in some respects, his liberalism was more principled than that of his superior. Nowhere did the difference between the two men show itself more than over the issue of the wartime relocation of Japanese Canadians. As former residents of British Columbia, both Robertson and Keenleyside were appalled by the racist passions stirred up by the demagoguery of British Columbian politicians in the aftermath of the Japanese attack on Pearl Harbor. Both men tried, unsuccessfully, to resist the drive toward relocation. But Keenleyside seemed to try harder. Early on, as relations between the western democracies and Japan deteriorated, Keenleyside had been a force for moderation, convincing fellow members of the Committee on Orientals to recommend a halt to all anti-Japanese propaganda. Throughout the summer of 1941, with war in the Pacific looming on the horizon, Keenleyside had continued to advocate tolerance. There was no containing the public's anti-Japanese impulses after Pearl Harbor, but Keenleyside persevered, antagonizing the province's politicians with his vigorous opposition to the proposed internment of Japanese Canadians.[54]

Like Robertson, Keenleyside's liberal impulses were tempered by security concerns. Though an early supporter of the admission of European refugees, this was for him as much a means of ensuring that Canada would get the best immigrants as it was a humanitarian gesture.[55] When confronted with the problem of how to prevent German- and Italian-Canadian wartime traitors from reasserting their Canadian citizenship, Keenleyside took a hard line, suggesting they be warned that they were liable to prosecution for treason should they ever attempt to return to Canada.[56] As advisor to the Cabinet Committee on Immigration Policy, he convinced a majority of its members that any European refugee who had been rejected for admission to the United States should automatically be excluded from Canada.[57] During the influx of Baltic 'boat people' in 1948–9, Keenleyside, while sympathetic to the plight of these anti-Soviet refugees, advocated the introduction of tough measures aimed at deterring additional landings.[58] Finally, when the government began to contemplate relaxing the regulations that prohibited most German nationals from emigrating to Canada, he argued strenuously for the maintenance of the status quo.[59]

Before Canada reopened its visa-issuing offices in Europe, the processing of immigrants, as we have seen, was handled on an ad hoc basis by Canada's military mission in Berlin. The mission was headed by General Maurice Pope, while its consular operations were run by S. Morley Scott. Like Robertson and Keenleyside, both men held liberal views on immigration.[60] Yet their liberal impulses were tempered by security concerns. A member of several government committees during the 1930s, Pope was instrumental in the formulation of Canada's plans for the imposition of censorship and the internment of enemy aliens in the event of the outbreak of war.[61] Scott's wartime role, in turn, was to oversee the implementation of some of the same regulations that Pope had helped to draft. Scott was a relative newcomer to the civil service, his first assignment being to the branch at External responsible for all 'matters relating to enemy nationals in Canada, in particular, prisoners of war, civilian internees and interned refugees.'[62]

During the late 1940s, the Immigration Branch of the Department of Mines and Resources was run by a group of four men. All but one had worked in the immigration bureaucracy throughout the turbulent years of depression and war. Immigration Branch was headed by Arthur L. Jolliffe, a career civil servant whose first government job had been as controller of Asian immigration at Vancouver.[63] Appointed director of immigration in January 1944, he inherited an agency weakened by budget cuts and mired in the restrictionist dogma of his predecessor, the avowedly racist Frederick C. Blair.[64] With fears of Nazi infiltration still running high, Jolliffe spent much of the remainder of the war coordinating the operations of Immigration Branch with those of military intelligence.[65]

Jolliffe's deputy was Charles E.S. Smith. Like his boss a former controller of Asian immigration, Smith took over as commissioner of immigration shortly after Jolliffe's promotion to director.[66] Smith's counterpart in Europe was Laval Fortier, one of only two immigration bureaucrats who was not a career civil servant. A successful lawyer before the war, Fortier rapidly moved up the ranks of the immigration bureaucracy, reaching its pinnacle in January 1950 with his appointment as deputy minister in the newly formed Department of Citizenship and Immigration.[67] The last man atop the immigration hierarchy was Georges R. Benoit. Though originally contracted as a translator by the Department of Mines and Resources, Benoit was permanently assigned there in the autumn of 1947. Within a few years, he had risen to the post of chief of operations at Immigration Branch.[68]

With the relaxation of PC 695 in the spring of 1946, the reopening of Canadian immigration inspection offices in Europe was only a matter of time.[69] Immigration field officers would be needed to staff the new facilities. Hand-picked to supervise their operations were Odilon Cormier and Philip W. Bird. Like Jolliffe, Smith, and Benoit, both Cormier and Bird spent their entire careers in the immigration bureaucracy. Known as a stickler for the regulations, Cormier was, from the security point of view at least, an excellent choice to head up Canada's first postwar immigration mission, which was located at Heidelberg in western Germany. Bird took over from Cormier as inspector-in-charge early in 1948. Unlike his predecessor, Bird had never been stationed in Europe. Nonetheless, he had extensive experience as an immigration field officer.[70]

If the immigration bureaucrats had been jaded by depression and war, events would transpire in the early postwar period that only deepened their cynicism and mistrust. On 5 September 1945, a frightened young cipher clerk named Igor Gouzenko walked out of the Soviet Union's Ottawa embassy for the last time. In the defector's trembling hands were a number of classified Russian-language cables and reports. The documents were political dynamite. Deciphered by the RCMP within thirty-six hours, they revealed that Soviet intelligence had been running an espionage ring in Canada for some time. More than a dozen Canadians, including civil servants, were linked to the ring's activities. A royal commission was convened to investigate this unprecedented breach of Canada's national security. Well before they submitted their final report, the commissioners had concluded that the situation was of sufficient gravity to warrant immediate countermeasures. Thus, on the morning of 15 February 1946, all those named in the Soviet documents were arrested and taken to RCMP headquarters for questioning.[71]

What became known as the 'Gouzenko affair' had profound implications for the way Ottawa dealt with security questions. The Cold War had come to Canada with a vengeance, replacing the euphoria that attended the defeat of the Axis with an atmosphere of crisis, betrayal, and fear.[72] For the government, the most shattering revelation to emerge from the royal commission's hearings was that Canadian public servants had violated their oaths and spied for a foreign power. Impelled by a collective reflex, official Ottawa resolved to prevent this from happening again. Accordingly, during the winter of 1945–6, senior bureaucrats took up the question of how to improve security-clearance procedures within the civil service.

In a continuation of wartime practices, the matter of governmental security was referred to the cabinet's defence committee. By the spring of 1946, the committee had narrowed its options down to two proposals. One, which had been submitted by Charles Foulkes, the army's chief of the general staff, envisioned the creation of an elaborate security and intelligence-gathering organization modelled along American lines and subordinated to the military. The other proposal, which had been crafted by Robertson, called for the establishment of a more modest security advisory panel comprising representatives from government departments, the RCMP, and military intelligence. Unlike the agency suggested by Foulkes, the panel proposed by Robertson was to be closely supervised by cabinet. After much discussion, Robertson's idea was accepted, probably because it ensured that security policy would be kept under civilian control. By late spring 1946, the innocuously named but influential Security Panel had been established.[73]

The panel's original mandate was to advise the government on ways of improving the vetting of prospective civil servants.[74] Its involvement in immigration came about as a result of the relaxation of PC 695 and the accompanying need to reopen Canadian immigrant-examination facilities abroad. With the drastic curtailment of immigration during the 1930s, what little screening of newcomers there was had been carried out by Canadian immigration offices, or, where no such facilities existed, by the British consular service. Shortly after the outbreak of the Second World War, Canadian immigration offices on the European continent were closed. In order to process repatriates and the few immigrants still eligible for admission to Canada, arrangements were

made with British military intelligence to conduct immigration screening. With the termination of hostilities in Europe, London informed
Ottawa that it would no longer be able to assist in the examination of
prospective immigrants to Canada.[75]

Britain's decision to discontinue immigration screening on Canada's
behalf meant that new arrangements had to be made. The problem was
discussed at the initial meetings of the Security Panel, which were held
in the summer of 1946. A subcommittee was formed to study alternatives. Its report, presented to a meeting of the full panel on 8 July, proposed that the RCMP be made available to Immigration Branch for the
purpose of conducting security examinations of prospective immigrants. Panel members ratified the subcommittee's recommendations in
August and passed them on to cabinet. After several more weeks of
deliberation, cabinet approved the dispatch of RCMP personnel overseas to assist in immigration screening.[76] According to the instructions
issued by RCMP headquarters, the job of its officers would be to make
security inquiries about prospective immigrants with a view to denying
admission to 'any ... who, from their known history and background,
would be unlikely to adapt themselves to the Canadian way of life and
to our system of democratic government.'[77]

In the aftermath of the Gouzenko affair, it might be assumed that the
primary aim of the new system of immigration screening would have
been the weeding out of suspected communists.[78] Yet this was not the
case. While Gouzenko's revelations had raised the spectre of Soviet
infiltration of the Canadian government, contemporary documentation
makes it clear that the immigration bureaucrats were not overly influenced by anti-communist hysteria. Rather, their immediate reaction
seems to have been a heightened preoccupation with subversives in
general, regardless of their political orientation. If there were a bias at
all within the immigration bureaucracy, it tended to manifest itself in
the formulation of screening criteria aimed at keeping out Nazis and
Nazi sympathizers, not communists.[79]

To be sure, Canada's immigration regulations did not contain an
explicit ban on suspected Nazi war criminals and collaborators. In the
immediate postwar period, such a prohibition did not appear to be
necessary. Shortly after Canada's declaration of war on Germany in
September 1939, the government had enacted an order-in-council that

barred enemy aliens from entering the country. Included in this prohibited class were residents of any territory occupied by the enemy.[80] Not only were enemy nationals thereby proscribed from landing, but also nationals of countries allied with Canada, if these had been overrun by the Nazi juggernaut. The aim was to prevent the infiltration of Canada by Nazi agents disguised as refugees. Together with the draconian provisions of PC 695, the closure of Canada's borders to such a broad range of enemy aliens excluded most European refugees from consideration as immigrants. The removal of the ban on nationals of countries occupied by Germany in May 1941[81] did little to rectify the situation. For the duration of the war, the only Canadian visa-issuing office on the continent was located in Lisbon, Portugal,[82] which was practically inaccessible, except through North Africa.

The prohibition on the entry of enemy aliens was maintained even after the termination of hostilities in Europe. Indeed, it was not until autumn 1945 that the government began to consider loosening the wartime ban.[83] When changes were finally adopted, they were so minor as to be almost meaningless. According to PC 1373, which was enacted in April 1946, enemy aliens were still to be denied admission to Canada. Exceptions might be considered, but only if the individuals in question were able to satisfy Canadian authorities that they had been opposed to an enemy government during the war.[84] Since opposition to dictatorial regimes is by necessity carried out underground, away from the prying eyes of secret police and government informers, prospective immigrants from former enemy countries would have had a great deal of difficulty establishing that they had opposed Nazi rule, even if their claims were true.[85] Without a witness to or documentary evidence of a visa seeker's anti-Nazi credentials, which in most cases was impossible to produce, Canadian immigration officers would have had little recourse but to reject such applications.[86] For many Europeans, then, Canada's doors remained closed.[87]

Properly enforced, the ban on enemy aliens should have gone a long way toward preventing the admission to Canada of suspected Nazi war criminals and collaborators. Yet it was not the only means of barring their entry. According to long-standing provisions of the Immigration Act, persons who, upon examination, were found to advocate the overthrow of the government of Canada, or to have done so in the past, or to be or have been affiliated with organizations that advocated violent opposition to any duly constituted government, or to have been found guilty of espionage or high treason, were to be denied Canadian visas.[88] By definition, war criminals and collaborators fell within these prohibited classes. Many wartime traitors, after all, had been implicated in radical right-wing opposition to the governments of their countries of origin long before their conquest and occupation by the Nazis. Moreover, some had already been tried for treason in absentia, while others were listed on international arrest warrants.

There was always the danger, of course, that war criminals or collaborators might be able to exploit loopholes within the broad anti-subversive clauses of the Immigration Act. Accordingly, officials charged with its enforcement quickly realized that, to be truly effective, the regulations had to be amended to deal specifically with prospective immigrants whose activities during the Second World War had rendered them undesirable or security risks. In keeping with their essentially reactive approach to the European refugee crisis, the bureaucrats fashioned rejection criteria based on standards set by Canada's wartime allies.

In January 1946, the powers occupying Germany enacted Allied Control Council Directive No. 24. A first step in the western Allies' sincere, if ultimately impractical, attempt to denazify German society,[89] Directive No. 24 called for 'the removal from office and from positions of responsibility [in Germany] of Nazis and all persons hostile to Allied purposes.' A preliminary list of 'formations' of the Nazi Party and its affiliated organizations was included. To assist in the identification of the members of such organizations, every German over the age of eighteen was required to fill out a questionnaire. Crafted by the Office of Strategic Services (OSS), the twelve-page questionnaire was designed to elicit the full details of an individual's career under the Third Reich, especially his or her memberships in the Nazi Party and affiliated organizations.[90] Based on the answers provided, which were to be checked against captured German civil and military records, every adult in Germany would then be placed into one of five categories: major offender, offender, lesser offender, follower, or exonerated. An individual determined to have been in any of the three offender categories would automatically be removed or enjoined from holding public office.[91]

Within weeks of the enactment of Directive No. 24, consultations began in Ottawa about how to apply the criteria contained therein to Canadian immigration screening. The policy that emerged was a hybrid of existing Canadian regulations and the Allied directive. The search for made-in-Canada rejection criteria was initiated at a meeting of External Affairs bureaucrats held on 6 February 1946. Discussion at the meeting was wide-ranging, but agreement was reached on several broad categories of prospective immigrants whose background would render them 'unsatisfactory' from a security point of view. These included anyone who had collaborated with the enemy during 1939–45, had past connections with a foreign intelligence service, had demonstrated sympathy with fascism, Nazism, or any other undesirable political tenets (including, presumably, communism), or was seeking asylum from a country with a duly constituted government.[92] The last category is noteworthy in that it reveals officialdom's suspicions about eastern European and Soviet refugees, some of whom were known to have been Nazi collaborators. The asylum-seekers category would be dropped, of course, in the wake of the UN's repudiation of the policy of mandatory repatriation. The other categories would undergo considerable alteration. Nevertheless, the 6 February meeting signalled the Canadian government's intention to take a hard-line approach to the screening of prospective immigrants for war criminal or collaborationist backgrounds.

The lengths to which Ottawa was prepared to go to prevent the influx of suspected Nazi collaborators is illustrated by the case of a former private in the Waffen-SS. In many ways, Jan Jesionek was an ideal candidate for immigration to Canada. Of partial Volksdeutsch origins, he had never renounced his Polish citizenship. Thus, he was a national of a country that had been allied with Canada throughout the war. In addition, he had solid and verifiable anti-Nazi credentials, his father having been imprisoned by the Germans for refusing to use the so-called Hitler greeting. Though he had served for several months with the 12th SS Panzer Division 'Hitler Youth,' Jesionek had been a reluctant conscript. Furthermore, he had deserted before the end of hostilities. Most importantly, his testimony before a Canadian military court had helped to convict SS Brigadier-General Kurt Meyer, his divisional commander, of the murder of Canadian prisoners of war in Normandy in June 1944.[93]

At the conclusion of the Meyer trial, Jesionek, who despaired of repatriation to his communist-dominated homeland, had expressed the desire to start a new life in Canada. Lieutenant-Colonel Bruce J.S. Macdonald, the prosecutor who had obtained the conviction against Meyer, promised the young Pole he would intercede on his behalf. True to his word, Macdonald wrote to the Canadian High Commission in London asking that special consideration be given in Jesionek's case.[94] He lavished praise on his former star witness, reminding the diplomats of Jesionek's invaluable contribution to the winning of the Meyer case and affirming that he would make 'an excellent Canadian.'[95] Impressed by Macdonald's sponsorship of Jesionek's application, the high commissioner passed it on to Immigration Branch with a favourable recommendation. The expressions of support proved to be of no avail. In characteristic fashion, the immigration bureaucrats rejected the application, citing Jesionek's inadmissibility on several grounds, including his service in the German armed forces. Even temporary admission on a non-immigrant basis was denied.[96]

Perhaps the clearest indication of the government's intentions with respect to Nazi war criminals and collaborators came on the eve of the resumption of European immigration to Canada. In the summer of 1946, a committee of the Security Panel offered an amendment to the Immigration Act that would have expanded its prohibited classes to include 'persons who are, or at any time have been, members of the Nazi Party or of the Fascist Party or of the Gestapo or of the Schutzstaffel or of the Sturm Abteilung [sic] or of any organization or party auxiliary to or supporting Nazism or Fascism or persons classified as war criminals.'[97] Cabinet rejected the proposed amendment on the grounds that there would be strong opposition in Parliament.[98] Undeterred, the immigration bureaucrats then sought to secure via 'departmental administrative action' what had been denied to them in the legislative realm – namely, an effective means of preventing subversives, including Hitler's former henchmen, from gaining admission to Canada. At a subsequent meeting of the Security Panel, it was suggested that this could be accomplished by making security checks a routine part of the immigrant-examination process.[99] Cabinet was satisfied with this solution and approved its implementation in the autumn of 1946.[100] Henceforth, it would be left to the discretion of the RCMP to interpret the Immigration Act in cases of suspected Nazi war criminals and collaborators.[101]

To assist security officers in their task, the RCMP prepared and circulated a paper titled 'The Nazi Party, Its Formations and Affiliated Organizations.' A virtual carbon copy of Allied Directive No. 24, right down to its division of the party into the Gestapo, formations like the Storm Troopers (SA), the SS, Waffen-SS, and so-called Death's Head units, as well as 'affiliated,' 'supervised,' and 'other' organizations, the paper attempted to distinguish between active and passive Nazis. While conceding that 'the mere fact that an individual was a member of the [Nazi] Party damns him in the eyes of the democratic world,' the Mounties also believed that membership was 'indispensable to everyone who wished to earn his living and who wished to be left undisturbed by the Police.' Accordingly, the level of one's complicity in Nazi crimes depended upon the number and nature of organizations to which one had belonged. The paper would form the basis of the instructions issued to Canada's first overseas visa-vetting officers.[102]

By the autumn of 1946, Canada was preparing to set up provisional visa-issuing facilities on the European continent.[103] For the RCMP and Immigration Branch personnel assigned to those facilities, a key part of their training was familiarization with the criteria and procedures they were to employ in the screening of prospective immigrants. There was some urgency to the training regime. Before the year was out, immigration from Europe to Canada would be resumed. Included in the first wave of applicants would be several hundred European refugees with close relatives in Canada. A much larger group of refugees would seek entry under the auspices of a special labour program. Finally, immigration from traditional sources like Britain and the United States, dormant for so long, would begin to pick up again. Each movement of immigrants became a test of the new system of immigration screening. The story of these early movements, and the effectiveness of the RCMP in excluding Nazi war criminals and collaborators therefrom, are the subjects of the next chapter.

CHAPTER THREE

Test Cases

In October 1946, more than four months after the relaxation of PC 695, Ottawa finally put the close relatives scheme into motion. In keeping with Robertson's original recommendations, the first contingent of immigrants from Europe would be a modest one. By special cabinet directive, Canadian visas were allocated for a maximum of 650 European refugees. All had to have family in Canada who were able and willing to sponsor them. Moreover, all had to be known to the government, with applications on their behalf already pending.[1]

The admission of the refugees was planned as a three-step process. First, a list of prospective immigrants would be compiled from the thousands of applications received in Ottawa. Second, the list would be submitted to the Intergovernmental Committee on Refugees (IGCR), under whose temporary care the refugees had been placed during the interval between the winding down of the United Nations Relief and Rehabilitation Administration (UNRRA) and the inauguration of the International Refugee Organization (IRO).[2] Upon receipt of the list, IGCR, with the assistance of the Canadian military mission in Berlin, would locate the nominated refugees and gather them at a mutually convenient site. Once the candidates had been assembled, the Canadian government would proceed with step three, the dispatch of consular officers to conduct civil and security examinations. Upon completion of the examinations, those refugees who had been accepted as immigrants were to be issued visas and provided with passage, the costs of which would be shared between the refugees' relatives and IGCR.[3]

The first two steps were carried out according to plan. The refugees were selected and assembled, consular officers were sent to the assembly camps, and the examinations began. The process soon hit a snag, however. In the course of carrying out their security inquiries, the Canadian officials discovered that approximately one out of three of the would-be immigrants were Soviet Mennonites who had been granted German citizenship during the war. Further investigation revealed that most of the German-naturalized Mennonites had not been inmates of refugee camps, but rather had been found residing on farms.[4] There is evidence that General Pope, the head of the Canadian military mission, was aware of the Mennonites' questionable immigration status.[5] Regardless of what Pope knew, the fact that the Mennonites had not been admitted to the refugee camps should have raised a red flag. Nonetheless, the Canadian mission attempted to pass them off as legitimate refugees.

Mennonites who had obtained German citizenship prior to the end of the war were, by definition, enemy aliens. As such, they were ineligible for admission to Canada, unless, of course, they could prove they had opposed the German government. Resorting to a tactic that would be used often by immigration lobby groups working on behalf of Volksdeutsche, the Canadian Mennonite Board of Colonization claimed that those of their religious brethren who received German citizenship during the war had been naturalized by the Nazi regime against their will.[6] When this explanation failed to garner any sympathy in Ottawa, the organization tried another approach, suggesting that the Mennonites had been evicted from their homes in Russia and forcibly resettled in Germany.[7] Like the involuntary-naturalization argument, this claim, too, was spurious.[8] Though some ethnic Germans were evacuated from the occupied eastern territories and interned in Nazi Germany as stateless persons during the latter stages of the war, the vast majority had come voluntarily.[9]

Apprised of the problem that had cropped up in Germany, the Department of External Affairs intervened. Conceding that the eligibility of the Mennonites was moot, the department suggested that a more liberal interpretation of the immigration regulations might enable some to be admitted to Canada. Several options were available, but the most practical, in External's view, was to confer 'opponent to an enemy government' status on those Mennonites who had relatives in Canada.[10]

Needless to say, this attempt to circumvent the ban on the admission of enemy aliens was not well received by Immigration Branch. Perennial sticklers for the regulations, the immigration bureaucrats instructed the Canadian mission not to issue visas to persons whose nationality was in question. Consequently, only a handful of the Mennonites selected for the first close relatives movement were granted admission to Canada.[11]

With the examination of a contingent of European refugees in the autumn of 1946, the system of immigration screening had passed its first test. Security checks had revealed that a considerable number of the applicants were ineligible, and they were promptly removed from the pool of prospective immigrants. Admittedly, this first test was an easy one. The number of applicants was quite small, and the government had been given their names well in advance. More importantly, the claims of refugee status advanced by the suspect Mennonites were easily verified against extant German records.

Concurrent with the selection and assembly of the first group of close relatives from Europe, a second movement of refugees was being contemplated. Their case would prove to be a much more serious test of Canada's system of immigration screening. For one thing, the number of prospective immigrants in the second group was substantially higher. Also, Ottawa would have no advance notice as to their identities. Finally, all of the refugees were of eastern European extraction, thereby complicating the task of carrying out security checks.

On 13 November 1946, 1,700 Polish men disembarked from the ship *Sea Robin* at Halifax.[12] Eleven days later, Halifax harbour welcomed the *Sea Snipe*, on board which were an additional 1,200 Poles. Like their compatriots from the *Sea Robin*, the passengers of the *Sea Snipe* were recently demobilized soldiers who had served in the Polish 2nd Corps of the British Army during the war. All had been promised admission to Canada in return for their commitment to work on family farms.

Upon arrival and disembarkation, the Polish veterans were marched to Halifax's naval depot, where each received blankets and some spending money. From the depot, they were taken to nearby railway marshalling yards and placed on specially designated trains. Once loaded, the trains moved out, some destined for Montreal, Kingston, and Toronto, others headed for points farther west, like Winnipeg, Edmonton, and Chilliwack, British Columbia. At each stop, the Poles were dropped off in groups of not less than one hundred and not more than three hundred. Met by Canadian military personnel, they were hustled into waiting buses and driven to the nearest army depots, where they were issued sets of work clothes. Outfitted for their sojourns in Canada, they were taken by car or rail to the farms to which they had been assigned.

To understand how and why 2,900 Poles were granted admission to a country whose doors were still closed to most European refugees, it is necessary to go back to Poland in August 1939, to the tense hours just prior to the outbreak of the Second World War. Like much of the Polish Army during the last summer of peace in Europe, the cavalry brigade commanded by General Wladyslaw Anders was unprepared for the storm that was about to break.[13] Holding forward positions along Poland's western frontier with Nazi Germany, Anders's men had been prevented from carrying out effective reconnaissance because of the Polish government's determination not to provoke Hitler. Accordingly, when massed German armour and infantry violated Polish territory on 1 September, the Anders brigade was caught by surprise and forced to withdraw. Thus began a month of almost continuous eastward retreat, interrupted only occasionally by courageous but futile counterattacks that pitted horse cavalry against mechanized German forces.

Harassed by the powerful German air force and slowed by refugee-clogged roads, Anders nevertheless managed to lead his troops to apparent safety along the Polish–Byelorussian border. Then a second disaster befell his beleaguered country. By virtue of secret annexes to the recently concluded Nazi–Soviet pact, the armed forces of the Soviet Union invaded Poland on 17 September. Facing little resistance from its demoralized foes, the Red Army quickly occupied Poland's eastern territories up to lines that had been pre-arranged with the Germans. Hungry, exhausted, and surrounded by hostile forces, Anders and the remnants of his brigade surrendered to Soviet units at the end of the month.

This was the start of one of the more remarkable individual odysseys of the Second World War. As a high-ranking officer, Anders was separated from his men and placed in the custody of the dreaded People's

Commissariat of Internal Affairs, or NKVD. After several weeks of almost daily interrogation, his captors concluded that he was a source of valuable intelligence and ordered him transported to Moscow. Locked away in the bowels of the city's infamous Lubianka prison, Anders was certain he would die there. Then fate intervened. On 22 June 1941, Nazi Germany launched Operation 'Barbarossa,' the invasion of the Soviet Union. Repeating the Blitzkrieg tactics that had proven so successful against Poland and France, Hitler's legions destroyed dozens of Red Army divisions and penetrated deep into Soviet territory. Reeling from these early defeats and the loss of so many front-line units, Stalin was compelled to release his Polish POWs for use against the invaders.[14]

Despite Anders's less-than-cooperative attitude toward his captors, the Soviets offered him the job of leading the restored Polish forces. After having endured the humiliation of defeat, capture, and imprisonment, the general welcomed the opportunity to command troops again, even if it were under the auspices of the hated Soviets. Over the next year and a half, several Polish divisions were organized and outfitted. On the eve of their return to action, however, matters took another turn. A stabilized situation at the front and disagreement over Anders's recruitment policies led Moscow to scrap plans for the deployment of most of the Poles in Russia. Instead, arrangements were made with Britain to evacuate them to Iran.[15] From there, the fledgling army made its way to the Iraqi desert, where it was reconstituted as a corps under British command.

The Polish 2nd Corps first saw action in Italy in 1944, during the Allied siege of the monastery that commanded the heights of Monte Cassino. The corps' baptism of fire was a bloody one. Of the approximately 37,000 Polish troops (two divisions) who went into battle on 11 May, 10 per cent were killed, wounded, or captured during the two weeks of fighting that ensued.[16] Nevertheless, the Poles impressed friend and foe alike with their daring and tenacity. Re-equipped and reinforced after Monte Cassino, the 2nd Corps became an integral part of the British Army in Italy. At peak strength comprising almost 160,000 men, the 2nd Corps continued to serve and fight there until the end of the war.[17]

While the nucleus of the 2nd Corps consisted of soldiers from the defeated Polish Army of 1939, over the course of the war its ranks were swelled by recruits whose Polish nationality and anti-Nazi credentials were questionable, to say the least. Probably the most suspect group of volunteers were several hundred Byelorussians from the disputed border area between Poland and the Soviet Union.[18] Situated in the centre of the eastern front, Byelorussia was essential to German military fortunes. With its dense forests and nearly impassable marshlands, the region afforded whoever occupied it good ground for defensive operations. It was also ideal terrain for guerrilla activity. After taking some time to get organized, Soviet partisans were operating with virtual impunity in Byelorussia by the spring of 1943.[19]

While the German forces who had invaded the Soviet Union were initially greeted as liberators, it was never Hitler's intention to grant the peoples of the occupied East even a modicum of national autonomy.[20] As an expression of the Nazis' determination to repress and exploit their new subjects, Berlin initially refused to countenance the establishment of indigenous military units.[21] This policy was rigidly enforced, even in the face of German setbacks at the front. Only in the spring of 1943, when the Soviet partisan movement began to threaten vital supply and communication lines, did the Nazi leadership reconsider.

Unable to spare manpower from the front for anti-partisan operations, the commander of the SS and police in Minsk acceded to a request by the Byelorussian puppet government to raise home-defence units. There were two conditions. First, the indigenous forces were not to be permitted to develop into a Byelorussian national army. Second, all such units that were raised in Byelorussia had to be committed to the fight against Soviet partisans.[22]

Designated the Byelorussian Home Guard (BKA), the new defence force began recruiting early in 1944. The objective was to raise forty-six battalions comprising upwards of 60,000 men. The BKA's ranks were to be filled by way of a general mobilization, but its complement of officers and NCOs was to be drawn from men who were already serving in the Ordnungsdienst (OD), or Order Service, the name given to the indigenous auxiliary police units formed in German-occupied Byelorussia.[23] During 1941–3, many of these OD units had participated in the slaughter of approximately two-thirds of Byelorussia's Jewish population, which before the war had numbered almost

400,000.[24] By incorporating the OD, then, the BKA became a dumping ground for some of the worst collaborationist elements of Byelorussian society.

Throughout the spring and summer of 1944, the BKA was heavily engaged in anti-partisan operations. Its presence behind the lines did little to influence the course of the war. Indeed, by autumn, the German Army had been all but driven out of western Byelorussia. Following on the heels of the retreating Germans were units of the BKA. Once they were safely ensconced in Germany, these ragtag forces were incorporated into the 30th SS Grenadier Division, a recently activated formation that consisted mainly of long-term Ukrainian and Byelorussian collaborators.[25] Soon after its establishment, the 30th SS was deployed to France, ostensibly to assist in the fight against the French underground.[26]

Within weeks of their transfer to the western front, the Byelorussians' commitment to the German cause showed signs of faltering. As long as they had been stationed in the East, the men of the BKA were fighting for their homes, their families, their lives. After Byelorussia was overrun by the Red Army, however, the thoughts of many turned to saving themselves. Aware that their best chance of survival lay in surrender to the western Allies, the Byelorussian puppet government, now in exile in Germany, lobbied the Nazi regime for the organization of the 30th SS's Byelorussian elements into a separate formation. Suspicious of the motives of the Germans' erstwhile allies but desperate for manpower, Reich Leader of the SS and Police Heinrich Himmler reluctantly agreed to the request.[27]

In January 1945, the SS Assault Brigade 'Belarus' was established. Two months later, this all-Byelorussian unit was thrown into battle against the spearheads of the U.S. 3rd Army, which was commanded by the legendary General George S. Patton. What happened next was predictable. Nowhere near full strength and bereft of fighting spirit, the Byelorussians offered only token resistance before surrendering en masse near Regensburg in southern Germany.[28]

With the Third Reich on the verge of collapse, the priority of the Byelorussian political leadership turned from support for the German war effort to keeping its soldiers out of Soviet hands. Envoys were dispatched to the American, British, and French armies to seek assurances that the men of the 'Belarus' brigade would not be repatriated. The hope was that the western Allies would overlook the unit's collaborationist record and embrace its members as staunch anti-communists. The Byelorussian diplomats were given a cordial reception, but no one was prepared to guarantee sanctuary for hundreds of former SS men. The only firm commitment came from General Anders, who promised that, if the remnants of the brigade could make their way to Italy, they would be absorbed into the Polish 2nd Corps. In offering his assistance to the Byelorussians, it seems unlikely that Anders knew of their SS affiliation or of the extent of their collaboration with the Germans. In any event, the general was concerned with more pressing matters. With the war in Europe over, he had undertaken negotiations with the British to prevent the return of the men of the 2nd Corps to Poland.[29]

Locked away as POWs, the Byelorussians would require assistance in getting to Italy. It was their good fortune to have fallen into Patton's hands. When Anders approached his ally with the idea of taking over control of the 'Belarus' brigade, the 3rd Army commander, whose anti-communist sympathies were well known, was very receptive to the idea. As a result of the Anders-Patton discussions, an agreement was reached whereby the members of the brigade would be surreptitiously transferred from American to French captivity as the first step in their evacuation to Italy. On a clear night in June 1945, the guards of the POW enclosure in Regensburg were withdrawn and the Byelorussians permitted to slip into the French zone of occupation. From there, French forces moved the brigade to Marseilles, the port of embarkation for ships to Italy. In a matter of weeks, then, hundreds of Nazi collaborators had gone from utter defeat and almost certain repatriation to sanctuary in the ranks of their former enemies.[30]

The Byelorussians were not out of the woods yet. In the months following the end of hostilities in Europe, millions of eastern Europeans and Soviet citizens were repatriated by the western Allies. It was not beyond the realm of possibility that the men of the 2nd Corps would be included in the wave of returnees. Notwithstanding its moral obligation to Polish soldiers who had served under British command during the war, the British government was committed to repatriation.[31] In an effort to fulfil the refugee provisions of the Yalta agreement without provoking a mutiny, the British Army tried to persuade its Polish soldiers to return home. Volunteers for repatriation were quickly segregated so as to forestall any last-minute change of heart.[32] For those less sanguine about the prospect of going home, London negotiated a number of guarantees with the Soviet-installed government in Warsaw, including a grant of amnesty for any Polish collaborator who had been conscripted into German forces.[33]

Satisfied by British assurances of safe passage, or simply homesick, a substantial number of the Polish soldiers elected to return to their native land. Between the German surrender in May 1945 and the end of the year, 82,000 of the approximately 205,000 Polish troops serving under British command, or 40 per cent, opted for repatriation. By the start of 1946, however, it was clear that the remainder had no intention of going back to Poland.[34] The hardliners included most of men of the 2nd Corps.[35] Faced with the intransigence and growing restiveness of its Polish soldiers, Britain was forced to shift from a policy of encouraging repatriation to one of colonization abroad.

The British government took responsibility for the resettlement of the Polish veterans in the hope that they could be dispersed among the various nations of the Commonwealth. Yet within a short time of launching its diplomatic offensive, London was forced to abandon the idea as a pipe dream. Despite considerable arm-twisting, the response from the Commonwealth was disappointing, to say the least. Of the various countries consulted, only New Zealand evinced any desire to help, and then only after its own servicemen had been repatriated.[36] It was clear that the problem of finding new homes for the men of the Polish 2nd Corps would have to be solved by Britain alone.

To meet this new obligation, London established the Polish Resettlement Corps (PRC) in May 1946. Created as an adjunct to the British armed forces, the PRC was envisioned as a temporary organization. Its mandate was to take over supervision of recently demobilized Polish soldiers and provide them with job training and whatever other assistance might be required to facilitate their integration into British society.[37]

In Canada, meanwhile, the end of the war, as was noted in the previous chapter, had brought with it a flurry of requests for family reunification from the relatives of European refugees. Some requests had been submitted by relatives of members of the 2nd Corps.[38] Like the overwhelming majority of such appeals, those submitted on behalf of the Polish veterans were rejected. Ottawa occasionally granted admission to a sponsored Polish ex-serviceman on a temporary, non-immigrant basis, but even such cases were few and far between.[39] For most Polish nationals, Canadian visas remained out of reach.

In light of the delays that had occurred in repatriating Canadian servicemen and of the anti-immigration sentiment that still pervaded official Ottawa, Canada in 1946 did not seem a promising destination for members of the 2nd Corps. But the Poles had an influential bene-factor – the Canadian business community. Suffering from the usurpa-tion of their workers by the armed forces, labour-intensive industries like mining and forestry were forced to get by with the help of German POWs. At the same time, the plight of the 2nd Corps was receiving extensive coverage in Canadian newspapers. Not surprisingly, then, some companies began to cast their gaze toward Italy. Sugar-beet growers, for example, lobbied Ottawa for the admission of a contingent of Polish ex-servicemen to help bring in the crop. The pulp-and-paper industry also expressed interest in Anders's men, hoping to use them in place of German POWs.[40]

The problem of labour in the early postwar period was twofold. First, a considerable part of Canada's workforce had been absorbed by the armed services. Delays in the repatriation of Canadian soldiers, sailors, and airmen from abroad and the generally unsettled economic conditions at home meant that labour shortages would persist for some time. Second, with the end of the war in Europe, the German POWs who had been making up the shortfall could no longer be kept in Can-ada. Their repatriation would only increase the pressure on the coun-try's already strained labour supply.[41] Indeed, it was the opinion of some within the business community that the loss of the POWs would cause the Canadian economy irreparable harm.[42]

As 1945 drew to a close, there were still some thirty-two thousand German POWs in Canada. Most had been used in logging operations or to bring in the harvest.[43] As late as March 1946, the Canadian govern-ment gave no indication that it was prepared to consider an extension of their stay. Nor did there appear to be any desire in Ottawa to accept applications from German POWs for permanent admission, except in rare cases.[44] Early in April, however, the government reversed itself.

Under increasing pressure from farmers in Ontario and the West, cabinet agreed to try to negotiate with Britain for the retention of a part of Canada's POW workforce.[45]

The repatriation of German prisoners had been a condition of the peace settlement between the Allied and Axis powers. Needless to say, the attempt by Canada to delay repatriation did not go over well in London. It was not long before the two countries were embroiled in a diplomatic tug of war. Just when the situation seemed hopelessly deadlocked, Norman Robertson came up with a way out of the impasse. Aware of the criticism to which the British government was being subjected for its promise to grant permanent admission to tens of thousands of Polish ex-servicemen, Robertson floated the idea of a trade. Canada would honour its commitment to finish repatriating the German POWs, he proposed, if Britain would agree to make available an equal number of demobilized Poles. In this way, the Canadian economy would not suffer unduly from the loss of POW labour, while the transfer of the Poles to Canada would take some of the wind out of the sails of the British government's critics. The idea, Robertson noted in uncharacteristically informal language, would effectively 'kill two or three birds with one stone.'[46]

With the squabble over POW repatriation souring relations between London and Ottawa, Robertson's proposal seemed like the ideal solution. Not only would Britain be placated, but Canada, having exchanged enemy POWs for Allied refugees, would be seen to be getting the better of the deal. With his keen eye for compromise, Prime Minister Mackenzie King quickly endorsed the idea.[47] Final government approval was contingent, of course, on the advice of the ministers who would be responsible for the deal's implementation.

At the weekly cabinet meeting held on 22 May 1946, Minister of Labour Humphrey Mitchell and Minister of Mines and Resources James A. Glen were informed of Robertson's proposal.[48] Both were receptive to the idea. Mitchell's only condition was that the Poles be as physically suited to agricultural labour as the Germans had been. Voicing the concerns of the immigration bureaucrats, Glen, on the other hand, wanted assurances that the Poles would be subjected to strict security screening. It would be most unfortunate, he observed, if 'Nazis or agents' were able to infiltrate the ranks of the new arrivals.[49]

Robertson's proposal was submitted for study to both the Department of Labour and Immigration Branch. After several days, both agencies concluded that their concerns could be addressed in the final agreement. With the interested departments on side, cabinet approval was just a formality. At its next meeting, cabinet authorized the commencement of negotiations with the British government regarding an exchange of German POWs for demobilized Polish soldiers.[50]

The response on the other side of the Atlantic was similarly positive. After receiving the prime minister's endorsement, External Affairs informally sounded out British authorities on the idea of a swap. Even before cabinet had finished deliberating the merits of Robertson's proposal, Canadian High Commissioner Vincent Massey was able to report that the British were amenable.[51] For the government in London, it was a question of domestic politics. The creation of the PRC and the anticipated introduction to Britain of large numbers of Polish workers had provoked considerable opposition in some quarters, particularly from the trade unions. Haunted by the memory of the Great Depression and reluctant to relinquish the strong bargaining position afforded by wartime labour shortages, the unions were railing against London's alleged betrayal of the British worker.[52] The transfer of four thousand Poles to Canada would not pacify the unions, of course, but it might deflect some of the criticism that Britons were being forced to bear the brunt of the influx of cheap foreign labour.

Once both sides had reached agreement in principle, all that remained was to hammer out the details. For the most part, the negotiations on substantive issues went smoothly, although a problem arose over logistics. The British government wanted Canada to take in demobilized Poles who had already been settled in Britain. Ottawa had other ideas. With anti-immigration feeling in the country still running high and with the dependants of many Canadians still stranded overseas, the last thing the King government wanted was to appear to be favouring the admission of foreign workers over the repatriation of its own nationals. Such a situation, Massey noted in a profound understatement, might 'give rise to very serious complaints and criticism.' From the public relations point of view, then, it was considered more prudent to screen the Poles in Italy and ship them directly to Canada.[53]

Though convinced the Canadians were unnecessarily complicating matters, the British relented for two reasons. First, they could not afford to do anything that might jeopardize what thus far had been the only substantial offer of help in resettling the Poles. Second, the Italian government was insisting that the 2nd Corps leave Italy before the national elections, which were scheduled to be held in the autumn.[54] The tight deadline meant that if the British government dallied, it would have to grant admission to an additional four thousand Poles, thereby negating the political benefits of the Canadian offer. Putting politics ahead of principle, London acceded to Ottawa's request that the transfer of the Poles from British to Canadian jurisdiction be carried out in Italy. The last hurdle having thereby been cleared, the two sides initialled the agreement early in June.[55]

The British–Canadian agreement called for Canada to exchange a contingent of German prisoners for soon-to-be-demobilized Polish soldiers. Since it had been anticipated that four thousand POWs would be required to assist Canadian farmers in 1946, mainly in the sugar-beet fields of Alberta, Manitoba, and Ontario, that was the number of Poles to be admitted to Canada. All had to be under thirty-five years of age, physically suited to agricultural work, and single. Each ex-serviceman was required to sign a contract committing him to work in Canada for three years. Prior to the start of the selection process, the contractual obligation would be reduced to two years. During this period of indenture, each man's admission to Canada would be on a temporary non-immigrant basis. Failure to fulfil the terms of the contract, either by premature termination, the commission of a crime, or the fomenting of anti-Soviet propaganda, would result in immediate expulsion.[56] Subject to good behaviour and the fulfilment of their contractual obligations, the Poles would be eligible for permanent admission. At that time, they would also be allowed to apply to have their relatives admitted.[57]

To facilitate implementation of the agreement, cabinet appointed an interdepartmental committee. The committee was given responsibility for all administrative matters pertaining to the agreement, such as the terms of the contracts into which the Poles would be entering, the establishment and dispatch overseas of the Canadian teams who would select the Polish contingent, and, most importantly, the formulation of the selection criteria to be applied. In seeking a committee chairman, cabinet took the somewhat unusual step of going outside of the career civil service. Raymond Ranger, to be sure, was not new to Ottawa. During the war, he had served both as director of mobilization and associate director of the National Selective Service. Immediately after the war, he had served as chairman of the Industrial Selection and Release Board. But his prewar experience had been in the private sector. Nevertheless, at the end of May 1946, Ranger was appointed special assistant to the deputy minister of labour with responsibility for the selection and admission to Canada of four thousand Polish ex-servicemen.[58]

Within two weeks of his appointment, Ranger's committee had worked out the details of the selection and screening process. One of the more contentious matters with which the committee had to deal was the size and composition of the Canadian selection teams. It was decided that two teams of three men, each comprising a medical officer, an employment officer, and an RCMP security officer, would be sent to Italy. The decision was a controversial one, as some committee members wondered whether six men would be sufficient to carry out the job of interviewing thousands of applicants. In the end, the dissenters put aside their concerns upon receiving assurances that the British Army would screen the Poles in advance of the Canadians' arrival.[59]

In terms of the personnel to be sent overseas, the committee nominated individuals with long experience in their respective fields. The medical officers were Dr Fred Parney and Dr George Audet, both distinguished members of the Department of Health and Welfare who had been seconded to Immigration Branch in the past. The employment officers – Joseph Meindl of the Department of Labour's Unemployment Insurance Commission (UIC) and Frank Dubenski of the department's National Employment Office – were also career bureaucrats. Staff Sergeants Kenneth Shakespeare and Archibald Stevenson, both RCMP veterans, were assigned to the Canadian teams as security officers. The mission would be headed by Harold Hare, a senior official at the Department of Labour.[60]

Cabinet approval for the admission of the Polish veterans had hinged on the assumption that they would be subjected to rigorous screening.[61] According to PC 3112, the order-in-council that authorized the government to bring in the Polish ex-servicemen, representatives of the

Department of Labour, Immigration Branch, and the RCMP were to be sent overseas to 'interview and examine' candidates.[62] In keeping with their end of the agreement, the British government promised to provide examination facilities to the Canadian selection teams, as well as access to British Army files on each of the Polish applicants. London also promised to screen the interpreters who would be detailed to the Canadian teams. In view of the wide dispersal of units of the 2nd Corps, it was agreed that applicants would be assembled for screening in two camps. One would be located near Naples, the other just outside of Ancona.[63]

At each assembly camp, British officials would be responsible for the preparation of nominal lists of applicants, copies of which were to be distributed to the examining Canadian medical, labour, and security officers.[64] For purposes of conducting examinations, an area of the camp was to be roped off, inside which tables were to be set up for each of the three examining officers, as well as one where the contracts would be signed. Upon arrival of the Canadian team, camp officials were to have the candidates line up and then feed them into the examination area in a more or less continuous stream. Each candidate would have with him his completed application form and his British Army file.

When his turn came, each applicant was to proceed, in sequence, to the medical, labour, and security officers. If he failed at any of the three stations, he would be informed on the spot. His name would then be struck from the Canadian lists and his file returned to the camp office. Successful applicants, on the other hand, would be given a personal identification form by the security officer. The form would bear the applicant's name, provisional immigration number, fingerprints, and signature. Form in hand, he would be waved on to the undertaking desk, where he would sign the contract obligating him to perform two years of agricultural labour in Canada. This would mark the end of Canadian screening procedures, although document checks were to be conducted both prior to departure from Italy and on arrival in Canada.[65]

In terms of screening for war criminal and collaborationist background, the admission criteria employed by the Canadian teams were among the most stringent ever applied to prospective immigrants.[66]

Each applicant was subject to the provisions of the Immigration Act, copies of which had been provided to RCMP officers Shakespeare and Stevenson.[67] The act, it will be remembered, expressly forbade the admission to Canada of persons who in the past had supported anti-democratic movements or engaged in treason.[68] Yet the teams' admission criteria went well beyond the act's broad anti-subversive provisions. According to PC 3112, service with the Allies against Axis forces was a precondition for eligibility. In practice, this was interpreted to mean that the Polish veterans could have no record of prior service in the German armed forces, regardless of whether it had been conscripted or voluntary. Even men who had been conscripted into German forced-labour detachments, a situation that could hardly be considered collaboration in the accepted sense of the term, were not eligible for admission.[69]

Taking a page from the UNRRA screening manual, Ranger's interdepartmental committee designed two questionnaires, both of which had to be completed prior to an applicant's examination. Admittedly, neither document directly asked about an applicant's wartime activities. The basic questionnaire, for example, contained eleven questions aimed at eliciting information regarding the applicant's nationality, his service with the 2nd Corps, and his agricultural skills. Of these, only one was relevant to the issue of criminal or collaborationist activity during the war. This was the form's final question, which asked: 'In what other occupations have you worked and for what periods?'[70]

The question about previous occupations was open-ended with respect to an applicant's employment history. If answered truthfully, it inevitably would have revealed information regarding his wartime activities. Of course, there was nothing to compel an applicant to tell the truth. For persons who had served in collaborationist units during the war, the temptation would have been quite strong to avoid any damaging disclosures. In the case of the Polish veterans, however, there was little chance that such a deception would succeed. Many of the men who joined the 2nd Corps after its arrival in Italy had been taken prisoner in German uniform.[71] As a matter of course, their British Army files would have included information gleaned from their identity discs, military papers, and interrogations after capture.[72] With full access to these records, it was unlikely that Canadian security officers would have been unaware of an applicant's prior service in German military or auxiliary police units.

The processing of the men of the 2nd Corps for examination began in mid-August 1946. Approximately 7,000 had filled out applications.[73] Preliminary screening by the Poles whittled the number down to 4,500.[74] Notwithstanding the assurances given to Ranger's interdepartmental committee, no British screening was carried out prior to the arrival in Italy of the Canadian selection teams.[75] Instead, the British Army merely assembled the applicants in three camps and prepared nominal lists. Yet that was sufficient for Canadian purposes. When Hare and his teams arrived in Italy at the end of August, they were able to start the process of selection almost immediately.[76]

With a pool of more than four thousand prospective immigrants, the 2nd Corps movement was the first serious test of Canada's postwar system of immigration screening. As a consequence, no one could be certain as to how effective it would be in weeding out undesirables. On the basis of contemporary reports, it appears that the two Canadian teams in Italy processed about 135 applicants per day.[77] Assuming that the teams worked a seven-and-a-half-hour day, the rate at which the applicants were processed would have been approximately nine per hour (eighteen in total), or one every six minutes.

Although it is difficult to conceive of such a rapid procedure having been effective, it may well be that a longer procedure was not required. After all, each Polish serviceman was required to bring both his completed application form and his British Army file to the examination. Any discrepancy between his declarations on the form and his army file would have been immediately noticed. This alone would have been grounds for his removal from the roster of candidates. In the event that the application form and personnel file were consistent, the RCMP security officer questioned the applicant as to his 'background and activities' prior to his joining the 2nd Corps.[78] On the basis of the answers provided, a determination was made as to whether the applicant's prior activities were in conformity with Canadian immigration criteria in general and with PC 3112 in particular. Whether the applicant was accepted or rejected, the entire examination should not have been more than a few minutes' duration.

If Ottawa harboured any doubts about the effectiveness of the screening procedures employed in Italy, these were quickly put to rest. Within days of the start of processing, the RCMP officers reported a problem. The ranks of the 2nd Corps, they had discovered, included more than just veterans from Russia and the Middle East. According to their British Army files, a substantial number of the Poles had joined the corps only after its arrival in Italy in 1944. More problematic was the revelation that some of the later recruits had not thrown their lot in with Anders until after the cessation of hostilities in Europe. Of the post-1944 recruits, screening revealed that at least 15 per cent had served in either the German armed forces or in German forced-labour detachments. Others had no record of overt collaboration with the enemy, but seemed to have derived material advantage from the German occupation of their country.[79] Citing concerns about the 'bona fides' of the men in these categories, the RCMP officers asked the Canadian mission for clarification of their instructions.[80]

The presence of collaborators in the Polish 2nd Corps should not have come as a surprise. During the final months of the war, almost sixty-nine thousand Poles in German uniform were taken prisoner by the Allies. Of these, more than fifty-three thousand, or 77 per cent, had found their way into Anders's force.[81] This meant that more than one-third of the men of the 2nd Corps had some record of collaboration with the Germans. To be sure, most, with the exception of the former BKA recruits, appear to have been coerced or conscripted into service. Nonetheless, under the terms of PC 3112, such men did not qualify for admission to Canada. If the criteria were not relaxed, the head of the Canadian mission warned, the number of Poles eligible for admission would fall well below the four thousand called for in the original British–Canadian agreement. Estimates as to the extent of the short-fall ranged from 25 to 50 per cent.[82]

Notwithstanding the problem that had arisen with respect to the screening of the Poles, the government's initial response was to hold firm. 'Under no circumstances,' External Affairs cabled the Canadian mission, should collaborators of any kind be accepted for admission to Canada.[83] In making the decision to exclude all Poles who had served in the German Army or in forced-labour detachments, Ottawa was cognizant of the fact that many had done so under duress. The government was also keenly aware that its quota of labourers would not be filled. Yet no weakening of the screening criteria was contemplated. Instead, the interdepartmental committee suggested that the shortfall might be made up from the ranks of the PRC in Britain. If additional ex-servicemen were required, cabinet indicated its willingness to reconsider the original decision to exclude married men.[84]

With so many of the Poles failing to meet the criteria for admission to Canada, it was not long before word of the problem got back to 2nd Corps headquarters. Viewing the tough Canadian screening regime as a betrayal of the original agreement, Anders and his staff went on the offensive. First, they withdrew all pending applications. Then, on 19 September, one of Anders's senior commanders addressed the troops at each of the assembly camps and called on them to 'hold together.' The implication was clear. Unless the Canadians went easy on its men, 2nd Corps would boycott the examinations.[85]

Surprised by the Poles' reaction but determined to forge ahead, the Canadian mission tried to negotiate a compromise. The problem was that Hare's hands were tied. As long as Ottawa refused to permit any relaxation of the screening criteria, he had nothing to offer.[86] Fearing the collapse of the entire scheme, the British government intervened in the dispute. The Poles were ordered to resume cooperating in the screening of eligible servicemen. At the same time, London flexed its diplomatic muscle. In a none-too-subtle attempt to pressure the Canadian government, the War Office reminded Ottawa that much more was at stake than the success of a single resettlement scheme. On the contrary, the War Office observed, failure to find a mutually acceptable solution to the problem would cause a 'loss of faith in British intentions,' with potentially grave foreign policy consequences.[87]

Ottawa was caught in a bind. On the one hand, its decision to admit four thousand Poles while there were still Canadians abroad awaiting repatriation had not been a popular one. Indeed, the only thing that had made it palatable to the Canadian public had been assurances that politically undesirable individuals would be kept out. On the other hand, the scheme had come about on Canada's initiative. Having pressed its ally for access to the Poles in the first place, the Canadian government was now under enormous pressure to keep its end of the bargain.

As the crisis deepened, the wires were hot with messages between

Ottawa and the Canadian High Commission in London. Once again, it fell to Norman Robertson to find a way out. Weighing the domestic political fallout of lifting the strict screening regime against the diplomatic consequences of maintaining it, Robertson, who had recently replaced Massey as high commissioner, crafted a compromise. The number of admissible Polish servicemen might be increased, he suggested, by extending eligibility to those who had deserted from the German armed forces or fled from German labour detachments and joined the 2nd Corps in time to participate in military operations. Surely this category of Poles, Robertson asserted, like the charter members of Anders's army, had established their anti-Nazi credentials. Moreover, the compromise did not in any way violate either the letter or the spirit of PC 3112. Under the revised screening criteria proposed by the new high commissioner, most 2nd Corps members who had a record of prior service in the German armed forces would still be excluded. In other words, participation in operations against the Germans would confer eligibility for admission to Canada only if the Pole in question had demonstrated his anti-Nazi sentiments by desertion or flight.[88]

In view of the high diplomatic stakes, Robertson's proposal was presented directly to Prime Minister King for consideration. As a face-saving way out of the impasse, the proposal had great appeal to King, but the prime minister was determined to avoid further complications. Accordingly, he decided, apparently on his own, that the boundaries of admissibility needed to be widened even more than had been proposed by his trusted servant. King's plan, in which then Minister of Justice Louis St Laurent concurred, called for the inclusion not only of deserters from the German Army who later fought with Anders, but also of any Pole captured in a German uniform who subsequently enlisted in the 2nd Corps and took part in its operations. In other words, the only Poles who would be barred from admission to Canada would be those members of the 2nd Corps who had joined too late to have fought against the Germans.[89]

The revised criteria were transmitted to Italy at the end of September and presented to the high command of the 2nd Corps on 1 October. While the Canadian offer did not go as far as the Poles had hoped, it was enough to end their boycott.[90] With Anders's approval secured, screening resumed on the basis of Robertson's proposal, as amended by the prime minister – that is, with the key criterion being the timing of a soldier's entry into the Polish 2nd Corps.[91] The process was back on track. Or so it seemed.

Almost immediately after the resumption of screening, another problem arose. In the course of re-examining the Poles, Staff Sergeants Shakespeare and Stevenson were a bit overzealous. Reading the revised criteria too literally, the RCMP officers interpreted them to mean that no one who joined the 2nd Corps too late to have fought the Germans was eligible for admission to Canada, irrespective of whether or not he had previously served in the German Army. The Poles were livid. The RCMP's interpretation, they complained, was actually favouring those members of the 2nd Corps who had served in the German armed forces over those who had not, such as Polish underground fighters or soldiers who had been captured in 1939 and who had spent several years in German POW captivity. If the situation were not rectified, 2nd Corps advised, its cooperation might be withdrawn yet again.[92]

Unlike the earlier disagreement over the stringency of Canadian screening, this time the Poles had a point. It made no sense to confer eligibility on former members of the German armed forces just because they had joined the 2nd Corps prior to an arbitrary deadline, while at the same time denying eligibility to persons who had never collaborated but who, through no fault of their own, had missed the deadline for enlistment. Still, the Canadian mistake was an honest one, and need not have resulted in new threats from the Polish side. In any event, cooler heads soon prevailed. Acknowledging the illogic and unfairness of the manner in which the revised criteria were being applied, Ottawa instructed Shakespeare and Stevenson to reject only those Poles who had joined the 2nd Corps too late to take part in operations against the Germans *and* who had previously served in the German armed forces or in forced-labour detachments.[93]

With the resolution of the second quarrel over screening, the selection process finally staggered toward completion. On 3 and 10 November, more than a week behind schedule, the first two contingents of Polish veterans sailed for Canada.[94] The landing of the *Sea Robin* at Halifax proceeded without incident, but disembarkation from the *Sea Snipe* was held up when irregularities were discovered on the identification papers of three of the passengers. Investigation at the scene revealed that all three men had lied about the timing of their enlistment in the Polish 2nd Corps. Bound by the provisions of PC 3112, the RCMP took the men into custody pending their return to Europe.[95]

After all of the controversy that had swirled around the scheme to bring the Polish veterans to Canada, the government could be excused if it assumed that the file was closed. Unfortunately, this was not the case. A few months after the admission of the first two contingents, the *Montreal Standard* obtained portions of the Canadian mission's final report. From the leaked excerpts, the newspaper learned that, at one assembly camp in Italy, the examination team had reinstated a substantial number of the Poles who had earlier been rejected because of their service in the German armed forces.[96] The story was too good to pass up. The next day, under the blaring headline '141 Nazi Poles on Farms Here,' the *Standard* ran an article that accused the Canadian government of having permitted the entry of dozens of Nazi collaborators.[97]

As was to be expected, public reaction was immediate and resoundingly critical of the government. So strong was the fallout from the *Standard* piece, in fact, that Ottawa was compelled to answer its charges. In a forceful statement delivered to the House of Commons on 5 May 1947, Minister of Labour Mitchell rejected the media's claims that screening of the Poles had been lax or careless. Addressing his remarks to the opposition, the minister gave a brief history of the 2nd Corps movement and described the screening procedures that had been employed. Then, turning to his own backbenchers, Mitchell assured them that 'every precaution' had been taken to prevent the admission to Canada of persons who held Nazi sympathies.[98]

The furore over the *Montreal Standard* article was a signal lesson in the danger of government leaks. For the purposes of this story, however, it is instructive for another reason. While its coverage was unquestionably sensational and exaggerated, the *Standard* had raised an important question – to what extent, if any, did the changes made to the admission criteria for the Polish ex-servicemen facilitate the entry into Canada of Nazi war criminals or collaborators? Based on the evidence, the answer would seem to be that they had little or no effect. The largest group of collaborators known to have infiltrated the ranks of the Polish 2nd Corps were the men of the SS Assault Brigade

'Belarus.' Since they had entered the 2nd Corps only after surrendering to Patton's 3rd Army, the Byelorussians would have remained ineligible for admission to Canada on the basis of the timing of their enlistment alone. In other words, even if they had successfully concealed their prior SS affiliation and auxiliary police service from the Canadian selection teams, their belated enlistment in the 2nd Corps had precluded their participation in military operations against the Germans, thereby rendering them inadmissible, even under the revised criteria.

As for collaborators who may have joined the 2nd Corps prior to the end of hostilities in Europe, they could, in theory, have been considered for admission to Canada. But to do so would have meant submitting to the full range of security screening procedures. Like all prospective immigrants, they would have been subject to the anti-subversive provisions of the Immigration Act. Furthermore, the declarations on their application forms, including the answer they had given to the all-important question about their previous occupations, would have been checked against their British Army files. Any discrepancy between the two would have been immediately detected. Thus, the only collaborators who had a chance to beat the Canadian screening system would have been those who had already deceived British Army interrogators about their prior wartime activities.[99] And even this was no guarantee of success. As Sergeant Shakespeare reported upon completion of the mission, he and Stevenson were often able to elicit additional information from applicants, including confessions that they had volunteered for service with the Germans, which meant automatic rejection.[100]

In evaluating the effectiveness of the Canadian security screening procedures to which the Polish ex-soldiers were subjected, an additional point needs to be made. It will be remembered that PC 1373, the April 1946 order-in-council that continued to bar most enemy aliens from entry into Canada, allowed for the admission of individuals who could prove they had been opposed to an enemy government. The number of such exceptions would necessarily have been low, but most assuredly would have included concentration or labour camp inmates, who, by definition, had been considered 'opponents' by the Nazi regime. Yet the Polish ex-servicemen, who were Canada's allies, were not granted even this minimum consideration, at least not initially.

According to the original criteria employed by the Canadian screening teams in Italy, a Pole who had previously been conscripted into a forced-labour detachment was automatically deemed ineligible for admission. Viewed in this light, the screening regime applied to the men of the 2nd Corps seems unnecessarily strict, even unfair. By extending admissibility, then, all that Robertson and the prime minister had really done was to bring the screening of the Poles into line with existing Canadian immigration criteria and practices.

When Minister of Labour Mitchell addressed the House of Commons early in May 1947, he was not only putting the best face on the government's handling of the Polish veterans' file. He was also trying to justify the completion of their movement to Canada. Under the provisions of PC 3112, Canada was obliged to take in an additional 1,100 Polish ex-servicemen. A dearth of transatlantic shipping and the need for a second round of selection meant that their admission would be deferred until the summer. In the interim, London asked the Canadian government if it would consider increasing its quota. Faced with the prospect of continued labour shortages, cabinet approved the admission of an additional five hundred men from the ranks of the 2nd Corps.[101]

Screening of the third and final contingent of Poles began in Britain in June 1947. In what was becoming a familiar refrain, 2nd Corps lobbied for consideration of those servicemen who had previously been rejected on security grounds. Ottawa did not cave in to the pressure. On the contrary, the Poles who applied for the remaining 1,600 spots were subjected to virtually the same screening regime as the earlier contingents. The only difference, in fact, was that the Canadian mission allotted more time for the RCMP security officer to interview each applicant. This may account for the somewhat higher rate of rejections than that which had marked the first round of screening. Of the 2,717 Polish veterans who were processed, 773, or 28 per cent, were turned away. The rejects included 500 on medical grounds, 119 on the grounds of insufficient agricultural experience, and 154 on security grounds. An additional 293 withdrew their applications during screening.[102]

Only one Nazi collaborator is known to have been included in the first contingent of European close relatives who were selected for admission to Canada in the autumn of 1946. The concurrent admission of Polish veterans was subsequently discovered to have been infiltrated by collaborators, but their number, too, was negligible. As far as European refugees were concerned, then, Canada's system of immigration screening had been put on a solid footing. The same could not be said of persons who entered Canada under ordinary immigration procedures. Indeed, screening of regular immigrants was rather haphazard by comparison. The double standard appears to have been based on the perception by many within the immigration bureaucracy that the risk to Canada was lower from traditional immigration countries like Britain and the United States than from war-torn Europe. It took two or three years for Ottawa to acknowledge that the regular immigrant stream was not free of security threats. In the interim, the government would be embarrassed by several high-profile cases of infiltration by Nazi collaborators.

One of the more glaring failures of Canada's early postwar system of immigration screening was the inadvertent admission of five French collaborators. In the summer of 1946, Jean Huc, Julien Labedan, and Dr André Boussat arrived in Canada from France. All were travelling on false papers, all were using aliases, and all had been convicted of war crimes or collaboration in absentia.[103] They were followed in November 1946 by Dr Georges Montel and Count Jacques de Bernonville. Like their countrymen, Montel and de Bernonville were travelling on false papers, using aliases, and had prior convictions for collaboration. The only difference was that Montel and de Bernonville came to Canada via the United States. Montel's admission had been facilitated by the American visa stamped in his false French passport, while de Bernonville had crossed the border at Lacolle, Quebec, disguised as a priest.[104]

Of the five fugitives, de Bernonville had by far the most odious war record.[105] According to evidence presented before the French court that convicted him, de Bernonville, a high-ranking servant of the collaborationist Vichy regime, had played a major role in the round-up of Jews in North Africa and the brutal repression of the French resistance in Lyon. There was even evidence he had volunteered for service in the Waffen-SS late in the war.[106]

For the first year or so after his arrival in Canada, de Bernonville kept a low profile, doing clerical work in Quebec City and St Pacombe before moving to Montreal in December 1947 to take a job as sales manager for a local dairy.[107] His quiet and anonymous life was shattered when a former member of the French resistance happened to recognize him in the street. Fearing he would be denounced, de Bernonville took pre-emptive action. In January 1948, he went to immigration authorities in Montreal, advised them of his true identity, and sought refugee status, claiming he had been hounded out of France by a communist-dominated government that had distorted his war record.[108] A board of inquiry was convened, found de Bernonville inadmissible under Canada's immigration regulations, and ordered his deportation.[109] His fate seemed sealed when the French government asked for his extradition.[110]

In dread of returning to France, de Bernonville solicited the aid of a Montreal law firm. To the surprise of the Canadian government, his attorneys were able to get the deportation order quashed on a technicality.[111] Thus began a two-year legal battle that pitted de Bernonville against the bureaucrats at Immigration Branch and External Affairs. His case became a something of a cause célèbre, with certain segments of Quebec society, which regarded him as the victim of a smear campaign, rallying to his defence.[112] The controversy resulting from his case also exposed the fragility of relations between English and French Canada, not to mention some very ugly racism. The matter finally came to a close in the spring of 1951, when de Bernonville, his final appeal having been rejected, availed himself of a last opportunity to leave the country voluntarily. On 17 August 1951, having secured a haven in Brazil through that country's consulate in Montreal, he boarded KLM flight 653 bound for Rio de Janeiro. He would never return to Canada.[113]

Like de Bernonville, the other four collaborators were exposed soon after their arrival. Their cases, too, were heard by boards of inquiry. The result was the same each time – the boards ruled them inadmissible and ordered their deportation. The difference in the cases of the lesser collaborators was that the French government was not actively seeking their extradition.[114] Accordingly, Ottawa was less inclined to push for their deportation.[115] On 22 September 1948, cabinet agreed to waive the immigration regulations in the cases of Huc, Labedan, Boussat, and Montel.[116]

The admission of the French collaborators pointed out two fundamental weaknesses in Canada's system of immigration screening. In
the cases of Huc, Labedan, and Boussat, their entry had been made
possible by the ease with which one could obtain false identity papers
in France.[117] The entry of de Bernonville and Montel, on the other
hand, was facilitated by the lack of proper screening at the Canadian–
U.S. border. At the time, it was possible for a person to enter Canada
from the United States without a Canadian visa. All one needed to be
admitted as a tourist, for example, was a travel document with a U.S.
visa inside.[118] U.S. visas could be obtained from American immigration authorities after only a short period of residence. This is clearly
what happened in Montel's case, and possibly in de Bernonville's as
well. Unfortunately, it was not until the de Bernonville case hit the
media that the government was alerted to these problems and took
steps to remedy them.[119]

As 1946 came to a close, Canada was still far from being immigrant-
friendly. Notwithstanding the relaxation of PC 695, only a handful of
European refugees had been able to obtain Canadian visas. To be sure,
the admission of 2,900 Polish ex-servicemen was a significant concession, but there was no indication it would become a precedent. Indeed,
official Ottawa seemed determined to prevent any repetition. Writing to
the minister responsible for immigration shortly after the arrival of the
first Polish contingent, Deputy Minister of Labour Arthur MacNamara
urged his colleague 'not ... to go too fast in the matter of encouraging
immigration.'[120] Norman Robertson was even more blunt. Decrying the
distinctly ethnic character of the 2nd Corps movement, the high commissioner warned that schemes of this kind would only encourage pressure groups to try to 'influence and distort' Canada's immigration
policy.[121]

Once again, Robertson's words would prove to be prophetic. Emboldened by their success with the Poles, the business community went
on offensive. Viewing the 2nd Corps movement as just the tip of an
immigration iceberg, Canadian business pressed for greater access to
the European refugees. The corporations were not alone in adopting
this position. To the associations representing Canada's various ethnic
communities, the admission of the Poles as indentured labourers

offered a strategy for the future. The message seemed clear – if you want to get your people into Canada, demonstrate their economic worth. Bound by their mutual interests vis-à-vis the European refugees, both the business community and the ethnic immigrant-aid societies intensified the pressure for a relaxation of Canada's remaining immigration restrictions. In the process, they would expose the country to the first real danger of infiltration by Nazi war criminals and collaborators since the end of the Second World War.

CHAPTER FOUR

The Door Ajar

The objectives of the immigration lobby in Canada were fundamentally altered in the wake of the 2nd Corps movement. Having originated as a principled response to the European refugee crisis, the lobby shed its broad international and humanitarian outlook in favour of narrow ethnic and economic considerations. The business community was an important catalyst in this transformation. During 1945–6, Canadian business had supported a more open immigration policy, albeit with reservations. In the aftermath of the admission of the Polish ex-servicemen, however, the economic benefits of cheap labour imported from Europe were simply too promising to forego. Taking their cue from the interests that had successfully lobbied for the admission of the Poles, industry and agriculture began clamouring for waivers from Canada's immigration restrictions.[1]

A similar tendency could be discerned among immigration advocacy groups. Throughout the war and in the immediate postwar period, most of the proponents of increased immigration to Canada had been non-partisan in their approach to the European refugee crisis. This changed after the admission of the Poles. While some groups continued to lobby on behalf of refugees without reference to their nationality or ethnic origin,[2] they were overshadowed by others with more parochial agendas. Before long, the immigration lobby would be dominated by a few large ethnic associations that competed for Canadian visas on what was, for all intents and purposes, a quota basis. The most active associations were those that worked on behalf of Balts,[3] Ukrainians,[4] and Germans[5] who had been displaced by the Second World War.

Concurrent with the change in the immigration lobby's aims was a shift in its power base. Whereas philanthropic and religious groups had dominated the lobby during the war, after 1945, and particularly after the 2nd Corps movement, corporate and ethnic interests took precedence. The extent to which the balance of power had shifted was demonstrated by the rapid rise to prominence of the Canadian Christian Council for Resettlement of Refugees (CCCRR). Founded in June 1947, CCCRR was an umbrella organization for the various German-Canadian immigrant-aid societies. Its mandate was to select prospective settlers from among the hundreds of thousands of refugees who were languishing in Allied-occupied Germany and Austria. In keeping with the postwar trend toward ethnic preference in Canadian immigration, CCCRR's assistance was restricted to refugees of German origin.[6]

During its first few years of operation, CCCRR was seized with the plight of the Volksdeutsche. Displaced from their homes in eastern Europe and the Soviet Union, most Volksdeutsche were ineligible for International Refugee Organization (IRO) assistance. Yet those who had not acquired German citizenship were technically admissible to Canada. The problem was that Canadian immigration teams were relying exclusively on IRO to assemble prospective immigrants for examination.[7] In the absence of changes to IRO's governing constitution, the only way in which significant numbers of Volksdeutsche might be considered for admission to Canada would have been through the establishment of a separate immigrant-processing system. Of course, any measure aimed at bypassing IRO required the support of the Canadian government and the approval of Allied occupation authorities.

In February 1947, representatives of the major immigrant-aid societies, including those that would come together under the CCCRR banner, met with Prime Minister Mackenzie King and lobbied for an expansion of Canada's immigrant-processing operations.[8] None of the organizations expected to take over screening.[9] Rather, their aim was to make it possible for those of their European brethren who were admissible to Canada to be examined by Canadian immigration teams. The plan was to gather applicants from among IRO-ineligible refugees, weed out the undesirables, and then arrange for examination of the remainder. What the immigrant-aid societies wanted, in effect, was to act as a kind of surrogate IRO.[10]

It took months of negotiation, but, in November 1947, CCCRR became the first of the immigration lobby groups to be recognized as an agent of the Canadian government.[11] In terms of the organization's prestige and credibility, such recognition was of inestimable value. Yet the real significance of this recognition lay in the higher priority that was accorded to Volksdeutsche immigration as a consequence. For the first time since the end of the war in Europe, admissible Volksdeutsche refugees would be able to compete for Canadian visas with their non-German counterparts on an almost level playing field. Though not formally sponsored by the government, CCCRR's overseas office was accorded many of the privileges of a Canadian immigration mission. To underscore the organization's new status, Ottawa requested that Allied occupation authorities provide whatever assistance was necessary to facilitate its operations.[12]

Apart from lending support through diplomatic channels, the Canadian government originally intended to maintain an arm's-length relationship with CCCRR. This arrangement worked well enough at first, as the number of Volksdeutsche applicants was manageable. Indeed, in keeping with its status as a voluntary organization, CCCRR was self-financing, its $25,000/year budget coming from the service charges it levied on the Canadian relatives of prospective immigrants. As the number of Volksdeutsche applicants increased, however, its budget proved to be inadequate. Aware that insolvency could scupper its operations, CCCRR went to the government with hat in hand early in 1948. Its arguments for assistance were compelling. As CCCRR's chairman reminded the minister responsible for immigration, the organization was providing the same service for IRO-ineligible refugees as IRO was lending to those who came within its mandate. Under the circumstances, he suggested, it was only fair to divert a percentage of Ottawa's IRO contributions to CCCRR's coffers.[13]

Having committed to the admission of IRO-ineligible German refugees, the Canadian government found itself confronted with a stark choice – either provide CCCRR with financial assistance, or take over its immigrant-processing operations. Neither option was particularly attractive. On the one hand, a bailout was likely to elicit charges of favouritism from the non-German immigrant-aid societies. Taking over CCCRR's work, on the other hand, would entail a major expansion of

Canada's overseas immigration operations. Its hands already full with the processing of non-German refugees, Ottawa opted for a bailout package. In March 1948, cabinet approved the issuance of an emergency grant of $50,000 to the beleaguered organization. To forestall any future financial difficulties, cabinet also agreed to pay for CCCRR's operations up to a maximum of $100,000 per year. When the Canadian dollar experienced a sudden drop in value against the German mark, the stipend was raised to $120,000 per year.[14]

Needless to say, the infusion of cash saved CCCRR's immigrant-processing experiment. It also marked the end of the arm's-length relationship between Ottawa and the organization. As Director of Immigration Arthur Jolliffe pointed out in a memorandum to Deputy Minister Hugh Keenleyside, the decision to finance CCCRR's operations put to rest any pretence of independence. Henceforth, Jolliffe commented, CCCRR would be a government agency in everything but name.[15]

As a result of the fourfold increase in its budget, CCCRR's overseas office was able to set itself up along the lines of a Canadian government immigration mission. Its first order of business was to acquire facilities. This problem was solved when authorities in the British zone of occupation offered CCCRR the use of a camp at Mühlenberg, near Hannover.[16] Next, the organization needed to procure its own transatlantic transportation. During the winter of 1947–8, CCCRR managed to secure a few berths on IRO-chartered passenger ships. When these proved insufficient for the number of Volksdeutsche who were being cleared for immigration, the organization negotiated the setting aside of 400 of the 773 berths available on the SS *Beaverbrae*, a former German submarine tender that had been converted for passenger service by Canadian Pacific. Eventually, the entire ship was placed at CCCRR's disposal.[17]

The extent to which lobbying influences government policy is invariably a matter of conjecture. Yet there can be little doubt as to the effectiveness of Canada's immigration lobby in the aftermath of the 2nd Corps movement. In January 1947, after almost seven months of inaction, cabinet undertook a review of the close relatives scheme under pressure from the various immigrant-aid societies. Referring to the numerous representations it had received as evidence of a 'general desire' for the further relaxation of Canada's immigration restrictions, the government enacted PC 371. By virtue of the new order-in-council, the close relatives category was expanded to include the married children of Canadian residents and any grandchildren under the age of eighteen. Shortly thereafter, the category was amended once again, this time to permit the admission of the fiancé(e)s of Canadian residents. But the most significant change was made at the end of April. Acting on a recommendation from its committee on immigration policy, the full cabinet approved the expansion of the close relatives category to include the immediate families of all persons admissible under the revised regulations. With each immigrant now able to bring along a spouse and all unmarried children under the age of eighteen, the number of potential admissions in this category increased exponentially.[18]

To be sure, the means test that had characterized all previous exceptions to PC 695 was left more or less intact. It could be argued, therefore, that even the widening of the close relatives category would have only a limited impact on immigration levels. However, this was not the only concession won by the immigration lobby in the aftermath of the 2nd Corps movement. Along with the expansion of the close relatives scheme came an enlargement of admissible occupational categories. Under pressure from labour-starved Canadian companies, the government opened Canada's doors to several new categories of foreign workers. According to the occupational provisions of PC 371, not only were homesteaders eligible for admission, but also the relatives of established farmers and agricultural workers who had secured employment. To satisfy the labour requirements of other key sectors of the Canadian economy, persons experienced in mining, lumbering, or logging who had been assured of jobs on arrival were also deemed eligible for admission.[19] By increasing the number of admissible occupations, then, PC 371 paved the way for an unprecedented influx of new immigrants.

In the first eighteen months since the end of the war in Europe, the Canadian government had gone a considerable distance in relaxing the restrictions on immigration. Yet for many immigration advocates, it was not nearly far enough. For example, in March 1947 Liberal Member of Parliament David Croll read a statement in the House of Commons that chastised the government for its 'vague, indefinite, [and] wholly inadequate' response to the European refugee crisis. Lamenting the plight of the displaced Europeans, Croll, who represented an ethnically mixed Toronto constituency, declared that 'we must all do our share.' For Canada, this meant opening its doors to a minimum of 100,000 refugees. Out of humanitarian considerations, Croll advised, close relatives of Canadian residents should still be given priority. Yet there was nothing, he suggested, that prevented Canada from extending admissibility in order to acquire the labour so desperately needed by Canadian industry and agriculture.[20]

Croll's speech was by no means the first critique of Canada's immigration policy. On the contrary, the government had been hearing rumblings from the Liberal backbenches for months. Chief among the detractors were MPs who represented constituencies with large central and eastern European populations. But this was the first time that a high-profile member of the Liberal caucus like Croll had openly broken ranks with the party. Beset by internal dissention, the government realized it had to do something dramatic. Accordingly, Prime Minister King, with the help of Keenleyside and Special Assistant Jack Pickersgill, set about drafting a statement to Parliament.[21] The speech would become a landmark in the history of Canadian immigration.

At 3:00 PM on 1 May 1947, King rose in the House of Commons to make his long-awaited statement on immigration. By any standards of measurement, his words were prudent and restrained. The prime minister began by promising that increases in immigration would be closely tied to Canada's 'absorptive capacity.' The strength of the Canadian economy, in other words, would determine the extent to which the country opened its doors. To emphasize the point, King reminded the House of the reason for the enactment of PC 695 back in March 1931 – the Great Depression. The improvement in economic conditions, he acknowledged, made it possible to interpret the regulations more generously than they had been in the past. But, King declared, there was no intention to revoke those restrictions that were necessary to maintain Canada's economic well-being and social equilibrium. Still, the country would accept its 'moral obligation' to Europe's refugees and permit the admission of 'some thousands' of them. Each prospective immigrant, he assured the House, would be examined on the basis of strict criteria, and only those found suitable would be selected.[22]

On its face, the prime minister's statement did not appear to signal a radical departure from the government's cautious approach to immigration. While Ottawa was prepared to admit more European refugees, the increase would be closely tied to economic conditions. As Keenleyside recalled many years later, the speech was vintage King, containing 'something for everyone, careful qualifications for each promise, a mildly progressive tone throughout, and [was,] on the whole, for that time, a reasonably sensible position.'[23] Yet it was clearly more than that. By pledging Canada's assistance in the search for a solution to the European refugee crisis, the prime minister was implying that the prewar policy of isolationism had been both an economic and a moral failure. King himself seemed to understand that a psychological barrier had been crossed. As he confided to his diary the same evening, 'I went as far as I could in indicating the danger facing us by saying that in a world of shrinking distances and international uncertainties, a small population could not expect to hold the heritage we have.'[24]

Notwithstanding the enactment of PC 371 and King's subsequent statement, some of the immigration bureaucrats continued to put up roadblocks, at least where European refugees were concerned.[25] The reasons are not entirely clear. Perhaps King had not been forceful enough in enunciating his government's intentions. A more likely explanation, though, was that Immigration Branch was still mired in the restrictionist dogma of the past. While careful not to contradict government policy, the sceptics occasionally let their true feelings slip out. One such misstep took place during a meeting between Charles Smith, who was commissioner of immigration and the number-two man at Immigration Branch, representatives of Canada's railways, and IRO's chief of resettlement.

In view of the limited availability of transatlantic shipping, Smith told his audience, priorities had to be set. According to Smith, admission of the British and Scandinavian relatives of Canadian residents ought to be given the highest priority. Special consideration might also be extended to Dutch homesteaders whom the government of the Netherlands was prepared to sponsor. Europe's refugees, in Smith's estimation, rated a distant third. Realizing he had overstepped the bounds of propriety, the immigration commissioner scrambled to qualify his statements, characterizing them as nothing more than his private opinions. But those in attendance were convinced he had spoken for the majority of his colleagues.[26]

Hampered by the immigration bureaucracy's continuing ambivalence, the movement of European refugees to Canada encountered repeated delays. This was about to change, however. The impetus for the new direction was the appointment of C.D. Howe as acting minister of mines and resources in place of James Glen, who had suffered a heart attack. As minister of munitions and supply between 1939 and 1944, Howe had been instrumental in mobilizing Canadian industry for a war effort that was the envy of the world. Having assumed the post of minister of reconstruction late in 1944, he was all too aware of the labour shortages plaguing the postwar Canadian economy.

Determined to avoid becoming entangled in red tape, Howe set about injecting the immigration bureaucrats with a new sense of urgency. 'The speeding up of the immigration movement,' he told Keenleyside, 'should be treated as a matter of high priority.'[27] One of Howe's first official acts as minister was to meet with representatives of IRO in order to better coordinate its operations with those of Canada's immigration teams. Upon learning that the shortage of transatlantic shipping was delaying the departure of refugees from Europe, he ordered Jolliffe to solve the problem. When the director of immigration proved unequal to the task, Howe intervened personally, speaking with the chief executives of the major shipping lines and winning their assurance that vessels would be placed at his department's disposal.[28]

As a result of Howe's prodding, the refugee movement gradually shifted into high gear. Still, not everyone was happy with his handling of the immigration portfolio. For example, unions saw in Howe's efforts to import European workers a threat to the strong bargaining position afforded them by Canada's labour shortages. Meanwhile, immigration advocates were disturbed by his adherence to a policy based on ethnic preference. As IRO's chief of resettlement lamented, Canadian companies 'want to pick and choose as to nationalities.'[29] But the main complaint seemed to be with Howe's apparent indifference to humanitarian considerations. No less an authority than Constance Hayward of the Canadian National Committee on Refugees (CNCR) expressed this concern, confiding to a senior IRO official her displeasure that Canada's immigration policy seemed to be based 'purely on our economic needs.' Of course, such criticisms were often tempered by the realization that the ends sometimes justified the means. As Hayward herself conceded, if allying with the business community was the only way to get Ottawa to fulfil its moral obligation to the refugees, it was a small price to pay.[30]

While C.D. Howe was trying to infuse the immigration bureaucrats with a 'can do' spirit, the man responsible for implementing Howe's will was Hugh Keenleyside. In a memorandum prepared in the wake of King's statement, the recently appointed deputy minister proposed the adoption of a policy he would later describe as having been based on 'enlightened self-interest.'[31] With the international community still dithering over the issue of resettlement quotas, the time was ripe, Keenleyside suggested in May 1947, for a bold Canadian stroke. A few thousand refugees, he suggested, could be admitted almost immediately. In Keenleyside's view, this kind of pre-emptive action would have two advantages. On the one hand, he predicted, it would enhance the reputation of Canadians as a 'humanitarian and practical' people. On the other hand, it would ensure that refugees could be selected 'in accordance with our own ideas as to who would be likely to make the best Canadian citizens.'[32]

Hard-headed in its objectives and yet compassionate in its approach, Keenleyside's memorandum became the blueprint of Canada's policy vis-à-vis Europe's refugees. Submitted to the Cabinet Committee on Immigration Policy in mid-May, his proposal was approved by the end of the month. In its report to the full cabinet, the committee recommended that Canada admit up to 5,000 persons from Europe's refugee camps. In view of the numerous requests being submitted by business and private individuals, it was suggested that the quota be filled with workers from various occupational categories. Lumbermen, tailors, and female domestics, the committee noted, were in greatest demand. On 5 June 1947, cabinet endorsed the committee's report and agreed to admit 5,000 refugees who were qualified for employment in the lumber and clothing industries or as domestics. The next day, the government enacted PC 2180, which formally authorized the refugee movement.[33] The decision marked a turning point in Canada's postwar immigration policy.

At first glance, PC 2180 appeared to be just another exception to the restrictive provisions of PC 695, no different from those that had been made for close relatives or the Polish ex-servicemen. Yet it had been enacted in a wholly different policy context. On the international front, IRO was a reality. Having supported the establishment of an organization whose *raison d'être* was the resettlement of European refugees, Canada, like other western countries, was under considerable pressure to lend practical assistance. Things were different at home as well. The most important development by far had been the changing of the guard within the immigration bureaucracy. Minister of Mines and Resources Glen, whose attitudes toward immigration were ambivalent at best,[34] was temporarily out of the picture, having been replaced by the staunchly pro-immigration C.D. Howe. Together with Keenleyside, another immigration advocate, Howe had given practical effect to the liberalization of Canada's immigration policy.

The extent to which the policy environment had changed was revealed within a month of the enactment of PC 2180. In a report to cabinet, Howe advised that the number of refugees cleared for admission to Canada already exceeded the quota provided for in the order-in-council. According to the acting minister, 2,720 forestry workers, 2,000 garment workers, 400 laundry workers, 100 textile workers, and 1,000 members of various other trades, or 6,220 in total, had been approved for immigration. Moreover, with so many industries experiencing labour shortages, requests for thousands more refugees were being actively considered. 'Under the circumstances,' Howe concluded, 'it is recommended that approval be given for the admission of a further five thousand individuals from the Displaced Persons Camps.'[35]

In keeping with the sea-change in official Ottawa's views on immigration, cabinet wasted little time in adopting Howe's recommendation.[36] This was the first in a series of initiatives that would result in a dramatic increase in immigration to Canada. Over the next year and a half, PC 2180 was amended five times, bringing the total of refugees admitted under the order-in-council to almost 50,000. The newcomers were drawn mainly from occupational groups requested by business and deemed essential by the government. They included electrical, garment, construction, lumber, farm, and domestic workers. Admitted concurrently, with the assistance of CCCRR, were more than 17,000 Volksdeutsche.[37]

Most of the refugees who arrived in Canada between 1947 and 1951 came under the auspices of two IRO programs. One program covered European refugees who were relatives of Canadian residents, the other refugees who had been allocated to Canadian companies as indentured labourers. Movements carried out under the relatives program began with the nomination of refugees by family members in Canada. Upon receipt of a predetermined number of nominations, Immigration Branch compiled a list of those admissible under the regulations and forwarded it to IRO. IRO then took the necessary steps to locate the nominated individuals and have them presented to Canadian immigration teams. Those applicants who passed medical, civil, and security examinations received Canadian visas. Once the visas had been issued, IRO chartered a ship and arranged for passage to Canada.[38]

Movements under the labour-selection program were carried out in a somewhat different manner. In order to evaluate the growing number of requests for European labour, Ottawa invited the associations representing agricultural, mining, and lumber interests to canvass their members as to their specific requirements. Upon receipt of these estimates, the associations referred them to an interdepartmental committee comprised of representatives of the Department of Labour and Immigration Branch. The committee's job was to advise cabinet on bulk-labour immigration. If the committee approved the estimates, a request based on specific labour requirements was sent to IRO's mission in Hull, Quebec, from where it was forwarded overseas. Addressed to the organization's headquarters in Geneva, the request was promptly distributed to its refugee-intake centres in Germany. IRO field officers then made a preliminary selection of potential labourers and assembled them for examination by Canadian immigration teams. The examination procedure was similar to that applied to relatives, except that, in the case of labourers, representatives of the Department of Labour and the industry concerned were on hand to assist in the selection process. Adhering to the precedent set by the 2nd Corps movement, successful candidates were made to sign an undertaking that committed them to work for a designated employer for a period of up to two years.

Once the Canadian immigration teams had completed their examinations, those relatives or labourers who had been granted visas were returned to the refugee camps. After a week or so, they were conveyed to the port of embarkation. Upon arrival at the port, a Canadian official verified each prospective immigrant's identity and ensured that his or her visa was in order. If the contingent were made up of labourers, it was at this point that their contracts were signed. Only then did embarkation proceed and the ship depart.

On the other side of the Atlantic, each contingent of refugees was met by a delegation consisting of a Canadian immigration officer, an RCMP constable, and an official from IRO, CCCRR, or other sponsoring agency. Each member of the reception committee was in possession of the passenger list as well as a list of the names of the sponsoring Canadian residents or organizations. During the first three years of its mandate, IRO advanced money to its representative for the purchase of railway tickets and meals for the new arrivals. In 1950, a new procedure was instituted whereby inland transportation and subsistence were prepaid by the sponsoring individual or agency. Once the ship had docked, the IRO representative met the refugees, distributed railway tickets and spending money, and ensured that everyone boarded the proper train. The procedure was the same for refugees who were part of a bulk-labour movement, except that, instead of an IRO official, it was a Department of Labour representative who met and took charge of the new arrivals.[39]

During IRO's first year of operation (1947–8), Canada admitted more refugees, in excess of 25,000, than any other country except the United Kingdom. Notwithstanding a slackening of demand for labour, the number of refugees who were let in actually increased by 40 per cent during 1948–9. Admissions declined somewhat in 1949–50, but remained steady over the next three years, averaging a very respectable 20,000 per year. By the end of IRO's mandate, more than 120,000 of the refugees under the organization's care had found homes in Canada. Another 30,000 IRO-ineligible refugees had also been granted admission. This total placed Canada fourth among all refugee-receiving countries, behind only the United States, Australia, and Israel.[40] For a nation as sparsely populated as Canada, this was a remarkable achievement.

Unfortunately, Canada's generosity was not without consequences. While the overwhelming majority of new immigrants were decent people who were only seeking a better life for themselves and their families, there was a tiny minority, perhaps totalling 1,500, who had less savoury motives for coming to Canada. A motley remnant of Hitler's legions of henchmen, this latter group, whose origins reflected Europe's deep national, ethnic, and religious divisions, made the overseas voyage in an attempt to flee the scene of their crimes. Most had been fortunate to evade repatriation at war's end. Most had received the assistance of IRO or some other immigrant-aid organization by concealing or misrepresenting their wartime activities. And most had secured passage to Canada by attaching themselves to bulk-labour contingents.

The infiltration of the refugee movement by Nazi war criminals and collaborators poses a dilemma for historians. On the one hand, the rate of infiltration was quite low, a mere 1 per cent of the total refugee movement to Canada. Indeed, were it 1,500 ordinary criminals and other undesirables who had evaded detection, they might be written off as statistically insignificant. But these were not ordinary criminals. As servants of the Nazi regime, they were all implicated, either directly or indirectly, in some of the most heinous crimes in history. Accordingly, it is fair to ask whether more could have been done to keep them out. That question can be answered only by an in-depth examination of Canada's immigration-screening system.

CHAPTER FIVE

No Safe Haven, 1947–1951

In the immediate postwar period, the screening of immigrants had been carried out by the Canadian military mission in Berlin. As long as its responsibility for screening was limited to returning Canadian servicemen and their dependants, the mission had been able to cope. Problems arose, however, once refugees became eligible for admission. Most refugees were restricted to camps in western Germany, and so could not get to the mission in Berlin. Conversely, the mission had insufficient staff to cover the camps. As a temporary measure, the British Army allocated some space for immigrant processing at a facility in Hannover. But even this proved insufficient for Canadian requirements.[1] Clearly, a serious commitment of personnel and resources was needed.

Annoyed by repeated delays in the movement of European refugees to Canada, Deputy Minister of Mines and Resources Hugh Keenleyside dispatched Director of Immigration Arthur Jolliffe overseas in July 1947. His job was to survey the situation and report back to Ottawa. As part of his fact-finding mission, Jolliffe travelled throughout Allied-occupied Germany, meeting with staff at the Canadian military mission, visiting refugee camps, and consulting with International Refugee Organization (IRO) officials.[2] After several days, he had gathered sufficient information to prepare his report. To no one's surprise, the picture that emerged was one of gross inefficiency and low morale.

The most glaring shortcoming, according to Jolliffe, was the lack of either a headquarters or accommodation. At the time of his visit, the director of immigration reported, he had been dismayed to see Odilon Cormier, who was supervising the work of the Canadian immigration teams, carrying files around in suitcases. Almost as troubling was the lack of transport. Without cars on stand-by, Jolliffe advised, immigration officers had to wait hours for a ride to the refugee camps. Finally, there was the matter of the low quality of the interpreters who were being supplied by the British Army. Not only were they wanting in language skills, the Canadian teams had complained, but some had not received security clearances.[3]

Having discovered an immigration operation in almost total disarray, Jolliffe recommended that a number of changes be instituted. First, he insisted on the establishment of a headquarters that would 'direct and control' the work of Canadian immigration teams in Germany. In part because of its proximity to the refugee camps and in part because IRO had its German headquarters there, Heidelberg was suggested as a possible site. Second, Jolliffe urged that permanent living quarters be acquired with sufficient space for forty Canadian immigration personnel. Third, he requested that eight cars be purchased, shipped overseas, and placed at the disposal of the new immigration mission. Fourth, he advised that the current pool of temporary interpreters be replaced by six permanent employees who had proven fluency in English, German, and at least one of the eastern European languages. Last, he proposed that a senior immigration officer be appointed to oversee the new mission's operations.[4]

His suspicions having been confirmed, Keenleyside made the overhaul of Canada's immigration operations abroad a high priority. The first step was to brief Acting Minister of Mines and Resources C.D. Howe. This was followed by some hard lobbying to ensure that immigrant processing was placed near the top of the government's agenda. The deputy minister's persistence paid off. At its 14 August 1947 meeting, cabinet agreed to implement each of Jolliffe's recommendations. The establishment of a Canadian immigration mission at Heidelberg was approved, as was the nomination of a senior official to manage it. Since Cormier had been fulfilling this function on an ad hoc basis, it was decided to formally appoint him to the post. It was also decided to approach Allied military authorities with a request for permanent billeting for Canadian immigration staff. Finally, cabinet made a commitment to supply the new immigration mission with a fleet of cars and a permanent detail of six interpreters.[5]

Notwithstanding the decision to expand Immigration Branch's overseas contingent, it was initially assumed that the two teams already working in Germany would be sufficient to carry out the processing of prospective immigrants. However, the high priority accorded to bulk-labour movements necessitated major increases in staffing levels. Over the course of the following year, nine teams were added. Each consisted of a physician, an immigration officer, a non-commissioned officer from the RCMP, an interpreter, and a driver. To assist in the selection of immigrant workers, most of the new teams also included an official from the Department of Labour and a representative from industry. By the end of 1948, the contingent at the Canadian immigration mission had swelled to seventy-one persons, including eleven security officers.[6] As regular immigration from western Europe resumed, eight more RCMP officers were added, one each for France, Belgium, the Netherlands, and Sweden, and two each for Austria and Italy. By 1949, there were nineteen Canadian security officers in the United Kingdom and on the European continent.[7]

The facilities and manpower that Canada devoted to immigrant processing in Europe were more than adequate for the task in 1947–8. However, the slackening of demand for labour on the part of Canadian business during 1948 prompted calls for substantial cuts to the immigration budget. Had these been enacted, they might have seriously impaired the ability of Canada's immigration teams to screen and process prospective newcomers. Fortunately, Immigration Branch was able to pre-empt deep cuts by streamlining its overseas operations. As a result of a review conducted by Keenleyside, only non-essential personnel were let go, while some immigration and RCMP officers were redeployed from Karlsruhe, where Canada's immigration mission had been moved after its brief sojourn at Heidelberg,[8] to the various Canadian consulates in Germany and Austria.[9] The impact of the cuts was therefore minimal. Significantly, all but one of the nineteen security officers originally assigned to immigration screening in Europe during 1947–8 were left at their posts.[10]

In terms of screening refugees for war criminal or collaborationist backgrounds, the admission criteria employed by Canada's immigration teams were kept fairly stringent. Indeed, of the various classes of immigrants previously barred from admission to Canada, only one –

enemy aliens – was relaxed to any significant degree. According to the provisions of PC 1373, nationals of countries that had aligned themselves with Germany during the war were classified as enemy aliens. As such, they were denied entry, unless, of course, they could demonstrate that they had been opposed to their own government. In practice, most were unable to offer proof of such opposition. Thus, only a small number of enemy aliens were granted admission to Canada in the first two years after the war.[11]

Facing mounting criticism for its refusal to revoke or modify the 'opposition to an enemy government' clause of PC 1373, Ottawa agreed to waive it for one group in the spring of 1947. Between their arrival in the United Kingdom in 1940 and their repatriation in 1946, some 47,000 Canadian servicemen had entered into marriage. While the vast majority of the war brides were British, more than 2,600 were of continental European heritage. Most were Dutch or Belgian, although there were also some French, Danes, and, despite the prohibition on fraternization, Germans and Italians.[12] Considered enemy aliens, the German and Italian war brides became British subjects upon marriage.[13] Nonetheless, they invariably found their departure for Canada held up while Immigration Branch and the RCMP reviewed their applications.

As a concession to the returning servicemen, an attempt was made to expedite the screening process. Instead of having to await a decision from Ottawa, the immigration officer on the scene could approve the bride in question if he were satisfied as to her anti-Nazi credentials.[14] This was, to be sure, a circumvention of the screening procedures normally applied to enemy aliens. Yet the war brides, as British subjects, ought to have been exempted from screening altogether. In any event, the number of prospective immigrants involved was so low that the danger of infiltration by Nazi collaborators was negligible.

As it happened, the exception made for war brides was just the first step in the removal of the ban on the admission of enemy aliens. Additional measures followed forthwith. In July 1947, Canada ratified peace treaties with four of Germany's wartime allies. As a result, the nationals of Finland, Hungary, Italy, and Romania had their status as enemy aliens formally revoked. Henceforth, they were to be treated, for immigration purposes, like applicants from any other country with which Canada had normal relations. Included in this new admissible class were prospective immigrants who had served in the Finnish, Hungarian, Italian, or Romanian armed forces during the war. Under the revised regulations, nationals of the former enemy countries could be denied admission only if they appeared on the UN's list of suspected war criminals or failed in some other way to meet the criteria set out in the Immigration Act.[15]

Of the four countries that benefited from the warming of diplomatic relations, two – Hungary and Romania – had adopted wartime policies of racial persecution and political repression rivalling those of their German allies. Accordingly, a significant number of Hungarians and Romanians were either directly implicated in the crimes of their governments or had abetted those of the Germans. In theory, then, it was possible that their removal from the category of enemy aliens enabled some Hungarian or Romanian war criminals to gain admission to Canada. Yet this was unlikely to have occurred very often. Occupied by the Red Army at war's end, both countries conducted extensive purges and trials of suspected Nazi sympathizers. Subjected to rough-and-ready justice, tens of thousands of Hungarians and Romanians were convicted of war crimes or treason. Hundreds were executed; thousands more were sentenced to long prison terms. Thus, to the extent that Canada was infiltrated by war criminals of Hungarian or Romanian nationality, it is unlikely that they would have come from their countries of origin. A far more plausible scenario is that they had evaded repatriation, passed themselves off as legitimate refugees, and found sanctuary in IRO-administered refugee camps.

Like their wartime allies, German nationals were also subject to the provisions of PC 1373. That is, they were ineligible for admission to Canada unless they could demonstrate their opposition to the Nazi regime. As has already been noted, this was an extremely difficult hurdle to overcome. Yet prospective German immigrants suffered from additional disabilities. For one thing, their status as enemy aliens was not revoked until September 1950. Moreover, as citizens of the country that had unleashed the war, German applicants tended to be subjected to closer scrutiny than the nationals of other former enemy states.

Included among those Germans who were inadmissible between 1947 and 1950 were Volksdeutsche who had acquired German citizenship during the war.[16] Once the Canadian Christian Council for Resettlement of Refugees' (CCCRR) mission in Germany began its processing operations, some of the obviously ineligible applicants were weeded out. Still, the number of rejections by Canadian authorities remained high. In the autumn of 1948, for example, CCCRR reported that about one out of every ten Volksdeutsche was being denied admission to Canada because of his or her wartime naturalization.[17]

In order to reverse or at least slow what its chairman described as the 'decided tendency toward shrinking,' CCCRR requested that the close relatives category be expanded for Germans.[18] Ottawa refused, with the result that the percentage of rejections kept rising. Things got so bad, in fact, that by September 1949, CCCRR was reporting a crisis in its immigrant-processing operations. This was no exaggeration. Under the close relatives scheme, one-third to one-half of all Volksdeutsche applicants were being rejected by Canadian immigration teams. The situation was even worse for bulk-labour contingents, where the rejection rate ranged from 50 to 75 per cent. Most visa applications were being refused on the grounds of acquired German citizenship. In view of their high rate of wartime German naturalization, it is perhaps not surprising that a majority of rejected applicants were Mennonites.[19]

Its immigration program under siege, CCCRR adopted a strategy born of desperation – it attempted to convince Ottawa that most Volksdeutsche had been naturalized against their will. Such arguments were not out-and-out fraud, of course, but they certainly verged on historical revisionism.[20] They also had no chance of success. IRO's investigations revealed that many Volksdeutsche, particularly Mennonites, had voluntarily accepted German citizenship during the war. Confronted with claims of forced naturalization, Canadian immigration authorities consulted IRO, with predictable results. Apprised of the true facts regarding the Nazi regime's citizenship policies, Immigration Branch let it be known that the representations being made on behalf of the Mennonites were 'inaccurate and specious,' and that, as a consequence, there would be no relaxation of the criteria for admission.[21]

Recognizing that Ottawa would not be moved by the involuntary-naturalization argument, the German-Canadian immigrant-aid societies abandoned that approach and concentrated instead on trying to get the restrictions on German nationals lifted altogether. Initially, at least, the change in strategy proved no more successful. Notwithstanding the relentless lobbying campaign undertaken by CCCRR and affiliated organizations, Ottawa refused to change the regulations until a formal peace treaty had been signed between the two countries.[22] At the same time, the government was not unsympathetic to the plight of would-be German immigrants. In recognition of the problem that German nationals were having in establishing their anti-Nazi credentials, cabinet briefly considered waiving the 'opposition to an enemy government' requirement in otherwise deserving cases. However, this initiative foundered in the face of resistance by the immigration bureaucrats, who argued that such exceptions would subject the existing policy to a kind of 'death by a thousand cuts.' A more palatable alternative, they suggested, would be to confer the right to apply for waivers on certain low-risk individuals. These could include the wife, unmarried children under eighteen, or aged parents of any legal resident of Canada, provided they 'were not active members of Nazi organizations or Communists ... and can otherwise comply with the requirements of the Immigration Act.' After some discussion, departmental approval was given and the Immigration Branch proposal submitted to cabinet. Cabinet's endorsement followed quickly.[23]

From the autumn of 1949 onward, the ban on German nationals was waived for persons who fell within certain spousal and parental categories and who had no obvious Nazi affiliations. The number of German enemy aliens who were thereby admitted was not significant. Moreover, most of those for whom the regulations were waived were women, children, and the elderly.[24] Needless to say, the threat of Nazi infiltration posed by these groups was negligible.

To be sure, waivers were occasionally granted to former members of the German armed forces. As far as can be determined, however, none of the few German veterans who were admitted by waiver had a war criminal background.[25] The case of O. W——— was typical. Born in Germany in 1909, W——— had migrated to Canada in 1930. A carpenter by trade, he had found work on construction sites in northern Ontario. In 1935, he married a Canadian woman, with whom he had two children. In the summer of 1939, W——— returned to Germany to visit his aging parents. He was still overseas when the war broke out. Having not yet been naturalized in Canada, he remained, for the Nazis' purposes, a German citizen. As such, he was liable for service in the German armed forces. Conscripted into the army, he served on the western front for four years before being captured by the Allies. Upon release from POW captivity, W—— found that, as an enemy alien, he could not obtain a visa to return to Canada. Based on his wife's application for a waiver, however, cabinet approved his readmission in January 1950.[26]

During the first few years after the war, the government of Canada had demonstrated a marked reluctance to relax the immigration restrictions on German nationals. In 1950, however, three factors conspired to make Ottawa more receptive to the idea. First, the lobbying by CCCRR and other German-Canadian immigrant-aid societies began to resonate with policy makers. Second, the refusal to issue even short-term visas to German nationals was inhibiting the restoration of trade between Germany and Canada. Third, Germans, particularly those with professional and technical skills, were increasingly seen as the most desirable of European immigrants. This was especially true as the refugee movement began to slacken off.[27]

In the interests of commerce, cabinet agreed late in 1949 that German businessmen could be granted short-term visitor's visas. But the real breakthrough came a few months later. In March 1950, Ottawa finally relented and made a major concession on the question of German immigration. Enacted as PC 1606, the new regulation authorized the admission of Volksdeutsche who had been granted German citizenship during the war. This was followed in September 1950 by the removal of German nationals from the category of enemy aliens.[28] Despite the absence of a peace treaty between Canada and Germany,[29] the effect of these measures was to finally put Germans on a more or less equal footing with prospective British, American, and French immigrants, except when it came to security screening, which remained somewhat more stringent.[30]

Generally speaking, Canada's early postwar policy on German immigration was strict but consistent. There was one aspect of the policy that caused some confusion, however. During the first two years after the war, Austrians were subjected to the same immigration restrictions as their German cousins. This was a consequence of Austria's absorption into the Third Reich in March 1938. Not consulted prior to the Nazi takeover, Austrians had had German citizenship conferred on them. For purposes of immigration, then, Canada considered them to be enemy aliens.

It soon became apparent that this interpretation was untenable. While Immigration Branch had classified Austrians as enemy aliens, External Affairs was taken in by the fiction that their country had been the first victim of Nazi aggression.[31] In External's view, Austria was no different from other countries that had fallen under the Nazi yoke. Accordingly, Canada had never been at war with Austria. If a state of war had not existed between Canada and Austria, then Austrians could not have been enemy aliens. Despite the obvious anomaly in the Canadian position, the difference of opinion between External and Immigration Branch was not immediately resolved. Indeed, it was not until the re-establishment of diplomatic relations between the two countries in 1948 that Ottawa agreed to allow its immigration teams in Austria – which were already processing IRO-eligible refugees there – to begin accepting applications from prospective Austrian immigrants. In terms of the criteria to be applied, the Canadian teams were instructed to accord Austrians the same treatment as the nationals of any other non-enemy state.[32]

Even after the change in Austria's diplomatic status, there remained the question of what to do about the almost one million of its citizens who had served in the German armed forces during the war.[33] In 1948, former German soldiers were still being denied admission to Canada. Yet the Austrian veterans posed a special problem. Once German citizenship had been conferred on them, they were rendered liable for service in Hitler's armies. Under Canadian immigration regulations, the only way in which former members of the German armed forces could be considered for admission was to prove they had been conscripted. This placed Austrians at a disadvantage vis-à-vis prospective immigrants from former enemy states like Italy and Hungary. If Austria had never been Canada's enemy, the immigration bureaucrats asked, then why should its nationals who had served in enemy forces be treated more harshly than the nationals of former enemy states like Italy, which had been at war with Canada and whose nationals had served in the armed forces of their countries? Arriving at an equitable solution required some creative thinking. After much debate, it was decided that the only way to accord Austrians who had served in the German armed forces the same immigration opportunities as Finnish, Hungarian, Italian, and Romanian ex-soldiers was to reclassify them as former enemy aliens.[34]

Approximately 150,000 Austrians, or one out of every seven who was eligible for military service, had joined the SS during the war. Austrians were similarly overrepresented in security police and concentration camp guard units, particularly in the leadership cadres.[35] Yet in contrast to countries like Hungary and Romania, Austria was less than vigorous in prosecuting its own citizens for war crimes. Accordingly, the removal of Austrians from the prohibited class of enemy aliens may have permitted some war criminals to gain admission to Canada. In the case of the Austrians, of course, Canadian immigration teams had a trump card that was not available to them when screening prospective immigrants from eastern Europe. Unlike the military and police archives of the Soviet bloc, those of Germany and Austria were accessible. It would have been rather difficult, then, for Austrians with dubious war records to completely evade detection.

Among the criteria on which both German and non-German immigrants were judged was service in the German armed forces. On paper, at least, such service was grounds for automatic rejection until the spring of 1950.[36] In practice, the prohibition had been considerably weakened by that time. Beginning in 1949, as we have seen, German nationals who had served in the armed forces of their country were admitted under special waivers. Of greater significance was the inclusion of former members of the German Army in the 2nd Corps movement. Unlike the isolated cases of German ex-soldiers who gained entry under cabinet waivers, the admission of the Poles set a precedent for all subsequent bulk-labour movements.

In seeking to fill their labour requirements, Canadian companies evinced a marked preference for Balts, who they regarded as the most desirable of the European refugees.[37] This created a problem. The rate of service in the German armed forces had been somewhat higher for Balts than for other eastern European peoples. Of course, wartime military service did not automatically render them ineligible for IRO assistance. Under Canada's immigration regulations, however, they were inadmissible.[38] As a result, a large percentage of the Balts whom IRO had approved for inclusion in bulk-labour movements were subsequently rejected by Canadian immigration teams.[39]

As had been the case with the selection of the first close relatives contingent back in the autumn of 1946, the interpretation of admission criteria became a matter of contention between External Affairs and Immigration Branch. External was under the impression that Canada was taking the same approach as IRO – that is, if a refugee could prove he had been compelled to join the German armed forces, his wartime service would not necessarily disqualify him from consideration. Immigration Branch had a different view. As Jolliffe explained to General Maurice Pope at Canada's military mission in Berlin, it made no difference whether a Baltic applicant had served 'willingly or unwillingly' – either way, he was inadmissible.[40] In fact, the ban was enforced until C.D. Howe weighed in. Unwilling to allow anything to interfere with the supply of European labour to Canadian business, the acting minister of mines and resources instructed his bureaucrats to bring Canadian policy into line with that of IRO. Henceforth, he insisted, Canadian immigration teams were not to disqualify Baltic veterans of the German Army from bulk-labour movements unless there was clear evidence they had been volunteers.[41]

Notwithstanding Howe's intervention, the problem persisted for a while longer. While Canadian immigration officials had been reined in, no one had consulted the RCMP. Thus, bulk-labour contingents destined for Canada, particularly those comprising large numbers of Balts, continued to be decimated by rejections. Included among those who were rebuffed were would-be immigrants who had received security clearances from British military intelligence. It appears that some RCMP security officers rejected Baltic refugees on the basis of their service in German forces alone, without ascertaining whether such service had been voluntary or conscripted. Others elected to ignore evidence attesting to conscription. Those who were more lenient when it came to conscripted service often found other grounds for rejection. For example, Baltic conscripts could be rejected if it were discovered they had obtained decorations or promotions over the course of their military service.[42]

The RCMP's hard line threatened to rupture the relationship between Canada and IRO that Howe had worked so hard to forge.

Accordingly, in January 1948, Ottawa launched an investigation. The aim was to determine why the rate of rejection on security grounds was so high among prospective Baltic immigrants. Briefs were accepted from representatives of the Latvian and Estonian refugees, the nationalities most affected by the strict screening regime. Then the RCMP was consulted. Within a month, the government had its answer. The reason for the high rate of rejections was the virtual impossibility of proving conscription.[43]

In an effort to placate both IRO and the Baltic lobby without weakening the system of immigration screening, Jolliffe suggested a compromise. IRO, the director of immigration reported, had adopted cut-off dates in order to determine whether former members of the German armed forces, particularly Balts who had served in Waffen-SS units, would be considered conscripts or volunteers. The same procedure, he suggested, could be employed by Canadian immigration teams. Since IRO was using 1 December 1943 as the date on which the Third Reich had invoked conscription in the occupied Baltic territories, Canada, Jolliffe recommended, ought to follow suit. The RCMP agreed. Henceforth, a Balt who had joined the German armed forces prior to 1 December 1943 would automatically be disqualified from consideration. A Balt who had joined after that date might be granted admission, provided he could demonstrate 'satisfactorily' that he had been conscripted.[44] As has already been noted, the volunteer versus conscript formula was employed until the spring of 1950, when, with the relaxation of restrictions on Volksdeutsche immigration, voluntary service in the regular German armed forces was no longer considered grounds for automatic rejection.[45]

Relaxation of the ban on Germans and other enemy aliens was offset by a tightening of the prohibitions on the entry of subversives. As defined by the Immigration Act, a subversive was anyone who currently advocated the overthrow of the government of Canada or had done so in the past, currently advocated violent opposition to any duly constituted government or had done so in the past, or had been found guilty of espionage or high treason.[46] In the 1940s and 1950s, subversion tended to be identified with the two dominant anti-democratic ideologies of the first half of the twentieth century – Nazism and communism. The preoccupation with threats of subversion from both the right and the left was confirmed in an RCMP memorandum to Keenleyside. When checking into the backgrounds of prospective immigrants, the RCMP commissioner advised, 'we are interested mainly in obtaining a satisfactory answer to two questions: first, what were the applicant's sympathies and activities during the late war, and second, is he sympathetic to Communism or any other form of subversive influence opposed to our democratic way of life?'[47]

During the early postwar period, Ottawa had been content to allow the RCMP to define the parameters of subversion. By 1948, however, disagreements over the Mounties' handling of cases involving attempted communist infiltration led to calls for greater accountability in the elaboration and application of immigration-screening criteria. Charging that the RCMP's anti-subversive training left much to be desired, Immigration Branch demanded that the police relay to Ottawa any information, no matter how trivial, that was uncovered regarding a prospective immigrant's political background. The immigration bureaucrats also insisted that the RCMP provide them with a list of the criteria being used to screen prospective immigrants. Finally, they called on the RCMP to place its officers under the authority of the immigration missions to which they were attached.[48]

Taken together, these demands constituted a serious threat to the autonomy from civilian control that the RCMP had carved out for itself in the area of immigration screening. For example, Immigration Branch's insistence on the release of information in specific cases directly contravened the Mounties' practice of withholding the results of their security inquiries.[49] The demand for a list of screening criteria, moreover, threatened to lift the veil of secrecy – deemed essential to preserve the anonymity of sources – under which the police had become accustomed to operating. In the face of this assault on its prerogatives, one would have expected the RCMP to launch a full-scale counterattack. Yet the anticipated turf war never materialized. There were two reasons. First, the exposure of holes in Canada's security apparatus left the Mounties politically weakened. Second, and more importantly, the demands for greater accountability in immigration screening had the blessing of cabinet.[50] After issuing a few desultory protests, then, the police had no choice but to give in to the bureaucrats' demands.[51]

In November 1948, after canvassing its officers abroad, the RCMP compiled a list of screening criteria and passed it on to Immigration Branch for review. The list contained thirteen grounds, each of which, 'if disclosed during interrogation or investigation,' was sufficient for rejecting a prospective immigrant. More than half of the criteria had nothing to do with political affiliations. Accordingly, an applicant could be denied admission to Canada if it were determined that he or she had a criminal record, was a professional gambler, prostitute, or black marketeer, had been evasive or untruthful under interrogation, was unable to produce valid documentation, or was using an alias. But the remaining criteria focused on subversives. As characterized by Norman Robertson, they reflected the government's intention to 'deny admission to any persons who, from their known history and background, would be unlikely to adapt themselves to the Canadian way of life and to our democratic form of government.'[52] In keeping with the intensification of the Cold War, known or suspected communists, as well as members of so-called revolutionary organizations, were to be denied visas. The other political criteria simply reiterated the existing ban on Nazis and fellow travellers. Thus, voluntary service in either the SS or the regular German armed forces, membership in either the Nazi or (Italian) Fascist Parties, and collaboration with the enemy continued to be grounds for rejection.[53]

Of the four rejection criteria specific to the Second World War, collaboration was the most vigorously enforced. As one commentator has noted, those who had assisted the Germans in the occupation of their native lands elicited a 'visceral and very negative' reaction from the RCMP.[54] The reasons are not hard to understand. It was one thing not to take up arms against Nazi occupation forces. Fearing reprisals, most people did not work actively against the Germans, preferring instead to wait out the war as quietly and unobtrusively as possible. Under the circumstances, this kind of passive acquiescence to Nazi rule was inevitable, perhaps even acceptable. On the other hand, active support for the Germans was not necessary for personal survival, and was therefore considered to be evidence of a flawed character. The essence of this distinction was captured by a Canadian diplomat stationed in Oslo, Norway. In explaining why his legation was refusing to issue visas to politically rehabilitated Norwegian collaborators, E.J. Garland stated that 'these people were faced with a moral test, which, by our standards, they failed to meet.'[55]

The severity with which the ban on wartime traitors was enforced did not result from emotionalism alone. Beyond the revulsion they evoked, there were practical reasons for preventing the admission of collaborators. These were elaborated during discussions about a proposal to relax the restrictions on persons who had engaged in so-called minor acts of collaboration. The head of the RCMP's Special Branch counselled against any abatement in vigilance, warning of potentially dire consequences for national security if his advice were to go unheeded. Speaking for the force as a whole, Superintendent George McClellan explained that 'we find it difficult to believe that proposed immigrants who are disloyal to the country of their birth would in fact be any more loyal to the country of their adoption.' Therefore, he advised, 'we feel that any large immigration of collaborators from German-occupied countries would materially increase our difficulties should a state of emergency [ever] arise.'[56]

Owing to their offensiveness on both moral and security grounds, collaborators had been singled out early on in the development of Canadian screening criteria. For example, at the first postwar meeting at which the resumption of immigration from Europe was discussed, External Affairs bureaucrats had recommended that collaborators be designated as a prohibited class.[57] During the 2nd Corps movement, moreover, Ottawa had initially set a very low threshold for collaborationist activity, including even conscripted service in the German Army or forced-labour detachments. In recognition that some forms of collaboration might have been elicited by compulsion, that threshold was subsequently lifted. Thereafter, it was possible for an individual who had been compelled to work for the Germans to obtain a Canadian visa, but he would have to demonstrate convincingly that his collaboration had been rendered under duress.[58] Apart from such cases, anyone determined to have collaborated willingly with Nazi occupation authorities or to have served voluntarily with the German armed forces was rejected out of hand.[59]

Other than the gradual elimination of the prohibition on enemy aliens, there was little relaxation of the Second World War–related criteria between 1947 and 1951. Up to 1948, service in the regular German armed forces was an automatic bar to admission. From 1948 to 1950, it could still bar an applicant if he had served voluntarily. Membership in the Fascist or Nazi Party was an automatic bar to admission until 1951.[60] Collaboration, no matter how inconsequential, continued to be an automatic bar until the following year.[61] Finally, the prohibition against former members of the Waffen-SS, with the exception of those who could prove they had been conscripted, was kept in place until the mid-1950s.[62]

The RCMP's list of thirteen grounds for rejection was not widely circulated. Indeed, other than the prime minister, his cabinet, and senior RCMP and Immigration Branch officials, few in the government were aware of its existence.[63] Even within the immigration bureaucracy, its dissemination was limited. According to the division of labour worked out between the bureaucrats and the police, the Mounties would inform Immigration Branch in the event that a particular individual had not received security clearance for admission to Canada. Their report would refer to the specific grounds for rejection (one or more of the list of thirteen). Ottawa would then inform the overseas mission to which the person had applied, but without citing the reason for the decision. Instead, the mission would be advised only as to which section of the Immigration Act applied. Thus, an individual rejected because of membership in the SS might be described as 'detrimental to the security of Canada' and therefore inadmissible.[64]

The development of a standardized list of rejection criteria was a watershed in the history of immigration screening in Canada. Still, it was not a panacea. After all, terms like 'Nazi Party' or 'collaborator' encompassed a plethora of organizations, agencies, and units. It is appropriate to ask, then, how the Second World War–related criteria were actually applied in the field. Initially, security officers assigned to overseas duty were given wide latitude in interpreting the Immigration Act and accompanying regulations. Concurrent with the 2nd Corps movement, however, a new document became available for use in screening for war criminal or collaborationist background. A comprehensive, and, for the most part, accurate depiction of the Nazi hierarchy, this document limited the need for interpretation.

In January 1946, as we saw in Chapter 2, Allied occupation authorities had undertaken to remove all Nazis and Nazi sympathizers from public office in Germany. To implement this policy, the Allies had enacted Control Council Directive No. 24. The directive created five categories – major offenders, offenders, lesser offenders, followers, and those who were exonerated – into which every German adult was to be assigned upon completion of a detailed questionnaire. Anyone falling within the first three offender categories was subject to automatic removal from the civil service or any other position of public trust. In this way, the Allies hoped, Germany would gradually be denazified.[65]

As set out in Directive No. 24, the categories were too broad to be of much assistance to Canadian authorities. But that would soon change. In the summer of 1946, as we have seen, the RCMP adapted the directive to the requirements of immigration screening.[66] Further refinements followed. On the basis of the mountain of evidence regarding Nazi criminality presented at the Nuremberg trials, the Allies were able to expand and clarify their earlier denazification procedures. Enacted in October 1946 as Control Council Directive No. 38, the supplementary procedures listed all Nazi organizations and agencies considered to be criminal or dangerous to the Allied occupation. Though its primary intent was to facilitate the 'arrest and punishment of war criminals, Nazis and militarists and the internment, control, and surveillance of potentially dangerous Germans,'[67] Directive No. 38 was also well suited to immigration screening. Not surprisingly, then, Inspector William H. Kelly, the head of RCMP visa control in Europe during the early 1950s, described it as the key document for interpreting Ottawa's postwar screening criteria.[68]

Directive No. 38 was like a telephone registry of the Nazi regime. The organizations listed included the Germans' various wartime intelligence agencies, security and regular police units, the Nazi Party and its affiliated organizations, most notably the Waffen- and general SS, governmental and military institutions, and all economic, social, and professional bodies that had come under Nazi control during the Third Reich. Assuming that an individual had been affiliated with any of these organizations, he or she was considered an offender for Allied purposes. Whether that individual was a major offender, offender, or lesser offender depended on the extent of the organization's criminality and his or her rank or position therein. In the case of the Waffen-SS, for example, all officers down to rank of SS major were automatically classified as major offenders. So were all concentration camp guards, regardless of rank. All remaining members of the Waffen-SS – that is, anyone below the rank of SS major – were classified as offenders, except for those rank-and-file troops who had been conscripted. On the other hand, Waffen-SS conscripts could be classified as offenders if there were evidence that they had been promoted to NCO or officer rank after enlistment.[69]

Between 1947 and 1953, the RCMP's use of Allied directives was limited to providing its officers with as comprehensive a list as possible of Nazi and affiliated organizations.[70] Since membership in such organizations constituted almost blanket grounds for rejection, there was no need to differentiate among the various offender categories. This changed once the Second World War–related criteria began to be relaxed. In the wake of a series of Security Panel decisions issued in the spring of 1952, the RCMP integrated the directives into its list of grounds for rejection. The result was a tightening of the existing criteria. For example, all former members of the Waffen-SS down to the rank of NCO, even if their service had been conscripted, were considered to be major offenders or offenders and therefore inadmissible. Rank-and-file Waffen-SS men were similarly classified, unless there were 'reasonable grounds' for believing they had been conscripted.[71]

The process whereby prospective immigrants were screened was a combination of everything Ottawa had learned from the United Nations Relief and Rehabilitation Administration (UNRRA), IRO, and 2nd Corps experiences. In the system devised by the immigration bureaucrats, screening was divided into three stages. Stage A was a medical examination conducted by the immigration team physician; Stage B the security examination conducted by an RCMP officer; and Stage C the civil examination conducted by the immigration officer. The decision whether to issue or deny a visa ultimately rested with the immigration officer, although he would, as a matter of course, put a great deal of stock in the security officer's Stage B recommendation. Indeed, in the early postwar period, immigration officers never accepted an applicant who had not been cleared for security. This changed in the wake of the problems uncovered in 1948. Thereafter, the RCMP ceded some authority to the civilians. Stage B recommendations continued to be followed in cases where subversion, including Nazi affiliation, was discovered or suspected. However, in all other cases where there were grounds for rejection, the security officer merely passed the information on to his immigration counterpart, who, in turn, determined whether or not the individual should be admitted to Canada. More importantly, Immigration Branch could review RCMP rejections, and, if it was deemed appropriate, overturn them.[72]

Screening of prospective immigrants began with the submission of an application form. When European immigration to Canada resumed late in 1946, prospective immigrants were required to have a visa application completed on their behalf. Known as the IMM-55, the form comprised two pages, and consisted mainly of questions regarding the applicant's Canadian sponsor. These were clearly intended to establish the sponsor's willingness and ability to provide financial support to the nominated immigrant until he or she was established in Canada.[73] As for the immigrant, the IMM-55 sought only the most basic biographical data.[74]

As the volume of immigration from Europe increased in 1947–8, Ottawa opened visa offices throughout the western half of the continent. Full access to Canadian immigration facilities was thereby expanded beyond refugees to the nationals of the countries of western Europe. With the resumption of regular immigration, the all-purpose IMM-55 was supplemented by application forms that could be completed by non-sponsored immigrants. For example, Canadian immigration authorities in the United Kingdom and France employed local versions of a form known as the IMM-362.[75] At Stockholm, Sweden, prospective immigrants were initially required to complete something called the IMM-359.[76] At Brussels, Belgium, where there was comparatively little traffic,[77] the visa section of the Canadian embassy used a generic 'Application for Immigration Visa.'[78] A similar form was used by the Canadian immigration office in The Hague, the Netherlands.[79] The one exception was Germany, where the IMM-55 remained in general use because of the ongoing requirement for sponsorship.[80]

From 1947 to 1950, persons seeking to obtain visas to Canada used one of two types of application form. Sponsored immigrants had the IMM-55 completed on their behalf, while non-sponsored immigrants usually completed a local version of the IMM-362. Only two categories of immigrant were not covered by the existing forms. Specialized forms were developed both for prospective homesteaders sponsored by the Canadian railway companies and for Volksdeutsche applicants. In the case of the former, a questionnaire known as the IMM-357 was in use almost from the outset of Canada's immigration-screening operations in Europe.[81] In the case of ethnic Germans, they had the added burden of having to complete two forms. One, of course, was the IMM-55. After the latter had been submitted and accepted, all CCCRR-assisted Volksdeutsche also had to fill out the organization's internal processing form, known as the ML-10.[82]

During the latter half of 1950, Ottawa attempted to rationalize the visa-application process by introducing a standard form. Known as the IMM-OS.8 (OS meaning overseas), the new form was to render all of its predecessors obsolete. While it was assumed that the practice of having forms printed locally would continue with the OS.8,[83] so as to allow for its proper translation into the language of the applicant's country of residence, deviations in content were no longer to be permitted. The government's aim, it seems, was to ensure that immigration processing, regardless of where on the European continent it took place, would be uniform. Intended for the exclusive use of non-sponsored immigrants, the OS.8, like its predecessors, would come to be used by most visa seekers.[84]

All of the forms in use between 1947 and 1951 required that the applicant provide basic biographical data – date and place of birth, current address, citizenship, a list of dependants, and occupation. Yet most were not geared to immigration screening, at least not initially. Though all asked for residency and employment information, most neither specified the manner in which it should be presented nor allocated sufficient space for a detailed listing.[85] The IMM-55, for example, provided only a single line for that purpose.[86] Subsequent forms were not much better. A dubious standout was the UK office's IMM-362, which allocated only two lines in which the applicant was to provide a 'summary of previous employment.'[87] The introduction of the OS.8 brought only marginal improvement. While the new form included a separate employment-information sheet, this too contained insufficient space for a complete accounting of previous jobs and residences.[88] Indeed, up to 1954, only two Canadian visa offices in Europe used a form that explicitly required and provided space for detailed residency and employment information. The first to do so was the visa section of the Canadian embassy in Paris, the second the visa section of the legation in Stockholm.[89] The only other exception was an occupational one. In addition to the OS.8, the handful of immigrants who were recruited for work in Canada's defence industry were required to complete a form that asked for a year-by-year accounting of residences and jobs over the previous decade.[90]

The specialized forms were also inadequate for the task of immigration screening. Intended as a means of weeding out ineligible Volksdeutsche, CCCRR's ML-10 required applicants to state whether they had served in the German armed forces, had the SS blood-group tattoo, or had previously been declared ineligible for IRO assistance.[91] Such information was readily obtained by other means, of course, but the requirement to provide it at the outset of the screening process did simplify matters for Canadian security officers.[92] The IMM-357, on the other hand, was almost completely useless from the security point of view. A single sheet with no questions about the prospective immigrant's prior residences outside of the British Commonwealth and with space for current occupation only, the form offered little data on which to base Stage B inquiries.[93]

In the absence of security-friendly forms, it is fair to ask how prospective immigrants, except those who came through Paris or Stockholm, could have been properly screened for war criminal or collaborationist background during the early postwar period. The answer is that the form was not the decisive factor in determining the effectiveness of Canadian immigration screening. From the outset, security checks were based on whatever information could be gleaned regarding a prospective immigrant's prior residences and jobs.[94] As the head of RCMP visa control in Europe reported to his superiors in 1953, 'when the original, 1947, policy was set up to obtain information on which to base a security check, it was considered that the addresses and occupations for the past ten years was [sic] sufficient.'[95] Thus, it was the duty of a security officer to elicit residency and employment information going back ten years from the date of a visa application. At posts where no security officer was present, the task fell to the immigration officer.[96] Moreover, the layout of the form was not to be an impediment. If no space were provided for a detailed listing of residences and jobs, the immigration officer was expected to type it on the back.[97]

Submission of the completed application form started the process of security examination. In carrying out their Stage B inquiries, security officers refined the procedures developed by the Canadian military mission in Berlin during its immigrant-processing days. Accordingly, in the case of IRO-assisted refugees, information regarding their prior jobs and residences was gleaned from their IRO application forms, which, as has already been noted, were more security-friendly than their Canadian equivalents.[98] Any additional relevant information not reported on these forms was elicited by way of interview.[99] Though interview techniques varied, security officers typically asked applicants specific questions about their wartime activities.[100] After completing the interview, the security officer would attempt to verify all details by consulting a variety of sources. The process was the same for non-sponsored prospective immigrants who were nationals of the country from which they applied, except that, prior to 1951, there was rarely an RCMP interview in advance of the initiation of Stage B inquiries. In such cases, checks with local authorities were deemed sufficient.[101]

In carrying out the requisite checks, security officers adhered to the rule that a prospective immigrant had no fundamental right to a visa, and that, if there were any doubt as to his or her bona fides, the issue was to be resolved 'in favour of Canada.' In other words, even the suspicion of a subversive background was sufficient grounds for rejection.[102] If the checks revealed nothing untoward, the applicant received a security clearance and the application was marked 'passed Stage B.'[103] He or she then proceeded to Stage C, the final interview by the immigration officer. If the officer were satisfied with the answers provided, he would approve the issuance of a visa. If not, the applicant could still be rejected. Unlike IRO's eligibility procedures, there was no formal process of appeal; rather, a rejected applicant's only recourse was intervention by the Canadian sponsor. Compounding the problem was that the name of every person rejected on security grounds was entered on a blacklist, which was circulated to all Canadian immigration missions.[104]

When screening prospective immigrants for prior Nazi affiliations, the examining RCMP officer could consult an array of police and intelligence offices. If an applicant was a refugee in Germany or Austria, verification of the information supplied on the application form and during the interview was invariably sought from Allied occupation authorities. The specific agency consulted depended on the location of the camp of which the applicant was an inmate. For refugees living in the American zone of occupation, the RCMP made inquiries with the U.S. Army's Counterintelligence Corps (CIC). For refugees residing in the British zone, British military intelligence (MI5) was consulted. Inquiries in the French zone were submitted to the Surêté.[105] In the case of nationals seeking admission from 'friendly' European countries – principally France, the Netherlands, Belgium, Italy, Denmark, Norway, Sweden, and, eventually, Germany – the RCMP contacted the local police.[106] Regardless of the applicant's country of origin and declared nationality, German civil and military records were consulted as a matter of course.[107] Occasionally, private sources were used.[108] Individuals who may have known the applicant were sometimes questioned in the absence of any alternative. Yet they were also consulted as a means of verifying or supplementing information supplied by foreign intelligence or police agencies.[109]

Assuming that the prospective immigrant was cleared for security, he or she was then subjected to a medical examination. Though referred to as Stage A, in practice the physical was often administered only after results of security checks had been obtained.[110] The discovery of a chronic health problem or communicable disease was grounds for automatic rejection. Medical examination could also serve a useful purpose in screening for war criminal or collaborationist background. The members of many, though by no means all, SS units had had their blood group tattooed on the inside of their left arms, near the armpit. Under early Canadian screening procedures, any non-German found to have such a tattoo was immediately assumed to have been a member of the SS and was automatically removed from consideration as an immigrant.[111] From 1948 on, the tattoo was still used as a means of detecting SS membership, but it no longer was grounds for automatic rejection. Instead, admissibility, as we have seen, was based on whether the applicant's Waffen-SS service had been conscripted or voluntary.[112] In order to avoid detection by the examining physician, some former SS men tried to have the tattoo removed. As such procedures invariably left tell-tale scars, they were rarely successful.[113]

Apart from Stages A, B, and C, all refugees and German and Austrian nationals had to clear an additional layer of screening. Germany and Austria, it will be remembered, were divided into various zones of Allied military occupation. From 1945 through 1950, no one was able to travel between or out of the western zones of occupied Germany and Austria unless he or she could obtain the necessary documents and exit permits. According to Allied regulations, anyone who wished to leave a zone of occupation had to apply for a Temporary Travel Document (TTD). Issued by the Combined Travel Board (CTB) under an agreement worked out among the American, British, and French military governments, the TTD served as a substitute travel document for persons unable to obtain a passport from their country of origin. Uniform in colour (green), size (6 × 4½″), and length (twenty-four pages), with ample space for the bearer's photograph and personal information, the TTD looked like an ordinary passport, except that the issuing agency was the Allied military government of the zone in which the bearer resided. Each IRO-assisted refugee was also issued a replacement passport, which was known as the Certificate of Identity, later renamed the London Travel Document (LTD). CCCRR-assisted refugees were issued a similar document, known as the ML-101. Unlike non-sponsored immigrants, the IRO- and CCCRR-assisted refugees did not have to apply for a travel document; it was automatically issued to any refugee whose immigration visa had been approved.[114]

Notwithstanding their widespread acceptance as valid passports, neither the TTD nor the LTD was sufficient in and of itself for Allied military governments to permit the departure of a prospective immigrant. Regardless of the travel document in his or her possession, the immigrant was required to get it stamped with an exit permit from the occupying authorities. To obtain this stamp, it was necessary to apply to the CTB. The application had to be accompanied by a visa from the country of final destination, or, failing that, a statement from that country's consular authorities that the applicant had in fact been granted admission. Upon receipt of such an application, the CTB then forwarded it for security inquiries to the appropriate zonal military government. The vetting process could take anywhere from three weeks to two months, and included checks for Nazi background in various archival repositories. Only when his or her TTD, LTD, or German or Austrian passport was stamped with an exit permit was a prospective immigrant free to leave.[115]

It cannot be emphasized too strongly that the issuance of travel documents and exit permits was not a substitute for Canadian visa-vetting procedures. On the contrary, the travel document/exit permit requirement was an additional layer of screening through which both refugees and German nationals had to pass if they were to be permitted entry to Canada. This was just as well, as the western Allies were somewhat uneven in the application of exit-screening procedures. While checks for Nazi background were done as a matter of course in the American and French zones as early as 1946, it was not until March 1950 that British military authorities began to follow suit.[116] Few ineligible immigrants appear to have been admitted to Canada as a consequence, however. Owing to concerns about the laxity of screening in the British zone, Canadian immigration teams often conducted security inquiries independently of their allies. Accordingly, they were able to identify otherwise ineligible persons who had already been granted exit permits. Indeed, the number of Canadian rejections of would-be immigrants who had been passed by British military intelligence sometimes reached 30 per cent of all applicants.[117]

With its strict rejection criteria, automatic background checks, and built-in redundancies, the Canadian system of immigration screening posed a formidable obstacle to the entry of subversives and other undesirables. Still, it was not without problems. Like the screening operations of UNRRA and IRO, those conducted by Canadian immigration teams could be compromised by human frailty. For example, to meet the organization's resettlement quotas, some IRO officials were unable to resist the temptation to conceal adverse information about a prospective immigrant. Others failed to inform their Canadian counterparts that a particular refugee had already been rejected by other countries.[118] To be sure, Canada's immigration teams in Germany were able to counter such tactics by the circulation of a blacklist. However, the success of blacklisting depended on timely updates, which were not always possible.[119]

Fraud was not limited to IRO officials, moreover. When screening immigrants from western Europe, for example, Canadian officials had to be on constant lookout for forged identity papers and passports. What made this problem particularly vexing was that the trade in counterfeit documents occasionally proceeded with the connivance of local authorities.[120]

More serious than the fraudulent practices of some IRO or European government officials were instances of corruption on the part of Canadian immigration personnel. Contemporary documents reveal that a handful of immigration officers in Canada and overseas had to be dismissed from their posts for professional misconduct, including illegal activities. At least one of the culprits had been stationed at the busy Canadian immigration mission at Karlsruhe, Germany. His case came to Ottawa's attention when it was discovered that seventy-six persons had obtained visitor's visas to Canada during the latter half of 1951 despite their rejection on security grounds. Under questioning by the RCMP, the officer responsible confessed that he had issued the visas in return for bribes. While subsequent investigation revealed that no subversives had entered Canada as a result of the sale of visas, the possibility of other such cases in which national security was breached cannot be discounted.[121]

Apart from instances of human weakness, Canadian immigration screening also suffered from systemic shortcomings. For example, with the resumption of large-scale screening operations in Europe, it was found that the RCMP's intelligence contacts could not handle more than twenty-five to thirty security checks per day. The result was a growing backlog of unscreened applications for Canadian visas.[122] Ottawa's initial response was to cease screening of prospective immigrants from Belgium, France, the Netherlands, Norway, Denmark, and Greece who had applied for Canadian visas prior to 10 November 1946. Shortly thereafter, the United Kingdom was added to the list of countries for whose nationals screening would be waived if their visa applications had been submitted prior to the 10 November cut-off date. As the number of immigrants from these countries was quite low at the time, such waivers could be granted without compromising Canadian security. However, any increase in the level of immigration, particularly if it involved European refugees, might permit the influx of subversives. Unable to agree on a solution, cabinet referred the problem to the Security Panel.[123]

The panel's first meeting with respect to the backlog was held on 30 January 1947. A number of options were raised at the meeting, ranging from the creation of a security organization large enough to effectively screen all immigrants to the abandonment of immigration screening altogether. In the end, panel members agreed that the extreme options were equally 'impracticable,' and sent the matter back to the RCMP for further study.[124] While opposed in principle to any relaxation of immigration screening, the Mounties had already come to the conclusion that some modification of their procedures was inevitable.[125] Accordingly, they recommended that a system of spot checking be instituted. Under such a system, approximately 20 per cent of all prospective immigrants would be examined, with the question of which ones to be left to the discretion of security officers in the field. Seeing no useful alternative, the panel agreed to the RCMP proposal and submitted it to cabinet.[126]

After a lengthy discussion, cabinet went along with the panel's recommendation, but left its implementation to the bureaucrats. In subsequent meetings, officials of Immigration Branch, the RCMP, and External Affairs developed a new procedure for the screening of prospective immigrants from Europe. Though based on the principle of selective screening, it differed from the Security Panel's recommendations in two important respects. First, the streamlining of immigration procedures would apply only to non-sponsored immigrants from the United Kingdom and western Europe. Refugees and the relatives of Canadian residents, other than wives and children, would continue to be screened in the usual manner. Second, while screening would be expedited for immigrants from the United Kingdom and western Europe, there would be no spot checking.[127] Instead, the issuance of Canadian visas to British subjects and western European nationals would not be held up pending completion of security inquiries, except when this was specifically requested by the RCMP. If, after two weeks, no adverse information was forthcoming, a prospective immigrant could come forward for his or her Stage C interview with the immigration officer.[128]

What became known as the fourteen-day procedure was in operation approximately three years.[129] During that time, some persons who were undesirable from a security point of view undoubtedly gained admission to Canada before the RCMP had had a chance to complete its Stage B inquiries.[130] But the number of war criminals or collaborators who would have been admitted as a result likely was quite low. After all, refugees and most close relatives of Canadian residents still had to await security clearance before they could be admitted. Of the wives and unmarried children of Canadian residents for whom the normal waiting period was waived, it is hard to imagine that there many war criminals among them. Furthermore, the number of immigrants who might have benefited from the fourteen-day procedure was limited. German nationals, for example, had to await the issuance of exit permits from Allied military authorities. The resulting delay gave the RCMP an additional few weeks to complete their security inquiries. In the event such inquiries took longer than expected, Germans with subversive backgrounds might still be caught as a result of exit-permit screening. Indeed, the only people who were in a position to take advantage of the fourteen-day procedure would have been nationals of the countries of western Europe. To be sure, there had been collaboration among the populations of these countries. But it was well below the level in the countries of eastern Europe and the Soviet Union, whose nationals were trying to enter Canada via the refugee pool. Thus, to the extent that collaborators were able to evade detection because of the fourteen-day procedure, they were likely to have been minor functionaries. Typical of the kind of collaborator who benefited from the procedure was a former Dutch Nazi who was granted a visa as a homesteader and who arrived at Montreal in September 1947.[131]

In addition to hampering the screening efforts of Canada's immigration teams in western Europe, the backlog also had the effect of increasing the pressure on the RCMP to speed up its rate of security clearance. As the Mounties tried to accelerate their screening procedures, mistakes were inevitable.[132] The number of errors that resulted from rushed clearances is unknown, of course. Yet there is anecdotal and documentary evidence that at least a few undesirables may have gained admission to Canada as a consequence. In 1950, for example, the Canadian immigration mission at Karlsruhe reported that, owing to a rush order for four hundred farm labourers, security officers had to confine themselves to spot checks. The following year, pressure from the farm lobby and the Department of Labour enabled 'a considerable number' of Italian agricultural labourers who had not been cleared for security to obtain Canadian visas. In 1952, the lobbying efforts of the Engineering Institute of Canada resulted in the admission of at least one German national whose security status was questionable.[133]

Another problem inherent in the system of immigration screening was the inadequacy of the anti-subversive training given to security and immigration officers, particularly where Nazi affiliations were concerned.[134] To some degree, this problem was offset by the almost blanket rejection criteria in effect early on and the use of Directive No. 38 once the grounds for rejection began to be narrowed. Unfortunately, the Allied directive, while certainly comprehensive, was characterized by one omission and one error, each of which may have led to a downgrading of certain Nazi perpetrators and collaborators to lesser offender status. This, in turn, increased the possibility, however remote, that war criminals or collaborators would have been cleared for security.

Since Directive No. 38 was originally intended as a means of classifying German nationals, it omitted the Schutzmannschaften, indigenous auxiliary police units that the Germans had raised in the occupied eastern territories and that had been integral to the implementation of their genocidal policies. This omission was not necessarily fatal, as the non-German rank-and-file of the Schutzmannschaften came under the general prohibition against collaborators. The second error was more serious, however. Among the units listed in the directive were the Einsatzgruppen, or operational task forces of the German security police. These special formations, which comprised approximately three thousand members in total, are estimated to have murdered more than two million Jews, communists, and other so-called undesirables in the Soviet Union during 1941–2.[135] Not only did the directive mistakenly identify the Einsatzgruppen as combat formations of the security police (they in fact operated in the rear of the German Army), but it also classified them as ordinary, rather than major, offenders. Such a description may well have minimized the criminality of the Einsatzgruppen in the minds of Canadian security officers.[136]

Despite its systemic shortcomings and the problems of corruption or sabotage that cropped up from time to time, Canada's postwar system of immigration screening was a well-administered, good-faith effort to prevent the entry of subversives and other undesirables. Nonetheless, some 1,500 Nazi war criminals and collaborators were able to evade detection and gain admission to Canada between 1947 and 1951. How was this possible? The fact is that while strict criteria and sound procedures were important, they were no substitute for adequate corroborating sources. As a consular official attached to the Canadian military mission in Berlin explained, no prospective immigrant, except, perhaps, one whose mind had been 'damaged a bit,' would have confessed to a war criminal or collaborationist background.[137] Assuming that such persons would have lied or dissembled about their wartime activities, the only way they could have been barred from entry was by independent verification of the information they provided. In other words, Canada's system of immigration screening was only as effective as foreign archives, police forces, and intelligence agencies permitted.

In this regard, Canadian security officers suffered from the same handicap as their UNRRA and IRO counterparts – the lack of access to reliable corroborating sources in the countries of the Soviet bloc.[138] While Canada had acquired some intelligence assets in eastern Europe in the immediate aftermath of the war, these were lost once the Iron Curtain descended.[139] A system of delayed immigration was put in place to try to deal with eastern European and Soviet immigrants.[140] That was fine for the few genuine anti-communist refugees who periodically escaped to western Europe. But it was impractical for the great mass of displaced persons who had made their way to Germany at the end of the Second World War. Denied access to police files and military archives behind the Iron Curtain, Canadian security officers and their contacts were forced to rely on those German military and civil records available to them in the West. As has already been noted, these records were of limited value in piecing together the wartime activities of collaborators from eastern Europe and the Soviet Union. Thus, while checks in German and Austrian records made it possible, perhaps even likely, that a Volksdeutsch or German national would be caught in the act of lying about his or her wartime activities, the inability to check sources behind the Iron Curtain increased the chances that collaborators from eastern Europe and the Soviet Union would evade detection.[141]

Based on the sources available at the time, there was only one truly preventable case of a major war criminal entering Canada between

1947 and 1951. On 30 December 1950, the *Beaverbrae* docked at Saint John, New Brunswick. Among those who disembarked was Albert Helmut Rauca. Like most of his fellow passengers, Rauca had signed a contract that obligated him to perform agricultural labour for a year before he was free to seek other employment. After being issued a ticket and some spending money, he boarded a train bound for the town of Otterville, Ontario. Upon arrival at his destination, he was taken by car to the farm of his assigned employer, where he was to spend the next year planting and picking tobacco.

Unlike the rest of the *Beaverbrae*'s contingent, Rauca was harbouring a dark secret. Having served as an SS officer during the war, Rauca was alleged to have participated in the murder of ten thousand Jews at Kaunas, Lithuania, in October 1941. Eventually transferred to the western front, he was captured by U.S. forces and held as a POW. Subsequently, he was placed in a detention camp for former SS and Gestapo officers. However, on 11 November 1945, he was transferred to the American military hospital in Karlsruhe, where he was employed as an orderly. After eight months, Rauca moved to Duisburg in the Ruhr valley, where he found occasional work as a coal miner. Like many Germans who emigrated to Canada during this period, he was sponsored by CCCRR.

As soon as the 1951 tobacco crop was in, Rauca left Otterville and made his way to Toronto. During his first few months there he worked as a bricklayer. Then, through a friend, he was offered a job managing a small banquet hall in Kitchener, Ontario. With no real ties in Toronto, Rauca moved to Kitchener in 1952. For several years, he put down roots in the city's substantial German-speaking community. In 1956, however, the banquet hall was sold. Seeing no other opportunities locally, Rauca decided to start over again in Toronto. For several years, he tried to make a go of it as a small businessman. After the failure of his dry-cleaning outlet, he moved to Huntsville, some three hours north of Toronto, where he operated a motel. Rauca lived quietly in Ontario's Muskoka region until 1982, when the government of the Federal Republic of Germany (FRG) formally requested his extradition. He was arrested by the RCMP on 17 June 1982. The evidence compiled by FRG officials was more than sufficient to establish a prima facie case of war crimes against him. After exhausting his appeals, Rauca was returned to Germany. He died of cancer in prison in 1983 while awaiting trial.[142]

How had Rauca, a former SS officer and an alleged war criminal, been able to gain admission to Canada? There can be little doubt that he had not been candid about his wartime activities. No one with Rauca's résumé would have been granted a visa had he been truthful on either his ML-10 form or when interviewed by Canadian immigration authorities. Still, he should not have evaded detection. After all, his personnel file was included among the thousands of SS officer dossiers captured by the Allies at the end of the war, dossiers that were consulted by Canadian security officers as a matter of course. Moreover, as a German national, Rauca required an exit permit to leave the country, which meant screening by Allied occupation authorities. Even if the Canadians had failed to locate his SS dossier, surely British military intelligence would have. Finally, as a German citizen by birth, Rauca also would have been subjected to Allied screening under Control Council Directive Nos 24 and 36.

In view of the long and readily accessible paper trail that existed on Rauca, there can be only three explanations for the breach of security that permitted him to obtain a Canadian visa. The most tempting, but least plausible, is negligence. It is extremely unlikely that *both* the Canadian immigration team that examined him and the Allied authorities who issued his exit permit would have failed to carry out checks on a German national who obviously had been of military age during the war. A second explanation is that checks were done, but that an incorrect spelling of Rauca's name had been used. This may seem farfetched, but it was the explanation given by the RCMP for its failure to locate him in the decade after the FRG first made inquiries as to his whereabouts.

There is another intriguing explanation, however. It is possible that Canadian immigration teams and Allied military authorities had a reason not to check Rauca's name with the usual sources. One of the more suspicious aspects of his case is that he was released from internment in a camp for SS officers to work in an American military hospital. At a time when Allied authorities were still deeply concerned about the loyalties of the German population at large, it was quite unusual that a former SS officer would be given daily access to a sensitive facility.

The most likely reason is that he had already received some kind of security clearance from Allied occupation authorities that nullified the need for further inquiries.[143] Perhaps Rauca was considered to be a source of intelligence by virtue of having grown up in eastern Germany. We cannot know for sure, of course. Yet in view of the thoroughness with which most German nationals were screened, this would seem to be the most plausible explanation for his admission to Canada.[144]

CHAPTER SIX

Exceptions That Proved the Rule

The process of lifting the restrictions on immigration to Canada was slow and methodical. Nonetheless, some cases were fast-tracked. Individual applicants tended to be the primary beneficiaries. Yet cabinet waivers were granted to groups as well. Between 1947 and 1951, there were three such cases. The first involved scientists and technicians from Germany, the second Estonian refugees from Sweden, and the third former members of a Ukrainian SS division. In each case, Canadian officials had to bend or set aside the immigration regulations in effect at the time. But, as we shall see, their actions did not result in any relaxation of screening for war criminal or collaborationist background.

On Tuesday, 6 June 1944, Allied forces landed on the Normandy coast of German-occupied France. What General Dwight D. Eisenhower called the 'Great Crusade' – the deliverance of western Europe from Nazi tyranny – had begun. As the Allies fought their way through France, Belgium, and the Netherlands into Germany, they liberated not only towns, but strategic installations as well. Among the sites that came under their control were factories, power plants, radio transmitters, and laboratories. The capture of such sites not only deprived the enemy of the wherewithal to continue the war, but also afforded the Allies unprecedented access to the enormous scientific and technical expertise of the Third Reich. Determined to exploit this resource both for the war effort and in the peace that was to follow, Eisenhower made the seizure and safeguarding of strategic installations a high priority.

Initially, the task of protecting captured installations was assigned to ordnance, signals, and chemical-warfare units of the Allied armies. It soon became apparent, however, that these formations were unequal to the technical requirements of the job. In their place, Supreme Head-quarters of the Allied Expeditionary Force (SHAEF) established special exploitation detachments known as T-Forces, the 'T' being short-hand for Technical Industrial Investigating Committees. Differentiated from the regular troops by the large red Ts painted on their helmets, the approximately three thousand T-Force members included medical and signals personnel, intelligence operatives, and special guard details. Their mission was to inventory and protect all captured industrial and scientific assets.

Unlike the regular army units they replaced, the T-Forces operated outside of the military chain of command. Though dependent on the Allied armed forces for logistical support, they took their orders from an agency known as the Combined Intelligence Objectives Staff (CIOS), which had been mandated by SHAEF to administer its pro-gram of scientific and technical exploitation. CIOS compiled the list of targets that were to be secured by the T-Forces, supplied them with technical personnel, and served as an information clearing-house. Working out of its headquarters in London, the agency dispatched its first team to France on 28 August 1944. By the end of the year, almost two hundred CIOS investigators were attached to T-Forces in the field.[1]

In material terms, the Allies' haul of strategic assets was impressive. Generators, heavy machinery, and experimental weapons, for example, were commandeered in staggering quantities. But CIOS's most im-portant accomplishment was the apprehension of the Third Reich's scientific elite. In an operation code named 'Paperclip,' the T-Forces captured many of Germany's top scientists and technologists. On occa-sion, they were taken prisoner en masse, such as happened when Nord-hausen, the Nazi centre for rocket development located in the Harz mountains, surrendered to the U.S. 3rd Armoured Division in April 1945. Over four hundred scientists and technicians, including many of Germany's best and brightest, fell into Allied hands at the Nordhausen facility. Most of the others, however, were arrested individually or in small groups.[2]

While Paperclip's immediate goal was the crippling of Nazi Germany's military-industrial complex, it had longer-term objectives as well. Suspicious of the motives of their Soviet allies, Washington and London resolved to deny them access to German scientific and technical expertise. In an operation subsidiary to Paperclip, code named 'Matchbox,' the T-Forces engaged in commando-style raids on the homes and suspected hideouts of top Nazi scientists. No risk was deemed too high in the effort to limit the transfer of German technology to the Soviet Union. Thus, on one occasion, a T-Force team infiltrated the Soviet zone of occupation and spirited forty-nine German chemists and their families right out from under the noses of their Red Army guards. Incidents like this prompted Moscow to decry the 'kidnapping' of German scientists and technicians by the Allies. The Soviets were being disingenuous, of course, as they were pursuing their own program of scientific exploitation. Code named 'Osavakim,' the Soviet program was responsible for the forcible evacuation of hundreds of scientists and technicians from eastern Germany. Once in Russia, the Germans were offered a choice – work for their captors, or sign a document declaring their unwillingness to assist in the 'reconstruction of the Soviet Union.' Having experienced twelve years under the Nazi dictatorship, few of the scientists were rash enough to opt for the second choice.[3]

Ottawa first learned of Operation Matchbox in the summer of 1945. According to reports filed by Canada's CIOS delegation, scientists and technicians were being removed from Germany by the Americans and the British almost daily, ostensibly to help in the development of new weapons for the war against Japan. As a partner in the war effort, Canada had an interest in the allocation of this scientific talent. That, at least, was the view of the National Research Council's (NRC) representative in the United Kingdom. Back in Canada, the scientific community seemed to agree. In a memorandum to the government, NRC President Dr Chalmers J. Mackenzie suggested that Ottawa make some discreet inquiries with the British. While bidding for the services of Hitler's scientists would be politically unpopular, Mackenzie conceded, 'it would be very shortsighted ... to make it impossible for Canadian science to benefit.'[4]

The British decision to employ German scientists had been predicated on the assumption that none of the individuals selected would have a record as 'a convinced Nazi.' This was a key factor in Ottawa's calculations as well. As the Department of External Affairs advised Dr Mackenzie, the obvious benefits of acquiring German scientists had to be weighed against the 'policy implications.' In the context of the immediate postwar period, this was a reference to the political backlash likely to result from any attempt by Canada to take part in the division of the scientific spoils of war. Faced with the reality of a Canadian public not yet ready to forgive and forget, NRC's enthusiasm waned noticeably. Within days of launching his trial balloon, Mackenzie announced that he had reversed his position on the acquisition of German scientists. 'It may be that later on we will wish to obtain the services of such people,' the NRC president speculated in a follow-up memorandum, but that would have to await more favourable political circumstances. In the wake of NRC's about-face, Ottawa advised London that it did not intend to make any requests for German scientists for the foreseeable future.[5]

True to its word, the Canadian government did not change its policy with respect to the German scientists for almost a year. Then, in September 1946, the issue began to be debated again by senior policy makers.[6] The catalyst for the resumption of discussions was a change of heart at NRC. As Dr Mackenzie advised Norman Robertson, the most recent reports from Canada's representatives on CIOS indicated that there had been a haemorrhage of scientific talent from Germany. The implication was clear. If Ottawa did not act quickly, Canada would be deprived of the services of men who were engaged in leading-edge research and development. Less concerned with the political implications than were his colleagues at External Affairs, the high commissioner advised Mackenzie to approach C.D. Howe. As the minister responsible for Canada's postwar economic development, Howe, Robertson opined, was likely to be sympathetic to the idea of acquiring German scientists.[7]

Mackenzie approached Howe at end of September. Referring to 'certain individual cases brought to our attention,' the NRC president declared that he now favoured the admission to Canada of 'a few well vetted scientists for specific work for which there are no Canadian specialists available.' The individuals in question, he assured the minister, were all known within the Canadian scientific community. Besides, only one was required immediately. That was K. S——, a chemist from Heidelberg who was being courted by McMaster University in Hamilton.[8]

As Robertson had predicted, Howe did not require much prodding. Upon receipt of Mackenzie's request, he placed the matter before the full cabinet. There was some resistance from External Affairs, whose officials wondered why it was necessary to make special arrangements to bring in German specialists when there were skilled technicians among the German POWs not yet repatriated. Armed with preliminary results from a National Defence Headquarters (NDHQ) survey of German prisoners still being held in Canada, Howe countered that the POW pool did not contain the kind of technicians required.[9] That seemed to satisfy the External bureaucrats. Yet there was also a broader desire to ensure the political credentials of any scientist who might be sought. Accordingly, at its 2 October 1946 meeting, cabinet approved the admission of 'a few' German scientists, but only on condition that each would be 'thoroughly investigated.'[10]

Cabinet's decision was based on the assumption that the number of scientists or technicians involved would be limited. As far as universities and public research facilities were concerned, this was true. But Ottawa underestimated private-sector interest. As it happened, several Canadian companies, each operating with the approval of the Department of Trade and Commerce, had already made inquiries with Canadian Military Headquarters (CMHQ) in London regarding the availability of German specialists. In one or two cases, firms had actually sent recruiters overseas. Within weeks of the cabinet's decision, then, the number of German scientists and technicians under consideration had risen to fifteen. Based on the business community's initial response, it was anticipated that the number could reach as high as fifty, perhaps as high as one hundred.[11]

With the prospect of dozens of German scientists being admitted, the question of their immigration status took on greater importance. Immigration Branch advised the government that the scientists and technicians, as German nationals, were enemy aliens under the existing regulations. As such, they were inadmissible. There were only two ways around the prohibition. If a particular scientist or technician were required for a limited period of time, he could be granted temporary entry under a ministerial permit. If permanent admission were the objective, an order-in-council waiving the regulations would be required. The immigration bureaucrats favoured the ministerial-permit option, since such action left the way open to require the individual to return to Germany at the end of his sojourn while at the same time not precluding an offer of permanent admission, if that were deemed desirable.[12]

At their 12 November meeting, cabinet ministers considered the alternatives. After much discussion, they elected to supplement their previous decision by permitting the temporary admission of at least fifteen German technicians and scientists required for research and industrial purposes. Candidates were to be recommended by the president of the NRC and the director-general of research at the Department of National Defence (DND). In keeping with their earlier decision, the ministers reiterated that no scientist or technician could be admitted until he had been carefully investigated from the security point of view.[13]

Most of the scientists apprehended under Operation Matchbox had been selected for their prowess in various areas of defence research. Accordingly, decisions as to their allocation required the agreement of the chiefs of staff of both the American and British armed forces. Though the bidding for their services was supposed to be conducted on the basis of 'approximate equality' between the United States, the United Kingdom, and the nations of the Commonwealth, in practice any Commonwealth country, including Canada, that wanted a German scientist had to reserve him through an agency called the British Intelligence Objectives Sub-Committee (BIOS). In the event that disputes broke out over allocation, these were to be resolved by negotiation between the competing parties. In cases involving scientists required for defence research, Canada's military liaison in London and the British War Office would represent their respective countries' interests. In cases involving scientists required for industrial research, the Canadian High Commission and the British Board of Trade were to work out a solution. All requests, whether for defence or industrial-research scientists, then had to be channelled through the Joint Staff Mission (JSM) in Washington, DC. If a Canadian request conflicted with American priorities, the dispute was supposed to be resolved by the flip of a coin.[14]

Notwithstanding the bipartite nature of the process, it proved almost impossible to enforce 'approximate equality' in the allocation of German scientists and technicians. This is hardly surprising. In the atmosphere of the Cold War, the acquisition of scientific talent was a high-stakes game of international diplomacy. Thus, whenever British or Commonwealth requirements conflicted with those of the United States, American interests almost invariably prevailed.[15] Indeed, the Americans demonstrated a willingness to go to any lengths to secure access to Germany's scientific elite, including violating their own laws. On more than one occasion, U.S. military authorities resolved conflicting claims on a scientist by spiriting him out of Germany and worrying about proper exit and immigration procedures later.[16]

In an attempt to put an end to such abuses, a special Bipartite Allocation Committee (BAC) was set up to take over from the discredited JSM. Under the BAC system, which was inaugurated late in 1948, Canadian representatives in Germany could approach a scientist or technician directly with an offer of employment. If the German were interested, he would provide the Canadian representative with his résumé, along with a statement from his employer releasing him from work, or, in the alternative, explaining why he could not be spared. The Canadian official would then submit a formal application for the scientist's services to Allied occupation authorities, who would forward it to BAC, where the final decision rested.[17]

Under the original procedures established by BIOS, to which the Canadian government had agreed, all applications for German scientists and technicians had to be presented to one of two British panels. In the case of scientists sought for defence research, the Canadian High Commission in London was required to submit the request to a panel of the Deputy Chiefs of Staff Committee (DCOS). In the case of scientists desired for industrial research, the High Commission had to submit the request to the Darwin Panel, which had been set up by the British Board of Trade. It was the task of both the DCOS and Darwin panels to screen the requested scientist for subversive background, in particular Nazi affiliations, determine whether he was qualified to contribute something new to the field in which he was slated to work, and decide whether his release would conflict with British priorities.[18]

As has already been noted, the request also had to be checked with the JSM in Washington (until the establishment of BAC) so as to ensure no prior American claim on the scientist in question. Assuming there were no conflicts over allocation, the scientist would be visited by an Allied security officer and subjected to a thorough investigation. In the case of a scientist sought for defence research, security investigation was the responsibility of the British army of occupation. In the case of a scientist sought for industrial research, the responsibility rested with the appropriate T-Force. If the investigation revealed nothing untoward, the Canadian military mission in Berlin was then free to negotiate the terms of the scientist's employment. Once the contract had been prepared, the mission was required to apply for an exit permit from the military-government authorities in the zone in which the scientist resided. This, as was noted in the previous chapter, involved yet another security check.[19]

Allocation procedures were streamlined with the establishment of BAC. This did not result in a relaxation of screening, however. No application was passed on to BAC for consideration until the scientist in question had been vetted by Allied military authorities. If BAC were uncertain as to an applicant's security status, it could order a security review. Since one of BAC's permanent members was an Allied intelligence officer, such reviews could be conducted internally.[20]

During the early stages of Matchbox, it was assumed that the scientist, once screened, would first be brought to the United Kingdom before making the transatlantic passage to Canada. In that scenario, he would have become the responsibility of Canadian immigration authorities in the United Kingdom, and thereby subject to the same visa procedures as any other resident alien.[21] As the allocation program evolved, however, many of the scientists went to Canada directly from ports in Germany or western Europe.[22] This may have been the result of Howe's efforts to expedite the movement of the scientists.[23] Regardless of the reasons for the change in transportation arrangements, there was no skirting or weakening of Canadian screening procedures.[24] Indeed, Canada's agreement to the BIOS procedure had been contingent on the application of a strict screening regime. The wisdom of this course was confirmed when Ottawa learned that attempts by American military authorities in Germany to circumvent U.S. immigration procedures had resulted in 'numerous vehement protests from veteran[s'] and patriotic associations.'[25]

Ottawa's decision to sign on to the BIOS procedure was made with the full knowledge and approval of the RCMP. After lengthy consultations with their liaison officer in London, the Mounties announced that the DCOS and Darwin methods of screenings were satisfactory. This did not mean they forfeited the right to conduct their own independent security inquiries. On the contrary, once the DCOS or Darwin and subsequent exit-permit screenings were completed, the prospective immigrant still had to go through regular Canadian immigration procedures. According to the RCMP, this was to be done 'in the usual way' – that is, by submitting the visa application to its liaison officer in London.[26] Since the scientist would have already passed through two layers of screening (Darwin or DCOS and exit permit), and since the checks involved would not have differed from those the RCMP officer could call for, the screening process was not likely to be initiated anew. But the RCMP officer certainly would have reviewed the results of the DCOS/Darwin and exit-permit screenings, and, if he had concerns, it was within his prerogative to resubmit the scientist's name. There was also a final security clearance in Canada at the port of arrival. If something came up at that time, the scientist or technician could still be denied his ministerial permit.[27] Thus, there was no real difference in the screening procedures undergone by the German scientists and those applied to other prospective immigrants residing in Germany.[28]

The RCMP gave its approval to the DCOS/Darwin screening procedures late in 1946. Other than trying to acquire Professor S——, however, Ottawa made no additional requests for several months. In view of the scientific community's concern that Canada was being left out of the allocation process, the government's reluctance to proceed more vigorously is difficult to understand. Perhaps it was a measure of the issue's political sensitivity that Ottawa did not immediately press Canadian interests. Whatever the reason, the first formal requests under the BIOS system were not submitted by the government, but rather came from the United Kingdom.[29] Intelligence reports that Operation Osavakim was being expanded to the western zones of occupation led British and American authorities to accelerate the removal of scientists from Germany. Seven soon-to-be-evacuated scientists had expressed an interest in emigration, and so Canada was given an opportunity to bid on their services.[30]

There was no interest in Canada for the UK-recommended scientists. Still, the British offer finally roused Ottawa from its lethargy. In response to the receipt of the seven names, the Department of Trade and Commerce decided to place them in a card index that could be consulted by interested Canadian firms. In addition, External Affairs clarified the BIOS procedures for the benefit of the Canadian Military Mission in Berlin. Most importantly, cabinet finally took measures to waive the regulations prohibiting the entry of German nationals. Enacted as PC 2047 in May 1947, the order-in-council provided for the admission of 'selected German scientists and technicians required [in Canada] for industrial and educational purposes.' Screening, according to the cabinet's decision, would be conducted on the basis of the BIOS arrangements.[31]

During the first two years following the enactment of PC 2047, fifteen German scientists were admitted to Canada. By 1951, another twenty-six had been admitted, bringing the total to forty-one. Most returned to Germany after the expiration of their contracts, although several, benefiting from extensions and the gradual relaxation of the regulations governing the admission of German nationals, elected to stay and become Canadian citizens.[32] Of the forty-one who were admitted, some had worked for the German armed forces during the war as engineers or in ordnance.[33] Most, however, had no Nazi affiliations. Of the handful who had been members of the Nazi Party, the decision as to whether to admit them or not was a judgment call on the part of the RCMP.[34] Thus, Hellmuth Walter, who specialized in submarine propulsion research, was rejected on the grounds of having been 'on very good terms with [Albert] Speer, the War Production Minister, and [with] Hitler.'[35] On other hand, Rudolf Funke, a technician denounced by former associates as 'Nazi No. 1 in the dental trade,' was granted admission after security investigation revealed that he had been thrown out of the Nazi Party in 1939 for having given sanctuary to the wife of a Jewish friend during Kristallnacht, the orgy of anti-Semitic violence and destruction perpetrated by the Nazis in cities and towns across Germany during the night of 10–11 November 1938.[36] A few of those admitted were even determined to have had strong anti-Nazi credentials.[37]

Indeed, of the forty-one German scientists and technicians known to have been granted entry to Canada between 1947 and 1951, only one had a suspicious wartime record. That was E. H——, an engineer who specialized in corrosion protection. H—— was admitted to Canada on a one-year contract. After its expiration, he returned to Germany. During the war, he had, by his own admission, worked on the Nazis' rocket program at Peenemünde on the Baltic coast. Like its successor operation at Nordhausen, Peenemünde exploited a large contingent of slave labourers.[38] As manager of the program's corrosion-resistance project, it is inconceivable that H—— would not have come into contact with these wretched prisoners. Whether he personally supervised any of them is unknown. However, in view of Peenemünde's infamous reputation, H—— probably should not have been admitted to Canada, at least not without further investigation.

The second case in which the immigration regulations were waived in order to admit an otherwise ineligible group involved Baltic refugees from the Soviet Union. By 1948, approximately twenty-three thousand Estonians were living in exile in Sweden.[39] Some had escaped to Sweden after the Soviet Union's annexation of the Baltic states in the summer of 1940. Others had fled there in the autumn of 1944, just ahead of the advancing Red Army. Since the end of the war, Moscow had been pressuring its neighbour to return them. This put the Swedes in a difficult position. On the one hand, the government in Stockholm had recognized the annexation of the Baltic countries. Accordingly, it considered the Estonians to be Soviet citizens. On the other hand, the Swedes were well aware of the fate awaiting the Estonians should they be repatriated. As a consequence, their response to Moscow's requests was ambivalent. While it would not force the Estonians to leave, the Swedish government let it be known that it would not be sorry to see them go.[40]

The ambiguity in Sweden's foreign policy made the Estonians feel very insecure. Their fears were heightened when the Swedish government did in fact repatriate some of their number. In response to a formal request from Moscow, Stockholm agreed to the extradition of 2,700 former members of the German armed forces to the Soviet Union in November 1945. Though most of the ex-soldiers were Volksdeutsche from Russia, between 150 and 200 were Balts. In the minds of the

Estonians, a dangerous precedent had been set. Their confidence in the Stockholm government all but shattered, many actively sought permanent refuge in the West.[41]

As the Cold War deepened, the Kremlin stepped up its demands for the return of people it regarded as Soviet citizens. The situation of the Estonians seemed to be increasingly precarious. Unable to secure guarantees from the Swedish government, some were driven to desperate measures. At the end of July 1947, for example, two dozen Estonians boarded the *Edith*, a forty-foot-long fishing vessel, and set sail for America from Sweden's Baltic coast. After a harrowing voyage of more than two weeks' duration, the *Edith* landed at Savannah, Georgia. In an effort to sort out their immigration status, passengers and crew were transported to Ellis Island in New York harbour. Sympathetic to their plight, U.S. immigration authorities nonetheless denied their applications for permanent residence. The Estonians were granted time, however, to find a country that would take them in.[42]

It was at this point that Canada became involved. Shortly after the landing of the *Edith*, Canadian Lutheran World Relief (CLWR), an agency founded a year earlier to care for its co-religionists among the displaced persons of Europe, was advised that the U.S.-based National Lutheran Council (NLC) was actively seeking a country in which the twenty-four Estonians could settle. CLWR promised to take the matter up with immigration authorities in Ottawa. With only a single day's notice, a delegation comprising two senior NLC officials and the Montreal representative of CLWR called on Director of Immigration Arthur Jolliffe in order to discuss the possibility of admitting the Estonians on 'compassionate grounds.' During the meeting, the Lutheran representatives emphasized the political nature of the *Edith*'s crossing and the jeopardy in which its passengers would find themselves should they ever be repatriated to the Soviet Union. To make its pitch more palatable, CLWR's representative advised that his organization would be willing to furnish Immigration Branch with a written guarantee that, in the event of favourable action on the part of the government, none of the group would be permitted to become public charges for five years after the date of their admission. Jolliffe commiserated with the visitors, but he made no promises. Instead, he offered only to look into the matter and report back to CLWR as soon as possible.[43]

CLWR's entreaties put Ottawa in a quandary. On the one hand, the Estonians were inadmissible under the existing immigration regulations. On the other hand, the *Edith*'s transatlantic crossing had received international press coverage, and so the appeals on the Estonians' behalf could not be dismissed without some political fallout. In the end, a final decision was deferred until the refugees could be screened. Operating through its liaison in London, the RCMP conducted inquiries into the backgrounds of the twenty-four Estonians. Hampered by the inaccessibility of sources behind the Iron Curtain, the Mounties could report only that 'nothing adverse' had been turned up. On the basis of this admittedly thin evidence, Minister of Mines and Resources James Glen recommended to cabinet that PC 695 be waived so as to enable the Estonians to settle in Canada permanently. After some discussion, cabinet went along with Glen's recommendation. On 19 November 1947, an order-in-council was enacted that permitted the admission of the twenty-four refugees.[44]

Ottawa had conceived of the *Edith* episode as a one-time gesture of humanitarian goodwill. The Estonian-Canadian community had other ideas. Taking a page from their German counterparts, the Estonians, working in concert with CLWR, began to lobby for a relaxation of the immigration regulations so as to permit more of their brethren in Sweden to be admitted.[45] As was the case during the earlier campaigns to ease Canada's restrictive immigration regulations, the Senate Committee on Immigration and Labour was pivotal in swaying public opinion. In response to the pressure, the government signalled its willingness to consider the dispatch of an immigration team to Sweden to process additional Estonians. Before that could be done, however, it would be necessary to send an official to Stockholm on a fact-finding mission. Deputy Minister of Mines and Resources Hugh Keenleyside was selected for the task.[46]

Keenleyside left for Europe in the summer of 1948. His first meeting was with representatives of the Estonian community in Sweden. In the course of a discussion held at the Canadian legation in Stockholm on 26 July, he was advised that two to three thousand Estonian refugees were prepared to come to Canada immediately. Next, he met with an official from the Swedish Foreign Office. The diplomat gave him a warm reception. As the Estonians were an irritant in their relationship with the Soviet Union, his government, the official admitted, was only too happy to let them go. There was one condition, however. Owing to Moscow's sensibilities on the issue of repatriation, the Swedish government insisted that there be no publicity attached to the dispatch of a Canadian immigration team to Stockholm. Indeed, so concerned were the Swedes about a possible Soviet reaction that they suggested the team be given some kind of diplomatic cover.[47]

Upon his return to Canada in August, Keenleyside filed a report on the Swedish situation. Based on his findings, the Cabinet Committee on Immigration Policy recommended that Canada permit the admission of up to five thousand Estonian refugees. To process the prospective immigrants, the committee noted, it would be necessary to send a team to Sweden consisting of an immigration officer, an RCMP officer, a physician, and a Department of Labour representative – in other words, the usual complement for a Canadian immigration team overseas. In deference to Stockholm's diplomatic concerns, the members of the team would have to be designated as extra legation staff. The committee also suggested that the International Refugee Organization (IRO) be approached to pay for the refugees' transatlantic passage, although IRO-chartered ships would not be used, again so as not to arouse Soviet suspicions. In the event IRO refused to pay, the committee members recommended that only those Estonians who could provide for their own transport should be considered for admission to Canada. At its 29 September 1948 meeting, cabinet agreed. Accordingly, PC 2180 was amended early in October to permit the admission of up to five thousand Estonians from Sweden.[48]

Events had moved relatively swiftly after Keenleyside's return from Europe. Once cabinet gave its approval, however, things began to bog down. Part of the problem was that the Canadian immigration team was not prepared to begin its processing operations until the spring of 1949.[49] A more serious obstacle to the rapid movement of the Estonians was the near impossibility of conducting security inquiries behind the Iron Curtain.[50] Already under enormous pressure because of the Swedish government's ambivalence, some of the Estonians decided to forego the drawn-out Canadian immigration procedures and instead emulated the passengers of the *Edith*.

Early in August 1948, a motor boat named *Astrid* and its twenty

Estonian passengers landed at Quebec City. Other small craft followed in its wake. In 1948 alone, more than five hundred Balts, mostly Estonians, arrived in Canada this way. Acting on the advice of Immigration Branch, the Cabinet Committee on Immigration Policy recommended that, in view of the 'exceptional' circumstances, the regulations be waived to permit the admission of all illegally landed Estonians. In a discussion held on 1 September 1948, cabinet agreed, deeming it 'unlikely' that there would be many more such landings in the future.[51]

Though motivated primarily by humanitarian considerations, cabinet appears to have based its decision on the likelihood that attempts to reach Canada by boat would subside once the country's Stockholm mission was up and running. Unfortunately, this was not the case. Despite the fact that visa applications were being accepted by the start of 1949, more than a thousand Estonians attempted the perilous transatlantic crossing that year. For a while, Ottawa continued to tolerate the illegal landings, merely holding the new arrivals in preventative detention in order to screen them. Assuming they passed Canadian immigration procedures, the Estonians were then granted admission. The government's humanitarian impulses were not boundless, however. In the spring, Immigration Branch advocated the issuance of warnings to the effect that any Estonians who landed at a Canadian port without having received a visa would be returned to Sweden. In a reversal of its previous position, cabinet approved the measure. Despite the danger of tipping off the Soviets, Canadian officials in Sweden were authorized to issue public warnings to the Estonian community that illegal landings would no longer be tolerated.[52]

The warnings had no effect. As the staff at Canada's Stockholm legation had predicted, Ottawa's earlier leniency with respect to illegal landings only emboldened the Estonians.[53] On 2 August 1949, for example, the vessel *Parnu* arrived at Halifax from Sweden with 154 refugees crammed on board. As had been the case with previous landings, most of the passengers were Estonians. This was the last straw. Acknowledging that Ottawa's policy of granting admission to aliens who arrived by boat had only encouraged others to do the same, Keenleyside admonished the government that the landings 'must be stopped.' He suggested two ways of doing so. First, Canada ought to return a few of the recent arrivals in order to deter other potential 'boat people.' Second, the captains and owners of the vessels that were bringing the Estonians to Canada had to be warned that they would henceforth be liable to criminal proceedings.[54] Cabinet agreed with the idea of prosecuting vessel owners and captains, but backed away from a policy of returning the illegal immigrants to Sweden. Subject to health and security checks, illegals would be permitted to remain, although anyone failing to meet the immigration requirements would, of course, be deported.[55]

In terms of screening for war criminal or collaborationist background, the Estonians from Sweden received no special dispensation. This was true both for Estonians who applied for visas through the immigration mission in Stockholm and for those who came to Canada's shores illegally. Since most of the Estonians who came legally from Stockholm required IRO's assistance in order to pay their passage, they first had to complete the organization's security-friendly CM/1 form with the assistance of Canadian immigration authorities.[56] Of course, those who landed illegally in Canada managed to evade this crucial step in the screening process. To prevent infiltration by subversives, they were detained while security inquiries were carried out. Some of the illegals were discovered to be security risks and were deported.[57] To be sure, RCMP security officers faced the same problem in screening the Estonians as they did with other refugees from eastern Europe and the Soviet Union – no access to reliable corroborating sources. Indeed, in some respects, the problem was even worse in the case of the Estonians, as there was no way to approach the Soviets for information without triggering a diplomatic incident. Consequently, several Nazi war criminals and collaborators were able to gain admission to Canada, most notably Haralds Puntilis, a chief of police alleged to have participated in the round-up and murder of Jews in Rezekne, Latvia, and Alexander Laak, who was alleged to have served as commander of a concentration camp in Estonia.[58] It must be emphasized, however, that the failure to detect such individuals was not the result of the waiving of security procedures, but rather the inability of the RCMP to conduct adequate checks behind the Iron Curtain.

The third exception made for an otherwise ineligible group of immigrants involved former members of a Ukrainian SS division who were residing in the United Kingdom. Unlike the German scientists and Estonian refugees, the Ukrainians did not benefit from the waiving of the immigration regulations. Rather, the Canadian government, after three years of steadfast resistance, finally brought its handling of the case into line with the policy then in effect regarding other non-German former members of the Waffen-SS. In so doing, Ottawa gave assurances that no ex-soldier would be admitted who could not pass 'the most rigid screening.'[59] Every effort appears to have been made to follow through on that promise. In fact, of the approximately 1,200–2,000 Ukrainian SS veterans who eventually came to Canada,[60] only a small fraction were subsequently discovered to have had prior service in German auxiliary police units.

In the aftermath of the defeat and capture of the German 6th Army at Stalingrad, a severe manpower shortage forced the Nazi regime to reverse its previous policy of not recruiting Waffen-SS units in the occupied eastern territories. Aware that Galicia, a border region extending from southeastern Poland into western Ukraine, was potentially fertile recruitment ground, Hitler consented to the organization of a Galician SS division in March 1943. Recruiting began shortly thereafter. Within a matter of weeks, Waffen-SS induction commissions were swamped with volunteers. Of the 80,000 Ukrainian men of military age who tried to enlist, almost 30,000 were rejected on the grounds of questionable political reliability. Another 20,000 were weeded out because they failed to meet the physical requirements. Of the 30,000 who remained, only about 8,000 were considered immediately suitable for service in the Waffen-SS.[61]

Approximately half of the initial complement of eligible recruits were inducted directly into the SS Volunteer Division 'Galicia,' subsequently renamed the 14th Galician SS Volunteer Division and the 14th SS Grenadier Division (Galician No. 1).[62] As troops of the Waffen-SS, they were given the rank of SS private and wore the SS runes and insignia on their uniforms.[63] Organization and training of the 4,000 men began in July 1943 on the SS's Heidelager troop-training grounds at Szebnie, a small town located about a hundred kilometres east of Cracow in southern Poland.[64] Concurrently, the remaining eligible recruits were organized into three police units known as Galician SS Volunteer Regiment Nos 1, 2, and 3.[65] Eventually, four more regiments were organized, one of which drew from members of Ukrainian police battalion no. 206, which had been stationed in Poland, the other three comprising volunteers from among Ukrainian forced labourers in France and Germany. After several weeks' training, regiment nos 1, 2, and 3 were incorporated into the division as well.[66] The others joined the division later, nos 6 and 7 being transferred from France to the Heidelager training grounds in December 1943 and January 1944 respectively, nos 4 and 5 from Germany and Poland respectively in June 1944.[67] This brought the 14th SS up to a strength of approximately 14,000 officers and other ranks. To fill the divisional reserve, Ukrainian police battalion no. 204, which had been stationed in Poland, as well as a Ukrainian coastal defence unit serving in France, were disbanded and their men transferred to the East.[68]

The 14th SS first saw action on the eastern front in the summer of 1944. Despite its inadequate training and second-rate equipment, the division was thrown into the middle of a major Soviet offensive at the beginning of July. Trapped in a pocket around Brody, the 14th SS disintegrated under the sledgehammer blows of the Red Army. Only three thousand men were able to break out. These shattered remnants were withdrawn to Hradischko in what was then the Nazi protectorate of Bohemia and Moravia, about a hundred kilometres north-northeast of Bratislava, the capital of Slovakia. While at Hradischko, the ranks were filled with a new levy of Ukrainians and reinforced with German NCOs. Early in the winter of 1944, the division, shortly to be renamed the 1st Division of the Ukrainian National Army, was sent to Slovakia to help the Germans put down a national uprising. In March 1945, it was transferred to Slovenia to participate in anti-partisan operations. From Slovenia the division made its way to Austria, where it surrendered to British forces in May 1945.[69]

The extent of the 14th SS's criminality is difficult to ascertain. If prior service in auxiliary police units is used as a measure, then the 14th SS was far less permeated by criminal elements than, say, the 30th SS, members of which, as we saw in Chapter 3, were later incorporated into the Polish 2nd Corps. As has already been noted, more than half of the division's original complement of men were drawn from a grass-roots recruitment drive in western Ukraine, with the remainder coming from the ranks of Ukrainian forced labourers in Germany and France.

Only a small percentage were men transferred from established auxiliary detachments.[70] Of the transfers, some were members of a coastal defence unit that had been stationed in France since its formation in January 1944. The others came from two auxiliary police units – Schutzmannschaft battalion nos 204 and 206 – that had not been established until the spring of 1944.[71] These units were formed too late to have participated in the Nazi slaughter in 1941–2 of approximately 60 per cent of Ukraine's Jewish population, which had numbered in excess of one and a half million before the outbreak of the war.[72] Moreover, there is no evidence that these units took part in anti-partisan operations or reprisals prior to their incorporation into the 14th SS.

This is not to suggest that the 14th SS deserved the clean bill of health conferred on it by a Canadian royal commission in 1986.[73] At least one of the police regiments into which divisional recruits were initially inducted appears to have perpetrated atrocities. That was Galician SS Volunteer Regiment No. 5, which was employed in anti-partisan operations in eastern Poland prior to its incorporation into the 14th SS. According to reports by the Armia Krajowa (AK), the main Polish resistance army, the regiment was involved in several massacres of civilians during the first few months of 1944.[74] Furthermore, a significant number of the division's recruits, particularly those who served in Schutzmannschaft battalion nos 204 and 206, appear to have seen prior service in Ukrainian irregular formations that were known to have perpetrated atrocities against Jews and communists during the early days of the German occupation.[75] A few members of the 14th SS had even served with German security police detachments in western Ukraine.[76] In view of the brutality with which the Germans suppressed the Slovak National Uprising in the autumn of 1944, it is possible that elements of the division were implicated in crimes against civilians during its tour of duty in Slovakia.[77] Finally, there are circumstantial links between the division and the Nazi concentration camp system. Contemporary documents reveal that both the division's Heidelager and Hradischko training grounds were adjacent to forced labour camps.[78] There is no direct evidence linking the division with the day-to-day operation of the camps. Yet it would not have been unusual for Waffen-SS recruits to have taken guard and prisoner-escort training there.[79]

After surrendering to the British, the approximately eleven thousand men of the 14th SS were transferred to Italy and interned at the Rimini POW camp, north of Rome. Having been captured in German uniform, most faced certain repatriation to the USSR. In the end, however, only about three thousand were actually sent back.[80] The reason was the intervention of powerful forces. Shortly after the termination of hostilities in Europe, General Pawlo Shandruk, the former leader of a Nazi-sponsored Ukrainian 'national liberation committee,' contacted Archbishop Iwan Buchko, a high-ranking prelate in Rome who specialized in Ukrainian affairs. Describing the former SS soldiers as good Catholics and fervent anti-communists, Shandruk implored Buchko to intervene on their behalf. The archbishop agreed to try. During a special audience with Pope Pius XII, Buchko pleaded the division's case. The pontiff was very sympathetic and promised to contact the appropriate British authorities. As a result of the Vatican's efforts, London agreed to change the Ukrainians' POW status to that of surrendered enemy personnel, a seemingly minor distinction, but one that freed the British from their repatriation obligations under the Yalta agreement.[81]

The men of the 14th SS owed their freedom, and possibly their lives, to Shandruk and Buchko. Yet their respite would be short-lived. By the beginning of 1947, the negotiation of a peace settlement with Italy was in its final stages. Once the treaty was signed, British and American occupation forces would be withdrawn from Italy, leaving the Rimini camp, as well as all other POW facilities, in the hands of the Italians. Though dominated by right-of-centre parties, the government in Rome had already signalled its willingness to cooperate with the USSR in the repatriation of Soviet citizens still interned on Italian soil. With time running out on the Ukrainians, officials of the British Foreign Office debated their fate. One faction advocated granting sanctuary to the men of the 14th SS until the issue of their final status could be worked out. Another rejected the idea, arguing that only genuine allies, like Anders's Poles, ought to be assisted, not people who had fought for the Germans. Ultimately, the views of the pro-Ukrainian faction held sway, in large measure because of the skilful campaign waged on behalf of the SS veterans by the Ukrainian communities in the United Kingdom, the United States, and Canada. Accordingly, in February 1947 London decided to admit the eight thousand men who remained at Rimini.[82]

With the war still fresh in the public memory, the British government was aware that its decision to admit the Ukrainians would not be a popular one. In an effort to pre-empt the critics, London launched a two-pronged public relations offensive. First, the official reason given for the transfer of the Ukrainians to the United Kingdom was the need to replenish labour forces lost as a result of the repatriation of German POWs. Second, the British public was assured that the former Ukrainian soldiers would be subjected to rigorous screening. This, London announced, would be carried out by Brigadier Fitzroy Maclean's Special Refugee Commission (SRC), which was already in Italy conducting security examinations of Yugoslav refugees.[83]

On the surface, at least, Maclean's presence in Italy seemed to ensure that the vetting of the 14th SS would be conducted with the requisite vigour and thoroughness. Unfortunately, the team selected to screen the Ukrainians faced problems that simply did not factor into SRC's Yugoslav operation. For one thing, Maclean was personally involved in screening the Yugoslavs, which meant that he had to delegate command of the 14th SS operation to his assistant, D. Haldane Porter. Second, whereas Maclean had access to Yugoslav government archives, Porter's team would have little in the way of corroborating documentation. Third, there simply was not enough time to do an adequate job. Despite Porter's estimation that it would take months to screen the Ukrainian contingent, the British government set a deadline of mid-March 1947.[84]

Notwithstanding the lack of access to reliable sources and the unrealistic time limits imposed by London, Porter's team made a good-faith effort to screen the Ukrainians. Of course, with less than a month to carry out its inquiries, SRC was able to examine only a fraction of the 8,272 men interned at Rimini. Supplied with nominal rolls and a short history of the 14th SS, Porter's team tried to screen a representative sample of the division's rank and file. During these spot checks, the persons selected for interview were asked a series of questions designed to elicit information regarding the nature of their recruitment, the duration of their service, and the activities of their particular sub-unit. Once an individual had been screened, his statement was checked for discrepancies against those of his comrades and the divisional history.[85]

Porter had no illusions about the effectiveness of such methods. In an interim report, he admitted that few of the men examined had German military identification documents. He was also deeply suspicious of the divisional history, which, as he noted, had been compiled 'entirely by the Ukrainians themselves.' Even the interviews were of questionable value. Those men whom his team had examined, Porter conceded, 'may be all or in part lying.' It was for these reasons that he recommended verifying their stories against UN, and, if necessary, Soviet lists of suspected war criminals. He also suggested that independent confirmation of the divisional history be obtained.[86]

On the basis of an admittedly incomplete job of screening, the men of the 14th SS were brought to the United Kingdom during May and June 1947. Upon arrival, they were put to work on projects that had formerly utilized German POW labour. While the Ukrainians proved to be good workers, there was no intention to grant them permanent status. Indeed, almost immediately, London began working out plans for their resettlement elsewhere. Over the course of its deliberations, the British government consulted closely with the Central Ukrainian Relief Bureau (CURB), which had been established at the end of hostilities in Europe to tend to the needs of Ukrainian refugees.[87] Headed by Gordon R. Panchuk, a Canadian flight lieutenant stationed in London, CURB recommended that the Ukrainians be permitted to emigrate to Canada en masse as 'the quickest and best solution.' London agreed. Having won British approval, Panchuk then contacted Immigration Branch, the Department of External Affairs, and the Canadian High Commission to the United Kingdom, asking each in turn to consider permitting the Ukrainians to migrate to Canada 'in bulk.'[88]

Taking a page out of CCCRR's book, CURB adopted the strategy of trying to portray the Ukrainians' wartime service in the best possible light. A key element in that strategy was to minimize the division's SS affiliation. In his early dealings with the immigration bureaucrats, Panchuk referred to the division by its last and non-SS designation (1st Division of the Ukrainian National Army) and alleged that the use of SS terminology in its case was little more than Soviet propaganda. He also glossed over the voluntary nature of its recruitment, focusing instead on those Ukrainians who had joined as an alternative to forced labour. The Germans, he suggested, did not have much success in attracting volunteers. Citing these so-called facts, Panchuk informed Ottawa that 'as far as the British are concerned, there is no security objection to a single individual in the group in question.'[89]

Did Panchuk know that much of the information he was passing on to the immigration bureaucrats bordered on historical revisionism? This is a difficult question to answer. At the time the resettlement of the 14th SS was first broached with Canadian officials, the information on which Panchuk based his reports had been gleaned from a history prepared by Andrij Palij, a former member of the division's welfare organization. There can be little doubt that Palij's apologist tract suited CURB's strategy of portraying the Ukrainians as innocent victims of war. It is not clear, however, whether Panchuk knew that specific aspects of the story were questionable or out-and-out lies.[90]

Regardless of the extent of Panchuk's knowledge at the time, Ottawa was not receptive to his arguments. During a meeting with representatives of the Ukrainian-Canadian community held on 9 October 1947, Keenleyside advised them that nothing was likely to be done for the eight thousand former SS men for the foreseeable future. The reason, as he later explained to Jolliffe, was that 'we want to give a preference to those who did *not* take an active part in the war against us' (italics added).[91] Close examination of the government's internal correspondence makes it clear that Ottawa's objections to the Ukrainians went well beyond their service in the German armed forces. In keeping with their jaundiced view of collaborators, the immigration bureaucrats opposed the admission of former members of the 14th SS on the grounds that their service appeared to have been voluntary. As Keenleyside advised his counterpart at External Affairs, 'a number of these persons may be listed by the U.S.S.R. as war criminals and indeed may be war criminals according to our own standards.'[92]

Based on the advice it was receiving from senior officials, cabinet leaned toward outright rejection of the 14th SS. Yet in view of the very public representations made on behalf of the division by the Ukrainian-Canadian lobby, the government was loath to close the door completely. Hoping to take the decision out of the realm of politics, cabinet acted in time-honoured fashion: it referred the matter to committee.[93] Charged with advising the government on what to do with the Ukrainians, the Cabinet Committee on Immigration Policy took a long time to come up with recommendations. Part of the reason for the delay may have been the government's desire to avoid offending the Ukrainian-Canadian community. But it was also the case that the committee found its inquiries blocked at every turn. Beyond a reiteration of its statement that the Ukrainians were unobjectionable from the security point of view, the British government did not provide much in the way of useful information.[94]

Stymied in London, the committee tried a different approach. As it happened, there were 25,000–30,000 Ukrainian refugees in Germany in the British zone of occupation, some of whom were also vying for admission to Canada. These Ukrainians had not served with the 14th SS, of course, but they could provide some insight into the motivation of their UK–based brethren. In particular, they might be surveyed with a view to determining the extent to which the Ukrainian population had collaborated during the war. Accordingly, in November 1947 the Canadian military mission in Berlin contacted British occupation authorities and asked them three questions: how many of the Ukrainians who were currently residing in Germany had previously served in the Red Army, how many had been evacuated to Germany as forced labourers, and how many had served in the German armed forces? The answers, the committee members believed, would enable them to better assess the claims being made by Panchuk and the Ukrainian-Canadian lobby.[95]

The committee's calculations were thrown into disarray upon receipt of the report by the British occupation authorities. The reason for the confusion was that the survey on which the report had been based was hopelessly flawed. According to the British Control Commission for Germany, very few Ukrainians had served in the German armed forces during the war. On the contrary, most claimed to have been evacuated to the Third Reich as forced labourers. Unfortunately, the British conceded, it was impossible to verify the accuracy of such claims. For one thing, they had no way of compelling the Ukrainians to be truthful. Moreover, many of those questioned may have had a very strong motivation to lie. Though the Yalta accords were by this time a dead letter, most refugees still feared repatriation if they admitted to either desertion from the Red Army or service in the German armed forces.[96]

Unable to obtain objective information as to the wartime sympathies of the Ukrainians, the committee did not report to cabinet until the spring of 1948. When it finally submitted recommendations, these were based to a considerable degree on conjecture. Rejecting British assurances as unreliable, the committee advised cabinet to consider the Ukrainians as voluntary collaborators for purposes of immigration. Those who could prove that their service had been rendered 'under compulsion' might be considered for admission, but the remainder ought to be rejected.[97] This was in keeping with the policy already in effect for non-Germans who had served in the regular German armed forces. Significantly, it was also part of an evolving consensus regarding non-Germans who had served in the Waffen-SS. Its initial suspicions having been confirmed, cabinet approved the committee's report, although no official action was taken to implement it. Instead, Panchuk and the Ukrainian leaders in Canada were quietly informed that the ban on the men of the 14th SS was still in effect.[98]

If the immigration bureaucrats thought the matter was closed, they were mistaken. CURB and the Ukrainian-Canadian lobby continued their campaign to get all or at least part of the 14th SS admitted. Aware that Ottawa's main objection to the division was the apparently voluntary character of its recruitment, those lobbying on its behalf changed their tactics. Henceforth, no effort would be spared in advancing the claim that the rank and file of the 14th SS had been 'forcibly conscripted.'[99] The change in tactics evoked no sympathy in Ottawa. Indeed, the immigration bureaucrats began to betray a certain weariness and annoyance with the lobbying on behalf of the Ukrainian ex-soldiers. For example, at the conclusion of a meeting with the head of the Ukrainian-Canadian Committee (UCC), Jolliffe told him that he did not want to hear anything more on the subject for at least three months. Upon receipt of yet another UCC missive, Keenleyside testily advised the director of immigration not to respond.[100]

At an apparent dead end with the Canadian government, Panchuk tried to enlist the aid of the authorities in the United Kingdom. During discussions with officials of the War Office, he was advised that Canada might reconsider its position on the Ukrainians if they were able to shed their POW label entirely.[101] Armed with this new information, CURB expended considerable energy trying to get the former 14th SS personnel upgraded from surrendered enemy to civilian status. After several months of lobbying, the organization was successful. In August 1948, London formally released the Ukrainians from POW captivity and granted them civilian status.[102]

The civilianization of the 14th SS seemed to galvanize the Ukrainian-Canadian lobby. In stories run in community newspapers in Winnipeg and Edmonton, UCC heralded the British government's action. More importantly, the organization announced that Ottawa was prepared to issue visas to members of the division who were able to produce evidence attesting to their civilian status.[103] This was not the case, of course. Notwithstanding the civilianization of the Ukrainians, there had been no change in policy on the Canadian side. The response of the immigration bureaucrats to the erroneous reports was swift and angry. Denouncing UCC for its apparent attempt to embarrass the government, the superintendent of immigration in western Canada advised that, at a minimum, some sort of retraction be issued.[104] Unwilling to alienate its Ukrainian-Canadian constituency, the government did not publicly rebuke UCC. However, it did advise those lobbying on behalf of the Ukrainian ex-soldiers that no change in policy had been made, nor was any forthcoming.[105]

The new civilian status of the Ukrainians did not lead to a lifting of the ban, but it may have been of some assistance in helping individual members of the 14th SS gain admission to Canada. At least a few of the Ukrainian veterans had been able to obtain IRO sponsorship by claiming that they had been civilians during the war.[106] Their success convinced Panchuk that the same tactic might be used to slip some of the men through Canadian immigration screening. 'If applications are made now without any mention of the fact that they were previously confined as PWs,' he advised a representative of the Ukrainian-Canadian lobby, 'no questions are asked.'[107] There is no way of determining how many former members of the 14th SS evaded detection in this manner. But the number may have been significant. After the change in their status, the Ukrainians were transferred to boarding houses, YMCAs, Salvation Army hostels, and work camps throughout the United Kingdom – in short, wherever there was room.[108] Their dispersal deprived immigration officers of a key screening tool. Prior to civilianization, the Ukrainians could have been identified as surrendered enemy personnel by comparing their addresses with a list of the various POW camps on British soil. Once their addresses changed, all trace of their previous status was erased.[109]

After the UCC newspaper fiasco, the immigration bureaucrats were less inclined to listen to the Ukrainian-Canadian lobby.[110] The overtures coming out of London were another matter. During a June 1948 meeting attended by the Canadian high commissioner, several members of his staff, and the RCMP's liaison officer in the United Kingdom, a representative of the Department of Labour was informed that the British government had made 'unofficial' inquiries about the possibility of Canada taking some of the 14th SS men off its hands. The Labour representative advised his audience that he was unable to give a definite answer without first consulting Ottawa. He suggested, however, that individual members of the division, 'if otherwise admissible,' might be used to make up for the shortfalls that periodically affected bulk-labour movements from Europe.[111]

Upon his return to Ottawa, the Canadian representative advised his department of the British government's trial balloon. As the inquiry had been unofficial, it went unanswered. Still intent on resettling at least part of the 14th SS, in the autumn of 1948 the British Foreign Office formally requested that the Canadian government accept 'a proportion' of the otherwise fit Ukrainian ex-soldiers who were unsuitable for employment in the United Kingdom. In the wake of this new development, the matter was once more referred to the Cabinet Committee on Immigration Policy. With nothing to contradict their earlier impressions of the division, the committee members again recommended rejection. Cabinet agreed.[112]

Despite having failed for a second time, the Ukrainian-Canadian lobby did not withdraw quietly into the background. On the contrary, Panchuk, who complained that 'the Canadian government and authorities have not given fair and just consideration to this serious problem,' advised UCC to intensify its lobbying efforts. A concerted national campaign was launched in 1949 involving members of Parliament and grassroots supporters.[113] It had no appreciable effect. Despite rumblings in the Liberal caucus about a double standard when it came to Ukrainian immigration, the government would not relent. Indeed, after further consultation with Jolliffe, Keenleyside, and its committee on immigration policy, cabinet upheld the ban on members of the 14th SS.[114]

There would be no change in Ottawa's attitude until mid-1950. When relief was finally granted to former members of the 14th SS, it was not as a result of the efforts of the Ukrainian-Canadian lobby,[115] but rather because the situation of the Ukrainians had become anomalous vis-à-vis another prohibited group. Volksdeutsche who had served in the German armed forces, it will be remembered, were not admissible until the lifting of that restriction in April 1950.[116] In the discussions that led up to their decision regarding former Volksdeutsche auxiliaries, the immigration bureaucrats recognized that it might necessitate a change in the status of the former Ukrainian enemy personnel.[117] Walter Harris, the new minister of citizenship and immigration, agreed. In the wake of the change in policy toward the Volksdeutsche, he advised his cabinet colleagues, the case of the 14th SS ought to be reconsidered. For his part, Harris recommended that 'Ukrainians who were in the United Kingdom as prisoners of war be admitted to Canada notwithstanding their service in the enemy forces, provided that they come within the admissible classes ... and otherwise comply with the provisions of the Immigration Act.'[118]

Interestingly, cabinet took note of the minister's arguments, but deferred a final decision pending receipt of an updated intelligence report on the division.[119] In the course of conducting its own inquiries, External Affairs had learned of possible links between the 14th SS and the Organization of Ukrainian Nationalists (OUN). Long regarded by the RCMP as having 'Nazi' and 'extremist' tendencies,[120] adherents of the OUN were considered security risks. Accordingly, cabinet would not give its approval for the admission of members of the 14th SS until the nature of the relationship between the division and the OUN could be determined.[121]

The Joint National Defence–External Affairs Intelligence Board (JIB) had a preliminary report ready by mid-April 1950. On the basis of information amassed by DND's Directorate of Military Intelligence, the JIB presented a reasonably accurate picture of German recruiting practices in occupied Ukraine, although it underestimated the extent to which enlistment in Ukrainian auxiliary units had been voluntary. The way was clear, it seemed, to lift the ban on the Ukrainian ex-soldiers. Yet despite the lack of evidence supporting an organizational link between the OUN and the 14th SS, the government was not satisfied. After reviewing the JIB report, cabinet asked the RCMP to investigate the matter further. These inquiries took another month. Thus, it was not until the Mounties confirmed JIB's findings late in May that cabinet finally agreed to the admission of the Ukrainians. There was one proviso. All applicants would have to undergo 'special' security screening measures.[122] It is not clear precisely what was meant in this regard, although Immigration Branch's subsequent instructions to its officers in the field called for each former SS man to be subjected to 'full security screening.'[123]

Although the decision to admit the Ukrainian SS veterans was made at the end of May 1950, the government waited more than two weeks before going public. Indeed, it was mid-June before the change in policy was announced. Word of the change came during Question Period in the House of Commons. In response to a query from a Liberal backbencher, Harris advised the House that, henceforth, former members of the 14th SS Division would be eligible to apply for admission to Canada, 'provided they come within the ordinary rules with respect to immigrants.' The decision had been based, he stated, on an investigation of the division 'as a whole,' not of individual members.[124]

Harris's answer was forthright, truthful, and wholly defensible from the public policy point of view. Yet it provoked a firestorm of protest. In a telegram to the minister, the president of the Canadian Jewish Congress (CJC) expressed the organization's dismay at what it regarded as the government's clearance of the 14th SS en masse. Citing the Nuremberg tribunal's condemnation of the SS as a criminal organization, the CJC implored Harris to delay admission of members of the division until a 'full and complete investigation' could be carried out.[125]

The CJC's concerns were not without justification. After all, Harris's statement to the House was the first public acknowledgment that former SS men were being considered for admission to Canada. Yet it was clear that the organization had overreacted. Nothing in Ottawa's handling of the matter suggested that the 14th SS was to be admitted en masse, or that individual members of the division who failed to meet the immigration criteria would nonetheless be granted visas. All that had changed was that membership in the division would no longer be grounds for automatic rejection. Harris alluded to this in his response to the CJC. At the same time, he did not close the door to further investigation. Seeking to reassure the CJC and, through it, the Canadian-Jewish community, the minister advised that 'I shall be pleased to receive any information you have about individuals in this Division as we have no intention of admitting anyone who cannot pass the most rigid screening.'[126]

While CJC's intervention did not ultimately lead to a reversal of the cabinet decision, it did prompt a delay in the acceptance of visa applications from former members of the 14th SS. During the interval, the government conducted additional inquiries into the activities of the division. CJC also compiled a brief. Unfortunately, the organization was unable to produce hard evidence to support the proposition that the 14th SS was rife with criminal elements. Nor did any information of an adverse nature result from the government's supplementary inquiries. Confronted with serious but unsubstantiated allegations against individual members of the division, the government saw no reason for further delay. Accordingly, Ottawa approved the resumption of the application process at the end of September.[127]

To say that CJC was disappointed with this decision is an understatement. From an objective point of view, however, the organization seems to have been applying a standard for admission that deviated sharply from contemporary immigration practices, not to mention the Canadian sense of fair play. Leaving aside the state of the evidence regarding the 14th SS's criminality, which, as the discussion above has demonstrated, is far from conclusive, it is clear that the CJC would have been satisfied only with a continuation of the outright ban on the division. As the organization's president complained to Harris, the resumption of screening 'would be futile if your action is based on ... individual names rather than on the totality of the evidence against the ... Division.'[128] The meaning here is unmistakable. Regardless of whether they had joined the 14th SS voluntarily or under duress, regardless of whether or not they had served in auxiliary police units prior to enlisting, regardless of their individual conduct, members of the division, according to the CJC, shared equally in its generally objectionable character. Taken to its logical conclusion, adoption of screening along the lines advocated by the organization could have only one result – perpetuation of the ban on the 14th SS.

The nature of the screening applied to members of the division can no longer be determined with precision. Ottawa had called for the Ukrainians to be subjected to the full range of screening procedures at the disposal of immigration and security officers. Assuming the government's instructions were followed, it can be surmised that the RCMP would have tried to elicit answers to three basic questions. First, had individual Ukrainians enlisted in the 14th SS voluntarily or under duress? Second, had they served in auxiliary police units prior to their enlistment in the Waffen-SS? Third, what was their rank at the conclusion of the war? Such questions would have conformed with the screening procedures in effect at that time. They also would have been in keeping with the criteria for offender status contained in Allied Control Council directives.

The effectiveness with which former members of the 14th SS were screened is also a matter of speculation. We know that only a few dozen of the 1,200–2,000 former members of the division who were admitted to Canada were subsequently revealed to have had prior auxiliary police service. There are two possible explanations. The first is that Canadian security officers were successful in weeding out longer-term collaborators.[129] The second is that relatively few of the Ukrainians in the United Kingdom, most of whom did not join the 14th SS until after the debacle at Brody, had in fact served in auxiliary police units prior to their enlistment. In view of the lack of access to captured German records in the Soviet Union, which were (and remain) the best source of information on the Ukrainian auxiliary police, the second explanation seems more plausible.

As regards screening for voluntary enlistment in the 14th SS, the picture is even less clear. If security officers based their decisions on the historical reports prepared by the JIB and the RCMP, then they were more likely to have accepted assertions of conscription. If, on the other hand, they resorted to the rule that was being applied more generally to Waffen-SS membership, that is, that enlistment prior to 1 December 1943 was likely voluntary, whereas enlistment after that date tended to indicate conscription, then the onus would have been on the Ukrainians to prove that their service had been compulsory. Without access to their individual visa applications, the most that can be said about the screening of the division was that it likely conformed to the procedures applied to all other refugees at the time. Thus, to the extent that the 14th SS movement was infiltrated by voluntary collaborators or war criminals, it was not the result of laxity or bad faith on the part of Canadian officials, but rather was caused by the limitations inherent in Canada's immigration-screening system.

By the time former members of the 14th SS were permitted to apply for admission to Canada, the Second World War had begun to recede from public memory. Moreover, the threat of Soviet expansionism far out-weighed fears of a Nazi revival. The decision to admit members of the 14th SS was thus a watershed in the history of Canadian immigration. Henceforth, Nazi affiliation would no longer be considered from the point of view of subversion. Indeed, with the exception of collabora-tors, the determination as to whether to admit or reject a prospective immigrant on the basis of his conduct in the war was considered to be more a matter of politics than of security. In a policy environment increasingly dominated by the Cold War, some relaxation of Second World War–related criteria was inevitable. Did this mean that it was easier for war criminals or collaborators to gain admission to Canada after 1950? That question can be answered only by an examination of the changes made to Canada's immigration-screening system in the wake of the 14th SS movement.

CHAPTER SEVEN

The Diminishing Threat

From 1945 to 1950, Canada took in a total of 453,111 immigrants. One-third of the new arrivals were European refugees. By 1950, however, the refugee movement was losing momentum. Having gone a long way toward fulfilment of its international obligations, the Canadian government decided to cut the immigration budget for the fiscal year 1949–50. Particularly hard hit was spending allocated for assisted passages, without which many would-be immigrants could not afford to make the transatlantic crossing. The result was a precipitous decline in the overall level of immigration to Canada. After reaching a postwar high of 125,414 in 1948, the number of new arrivals decreased over the next two years by 24 and 22 per cent respectively, bottoming out at a meagre 73,912 in 1950.[1]

Ottawa's sudden bout of stinginess did not bode well for the future of immigration to Canada. Not only did the government seem to be signalling a return to the restrictionist policies of the recent past, but immigration's staunchest defenders, most notably C.D. Howe and Hugh Keenleyside, were now out of the picture, both having been transferred to other portfolios. Yet there were hopeful signs as well. In 1950, Ottawa took three steps that indicated immigration would remain a priority. The first was the expansion of the immigration bureaucracy. In January, Immigration Branch was removed from the jurisdiction of the Department of Mines and Resources and elevated to departmental status. Shortly thereafter, cabinet dramatically increased the budget of the new Department of Citizenship and Immigration. Allocated a paltry $5 million in 1949–50, immigration would benefit from an additional

$4 million in spending in 1950–1. Included in the supplementary expenditures was a discretionary fund of approximately $1 million, most of which was earmarked for assisted passages from the United Kingdom and other Commonwealth countries. At $30 a head, the fund would enable as many as 33,000 additional persons to come to Canada.[2]

The second major step toward reversing the downward trend in immigration was the widening of admissibility. In June 1950, cabinet authorized a major relaxation in the immigration regulations. Enacted as PC 2856, the order-in-council eliminated the various restrictive familial and occupational categories and substituted a general requirement as to suitability. While in theory a prospective immigrant could be rejected if found 'undesirable' on any number of social or cultural grounds, in practice the new regulations offered the opportunity of admission to any person without regard to economic circumstances and almost without regard to ethnic background (provision was made for the continued exclusion of 'immigrants of any Asiatic race').[3] So profound was the change that the immigration bureaucrats bolstered themselves for a record influx. According to one Immigration Branch estimate, immigration from Europe alone was expected to reach almost 130,000 in 1951.[4]

The third step toward restoring immigration to 1948 levels was the lifting of the ban on German nationals. In 1949, the last full year of the ban, only about six thousand Germans had been able to obtain Canadian visas, most of which were issued on the basis of cabinet waivers. All of this changed in the autumn of 1950. Despite the absence of a formal peace treaty with the government in Bonn, Germans were at last removed from the prohibited class of enemy aliens. For the first time in more than a decade, they were, from the point of view of immigration eligibility, on a more or less equal footing with the nationals of other European countries. The effect of the change in their status was predictable. Within the space of about sixteen months, the number of German nationals who emigrated to Canada increased more than fivefold.[5]

Instituted in rapid succession, PC 2856, the assisted-passage program, and unfettered German access unleashed a wave of new immigration to Canada. In 1951, the country welcomed 194,391 newcomers, a 166 per cent increase over the previous year and the highest total

since before the First World War. With the end of the refugee movement, the influx of immigrants tapered off somewhat, settling at just
under 165,000 in 1952. For each of the next two years, it hovered
around the 160,000 level. As a consequence of waning demand for foreign workers, immigration fell off by some 30 per cent in 1955. But
this time the decline would be short-lived. The following year, immigration again climbed over the 160,000 level, with much of the increase
attributable to expanded farm-labour contingents.[6]

With the elimination of the last of the depression-era and wartime
restrictions, immigration to Canada experienced a veritable renaissance
during the 1950s. In the first half of the decade alone, the country
absorbed nearly a million new Canadians. Included in this mass migration were an estimated five hundred Nazi war criminals and collaborators, or approximately one-third of the number who had gained
admission between 1945 and 1950. Why was Nazi infiltration so much
lower during a period of comparatively freer access? The question
affords no easy answers. One explanation is that Canada's system of
immigration screening had improved with the passage of time. Another
is that traditional immigrant-receiving countries like the United States
and Australia gradually supplanted Canada as the destination of choice
for European emigrants.[7] But the most likely reason was the winding
down of the refugee movement and a compensatory increase in immigration from the United Kingdom and western Europe. The refugee
camps had been rife with Nazi and collaborationist elements, many of
whom had fled from the formerly German-occupied territories in eastern Europe and the Soviet Union, where evidence of their crimes
remained largely inaccessible behind the Iron Curtain. By definition,
then, the end of the refugee movement meant an immigration pool less
tainted by war criminals and collaborators. To be sure, the shift in priority from eastern European refugees to British and western European
immigrants did not end the danger of Nazi infiltration. It did, however,
substantially improve the chances of detection.

With settlement from overseas attaining levels not seen since the
turn of the century, it seemed that Canada's immigration policy had
finally weathered the political and economic storms of the 1930s and
1940s. One cloud remained on the horizon, however. As immigration
increased, so too did the number of unprocessed visa applications. The

problem was not a new one. As early as 1947, Ottawa had recognized that its cumbersome system of immigration screening was creating a backlog of unprocessed applications. In an attempt to deal with the problem, the immigration bureaucrats had introduced a system of selective screening. Under this new system, screening was waived for low-risk groups such as the wives and young children of refugees, while British and western European nationals had their visas issued after fourteen days, regardless of whether or not Stage B inquiries had been completed. In this way, it was thought, the movement of immigrants to Canada could be expedited without compromising security. Unfortunately, these measures had little effect on the rate of security clearance, and thus were quietly abandoned. Unable to keep pace with the high volume of applicants, Canada's overseas immigration missions watched helplessly as the backlog grew to unmanageable proportions.[8]

By 1951, Canada's system of immigration screening was strained to the breaking point. The government was faced with a stark choice – reduce the backlog, or be forced to call a temporary halt to further immigration. In view of the public outcry that was sure to accompany any moratorium, Ottawa took a proactive approach, insisting that the bureaucrats look for ways to accelerate the processing of new immigrants.[9] Streamlining the system of immigration screening would not be easy, of course. But solutions were at hand. Unlike its first encounter with the ubiquitous backlog, this time, at least, officialdom would be able to draw on almost five years of experience.

As they contemplated new screening procedures, the immigration bureaucrats realized they were walking a fine line. According to RCMP reports, any attempt to speed up clearances would increase the likelihood of infiltration by subversives, including Nazi war criminals and collaborators.[10] Yet there was no alternative. If a high volume of immigration was to be maintained, security would have to be balanced with efficiency. Immigration screening would have to become, in effect, an exercise in risk management.

The bureaucracy's efforts to deal with the backlog were reflected in a series of changes to the system of immigration screening introduced during the early 1950s. Each stage of visa vetting – from submission of an application to investigation of the applicant to evaluation of the results – was subjected to some measure of reform. So wide-ranging were the changes, in fact, that the RCMP felt compelled to circulate them in the form of a manual to its officers overseas. Compiled during the latter half of 1953, the new manual was a consolidation of all previous and current directives into a single, easy-to-use binder. Highlights included the latest interpretation of the Immigration Act, suggested interview techniques, instructions for obtaining a prospective immigrant's past residence and employment information, and guidelines for dealing with foreign contacts.[11]

The extent to which the manual enhanced the system of immigration screening is difficult to ascertain. On the one hand, the manual was at least somewhat redundant, since Canada's overseas missions had already compiled their own local versions. On the other hand, such improvisation had led to inconsistencies in the application of screening procedures.[12] To the extent that this may have caused certain Canadian immigration offices to become targets for subversives, the circulation of the manual was probably a useful countermeasure. At the very least, it ensured that all RCMP personnel assigned to visa-vetting duty overseas would be trained to the same standard.

During their audit of the immigration-screening system, the bureaucrats identified two major problems. One was the breakdown of screening behind the Iron Curtain, the other inefficiency in carrying out security checks. Both contributed greatly to the growth of the backlog. Prior to the end of the ban on German immigration, 85 per cent of the backlog had consisted of unscreened applications from eastern European nationals and Soviet citizens. That was sufficient on its own to trip alarm bells in Ottawa. Yet the problem went beyond sheer numbers. Owing to the paucity of contacts and the various other difficulties that attended Stage B inquiries behind the Iron Curtain, security checks often were of interminable duration. Moreover, even when they were completed, the results tended to be less than satisfying. In the absence of a viable network of contacts, the information obtained on individuals from the Soviet bloc usually was scant and unreliable.[13]

The 1951 audit was not the first attempt to deal with the problem of screening behind the Iron Curtain. Increasingly wary of communist infiltration, Canada's overseas immigration missions had already established a system of delayed processing for eastern European nationals and Soviet citizens. Acting on a September 1949 cabinet directive, the missions had let it be known that applicants from the Soviet bloc would no longer be considered for entry into Canada unless they first made their way to a Canadian immigration office in the United Kingdom or western Europe. Under the repressive regimes of the Soviet satellites, permission to travel for the purpose of immigration was almost impossible to obtain. The message to prospective immigrants was clear. Any eastern European national with an exit visa from his or her country of origin would be viewed suspiciously, perhaps even as an agent of that government, and thus would not be welcome in Canada. This unforgiving policy did not apply to genuine refugees, of course. The problem was that the only way for refugees to establish their credentials was to present themselves at a Canadian immigration mission in the West, an act that required escape from behind the Iron Curtain at considerable personal risk.[14]

While it slowed the rate of visa application from the Soviet bloc, the funnelling of prospective immigrants through western Europe was hardly a panacea. For one thing, the burden was not evenly distributed. Owing to their proximity to the Baltic states and East Germany, from where the stream of refugees was unrelenting, Canadian visa offices in Sweden and Germany bore the brunt of the exodus.[15] More importantly, the new policy did not address the problems attending Stage B inquiries behind the Iron Curtain, but merely deferred them. In recognition of the limitations of the system of delayed processing, the head of Canada's diplomatic mission in Stockholm proposed an alternative. Until such time as Ottawa restored Canadian visa offices behind the Iron Curtain to full-service status,[16] he could, he suggested early in 1952, withhold consideration of applications from eastern European nationals and Soviet citizens until they had lived in Sweden for a period of at least two years. This would further slow the rate of application from the Soviet bloc, while at the same time allowing for a more thorough screening of those few prospective immigrants who managed to get to the West.[17]

Having grappled with the problems of screening behind the Iron Curtain without much success, the Mounties were quick to endorse the idea. In their view, the residency requirement would allow for the development of a 'record' on which to base screening of prospective immigrants who were not nationals of the country in which they were resident. Others were less sanguine. For example, there was strong resistance on the part of the Department of Citizenship and Immigration. According to senior immigration bureaucrats, the residency requirement would place an unfair burden on genuine Soviet-bloc refugees. With the RCMP on side, however, there was little doubt that the proposal would be adopted. Indeed, after a brief discussion, cabinet approved the two-year residency requirement in June 1952.[18]

As far as immigration to Canada was concerned, the two-year residency requirement drastically curtailed the options of eastern European nationals and Soviet citizens. In so doing, it enabled Canadian authorities to turn their attention to the enormous backlog of unscreened applications. Its effectiveness in preventing the entry of subversives was another matter. After all, if an eastern European with a subversive background managed to get to a third country (Sweden, for example) and stay out of trouble for two years, Canadian immigration authorities would have no basis for rejecting that person's application. In such cases, the former head of RCMP visa control in Europe conceded, the mandatory waiting period amounted to little more than a 'stalling tactic.'[19] Still, it was more prudent than granting immediate admission. Moreover, the prospect of a two-year delay might have been enough to persuade some dubious individuals to apply to countries where conditions of entry were less stringent.

In terms of screening for war criminal or collaborationist background, the residency requirement was likewise of little value. Regardless of where they came from, all European applicants for Canadian visas were questioned about their wartime activities. Thus, whether war criminals or collaborators submitted their visa applications from their homeland or from a country of temporary refuge, the RCMP's ability to ferret them out rested mainly on the availability of corroborating sources. There was always the chance, of course, that a collaborator from eastern Europe or the Soviet Union might be exposed during the two-year waiting period. Yet without access to captured German records behind the Iron Curtain, this was highly unlikely. In the final analysis, eastern European war criminals or collaborators who were determined to settle in Canada needed only patience and the wherewithal to sustain themselves in order to circumvent the two-year residency requirement.

If the residency requirement only delayed the admission of subversives and other undesirables, it did have one immediate effect. As a result of the extension of the waiting period, a number of otherwise eligible relatives of Canadian residents had their admission to Canada postponed. This was quickly recognized as a humanitarian and public relations disaster. Hoping to avoid a political backlash by the ethnic constituencies most affected, the government of the day solicited the opinion of the RCMP. In response, the Mounties suggested that if screening were waived for low-risk categories of immigrants from eastern Europe, the residency requirement might be dispensed with in their cases. Ambivalent about the waiting period to begin with, the immigration bureaucrats gave their enthusiastic assent to the RCMP's proposal. In fact, by the time the Security Panel met to discuss the matter in March 1953, there was unanimous agreement that screening ought to be waived in the case of a Canadian resident's wife, children under the age of eighteen, or elderly parents who hailed from any of the communist-dominated countries of eastern and southeastern Europe, the Baltic states, the Soviet zone of Germany, or, of course, the USSR.[20]

Notwithstanding the fact that the panel's recommendation had the backing of the RCMP, the government initially rejected it. Indeed, more than two years went by before Ottawa consented to this relatively minor relaxation of the immigration regulations. It was not until July 1955 that cabinet finally waived screening for those categories of close relatives suggested by the RCMP and in which the Security Panel had concurred. After a few more months of deliberation, cabinet extended the waiver to ordained ministers and the fiancé(e)s of Canadian residents. There were two conditions, however. First, the prospective immigrant had to be otherwise admissible under the provisions of the Immigration Act. Second, the Canadian relative or sponsor had to submit to security screening.[21]

It is possible that the waiver for close relatives and clergy from eastern Europe and the Soviet Union enabled some undesirables to enter Canada. But the number of Nazi war criminals or collaborators who were admitted as a result was probably quite low. After all, it is hard to imagine that there were many war criminals among the wives, fiancé(e)s, and young children covered by the waiver. On the other hand, some of the elderly parents or clergy who were also exempted from screening may have had dubious war records. Yet the chance that there were any serious offenders among them was similarly remote. As nationals of countries that were occupied by the Red Army at war's end, they would have been subjected to the various purges of fascist and other 'politically unreliable' elements in which the Soviet satellites engaged during the late 1940s and early 1950s. Having survived this raft of denunciations, dismissals, and trials unscathed, it is reasonable to assume that most of the immigrants in the exempted categories were free of the taint of wartime collaboration.

As was noted above, there were two major factors in the growth of the backlog of unscreened visa applications. The first was the break-down of screening behind the Iron Curtain, which, as we have seen, was dealt with by limiting the number of applications from eastern European nationals and Soviet citizens. The second factor was ineffi-ciency in the carrying out of security checks. In theory, the search for solutions to this problem was the exclusive purview of the Mounties. Since the Immigration–RCMP conflict in 1948, however, the lines between civil and security investigation had become increasingly blurred. Not surprisingly, then, the immigration bureaucrats got involved. The result of their intervention was a revision of the OS.8 application form.

Prior to 1954, it will be remembered, the OS.8 had not contained space for a full accounting of a prospective immigrant's employment history. Instead, a separate employment information form was being used for that purpose. This worked well enough at first, with the form serving as a kind of résumé from which security officers were able to glean the data necessary to carry out their Stage B inquiries. By 1953, however, there were rumblings that use of the separate form was slow-ing the rate of security clearance. The form, it seemed, was eliciting a wide range of responses. Some prospective immigrants were providing ponderous life stories, while others were supplying only the barest details. The former required that security officers wade through a stream of verbiage in search of relevant facts, while the latter necessi-tated requests for additional information. Clearly, some attempt at stan-dardization was in order. In response to the Mounties' concerns, the

Department of Citizenship and Immigration revised the OS.8 by adding a section with space for a year-by-year listing of an immigrant's
occupations and employers going back to 1938.[22]

Inasmuch as it relieved security officers of the need to decipher or
supplement the information supplied by prospective immigrants, the
revision of the OS.8 probably hastened the process of security clearance to some degree. Its effectiveness in preventing the admission of
war criminals or collaborators is less certain. To be sure, a prospective immigrant's residency and occupational history constituted the
essential raw data on which Stage B inquiries were based. Yet such
information was being elicited long before the OS.8 was changed.
Accordingly, an applicant who filled out the pre-1954 OS.8 had as
strong a duty of candour to report his wartime activities as an applicant
who filled out the revised version. Conversely, if a prospective immigrant was going to lie about or attempt to hide his Second World War
activities, the post-1954 form would have been no more effective at
deterring such misrepresentation than its previous incarnations. At
most, the new OS.8 would have eliminated any confusion on the applicant's part as to the nature of the employment information being sought
and the manner in which it was to be presented.[23]

More relevant to the speed with which clearances were carried out
than the layout of the OS.8 was the manner in which security information was compiled and processed. On the basis of data supplied by a
prospective immigrant and supplemented, when necessary, by the
investigating officer, security checks were conducted through available
sources. During the early postwar years, Canadian security officers had
initiated their Stage B inquiries by submitting lengthy lists of the
names of visa seekers to their various contacts. The lists took a long
time to process, particularly when a large number of eastern European
nationals or Soviet citizens were involved. As a consequence, the officers had to await the results of all checks before being able to render
decisions in specific cases. More than any other factor, this delay in the
receipt of the results of security checks was responsible for the growth
of the backlog to unmanageable proportions.[24]

Frustrated by the slow pace of security clearance, the immigration
bureaucrats adopted two new procedures that dramatically streamlined
the system of checks. The first was intended to reduce the frequency

with which security checks were carried out. During a meeting between representatives of the RCMP and the Department of Citizenship and Immigration in February 1951, it was decided that British military intelligence would be consulted only in exceptional and potentially dangerous cases. The decision as to whether a prospective immigrant fell into this category was to be left to the investigating officer. His decision would be based, in the main, on the impressions he obtained from a face-to-face interrogation, to which all visa seekers from the United Kingdom and western Europe would now have to submit. The new procedure was, in effect, a reversion to the spot-check method that had been rejected four years earlier. To compensate for the resulting increase in the number of interviews, twelve additional security officers were assigned to visa-vetting duty overseas.[25]

There is no question that the change in emphasis from security checks to personal interviews accelerated the process of immigration screening. Its impact on the RCMP's ability to detect subversives is less certain. On the one hand, the Mounties were not happy about the new procedure. As the head of RCMP Special Branch lamented to his superiors, dispensing with the intelligence check reduced immigration screening in some countries to 'little more than a facade.'[26] Yet, he conceded, submitting the names of prospective immigrants to security agencies in the United Kingdom and western Europe had been of limited value in any event. He might have added that it had been even less useful for detecting Nazi war criminals and collaborators. After all, the best sources for determining the nature of an individual's wartime activities tended to be archival, police, and judicial records. To the extent that these were accessible, the chances of detection were fairly good. When they were not accessible, as happened in the overwhelming majority of cases of prospective immigrants of eastern European background or Soviet citizenship, western intelligence contacts were of little assistance. In all likelihood, then, the introduction of spot intelligence checks for immigrants from the United Kingdom and western Europe did not substantially increase the danger of Nazi infiltration.

The switch to an interview-based system reduced the number of security checks conducted by Canadian screening officers overseas. But it did nothing to expedite those checks that continued to be carried out. To shorten their turnaround time, a second new procedure was

introduced in the summer of 1953. Known as the 'Green Form' procedure, after the colour of print on the form on which it was based, it
required that a security officer enter a prospective immigrant's personal
data on a separate information sheet. After as much of the form as possible had been filled in, up to ten copies of the sheet were made and
sent off for checks to the RCMP's various contacts. Once a contact had
carried out the check for which he was responsible, he entered the
results on the sheet, which was then returned to the investigating
RCMP officer. Upon return of all of the contact sheets, the officer had
at his disposal an exhaustive record of the results of the security checks
carried out on a particular applicant. This enabled him to render a decision promptly, without having to await the completion of checks on
other would-be immigrants.[27]

While the Green Form system undoubtedly expedited the issuance of
security clearances (and rejections), its impact on screening for war
criminal or collaborationist background likely was minimal. True, use
of the form accelerated the carrying out of background checks. But it
did not improve their quality. Nor did it lead to any increase in the
number of contacts available to security officers. In other words, the
Green Form system did nothing to alleviate the main deficiency in
Canadian immigration screening – namely, the inability to carry out
adequate checks behind the Iron Curtain.

The changes made to the system of immigration screening during the
early 1950s had the desired effect. Security clearance proceeded more
quickly, thereby enabling the police to concentrate on the large volume
of previously unscreened visa applications. In the space of two years,
the backlog had been all but eliminated.[28] Still, the immigration
bureaucrats were not satisfied. Concurrent with their audit of Canadian
screening procedures, they also undertook a review of the various
screening criteria, most notably the Second World War–related grounds
for rejection. In the context of Ottawa's efforts to streamline the system
of immigration screening, this review seemed to be counterproductive.
After all, any relaxation of the criteria would render more people eligible for admission to Canada. As the number of visa applications
increased, so too, inevitably, would the pressure on Canada's immigration-screening machinery. Accordingly, the bureaucracy's review of

screening criteria appeared to run counter to the mandate it had been given by cabinet. The reasons for this apparent about-face, the changes in screening that resulted therefrom, and, most importantly, their impact on the ability of visa-vetting officers to detect Nazi war criminals and collaborators, are the subjects of the next chapter.

CHAPTER EIGHT

The Era of Risk Management, 1951–1956

During the early postwar period, Canadian immigration screening had been preoccupied with the threat of Nazi infiltration. Beginning in 1948, however, perceptions of the threat began to change. There is little question that the intensification of the Cold War was a major factor in altering perceptions. The crushing of Czechoslovakia's independence in March 1948, the Soviet blockade of Berlin during 1948–9, the communist takeover in China in the autumn of 1949, and the outbreak of the Korean War in June 1950 all served to heighten anxiety in Western capitals about the danger of Soviet expansionism. The corollary to these military and diplomatic apprehensions was a growing fear of communist subversion at home. As anti-communist hysteria increased, concerns about Nazi infiltration subsided.

Canada's immigration bureaucrats could not shield themselves from the shifting geopolitical winds. As the 1940s drew to a close, they too came to regard communist subversion as the principal threat to national security. Their change of heart was first reflected in the November 1948 list of immigration-screening criteria, which included communist affiliation and membership in so-called revolutionary organizations as grounds for automatic rejection.[1] But the turning point came two years later. At a meeting of the Security Panel held in October 1950, the primacy of the threat posed by communism was formally acknowledged. After discussion of a proposal to withhold Canadian citizenship from immigrants who had demonstrated subversive tendencies, there was general agreement among panel members that 'active' communists ought to be denied citizenship outright. 'Strong and still active' Nazis, on the other hand, should merely have their cases held in abeyance for two years, during which time, presumably, they would have the opportunity to reform themselves.[2] The meaning of these recommendations was unmistakable. For the first time since the end of the Second World War, communists were acknowledged to be a more serious threat to the immigration pool than were Nazis.

In the red-baiting atmosphere of the late 1940s and early 1950s, some lessening of vigilance regarding Nazi infiltration was inevitable. Yet it would be wrong to attribute it to the effects of the Cold War alone. Of more immediate relevance to the immigration bureaucrats were changes undertaken in Germany and western Europe with regard to the punishment and rehabilitation of war criminals and collaborators, changes that were only partly related to the conflict between East and West.

The most profound transformation occurred in Germany. During the first few years after the war, the Germans had cooperated dutifully, albeit sullenly, in the Allied program of war crimes trials. They had no choice – their country was prostrate and at the mercy of the occupation authorities. Their willingness to cooperate diminished with the merging of the western zones of occupation into the Federal Republic of Germany (FRG) in the spring of 1949. Henceforth, German compliance in the prosecution of suspected war criminals was no longer a foregone conclusion. Using the leverage afforded by Germany's strategic geographic location, the new government in Bonn began to reassert national sovereignty. In September 1950, for example, the Federal Republic advised the Allies that the price for its participation in the defence of central Europe was the winding down of war crimes trials and clemency for those Germans who had already been convicted. In the face of Bonn's trump card, the rate of prosecutions in both the American and British zones of occupation began to decline, while the number of pardons increased dramatically.[3] By the mid-1950s, the German government had achieved its goals. The Allied trials were over, and most convicted war criminals had been set free.[4]

The first shots fired in the FRG's assault on the Allies' war crimes policy were a series of parliamentary resolutions on the question of denazification. Passed with all-party support, the cumulative effect of the resolutions was that, as of 1 January 1951, the German government would no longer recognize the categories of lesser offenders and followers set out in Allied Control Council Directive No. 38.[5] Under the directive, persons so classified had been liable to a host of sanctions. As a rule, imprisonment had not been imposed in their cases. Instead, many lesser offenders and followers had been forcibly removed from the civil service, universities and schools, the media, and other positions of public trust. They had also been subjected to the loss of political rights, including the right to vote, the expropriation of their property, and restrictions on travel. Unless otherwise indicated, these sanctions were to be applied for a period of not less than two and not more than three years. If, during that time, the person under sanction behaved acceptably, he or she was eligible for reclassification and reinstatement to his or her former position.[6] Thus, punishment for lesser offenders and followers had often constituted little more than a two- or three-year period of probation.

Bonn's decision to rescind parts of Directive No. 38 did not come as a complete surprise to the Allies. Since the tribunals charged with enforcing the directive had completed their work by the end of 1947, the probationary period for many lesser offenders and followers had already expired. In keeping with their mandate, German denazification courts were immersed in the process of reclassification.[7] Thus, had the German government not intervened, the lesser offender and follower categories would eventually have been eliminated.

Passage of the various parliamentary resolutions threw the timetable for denazification into disarray. What Bonn was demanding, in effect, was an immediate remission of sentence for all lesser offenders and followers. If implemented, such an amnesty had the potential to wreak havoc with the Allied occupation regime. Included within the lesser offender and follower categories, after all, were many former members of the Nazi Party and its affiliated organizations. While they tended to have been on the margins of the Nazi movement,[8] reinstating such persons en masse into positions of public trust constituted a potential threat to the FRG's fledgling institutions. Short of conducting a second round of purges, however, there was little the occupation authorities could do. In the end, the Allies went along with the change in policy, hoping that the risk to German democracy could be contained.[9]

Concurrent with the German government's flexing of its new-found diplomatic muscle, the immigration lobby in Canada began to stir again. Having won removal of the ban on naturalized Volksdeutsche and German nationals, the Canadian Christian Council for Resettlement of Refugees (CCCRR) began to press for relaxation of other screening criteria. In a brief presented to the minister of citizenship and immigration in September 1950, T.O.F. Herzer, the organization's chairman, lamented the high rate of rejection that continued to impede German immigration to Canada. The problem, Herzer complained, was Ottawa's tendency to lump all former Nazis together. Resorting to an argument that had informed the German Parliament's various resolutions, the chairman assured the minister that most of those who were being rejected on the grounds of Nazi Party or Waffen-SS membership were not security risks. The vast majority, he claimed, had joined these organizations 'ignorantly, innocently, or under economic pressure.'[10] Accordingly, Herzer concluded, the just solution was to instruct Canadian security officers in Germany that 'nominal membership in the Nazi Party ... or the Waffen-SS shall not in itself constitute a barrier to Canada, if it can be reasonably established ... that the prospective immigrant comes within the class of ... nominal, ignorant or forced membership.'[11]

These developments could not help but prompt official Ottawa to re-evaluate its attitudes on denazification. While Canada, like other western countries, tended to view the issue mainly in terms of its effect on European defence,[12] denazification began to impinge upon other areas of joint German-Canadian interest, including immigration. Not surprisingly, then, receipt of Herzer's brief prompted a formal review of Canada's immigration-screening criteria.[13] The review exposed deep divisions within the bureaucracy. On one side, External Affairs supported a relaxation of the Nazi Party and Waffen-SS restrictions for lesser offenders and followers – that is, for those German nationals and naturalized Volksdeutsche whose nominal membership in the party or conscription into the Waffen-SS had rendered them low security risks in the eyes of Allied occupation authorities. On the other side, the RCMP adopted a much tougher line, particularly in the face of what it perceived to be the ongoing security risk posed by former members of the Waffen-SS. For their part, the immigration bureaucrats in Ottawa tended toward External's position, while immigration officers in the field lined up with the RCMP.[14] Caught between opposing views, the Department of Citizenship and Immigration settled on a compromise – German members of the Waffen-SS would continue to be rejected, but membership in the Nazi Party would no longer constitute an automatic bar to admission. As regards party members, only those considered to have been 'important and dangerous' would continue to be excluded.[15]

The relaxation of the screening criteria for former members of the Nazi Party was implemented in two stages. In the short term, Ottawa set up a process whereby all visa applications that had been rejected on the grounds of party membership could be reviewed. The process took a while to get on track.[16] Yet within the space of a few months, more than a third of such cases had been given a second look. On the basis of the substantially narrowed criterion of 'important and dangerous,' the decisions in all but 5 per cent of the reviewed cases were reversed.[17]

Over the longer term, there was an attempt to clarify what was meant by 'important and dangerous.' The Security Panel met to discuss the issue during the spring and summer of 1951. Unable to reach a consensus, the panel asked External Affairs to investigate Allied and German policies regarding the punishment and rehabilitation of ex-Nazis. The purpose of such an investigation, according to the panel, would be to provide some direction on the 'proper screening' of former Nazis among applicants for immigration from Germany.[18]

Over the next several months, the Canadian embassy in Bonn interviewed members of the German government, opposition politicians, and representatives from the various occupation authorities. Upon completion of its wide-ranging consultations, the embassy came up with a formula for determining the types of Nazis, who, in its view, 'should be excluded or subjected to special investigation.' The formula was based, in the main, on the German government's decision to rescind the lesser offender and follower categories of Nazis as outlined in Directive No. 38. Accordingly, any Nazi determined to have been a major offender or offender would continue to be barred from admission to Canada. Included in the major offender and offender categories would be persons who had held senior or intermediate-level positions in Germany's various wartime intelligence agencies; security and regular police units; the Nazi Party and its affiliated organizations, including the Waffen- and general SS; governmental and military institutions;

or any of the economic, social, and professional bodies that had come under Nazi control during the Third Reich.[19] On the other hand, screening might be waived or relaxed for less dangerous elements of the German population. Persons for whom the embassy suggested that security examination be waived included those born after 1 January 1919; those who fell within lower income groups; those who were more than 50 per cent disabled; those who had not been jailed for any reason, including wartime Nazi affiliation, since 1 January 1946; and former members of the German armed forces who had been held as POWs in Canada. Persons for whom the screening criteria might be relaxed, according to the embassy, included those whose sole party affiliation was determined to have been membership in a Nazi youth, trade, or professional association.[20]

The embassy's recommendations were put before the Security Panel in May 1952. During an extended discussion, it was agreed that Canadian visa-vetting officers required more specificity in evaluating applications from former members of the Nazi Party than the description 'important and dangerous' allowed. Accepting the proposition that major offenders and offenders ought to remain *persona non grata*, the panel proposed several new screening arrangements. First, the term 'Nazi' would henceforth apply to members of the party, the SS, the SD (the Nazis' security service), the Gestapo, and the Abwehr (German army intelligence). Second, members of the Nazi Party who had been classified as major offenders or offenders under Directive No. 38 would continue to be excluded from admission to Canada. In applying the directive, the panel advised, the RCMP ought not to be strictly bound by the definitions contained therein. Thus, in cases where the interpretation of the examining officer differed with that contained in the directive, the officer's decision would be final. Third, the panel recommended that anyone found on examination to have been employed in a concentration camp be subject to automatic rejection.[21]

Without a doubt, there was something unsavoury about the easing of immigration restrictions on members of the Nazi Party just a few years after the end of the war. Yet its effect on the screening of would-be immigrants for war criminal background likely was minimal. After all, non-Germans, who constitute the vast majority of suspected Nazi war criminals and collaborators known to be living in Canada, had not been permitted to join the party. Even among eligible German nationals, party membership never reached 10 per cent.[22] Of the approximately 6,000,000 Germans who did join the party, most were nominal or passive members, with less than 400,000, or under 7 per cent, having attained any sort of leadership position.[23] Furthermore, a majority, albeit a slim one, joined the party during the period between Hitler's rise to power and the outbreak of the Second World War, when the risks of membership were low and the potential economic or employment benefits were greatest.[24] Finally, there was no automatic correlation between party membership and the propensity to commit war crimes. For example, one of the most notorious killing units of the Second World War had a relatively low rate of Nazi affiliation. According to German records, only 25 per cent of Reserve Police Battalion No. 101, a Hamburg-based detachment that aided and abetted the murder of more than 80,000 Jews in Poland in the relatively short span of eighteen months, were party members.[25] Clearly, not all Nazis were war criminals, nor were all war criminals Nazis.

Around the time the FRG was trying to pressure the Allies into ending the trials of suspected war criminals, other European countries were re-evaluating their war crimes policies as well. In Belgium, for example, the status of so-called minor collaborators was under review. During the immediate postwar period, the government in Brussels had treated such persons in roughly the same manner as the Allies had dealt with lesser offenders and followers in Germany. In other words, any Belgian who had collaborated with the Germans in some minor way, such as engaging in pro-German propaganda or selling goods to the occupation forces, had been subjected to dismissal from positions of public trust, loss of political rights, expropriation of property, and restrictions on travel. Beginning in the late 1940s, however, the Belgian government undertook a process of national reconciliation. The cornerstone of its efforts in this regard was a reclassification and guardianship service established within the Ministry of Justice. The agency's mandate was similar to that of the German denazification courts – review the sentences of minor collaborators and determine their eligibility for rehabilitation. As a result of its work, hundreds of former collaborators had been restored to full political and civil equality with their compatriots by the end of 1950. Almost simultaneously, a similar process was initiated in France.[26] Gradually, the other countries of western Europe followed suit.[27]

Canadian immigration authorities first learned of the trend toward reconciliation during meetings with Belgian government officials in the autumn of 1950.[28] As had happened after the German Parliament issued its various resolutions, changes in the war crimes policies of the countries of western Europe prompted a review of Canadian immigration-screening criteria. During the spring and early summer of 1951, the immigration bureaucrats and the RCMP debated whether to ease the restrictions on minor collaborators. Owing to the Mounties' refusal to go along, little progress was made.[29] The matter was then taken up by the Security Panel, which likewise was unable to reach a consensus. Hopelessly deadlocked, the panel called on External Affairs to solicit the views of the governments in various western capitals. The rationale was that any revision of Canada's immigration-screening criteria ought to be in keeping with the policies of its wartime allies.[30]

Acting on the panel's request, Canada's embassies in France, Belgium, Denmark, the Netherlands, and Norway were ordered to report on the war crimes policies being pursued by their hosts. Their findings were somewhat unexpected. Despite the fact that the aforementioned countries had had different experiences while living under German rule, their treatment of those of their citizens who had sided with the occupiers was evolving along remarkably similar lines. Serious cases of collaboration, the embassies reported, continued to be prosecuted. On the other hand, there was a general trend toward leniency and rehabilitation for minor collaborators. On the basis of these reports, External concluded that immigration screening could be relaxed for such persons without any adverse effect on Canadian security. Major collaborators, of course, should continue to be banned. As defined by the embassies, major collaborators included persons who had been tried and found guilty of treason, been convicted of collaborationist crimes that had endangered Allied military personnel, served in concentration camps or in police units, or acted as informants against loyal citizens.[31]

Unlike its recommendations regarding the criteria for former members of Nazi organizations, External's report on the state of war crimes policy in western Europe was not well received. In what was perhaps their strongest statement of support for the Second World War–related screening criteria, the Mounties vehemently opposed any abatement in vigilance where former collaborators were concerned. The Department of Citizenship and Immigration agreed, arguing that there were sufficient immigrants 'of good character and background' without having to dip into the pool of former collaborators.[32] Once again, it would be left to the Security Panel to break the deadlock. Notwithstanding the fact that the issue was framed in such a way as to favour External's position,[33] panel members rejected the notion that rehabilitated minor collaborators no longer posed a security threat to Canada. At a meeting held in May 1952, the panel recommended continued rejection of all collaborators, except those whose acts of betrayal had been committed under duress.[34] In fact, there was to be no relief for voluntary minor collaborators until several years later. Even then, leniency was granted only in exceptional cases, usually on humanitarian grounds, at the discretion of Canadian immigration authorities abroad.[35]

To be sure, the Security Panel's decision constituted a retreat from the earlier policy of blanket exclusion. Yet it did not significantly increase the risk of infiltration by war criminals or major collaborators.[36] For example, persons whose collaboration had endangered the lives of Allied military personnel would continue to be excluded. By definition, this category comprised members of any military unit that had fought against the Allies. Yet it also included civilians who had turned in downed Allied airmen to German occupation forces. Service in an auxiliary police unit also constituted grounds for rejection. Members of the Schutzmannschaften, therefore, would continue to be banned. In short, collaboration remained an automatic bar to admission unless a prospective immigrant could prove that his or her act of betrayal had been minor and committed under duress.[37]

The modest relaxation of the criteria for former collaborators restored some equilibrium to Canada's immigration-screening system. As a result of the Security Panel's decision, collaborators would be accorded the same treatment as former members of the Waffen-SS – that is, they would be denied admission unless they could provide evidence that their collaboration had been compelled or elicited under pressure. With consistency, presumably, would come a greater degree of fairness. For some in Canada, of course, the changes did not go nearly far enough. Faced with continued high rates of rejection among

German would-be immigrants, CCCRR turned its attention to the vexing and seemingly insoluble problem of membership in the Waffen-SS.[38] It took weeks of intense lobbying, but, early in 1951, the organization finally detected some willingness on the part of the Canadian government to reconsider the status of the former SS soldiers. The sense of movement was confirmed in February, when Herzer was invited to Ottawa to present a brief on their behalf.[39]

Granted a second chance to plead the case of the Waffen-SS veterans, CCCRR was determined to make the most of it. Aware of the arguments advanced by the Ukrainian-Canadian lobby on behalf of the 14th SS, the organization adopted a similar strategy. Henceforth, no effort would be spared in attempting to prove the shopworn and somewhat revisionist claim that Waffen-SS troops had been subjected to the same military draft as their regular army counterparts. In keeping with the new strategy, a CCCRR delegation went overseas in March 1951 in order to review German military records.[40] Upon its return, the delegation claimed to have found evidence that most Waffen-SS units had consisted of conscripts, particularly from 1943 on, when Germany began to experience severe manpower shortages among front-line units. This was the breakthrough the organization had been looking for. After assembling the evidence in a second brief, Herzer cabled Minister of Citizenship and Immigration Walter Harris with the news and advised him of CCCRR's desire 'to re-state our proposal regarding membership in the Waffen SS with some modification and amendments.' The upshot of the new brief was that admissibility of former members of the Waffen-SS ought to be based solely on the timing of their enlistment. Since there was now evidence that most Volksdeutsche who joined the Waffen-SS after 1942 had been conscripted, the requirement to prove it in individual cases, he argued, had been rendered superfluous.[41]

Herzer's brief prompted a second round of consultations on the issue of Waffen-SS admissibility. Characteristically, External Affairs favoured relaxation of the criteria along the lines suggested by CCCRR. The Department of Citizenship and Immigration concurred. Yet this did not necessarily mean that the policy would be changed. After all, the same constellation of forces had argued much the same thing the previous autumn. But with the RCMP steadfastly opposed, the government had been reluctant to move. Events now took an unexpected turn, however. As a result of discussions between the RCMP commissioner and senior immigration bureaucrats, the Mounties signalled their willingness to countenance some loosening of restrictions where the Waffen-SS was concerned. Uneasy about the prospect of being flooded with applications from SS veterans, the force's agreement was contingent on the change being limited to cases involving compassionate grounds or when the age and circumstances of enlistment warranted special consideration.[42]

The RCMP's change of heart ensured that some relaxation of the rules governing Waffen-SS admissibility would be forthcoming. This was confirmed at the next meeting of the Security Panel. On 5 July 1951, panel members agreed that, in light of the new evidence supplied by CCCRR, the enlistment cut-off date by which former members of the Waffen-SS would be rendered eligible ought to be pushed back from 1 December to 1 January 1943. Non-Germans and non-naturalized Volksdeutsche who had joined subsequent to that date could have their cases reviewed on their merits. This was a significant weakening of the screening criteria, particularly in the case of non-Germans, since neither the Baltic formations of the Waffen-SS nor many of those raised in eastern Europe had begun recruiting until later in 1943. Indeed, the change meant that most former members of the non-German SS units would now be eligible for admission. Still, the panel's decision was not everything CCCRR had hoped for. While the date for automatic rejection had been pushed back, the onus remained on a prospective immigrant to prove that his Waffen-SS service had been conscripted. According to the instructions issued to screening officers overseas, 'members of the Waffen SS ... who joined after the 1st of January, 1943, will not be rejected automatically *if it can be established that a prospective immigrant was forced to join*' (italics added).[43]

For all Ottawa's efforts to appease CCCRR, it soon became apparent that the Security Panel's decision meant business as usual. To be sure, the revised cut-off date rendered more former members of the Waffen-SS eligible for consideration. But the hurdle of proving conscription remained. In a report that was likely indicative of the situation throughout Germany, Colonel E.J. Bye,[44] a security officer attached to Canada's immigration mission at Bremen, complained to his supervisor at

Karlsruhe in December 1951 that, even under the more liberal criteria, the rejection rate among Volksdeutsche and German nationals remained high. There were three reasons, he explained. First, citing a problem dating back to International Refugee Organization (IRO) days, Bye noted that ambiguities in the extant documentation made it almost impossible to prove conscription. Second, many Volksdeutsche who were eligible to apply for immigration to Canada because their Waffen-SS service began after the cut-off date of 1 January 1943 had also been granted German citizenship during the war, thereby rendering them ineligible for consideration on that basis alone. Third, among German nationals who were applying for admission to Canada were many young people who had been drafted into the Waffen-SS late in the war, thereby rendering them eligible in terms of the cut-off date, but whom he had to reject on the grounds that they were German-born members of the Waffen-SS.[45]

Bye was known to be a stickler when it came to enforcement of the immigration-screening criteria.[46] Nonetheless, he betrayed a certain sympathy for many of the would-be immigrants he had been compelled to reject. Indeed, in seeking guidance on how to interpret the rules governing the admissibility of former members of the Waffen-SS, he seemed to suggest that greater leniency was in order. This was particularly true with respect to his arguments on behalf of teenaged German nationals who had been conscripted into the Waffen-SS during the latter stages of the war. In their cases, Bye suggested, the decision ought to be left to the discretion of the examining officer. It was also true with respect to the 1 January 1943 cut-off date, which, he implied, was somewhat arbitrary. Finally, Bye asked whether it made sense to automatically reject Volksdeutsche members of the Waffen-SS who could otherwise meet the criteria simply because they had received German citizenship prior to enlisting.[47]

Whatever the bias that informed his report, the Bremen-based security officer had exposed some anomalies in the rules governing the admissibility of former members of the Waffen-SS. Accordingly, his report received wide circulation, working its way up the RCMP chain of command in Germany and Ottawa.[48] Initially, no action was taken. While of the view that the report should not be swept under the rug, Inspector William H. Kelly, the head of RCMP visa control in Europe, did not think that the time was right to make any changes in screening policy. He did not elaborate. For the moment, at least, the Security Panel's original decision regarding Waffen-SS admissibility would be allowed to stand.[49]

With Ottawa unwilling to reopen what had been a long and some-times acrimonious debate, the revised policy toward former members of the Waffen-SS remained in effect for several more months. As had been the case with former members of the Nazi Party, the impetus for change in the immigration status of the SS veterans came from outside the government. In April 1952, CCCRR received word that a substantial number of Volksdeutsche were being screened out of a bulk-labour contingent on the basis of their prior service in the Waffen-SS. Having lobbied for the new cut-off date on the assumption that it would render many more Volksdeutsche eligible for admission, the organization was greatly disappointed by the news. Suspecting either sabotage or incompetence, Herzer complained to the Department of Citizenship and Immigration. His suspicions were unfounded. As Deputy Minister Laval Fortier, the department's pointsman on the issue, assured the chairman, all of Canada's immigration missions abroad had been apprised of the change in the cut-off date to 1 January 1943. Still, he could not explain why the rate of rejection for Waffen-SS service remained high. In his exasperation, Fortier attempted to shift the blame to the German lobby. 'A lot of trouble and delay could be avoided,' he scolded Herzer, if only CCCRR would confine its processing operations to prospective immigrants who had *not* served in the Waffen-SS.[50]

Despite his dismissive attitude, the deputy minister had reason to be concerned. Thus far, the change in the cut-off date seemed to have had no appreciable effect on the rate of security rejections. The time was right, he concluded, for another review. Fortier's wishes were transmitted to the Canadian immigration mission in Karlsruhe. The head of the mission, in turn, approached G.A. Sincennes, Canada's chief security officer in Germany. Though Sincennes was already conducting an investigation into the specific rejections that had aroused the ire of Herzer, he dropped it in order to study the broader issue of Waffen-SS eligibility.[51]

The rigour with which Sincennes carried out his review can no longer be determined. In light of the fact that he had a report ready within a week, it may be assumed that his consultations were not particularly extensive. Indeed, the report constituted little more than a critique of Bye's conclusions. Like Bye, Sincennes acknowledged that it was all but impossible for former members of the Waffen-SS to prove they had been conscripted. Therefore, he advised, the requirement ought to be dropped. To prevent any abatement in vigilance, he suggested the adoption of a new voluntary/conscripted service cut-off date that would apply to all non-German or Volksdeutsche former members of the Waffen-SS. In Sincennes's view, 1 January 1944 was a more realistic date for the onset of compulsory service. If a prospective immigrant were discovered to have enlisted in the Waffen-SS prior to that date, it would be assumed that he had volunteered, and he would be rendered ineligible for admission to Canada. If he had entered Waffen-SS service after 1 January 1944, he would be cleared for security, provided, of course, there were no other blemishes on his record.[52]

Much of this was in keeping with Bye's earlier recommendations. Where Sincennes parted company with his subordinate was over the latter's suggestion that there ought to be an easing of the restrictions on German nationals and naturalized Volksdeutsche who had served in the Waffen-SS. With respect to German nationals, the head of security screening in Germany withheld comment, thereby implying that he was perfectly content with the policy of blanket exclusion. As regards the Volksdeutsche, Sincennes took the hard-line view that most had become enthusiastic subjects and willing servants of the Third Reich. Volksdeutsche in eastern Europe had profited from their German heritage, he argued, by eagerly supplanting local elites and greedily expropriating their property. The situation of the Volksdeutsche from the Soviet Union was more complicated, he conceded, but they too had certainly been supportive of the Nazi occupation, at least initially.[53]

Receipt of Sincennes's recommendations threw official Ottawa into a quandary. After all, there were now two complex and somewhat contradictory reports from which to choose – that prepared by Sincennes, as well as Bye's earlier effort. As was typical in such cases, the decision was left to the Security Panel. In framing the issue for his colleagues, Panel Secretary Peter Dwyer, a former British liaison to the U.S. intelligence community who was spending his retirement advising the Canadian government on security matters,[54] suggested adjustments along the lines proposed by Colonel Bye. This meant that there should be no change in the admissibility requirements for non-Germans who had served in the Waffen-SS. In their cases, Dwyer advised, the cut-off date of 1 January 1943 and the burden of proving conscription ought to remain in effect. On the other hand, there might be some room for manoeuvre with respect to German nationals and Volksdeutsche. For instance, those German nationals who had joined the Waffen-SS after 1 January 1944 while still under the age of eighteen could be considered for admission, when, in Dwyer's words, there were 'reasonable grounds' for believing they had been conscripted or had joined under duress. The same might apply to naturalized Volksdeutsche when there were grounds for assuming that German citizenship had 'not [been] of their own choosing' – in other words, when it had been conferred on them. Finally, Volksdeutsche who never obtained German citizenship might also be considered for admission when there was evidence that their Waffen-SS service had been elicited by conscription or as a result of pressure by Nazi occupation authorities.[55]

In commenting on the Dwyer/Bye proposals, the Department of Citizenship and Immigration's representatives on the Security Panel were sceptical, characterizing German nationals and Volksdeutsche who had served in the Waffen-SS as 'a dubious group.' Since there was a backlog of German applicants whose wartime records were not compromised by Nazi affiliations, the immigration bureaucrats wondered why it was necessary to select from former members of the Waffen-SS.[56] But other panel members took a more generous view. If non-Germans could have been conscripted into the Waffen-SS, they argued, then so too could German nationals. In the end, the panel adopted a compromise position. At their meeting in May 1952, panel members accepted Dwyer's recommendations regarding German nationals under eighteen and non-naturalized Volksdeutsche. Unlike Dwyer, however, the panel elected not to distinguish between German nationals and naturalized Volksdeutsche. Taking Sincennes at his word regarding the infrequency of forced naturalization, they lumped Volksdeutsche who had acquired German citizenship together with German nationals. That is, German-naturalized Volksdeutsche who had served in the Waffen-SS were to be denied admission to Canada unless they had enlisted after 1 January 1944 and had been eighteen years of age or under upon entry.[57]

On paper, the Security Panel's compromise acknowledged the existence of three categories of Waffen-SS men. One consisted of non-Germans whose eligibility for admission to Canada would depend on their having joined the Waffen-SS after 1 January 1943 and their being able to prove that their enlistment had been compulsory. A second category consisted of German nationals whose eligibility would depend on their having been conscripted into the Waffen-SS on or after 1 January 1944 and their having been eighteen years of age or under when they were drafted. The third category comprised Volksdeutsche who had never received German citizenship. Like German nationals, their eligibility for admission to Canada would depend on their having been conscripted into the Waffen-SS on or after 1 January 1944. Unlike German nationals, however, they would not have to prove they had been eighteen years of age or younger at the time of their enlistment.

What did the Security Panel's decision mean in practice? With respect to non-Germans who had served in the Waffen-SS, nothing had changed. Non-Germans who had joined the Waffen-SS prior to 1 January 1943 were automatically excluded from consideration as immigrants; non-Germans who had joined after that date might be considered for admission, but the onus would be on them to prove they had been conscripted. With respect to Germans or non-naturalized Volksdeutsche who had served in the Waffen-SS, most would still be excluded. There were two exceptions, however. One included Volksdeutsche who had been drafted on or after 1 January 1944. Formerly considered under the non-German category, non-naturalized Volksdeutsche now actually faced a higher bar of admissibility – a volunteer/conscript cut-off date of 1 January 1944 instead of 1 January 1943. In other words, this was not a relaxation, but in fact a tightening of the criteria for Waffen-SS membership. The other exception was for German nationals who had been drafted into the Waffen-SS on or after 1 January 1944 while eighteen years of age or under. This was a retreat from the previous practice of blanket exclusion, but a relatively minor one. After all, only draftees who had been eighteen years of age or under would be considered for admission to Canada. Coupled with the relatively late cut-off date for enlistment, the age requirement all but eliminated the possibility that war criminals could have infiltrated this particular Waffen-SS category.

The lack of substantive change inherent in the Security Panel's decision strained relations between Canada and Germany. In May 1953, the German government sent a note to the Canadian immigration mission in Karlsruhe protesting the rejection of two Volksdeutsche on the grounds of Waffen-SS service and asking for reconsideration of their cases on humanitarian grounds.[58] The cases involved J. P—— and A. S——, both of whom were former members of the 7th SS Volunteer Division 'Prinz Eugen,' which had been raised in northern Serbia during the spring of 1942 to combat the growing partisan threat and which, by the end of the war, had acquired a reputation for extreme brutality.[59] Both P—— and S—— were Volksdeutsche, both had ended up in Germany at the close of the war, and both had relatives in Canada. There the similarities ended, however. On the one hand, P—— was quite young, having just turned eighteen when he enlisted in March 1944. He had already been twice rejected by Canadian immigration authorities, once in December 1948 on the grounds of the blanket exclusion for Volksdeutsche members of the Waffen-SS, the second time in July 1951, apparently because he was unable to prove conscription. S—— was twenty-seven when he enlisted – under duress, he claimed – in June 1942. His application for a Canadian visa had been rejected in November 1950, apparently because his enlistment antedated the 1 December 1943 cut-off date then in effect.[60]

Dismissed as a tempest in a teapot by External Affairs, the German note caused real consternation among the immigration bureaucrats. Joseph R. Robillard, the head of Canada's immigration mission in Karlsruhe, forwarded the missive to Ottawa with a recommendation that the cases be reviewed. A review was required, Robillard urged his superiors, because the only grounds for rejection had been enlistment prior to the cut-off date of 1 January 1944. Since what he described as 'this arbitrary date' was preventing the admission to Canada of otherwise deserving Volksdeutsche, Robillard suggested that it be changed yet again.[61] His entire line of argument, of course, was utter nonsense. Both men were rejected before the 1 January 1944 cut-off date had even come into effect. Thus, a review was in order, not because the cut-off date was 'arbitrary,' but rather to determine whether either man

might benefit from the change in the rules of admissibility – specifically, the new cut-off date for enlistment – which had come into effect
since their previous rejections.

In a classic case of making the right decision for the wrong reasons,
Ottawa granted Robillard his review. In June 1953, the cases of
P—— and S—— were referred to the RCMP for 'further consideration.' There was also some discussion about Robillard's suggestion to
alter or scrap the 1 January 1944 cut-off date. With respect to the
Waffen-SS veterans on whose behalf the review was conducted, the
Mounties were unyielding; P—— and S—— were again denied security clearance. The decision was correct as it applied to S——, whose
June 1942 enlistment had rendered him ineligible, but it was incorrect
in the case of P——, whose induction into the 7th SS in March 1944
rendered him admissible under the Security Panel's revised criteria. A
follow-up request on his behalf pointed out the error, and, in October
1953, the RCMP finally passed P—— clear for security. Unable to
meet the cut-off date for compulsory enlistment even under the revised
criteria, S—— was rejected once more.[62]

Robillard did little better with his suggestion that the 1 January 1944
cut-off date be changed or scrapped altogether in cases involving non-
naturalized Volksdeutsche. Convinced that there was little to choose
between the Volksdeutsche and their German-born brethren, the RCMP
opposed the idea.[63] Nonetheless, Robillard's superiors in Ottawa, perhaps worn down by CCCRR's relentless lobbying, saw some merit in a
return to the previous cut-off date of 1 January 1943. Accordingly, they
asked that the matter be taken up by the Security Sub-Panel, which had
recently replaced the Security Panel as the main deliberative body on
the purely technical aspects of Canada's security policy.[64] The sub-
panel's members agreed to review their predecessors' earlier decision.
In its response to the Department of Citizenship and Immigration, the
sub-panel advised the immigration bureaucrats that the 1 January 1944
cut-off date should be dropped for non-naturalized Volksdeutsche, but
kept for German nationals.[65] This meant that there were now only two
categories of former Waffen-SS men recognized in Canadian immigration-screening criteria – non-Germans and German nationals. Non-
Germans (a category that now included non-naturalized Volksdeutsche) who had joined the Waffen-SS prior to 1 January 1943 were to be

rejected out of hand; those who had been conscripted after 1 January 1943 were eligible for admission, but the onus remained on them to prove conscription or enlistment under duress. German nationals (a category that now included both persons born in Germany and Volksdeutsche who had received German naturalization) who had joined the Waffen-SS prior to 1 January 1944 were similarly to be rejected out of hand. Only German nationals who had been conscripted after that date and who were eighteen years of age or under at the time were eligible for admission.

After more than two years of discussion and debate, the screening criteria for members of the Waffen-SS had at last been placed on a rational and historically defensible footing. Volksdeutsche who had never received German citizenship were now to be accorded the same treatment as any other European nationals who had joined the Waffen-SS. For all intents and purposes, they were viewed as either voluntary or conscripted collaborators. To be sure, the date of 1 January 1943 was a bit early to be considered as the cut-off beyond which conscription had been automatic (1 December 1943 was more accurate), but the error in the date was more than offset by the fact that the onus was still on a prospective immigrant to prove conscription. As we have seen, the difficulty of proving conscription tended to result in the rejection of most former members of the Waffen-SS. Thus, retention of this requirement would have sharply limited the number of non-Germans and Volksdeutsche who were able to take advantage of the change in the cut-off date. Moreover, it ensured that hard-core Nazi sympathizers, those militants who had first served in auxiliary police units in the German-occupied territories before being transferred into Waffen-SS units, would continue to be rejected.

In the case of German nationals, the sub-panel's recommendations also placed the screening criteria on a sounder historical basis. Limiting eligibility for admission to Canada to those German Waffen-SS veterans who had been conscripted after 1 January 1944 at the age of eighteen or younger reflected the reality that, for German nationals, wartime enlistment in the Waffen-SS had almost always been compulsory. If anything, the 1 January 1944 date erred on the side of caution. After all, some members of the 12th SS Panzer Division 'Hitler Youth' had been conscripted as early as the spring and summer of 1943.[66] One is therefore tempted to agree with the judgment rendered by Inspector Kelly many years later – namely, that the attempts to modify the criteria for former members of the Waffen-SS had resulted in 'little change.'[67]

The sub-panel's decision of June 1953 was the culmination of more than two years of deliberation on the subject of Waffen-SS eligibility. Not surprisingly, then, there was no great desire to tamper with it. Accordingly, for the next two years, no further changes were contemplated. Ottawa held firm even in the face of renewed pressure by CCCRR to have the cut-off date pushed back earlier than 1 January 1943 so as to render still more SS veterans eligible for consideration. As the executive secretary of Canadian Lutheran World Relief (CLWR) lamented to its Ontario branch in 1955, since the Security Panel's decision back in July 1951, any suggestions for relaxation had been met with 'a considerable amount of firmness.'[68]

The next review of the rules governing Waffen-SS admissibility did not take place until 1955. When the opportunity for a review arose, it was not planned, but rather was the result of a fortuitous convergence of circumstances. First, immigration to Canada experienced a marked decrease in 1955. While cabinet had set a target of 150,000 immigrants, shrinking demand for foreign labour accounted for a reduction in admissions to less than 110,000.[69] Second, with the war an increasingly distant memory, the Waffen-SS restrictions came to be seen by some within the immigration bureaucracy as outdated wartime prejudice. Few officials dared to express such views openly, of course. Their reticence evaporated, however, in the face of Ottawa's failure to meet its immigration targets.

While domestic considerations drove Ottawa to consider relaxing the Waffen-SS restrictions, the catalyst for the change in Canadian screening policy was a major development overseas. In December 1954, the North Atlantic Treaty Organization (NATO) approved the admission of the Federal Republic of Germany into the alliance.[70] German rearmament, something that had been unthinkable just a few years earlier, was now about to become a reality. As a full-fledged partner in NATO, Germany naturally expected to be treated just like any other ally. From the point of view of the government in Bonn, equality would not be achieved until the last vestiges of Germany's criminal past had been obliterated. Since no issue represented the country's pariah status more than the continued stigmatization of its former soldiers, some relief would have to be forthcoming.

Most of NATO's member states were well aware of German sensitivities on the issue of the decriminalization of the Waffen-SS. It was for this reason that they had already granted clemency to a great many former SS soldiers. It also explained why they had removed restrictions on the emigration of Germans who had served in Hitler's armed forces, including the Waffen-SS.[71] As the last holdout, Canada was coming under increasing pressure to fall into line. The predicament was discussed at a meeting of immigration and RCMP officials held at Karlsruhe in February 1955. Citing NATO's recent decision to admit the Federal Republic as a full member, Robillard predicted that the German government 'will no doubt take a very dim view of the fact that we welcome their new soldiers into our family of nations but still refuse [to declare] eligible for migration to Canada those who in former times joined the elite of their armed forces in order to serve the Fatherland.' In light of the changing international circumstances, the head of the mission suggested, it might be time for Ottawa to reconsider its position regarding the admission of naturalized Volksdeutsche and German nationals who had voluntarily served in the Waffen-SS.[72]

If implemented, Robillard's proposal would have constituted a major departure from Canada's immigration-screening practices. Since the end of the war, Canadian authorities had always distinguished between voluntary and compulsory service with the enemy. The distinction had applied to enemy aliens, collaborators, and, of course, to members of the Waffen-SS. Predictably, Robillard met with strong resistance. However, the focus of the opposition was not, as might have been expected, the RCMP, but rather External Affairs.[73]

In a memorandum seething with moral indignation, Charles Ritchie, Canada's ambassador to the Federal Republic, rejected Robillard's suggestion. 'I find it hard to believe,' Ritchie stated in a none-too-veiled attack on his colleague's judgment, 'that we are so short of suitable candidates for immigration that it is necessary to start recruiting in a portion of the German and "Volksdeutsche" population whose war records are of the worst.' Dismissing as a red herring Robillard's prediction of dire diplomatic consequences, the ambassador urged Ottawa

to maintain the restrictions on German nationals who had served voluntarily in the Waffen-SS. Besides, he said, the government ought to be
more concerned with the public reaction in Canada, which, if Robillard's proposal was enacted, would almost certainly be 'of an adverse
nature.'[74]

Faced with Ritchie's vehement and principled opposition, the immigration bureaucrats gave only tepid support to Robillard.[75] Undeterred,
the head of the mission at Karlsruhe continued to press his case. In
response to Ritchie's attack, Robillard characterized Canada's policy
toward former members of the Waffen-SS as entirely wrong-headed.
To be sure, he conceded, thousands of German nationals and Volksdeutsche had been denied visas on the grounds of SS membership since
the start of immigration-screening operations in Germany. Yet hundreds had been admitted. This 'anomalous' situation could not continue, Robillard warned. Contrary to the ambassador's claim that there
were not likely to be any diplomatic consequences, the policy was
already causing Canada considerable embarrassment, he complained.
'Time and time again,' Robillard assured Ritchie, 'German authorities
... have raised the question of our arbitrary rejection of former members of SS units.'[76]

Once again, an attempt to relax Second World War–related screening
criteria was provoking sharp disagreements within official circles. As
had happened on previous occasions, Ottawa handed the matter over to
the Security Sub-Panel. Unfortunately, from the government's point
of view, the referral did not have the desired effect. At its meeting on
16 June 1955, the sub-panel mirrored the sharp divisions that existed
among the various interested parties. Unable to reach a consensus, the
sub-panel postponed a decision on Waffen-SS admissibility pending a
survey of Canadian embassies in Europe and RCMP inquiries with
American and British intelligence.[77]

Four months elapsed before the sub-panel had sufficient information
to render its decision. In view of Robillard's concerns about a negative
German reaction, one might have expected its recommendations to
have paid undue attention to diplomatic considerations. Yet this was
not the case.[78] On the contrary, the sub-panel's primary interest seems
to have been the assuaging of Canadian public opinion.[79] At their
18 October 1955 meeting, sub-panel members decided that voluntary

service in the Waffen-SS would no longer constitute grounds for auto-matic refusal of German nationals and naturalized Volksdeutsche. Instead, applications from such persons would be considered on their merits. However, only close relatives of Canadian residents would be eligible. Moreover, Waffen-SS veterans who, in the opinion of the examining security officer, were major offenders under Allied Control Council Directive No. 38, would continue to be rejected. After further consultation within the immigration bureaucracy, Minister of Citizen-ship and Immigration Jack Pickersgill finally approved the change in policy in February 1956.[80]

What was the effect of this change? In theory, the removal of the ban on Waffen-SS volunteers ought to have made it easier for Nazi war criminals and collaborators to gain admission to Canada. After all, the obligation to prove conscription had constituted an almost insurmount-able barrier to former members of the Waffen-SS. With the evidentiary burden lifted, many more German nationals and naturalized Volksdeut-sche were rendered eligible for consideration as immigrants. Yet the number of war criminals or collaborators who could have taken advan-tage of the revised criteria likely would have been quite low. The rea-son can be illustrated by an analysis of the manner in which the revised criteria were actually applied.

In assessing the impact of the new policy, it cannot be emphasized too strongly that no real change had occurred in the cases of non-Germans and non-naturalized Volksdeutsche SS veterans. To be sure, they, like their counterparts among German nationals, were absolved of the responsibility of proving conscription. But voluntary service remained a bar to their admission in another sense. While security officers were no longer permitted to distinguish between conscripted and voluntary Waffen-SS service in evaluating visa applications from non-German or non-naturalized Volksdeutsche, in practice they had to, since such service still constituted evidence of collaboration. Deprived of the volunteer versus conscript distinction in cases involving former members of the Waffen-SS, the RCMP instead began to apply the restrictions on collaborators more broadly.[81] In so doing, they were not implementing any directive to this effect. Rather, the change in RCMP practice was simply a logical outgrowth of the maintenance of immi-gration restrictions on most collaborators.

The extension of the ban on collaborators to former members of the Waffen-SS would not have applied in cases involving German nationals, of course. Still, even German nationals derived only limited benefit from the revised criteria. For one thing, major offenders among members of the Waffen-SS continued to be barred from admission. Under Directive No. 38, all officers down to the rank of SS major were considered to be major offenders.[82] As for junior officers and the rank and file, it remained within the discretion of Canadian immigration authorities to reject German nationals who had served in the Waffen-SS and who had odious or suspicious war records. Significantly, such cases were not to be decided until the RCMP had reviewed them.[83]

Concurrent with the relaxation of the criteria for German nationals and naturalized Volksdeutsche who had served in the Waffen-SS, the Security Sub-Panel also eased the restrictions for former members of other Nazi-affiliated organizations. Included in this group were former members of the general SS, the Stormtroopers (SA), the Abwehr, and the SD (membership in the Gestapo or service in a concentration camp remained automatic grounds for rejection).[84] In rendering its decision, the sub-panel recommended that persons who had been members of these organizations be treated in the same manner as the Waffen-SS veterans. Accordingly, only former members of the SS, SA, Abwehr, or SD who had relatives in Canada might be considered for admission. The major offenders among them, of course, were to be automatically excluded. This meant that senior and intermediate-level officials of these Nazi-affiliated organizations would continue to be rejected out of hand.[85] As for more junior members, the decision whether to clear or reject was left to the discretion of the examining officer. Any German national or Volksdeutsch who admitted to membership in one or another of these organizations could therefore expect to have to give a full accounting of his wartime activities, which would then be checked against extant German civil and military records.

Notwithstanding the years of tinkering to which the Second World War–related rejection criteria were subjected, Canada persevered in its efforts to deny Hitler's henchmen safe haven well into the 1950s. The vigour with which ex-Nazis continued to be barred from admission was perhaps best reflected by a case submitted to the RCMP more than a year after the relaxation of the screening criteria for former members of

Nazi-affiliated organizations. In the autumn of 1957, a German national applied for a visa at the Canadian immigration mission in Karlsruhe. The subsequent security investigation revealed that the applicant had been a member of the Nazi Party and the SS. Over the course of his service in the SS, he had attained the rank of captain. During the war, he had served with the security police in German-occupied Yugoslavia.

Under a strict interpretation of the Second World War–related criteria as revised during the 1950s, the applicant was admissible. That is, he was not a major offender under Control Council Directive No. 38. His rank (SS captain), his nominal membership in the Nazi Party, and his service in the security police placed him in the category of ordinary, not major, offender. Yet the RCMP rejected him in any event, claiming that his various affiliations constituted evidence that he was a 'fanatical Nazi' and therefore undesirable. Indeed, his war record was considered so odious that when his wife applied for a visa more than five years later, she too was rejected, the police fearing that the couple might use her residence in Canada as a means to get him admitted under the provisions governing close relatives. In the end, she was informed that she was eligible to apply for a visitor's visa only.[86]

The refugee movement that was an outgrowth of the Second World War ended with the expiry of IRO's mandate in 1951. Nevertheless, Canada's immigration bureaucrats had to deal with occasional refugee crises throughout the 1950s. While the United States and the Soviet Union abstained from direct military confrontation, the Cold War was played out around the world in numerous civil wars, proxy conflicts, and even superpower interventions. Like all wars, these regional clashes produced their share of devastation, persecution, and dislocation. The resulting torrent of refugees strained the resources of the international community to deal with them. Inevitably, traditional immigrant-receiving countries like Canada came under pressure to render assistance.

During the 1950s, the East–West conflict produced two major refugee crises in Europe. The first was occasioned by workers' protests and strikes that broke out in the Soviet zone of Germany in 1953, the second by a more organized uprising against Communist rule in Hungary in 1956. Both revolts were suppressed only after considerable bloodshed, with the result that East Germans and Hungarians fled their respective countries in droves. As it had done during the late 1940s, Canada set aside its immigration regulations in order to facilitate the admission of some of these unfortunate people on humanitarian grounds. Early in the spring of 1953, for example, the two-year residency requirement was waived for a token few of the thousands of East German refugees who were making their way to the Federal Republic.[87] Similarly, in 1957 Ottawa waived the residency requirement for a much larger contingent of Hungarian refugees who were scattered throughout southern and western Europe.[88] In neither instance was security examination dispensed with.[89] Unfortunately, as had been the case with the Estonian 'boat people' and the Ukrainian SS veterans, screening for war criminal or collaborationist background was again hampered by lack of access to records behind the Iron Curtain.

CHAPTER NINE

Undiplomatic Passports

Thus far, it has been demonstrated that the overwhelming majority of Nazi war criminals and collaborators who settled in Canada after the Second World War were admitted inadvertently, either as a result of the absence of information on their wartime activities or its inaccessibility. Nonetheless, some cases defied such conventional explanations. Helmut Rauca, for example, managed to slip past Canadian immigration screening despite the presence in German archives of a lengthy paper trail attesting to his SS membership. Count Jacques de Bernonville also evaded detection, even though the war crimes judgment that a French court had passed on him in absentia was a matter of public record. The temptation in such cases is to blame Canadian authorities. Yet factors other than incompetence may have been at work. As we shall see, on a few occasions, Hitler's fellow travellers had the assistance of powerful forces in escaping justice and making new lives for themselves in Canada.[1]

In the vocabulary of international espionage, 'ratlines' are networks of operatives who smuggle fugitives or undercover agents in and out of hostile territory. During the Cold War, the most active and controversial ratlines were those that spirited ex-Nazis and former collaborators out from behind the Iron Curtain or from Europe's refugee camps to the United Kingdom, the United States, Australia, and other immigrant-receiving countries, including Canada. Despite having been cloaked in the well-worn garb of political deniability, most of the Nazi ratlines were supported by western governments. The U.S. State Department and Central Intelligence Agency (CIA), British military intelligence, and other western intelligence services all had a hand in the business of finding safe haven for the motley remnants of European fascism. They were not alone. Functioning alongside the official ratlines were several unofficial ones. The most prominent of these was Intermarium, a Catholic lay group that conducted its operations with the approval and under the protection of the Vatican in Rome. Sometimes, the interests and operations of the official and unofficial ratlines converged, such as in the summer of 1947, when London and Washington conspired with the Vatican to keep several high-level Yugoslav collaborators out of the hands of Brigadier Fitzroy Maclean's screening commission.[2]

Motivated by the desire to strengthen anti-Soviet emigré communities in the West and blessed with virtually unlimited resources, the United States was the undisputed early leader in bringing ex-Nazis out of Europe. In theory, this policy ought to have been implemented by the Office of Strategic Services (OSS) and its successor organization, the CIA. However, as a result of the machinations of the Dulles brothers – John Foster, who eventually would be Secretary of State under Eisenhower, and Allen, who would head up the CIA – a separate Nazi-smuggling organization was established in 1948. Operating out of the State Department, the innocuously named Office of Policy Coordination (OPC) was headed by Frank Wisner, a prominent Wall Street attorney and a former OSS colleague of Allen Dulles. Officially, OPC's mandate was to offer logistical and financial support to any eastern European or Soviet emigré group that demonstrated the willingness and the capacity to carry out acts of subversion behind the Iron Curtain. Its real purpose, however, was to assist anti-Communist defectors and refugees in making their way to the West. In constructing the OPC ratline, Wisner was encouraged not to be too particular about the wartime political affiliations of his 'clients.' Not surprisingly, then, his first contacts were with senior Nazi officials who had coordinated collaborationist activity in the German-occupied eastern territories. By far the most important of the former Nazi spymasters was a general named Reinhard Gehlen.[3]

Gehlen was born in 1902 in southeastern Germany. The son of an obscure army lieutenant, he acquired social status and political influence by marrying into an aristocratic Prussian family. During the war, he headed up Foreign Armies East (FHO), the military intelligence section of the High Command of the German Armed Forces, which was responsible for assessing the enemy's strength on the eastern front. Though a Nazi by conviction, Gehlen was also a professional. Thus, he refused to give in to the temptation, so prevalent among his colleagues, to whitewash the true balance of forces in order to avoid incurring Hitler's wrath. This undoubtedly was the right thing to do, but Gehlen would pay dearly for his candour. In January 1945, the Führer, outraged by what he regarded as FHO's 'defeatist' prognoses, ordered its chief committed to an asylum for the criminally insane.

His faith in the Nazi cause irrevocably shattered, Gehlen wasted little time in burning his bridges. After having the orders committing him revoked, the former intelligence chief began to think in terms of the post-Hitler era. It did not take a great deal of insight on Gehlen's part to realize that his work in the occupied East might make him a valuable commodity. All he had to do was avoid falling into the hands of the Red Army. With the front drawing ever closer to Berlin, Gehlen fled westward in April 1945. At the first opportunity, he surrendered to a U.S. Army unit.[4]

It was during the standard questioning to which all German prisoners of war were subjected that Gehlen first floated the idea of putting his FHO network to work for the Americans. His interrogator had no authority to negotiate, of course, and the general was returned to his POW enclosure. But his luck would soon change. Just days before Germany's surrender, Allen Dulles, then an OSS officer on a secret mission to Switzerland, was briefed about Gehlen's offer. While Dulles was not disposed to make blind deals with Nazi generals, the possible intelligence benefits seemed too good to pass up. Accordingly, he encouraged the army's intelligence representatives to pursue the matter further. Dulles's support seemed to do the trick. Within weeks of the Switzerland briefing, Gehlen, his card index, and an impressive collection of Nazi records became the property of the U.S. Army.[5]

The reversal in Gehlen's fortunes was truly dramatic. One day he was just another prisoner, albeit a high-ranking one, destined to do time in an uncomfortable POW camp; the next he was a trusted ally who would soon find himself on the U.S. government's payroll. Indeed, not long after the end of hostilities in Europe, the former intelligence chief was brought to America. Much of his time there was spent in debriefings. On one occasion, however, he was provided with a U.S. Army uniform, flown to Washington, and driven to a high-level meeting at the Pentagon, where he regaled an audience of senior military officers with tales of FHO's infiltration of the Soviet Union's various secret services. By the time he left the United States, Gehlen had been completely co-opted, or so his hosts assumed. Upon the general's return to Germany in July 1946, Dulles placed him in charge of a secret facility that was being built at Pullach, a pleasant Bavarian village on the outskirts of Munich. Once construction had been completed, Gehlen's task would be to revive FHO's network of contacts and put it to work as an American ratline.[6]

The Gehlen organization seemed to hold great promise. Not long after it went into business with OPC, however, the CIA learned that the Nazi-smuggling ratline had been infiltrated by communist agents. The administration in Washington took immediate countermeasures. First, the U.S. immigration service was given the names of dozens of ex-Nazis whose arrival was imminent and was ordered to deny them entry. Second, after President Harry Truman's re-election in November 1948, the executive branch began to reassert control over U.S. policy on anti-communist subversion and defectors. In a series of National Security Council (NSC) directives enacted over the course of the following year, covert operations were taken away from the Dulles brothers and made the exclusive purview of the CIA. This did not mean the end of the OPC–Gehlen ratline. While much more discriminating than either Wisner or Gehlen about who it would consider helping, the CIA did nothing to stop the influx into the United States of ex-Nazis and former collaborators. Rather, the agency merely screened candidates more closely in order to ensure they had not been compromised by Soviet intelligence.[7]

As developed by OPC and perfected by the CIA, the system of ratlining was a relatively simple one. The Gehlen organization would locate important or potentially useful defectors – most of whom were languishing behind the Iron Curtain or in refugee camps in western Europe – remove them from any immediate danger, supply them with documentation, and then pass them off to an intermediary organization, which would, in turn, put them in touch with ratline operatives. The use of intermediaries was crucial, as it provided OPC and later the CIA with a layer of deniability. One of most frequently used intermediaries in the American zones of occupation in Germany and Austria was the U.S. Army's Counter-Intelligence Corps (CIC). Ironically, CIC was more often than not an unwitting accomplice in such operations. There were exceptions, of course. Perhaps the most infamous case involved the CIC unit that, throughout the spring and summer of 1950, shielded former Lyon Gestapo chief Klaus Barbie from extradition to France, helped him escape to South America, and then lied about it when questioned by U.S. government officials.[8] Yet most CIC units had nothing to do with the unseemly trade in ex-Nazis and former collaborators. In fact, on several occasions CIC actually tried to break up Nazi-smuggling operations, only to receive orders to back off, orders that, presumably, originated with either Wisner or John Foster Dulles.[9]

The Americans did not have a monopoly in the business of providing safe haven for ex-Nazis and former collaborators. British military intelligence, most notably MI6, was also heavily involved. The key figure in British operations of this kind was one Harold Adrian Russell Philby, more commonly known as 'Kim.' Born in India in 1911, Kim Philby was the son of a talented but terribly erratic agent of the British secret service. As a young man, Kim studied at Cambridge, where he adopted Marxism as his political creed and immersed himself in anti-fascist politics. Recruited by Soviet intelligence in the mid-1930s, he was ordered to sever his communist connections and to move instead into right-wing or fascist circles as a cover. For the rest of the decade, he worked as a special correspondent in Spain for the London *Times*. During his tenure as a journalist, Philby reported on the civil war between the Spanish republicans and Franco's fascists. Though publicly supportive of Franco, he used his access to the fascist camp to pass information to his Soviet handlers regarding its secret communications with pro-Nazi elements within the British monarchy.

Kim's entrée into British intelligence came via his father, who managed to get him cleared for work at MI6 despite his son's earlier dabbling with Marxism. After toiling for a time on the agency's Iberian desk, he was given responsibility for its Mediterranean and Balkan operations. From 1941 to 1944, while ostensibly engaged in counter-espionage against the Nazis, Philby supplied information to the Soviets that enabled them to penetrate virtually every fascist movement in the German-occupied eastern territories. With victory over the Third Reich looming, he informed Moscow of the West's probable reactions to Soviet moves in southern and eastern Europe. On the basis of Philby's information, Stalin learned that the West would meet any communist coup attempts in Italy or Austria with force, and he backed off. On the other hand, the Soviet dictator was advised that the West's response to the installation of puppet governments in eastern Europe was likely to be weak, and so he proceeded without fear of retaliation.[10]

Philby remained with MI6 after the war. While he continued to work in counter-espionage, much of his time in the months immediately following the end of hostilities was spent as a member of a secret service reorganization committee. Upon completion of the committee's work, he was returned to the field.

Dispatched to Turkey in 1946, Philby ran MI6's anti-Soviet operations out of Istanbul for the next two years. It was in Turkey where he first met Wisner. After a few meetings, the two men decided to merge their ratlines. Using as their cover the Anti-Bolshevik Bloc of Nations (ABN), an umbrella group of eastern European and Soviet emigrés who agitated for the overthrow of communist rule in their homelands, Philby and Wisner successfully spirited dozens of ex-Nazis to the West. Then, early in 1949, Philby was promoted to the rank of senior British intelligence liaison in North America. His transfer to Washington did not end his involvement with the Nazi ratlines. On the contrary, one of Philby's tasks in Washington was to assist in the covert resettlement of ex-Nazis in the United States and Canada.[11]

In view of their mutual interest in ratlining, it was hardly surprising that Philby would be courted by Wisner and his superiors. Of course, neither Wisner nor the Dulles brothers had any idea that their partner was a double agent, or worse, that ABN was riddled with communist spies. Thus, while the Wisner–Philby pipeline enabled substantial numbers of ex-Nazis to find sanctuary, it also compromised the West's security. In fact, U.S. support for Philby's ratlining operations proved to be a political and espionage fiasco of unprecedented magnitude. Politically, the Soviets were able to use the presence of ex-Nazis in the West to embarrass western governments. From the counter-espionage perspective, Philby's activities had enabled numerous Soviet agents to set up operations in the heart of enemy territory. Things got so bad that, shortly after his arrival in Washington, the CIA informed Philby that they no longer wanted anything to do with the ex-Nazis he had been palming off on them.[12]

There is no evidence that Canada was involved in either the establishment or the operation of Nazi ratlines. This does not mean that its hands were completely clean in the matter. For one thing, Ottawa was a willing participant in the U.S. government's Presidential Escapee Program (PEP). Directed out of the American embassies in Greece and Turkey, the program provided settlement opportunities to all bona fide anti-communist refugees who were able to escape from the Soviet satellite states in the Balkans. Escapees were first screened to ensure that they were not communist agents, then debriefed, and finally provided with whatever humanitarian assistance was necessary to get them back on their feet. In selected cases, they were paraded before the media in order to maximize the propaganda effect of their escapes. While there is no evidence linking this particular program with the Nazi-smuggling ratlines of OPC or the CIA, it certainly could have been used for such purposes.[13]

Of greater concern than Canadian participation in the PEP was the possible role of the Security Panel in facilitating the admission to Canada of dubious anti-communist defectors and refugees. At least one commentator has suggested that part of Peter Dwyer's job as panel secretary was to help prepare documentation that would allow persons who were security risks or otherwise undesirable to slip through Canada's immigration-screening system.[14] Dwyer, to be sure, is a shadowy figure. As was discussed in the previous chapter, he came to Canada in 1952 to assist the government in upgrading its security apparatus. This was not his first involvement in matters relating to Canadian security. In September 1945, he and another MI6 officer stationed in Washington had travelled to Ottawa to interrogate Igor Gouzenko.[15] Upon his return to the American capital, Dwyer was named senior British liaison officer in North America, a post he held until 1949, when he was replaced by Philby. Officially, Dwyer resigned upon receiving word of his replacement. Unofficially, he stayed on in order to ease Philby's transition into his new job.[16] It is this period of Dwyer's career that is most troubling. After all, it seems inconceivable that he would not have been made aware of Philby's role in Nazi-smuggling during the transitional period, if he had not already known about it.

The extent of Dwyer's involvement in ratlining once he came to Canada is unknown. There can be little doubt that Philby, upon discovering that official Washington was less receptive to his ex-Nazis than it had been in the past, would have had a strong motive to try to divert his smuggling operations to Canada. Yet he was exposed as a Soviet mole in 1951, several months before Dwyer, then in retirement, arrived in Canada. Whatever his prior involvement in the business of Nazi-smuggling, it is unlikely that Dwyer would have continued to employ Philby's ratlines once it became apparent they were hopelessly compromised by Soviet agents. The real question is whether he would have continued Philby's work using alternative methods. Until such time as classified documents are released, the answer will be consigned to the realm of speculation.

Another possible ratline for the admission to Canada of ex-Nazis and former collaborators was the High Command of the U.S. Army in Europe (USAREUR). In his testimony before the commission of inquiry that first looked into the problem of Nazi war criminals and collaborators in Canada in 1985–6, William Kelly gave evidence regarding a problem that had cropped up during his tenure as the head of RCMP visa control in Europe. Early in 1954, according to Kelly, he was advised by the Canadian immigration mission at Karlsruhe that it had received a number of suspicious visa applications from the address of USAREUR in the American zone of occupation. All of the applications were neatly typed and all were accompanied by what later turned out to be forged papers. Kelly testified that when he tried to make inquiries with the Americans, he was rebuffed. Without any proof as to their bona fides, the head of Canadian visa control in Europe had no choice but to reject the applicants. Unfortunately, Kelly lamented, other such applications had been cleared for security before the Karlsruhe mission caught on. The implication was clear. Undesirables had evaded Canadian immigration screening via the USAREUR ratline, although in what numbers is unknown.[17]

Most archival records relating to Canada's cooperation in western security and intelligence operations remain classified. Until they are released, there will be no way to estimate the number of Nazi war criminals and collaborators who were admitted to the country via ratlines. However, a few cases are now a matter of public record. For example, one ex-Nazi known to have gained admission to Canada via the Wisner–Philby pipeline was Ferdinand Durcansky. Having served for a time as foreign minister of the Nazi satellite state in Slovakia, Durcansky was tried in absentia after the war and sentenced to death by the Czechoslovak government. With the help of Intermarium, he went underground, thereby avoiding capture and repatriation. In the autumn of 1946, he resurfaced in Rome. During meetings with emigré circles there, he learned of the existence of ABN. Obsessed with restoring Slovakia to independent status, he sought out allies and financing for a *coup d'état*. All of this cloak-and-dagger activity brought him into contact with Philby.

From Philby's point of view, Durcansky was the ideal dupe. After all, the Slovak leader was deadly serious about the overthrow of the Czech government, yet completely ignorant of how riddled ABN was with Soviet agents. He therefore suited Philby's larger purpose. The MI6 double agent would support Durcansky's efforts to the hilt, and then, at the crucial moment, betray the plotters and await the inevitable political backlash. At the very least, the plot would expose the weakness of the democratic regime in Czechoslovakia, rendering it vulnerable to attack by the political opposition. With the right wing discredited by Durcansky's failed coup, the left, Philby thought, might be in a position to call the shots.

Philby's plans succeeded beyond his wildest expectations. Beginning in June 1947, Durcansky, with the support of ABN, began a series of almost daily radio broadcasts aimed at like-minded individuals in Slovakia. The broadcasts lambasted the central government in Prague and warned that a separatist coup was imminent. Subsequently, the government announced that its security forces had seized leaflets calling for the overthrow of Czech rule in Slovakia and its replacement with a regime headed by none other than Durcansky. This was followed in September by word that a plot to overthrow the government of Czechoslovakia had been uncovered in which a number of Slovak political leaders were implicated. The communists, who at the time constituted little more than a rump in the Czechoslovak national assembly, called for a complete purge of the bureaucracy and the judiciary. The central government did not go that far, but it did assign communist deputies to run several key ministries, including the Ministry of the Interior, which controlled the security forces. This move sounded the death knell of democracy in Czechoslovakia. Within a few months, the communists had seized control of the entire government.[18]

Philby must have made his Soviet handlers very happy. Not only had a fascist coup been foiled, but the sole surviving democratic government in eastern Europe had been overthrown, replaced by a communist regime that was all too willing to turn Czechoslovakia into yet another satellite of the USSR. As for Durcansky, his grandiose plans were in ruins. He had little time to dwell on his failure, however. Of more immediate concern was escape before the communists in Czechoslovakia demanded his extradition. Using his Intermarium contacts, Durcansky managed to secure passage to South America via the Vatican's ratline.

Having destroyed his hapless pawn, Philby reverted to type – he again assumed the role of MI6's protector of an ex-Nazi in need. First, he assisted in throwing everyone off Durcansky's trail by planting bogus stories in the press regarding his whereabouts. With his client safely ensconced in South America, Philby then tried to help him emigrate to the United States. This would prove to be the master spy's first significant failure. While under normal circumstances the Americans were more than willing to grant asylum to anti-communist 'freedom fighters,' they wanted no part of Durcansky. The CIA was in the business of supporting people who tried to overthrow communist regimes, not democratic ones. Accordingly, in September 1950, the U.S. immigration service was advised that Durcansky was *persona non grata* and should under no circumstances be issued a visa.[19]

With the door to the United States slammed shut, Philby had no choice but to look elsewhere. He suggested that Durcansky try Canada. This proved to be good advice. Whether Philby knew it or not, Canada's system of immigration screening in South America was simply not yet up to the standards of its European operations. Thus, just two weeks after he had been rejected by the Americans, Durcansky walked into the Canadian embassy in Buenos Aires, Argentina, filled out an application, and was granted a visitor's visa valid for three months.[20]

Notwithstanding the ease with which he had obtained his visa, Durcansky did not proceed to Canada immediately. Apparently, he first had to mend fences with Slovak emigré circles in the United Kingdom. British immigration authorities seem to have had no idea Durcansky was in the country until well after his arrival, which suggests that Philby may have pulled some strings. The would-be Slovak premier spent several weeks in London. Indeed, it was only when the expiry date on his Canadian visa drew near that Durcansky decided to leave. Prior to his departure, he went to the Canadian High Commission in London and sought to renew the visa. Inexplicably, Canadian authorities complied without conducting a security check. On 5 December, Durcansky's visa was extended to March 1951. He left for Canada a few days later.

The Canadian government was completely in the dark about Durcansky's proposed visit. This was the result of two unfortunate and entirely avoidable errors. The first error occurred when the British government's warning about Durcansky arrived at the Canadian High Commission the day *after* his visa had been extended. The second took place when the High Commission was slow to alert External Affairs in Ottawa about Durcansky's imminent arrival. Word was finally issued to the Department of Citizenship and Immigration, but it was too late to advise officials stationed at points of entry along the East Coast. On 15 December 1950, Durcansky disembarked from a British Airways flight at Dorval airport, just outside of Montreal.[21]

What was particularly frustrating about this case was that Durcansky was well known to Canadian immigration officials. Prior to his failed coup attempt, Durcansky had tried twice, both times unsuccessfully, to get Canada to recognize his Slovak 'national liberation committee' as a government-in-exile.[22] As a result of his exertions, a security dossier had been compiled on him. All of this went for naught, of course. Legally, there was nothing Canadian authorities could do once Durcansky had stepped on to Canadian soil. Determined to prevent him from agitating within the Slovak-Canadian community, Ottawa informed the RCMP of his arrival. It is not clear whether Durcansky knew he was under surveillance. In any event, he left in March 1951, after the expiration of his second visa. Yet Canada had not seen the last of him. While Durcansky divided his time between the United Kingdom and

Germany as one of ABN's leading activists, he was allowed to visit Canada on occasion, despite his wartime record.[23]

Durcansky was not the only former official of the Nazi puppet government in Slovakia to gain admission to Canada via a ratline. Another was Karol Sidor. Before the outbreak of the Second World War, Sidor had headed the Hlinka Guard, the paramilitary wing of the fascist party that took power in Slovakia after the Germans dismembered the Czechoslovak Republic in March 1939. Not long after the German coup, however, he fell out of favour with the new government and was removed as head of the Hlinka Guard. In order to prevent any opposition from rallying around him, Sidor was sent to Rome as Slovakia's ambassador to the Vatican. Although a short-term setback, the Vatican posting had definite long-term benefits. With the defeat of Nazi Germany and the collapse of the Slovak puppet state, Sidor was out of reach of the Czechoslovak authorities, who were anxious to try him for treason.[24]

In the first few years after the war, the Vatican did its best to find a permanent home for Sidor. The United States was approached several times, but without success.[25] The State Department's refusals were based on Sidor's wartime record, which, according to U.S. immigration regulations, rendered his admission 'prejudicial to the interests of the United States.'[26] After Sidor's last rebuff in the United States, a papal representative approached the Canadian government and asked for special consideration in his case. Perhaps fearing that Canadian immigration authorities would reject Sidor on the same grounds as the Americans, the representative appealed directly to Prime Minister Louis St Laurent. Citing the 'delicacy' of Sidor's situation and the 'serious inconvenience and vexations' that would accompany any attempt to settle him in Europe, he asked that Sidor and his family be permitted to enter Canada as soon as possible.[27]

St Laurent wasted little time in passing the Vatican's request on to the Department of Mines and Resources, which was responsible for immigration at the time. Evidently, the fact that the request came from the prime minister made little impression on the bureaucrats. In characteristic fashion, Immigration Branch was still considering Sidor's visa application more than two months after it had been submitted. The reason, as Deputy Minister Hugh Keenleyside explained somewhat sheepishly to St Laurent, was that the RCMP had not yet passed Sidor clear for security. The Mounties, it seemed, were troubled by some of his public writings and at the same time had not received any cooperation from the Czechoslovak authorities. Frustrated by cases such as Sidor's, which, in St Laurent's words, 'can drag on endlessly,' the prime minister then suggested none too subtly that the problem was not with Sidor but rather with the system of immigration screening.[28] That was the end of any further RCMP resistance. Despite the fact that the Mounties had not completed their investigation of Sidor, the immigration regulations were waived in his case and he and his family were approved for admission in mid-November 1949.[29] In an unmistakable though obviously unintentional reference to the ratline that had made it all possible, the order-in-council whereby Sidor was admitted noted that he 'would endeavour to combat subversive elements among all Slovaks in Canada.'[30]

The last and perhaps the most publicized case of a collaborator who gained admission to Canada via a Nazi-smuggling ratline was that of Radislav P. Grujicic.[31] Born in 1911 in Serbia, Grujicic studied law as a young man and even flirted briefly with leftist politics before joining the police. After Germany's invasion and occupation of Yugoslavia, Grujicic offered his services to the Nazis. He was named chief of the anti-communist section of the Special Police in Belgrade. In this capacity, he directed investigations into the activities of alleged Yugoslav communists. When left-wing affiliation was established, often on the basis of the flimsiest evidence or after brutal interrogations, in which Grujicic himself sometimes took part, his job was to decide on an appropriate punishment. This could range from simple imprisonment or internment in a concentration camp to execution. Thousands of innocent Yugoslav citizens were dealt with in this manner. Not surprisingly, then, Grujicic was sentenced to death in absentia by a Yugoslav military tribunal in 1947.

After the collapse of the Third Reich, Grujicic, who in 1944 had fled westward with the retreating German forces, entered a refugee camp at Eboli, Italy. At some point, he must have told Allied occupation authorities of his experience in security matters, because in 1948 he was transferred to Austria, where he worked for a CIC detachment. For reasons that are shrouded in mystery, but that have the unmistakable aroma of ratlining, the CIC unit in question provided him with a new identity before he was returned to Italy. Henceforth known as Marko Jankovic, Grujicic was able to obtain International Refugee Organization (IRO) assistance and inclusion in a bulk-labour contingent destined for Canada. He sailed from Italy late in July 1948 on the SS *Saturnia*, arriving in Halifax on 9 August 1948. After fulfilling his contractual obligations, he moved to southwestern Ontario, working at various jobs in Canada and the United States until his retirement. In the autumn of 1992, he was charged with conspiracy to commit war crimes by the Department of Justice in Ottawa. Unfortunately, the case had to be dropped in September 1994 when it became apparent that he was too ill to assist in his own defence. Grujicic died a few months later.

Much has been made of the fact that the RCMP learned early on both of Grujicic's true identity and of the allegations against him, and yet kept it all secret – going so far as to lie to Canadian immigration authorities – because of his perceived value as an intelligence source. Indeed, critics have pointed to his case as evidence of official Ottawa's long-standing indifference to the presence in Canada of Nazi war criminals and collaborators. They are only partly right. Whatever one might think of the RCMP's handling of the Grujicic case, and with the benefit of hindsight it does seem objectionable, the fact is that the Mounties had no part in or knowledge of his admission to Canada under false pretences. Canada allowed him to stay, but it did not open the door for him. That was done by a rogue CIC unit and an American ratline.

Conclusions

'How were two thousand Nazi war criminals and collaborators able to gain admission to Canada?' That was the disturbing but important question asked at the beginning of this book. In the search for answers, three possible contributing factors were identified: the immigration bureaucracy, the immigration lobby, and the western intelligence community. It has long been assumed that these interested parties, either individually or in concert, either because of their incompetence or purposefully, conspired to permit hundreds of Hitler's former henchmen to settle in Canada. By this point in the narrative, it should be clear that their responsibility was a great deal less than has generally been believed.

Only by distorting the historical record can the system of immigration screening and the men who supervised its operation be blamed for the presence in Canada of Nazi war criminals and collaborators. To be sure, Ottawa was not ready, either institutionally or psychologically, for the waves of immigrants who washed over Canada's shores during the early postwar period. Following on the heels of a decade and a half of the most restrictive immigration policies imaginable, this lack of preparedness, while regrettable, was certainly understandable. Yet once the government had signalled its intention to change course, most immigration bureaucrats did their best to accommodate the new reality. Drawing on the experiences of the United Nations Relief and Rehabilitation Administration (UNRRA) and the International Refugee Organization (IRO), they knew that undesirables of all political affiliations, but in particular the recently defeated Nazis and fellow travellers, would try to infiltrate the pool of prospective immigrants. They knew as well that the only way to stop such infiltration was to cast a net that would filter out undesirables without unduly impeding the flow of new Canadians.

The system of immigration screening was a work in progress. Beginning in 1947, teams consisting of immigration officers, Mounties, and support personnel were sent to Germany to interview and select immigrants from among the hundreds of thousands of European refugees who had been displaced by the Second World War. Insufficient in number, inadequately trained, and almost wholly at the mercy of international relief agencies and Allied occupation forces, the Canadian teams had to improvise screening procedures on the spot. In the prevailing atmosphere of crisis and confusion, mistakes were inevitable. Gradually, however, a system of immigration screening took shape. Within a matter of months, it had become a well-administered and largely effective means of selecting applicants for admission to Canada.

In terms of its modus operandi, the system of immigration screening was something akin to a series of trip wires in a minefield. Before they were accepted for admission to Canada, would-be immigrants had to negotiate a complex array of security procedures and clearances. Visa applications were required to include information on nationality, prior residences, and previous employment – all the raw data necessary for effective screening. This information was then checked for accuracy and weighed against the criteria for admission. Anyone found not to have told the truth was automatically rejected. Anyone who failed to meet the screening criteria was similarly disqualified. Except in rare cases, there was no chance for appeal. If a visa seeker was deemed unsuitable by immigration authorities at the point of examination, that usually scuppered the chances for admission. As Canadian officials overseas were constantly reminded, any doubts about the bona fides of a particular applicant were to be resolved in favour of Canada.

The main function of the system of immigration screening was to sift the pool of would-be immigrants for subversives and undesirables. Included within these categories were Nazi war criminals and collaborators. Indeed, concern with Nazi infiltration was reflected throughout the screening process, from submission of a visa application to investigation of the applicant to evaluation of the results. Applications had to include an accounting of an individual's whereabouts and activities during the Second World War. Investigation of an applicant invariably included checks on that person's wartime activities. Whenever possible, these checks were carried out using German civil and military records. Finally, the criteria upon which the results of security investigations were evaluated included an applicant's wartime political affiliations.

From the outset, membership in Nazi and kindred organizations figured prominently in Canada's immigration-screening criteria. By 1949, when the RCMP came up with a formalized list of thirteen grounds for rejection, four were directly related to an applicant's affiliations during the Second World War. After 1950, as official Ottawa came to the inevitable and justified conclusion that ex-Nazis no longer posed a threat to the security of Canada, some relaxation of the Second World War–related criteria was permitted.[1] Yet even in the absence of a discernible security threat, the immigration bureaucrats never failed to take account of the objectionable character of the Nazi regime. Thus, when changes were made to the screening criteria, they represented not so much a weakening of the resolve to ban ex-Nazis, but rather constituted a series of sensible and measured responses to changing international circumstances.

To be sure, the system of immigration screening was imperfect. Like the UNRRA and IRO procedures on which it was based, the Canadian system encountered several problems, ranging from inadequate training of visa-vetting officers to an overburdened security-clearance apparatus to occasional political interference. Some of the problems were systemic, others the result of human frailty. But the system's main weakness, as has been noted elsewhere, was inconsistency in the quality and availability of corroborating sources. Unlike the elaboration of screening criteria and procedures, the problem of sources, regrettably, was beyond the capacity of the Canadian government to rectify.

This is not to suggest that Canada's immigration authorities operated in an information vacuum where the Second World War was concerned. On the contrary, there were substantial materials relevant to collaborationist and criminal activity during the war that could be and were consulted. Over the course of their withdrawal from western and eastern Europe, the Germans left behind a treasure trove of documents relating to all aspects of their occupation regime, including its organizational structure and its policies. Included in this mass of documentation were records from Nazi units that had been implicated in some of the most horrific atrocities of the war. At minimum, such documents were a source of insight into the nature and extent of collaboration among the indigenous populations of the occupied territories. On occasion, they could be used to pinpoint the collaborationist activities of individuals. When accessible, as was the case throughout western Europe, they were invaluable as a means of evaluating both the truthfulness and the eligibility of applicants for admission to Canada. Unfortunately, much of this documentation, in particular that pertaining to eastern European and Soviet collaborators, was locked away in secret archives behind the Iron Curtain, out of reach of Canadian investigators. Without access to these records, it was difficult, if not impossible, for RCMP security officers to conduct inquiries into the wartime activities of many of the prospective immigrants they were charged with examining. In view of this perennial constraint on effective screening, mass immigration necessarily became an exercise in risk management.

Just as it is possible to underestimate the effectiveness of the system of immigration screening, it is also possible to overestimate the ability of the immigration lobby to subvert it. There is little question that lobby groups helped to make the policy environment more receptive to immigration in the years immediately following the Second World War. This was particularly true when the interests of Canada's business community and those of the immigration lobby converged, such as happened in the case of the 2nd Corps movement in 1946. Yet an examination of the lobby's record during the first postwar decade reveals that it usually was unsuccessful in its attempts to obtain relief from the immigration-screening criteria. A classic example was the Ukrainian-Canadian community's failure to persuade the government to reconsider its refusal to admit former members of the 14th SS Division. Three years of hard lobbying produced rebuke after rebuke against the overly zealous lobby, but no change in policy. In fact, it was only when the criteria governing the admission of Volksdeutsche auxiliaries were revised in 1950 that the Ukrainian SS veterans were at last considered for admission.

Of all the ethnically based lobby groups, only the Canadian Christian Council for Resettlement of Refugees (CCCRR) seems to have wielded any real influence in Ottawa. And even its record was mixed. On the one hand, the organization was able to win relief for certain marginal categories of ex-Nazis. On the other hand, there were definite limits to the government's benevolence in this regard, limits beyond which Ottawa simply did not respond, no matter how intensely CCCRR pressed its case. Moreover, it is not certain that such concessions as were granted can be attributed solely to the organization's efforts. The government's review and subsequent revision of the screening criteria for low-level Nazi Party members and Waffen-SS troops seems to have been initiated more in response to changing international circumstances – such as Germany's admission into NATO in 1954 – than to CCCRR's lobbying.

If the bureaucrats and the immigration lobby were not to blame for the presence in Canada of Nazi war criminals and collaborators, the degree of responsibility of western intelligence agencies is less clear. We have seen how several suspected war criminals and collaborators gained admission to Canada via intelligence ratlines. Undoubtedly, others did so as well. It will not be possible to determine their number, of course, until top-secret documents in Canada and elsewhere are declassified. Yet when the final chapter is written on the Nazi-smuggling operations of the western intelligence community, the number of war criminals and collaborators who gained admission to Canada in this fashion is likely to constitute only a tiny fraction of the total. The reason is not hard to understand. In attempting to locate allies in their propaganda and espionage war against the countries of the Soviet bloc, western governments tended to limit their recruitment efforts to high-profile Nazis and collaborators. However strong his anti-communist convictions, the average rifleman who had served in an auxiliary police unit in the German-occupied East simply did not have sufficient information or contacts to warrant a great deal of exertion on his behalf by the CIA, MI6, or other intelligence services. Surely it is no coincidence that, of the Canadian cases that have come to light thus far, all involved individuals who had been either high-ranking fascists or senior security operatives during the war. It strains credulity, therefore, to think that more than a select and 'elite' handful of ex-Nazis would have been accorded the privilege of admission to Canada via intelligence ratlines.

One way in which Canada might have overcome the difficulties inherent in immigration screening would have been to establish a counterespionage service with the capacity to conduct security inquiries behind the Iron Curtain. Another might have been to have moved more slowly in reviving immigration after the war. Yet both policies would have come with a steep price. For example, had Canada established a security apparatus comparable in size and mandate to that of its American ally, as was recommended and rejected during the winter of 1945–6, the country probably could have prevented the admission of a few war criminals and collaborators, but only at the cost of handing the government enormous power to pry into the lives of its citizens. Similarly, had Ottawa continued its restrictive immigration policy after the termination of hostilities in Europe, some war criminals and collaborators undoubtedly would have been denied entry, but at a considerable cost to the country's economy and cultural heritage, not to mention its international reputation.

In the end, Canadian policy makers seem to have taken the sensible middle path. After the failure of the isolationism of the 1930s, they concluded, as Prime Minister King confided to his diary in May 1947, that 'in a world of shrinking distances and international uncertainties, a small population could not expect to hold the heritage we have.'[2] In opening the country's doors to persons displaced by the Second World War, they recognized that some risk was involved. There was the risk that prospective immigrants would not be truthful about their past political affiliations, criminal records, and, yes, their wartime activities. The risk was compounded by the possibility that corroborating sources would be unavailable, and that some undesirables would slip through as a consequence.[3] Yet the risk must be viewed in its true historical perspective. Canada accepted a million and a half immigrants in the first decade after the Second World War. Almost two-thirds of the new arrivals were of European origin. Within that mass influx were perhaps two thousand Nazi war criminals and collaborators. When weighed against the contribution made by the overwhelming majority of postwar immigrants, the few failures of the system of immigration screening seem far less important. Indeed, by any standards of measurement, the benefit to Canada was well worth the risk.

Immigration Screening as a Research Problem: The Sources and Their Limitations

In the aftermath of the Second World War, security screening of prospective immigrants was directed by the RCMP's Special Branch. By the 1980s, however, the functions of Special Branch had been transferred to the Canadian Security and Intelligence Service (CSIS). Accordingly, retired Special Branch records were housed at the National Archives in Ottawa as part of the CSIS record group (RG 146). This poses a problem for historians. Access to CSIS files is highly restricted. Indeed, many files are considered so sensitive that even descriptions of their contents remain classified. Other files can be reviewed, but their release is subject to a myriad of conditions imposed by the Access to Information Act. Thus, when access to CSIS records is granted, many documents are withheld or released with substantial portions excised.

Archival files related to Canada's postwar immigration-screening operations contain two kinds of documentation – policy correspondence and reports on individual cases. The former can be accessed, while the latter are, for all intents and purposes, closed. Owing to the receipt of numerous Access to Information requests over the years, the National Archives has released some Special Branch documents regarding immigration screening. Others have been made public as exhibits in the federal government's denaturalization cases against suspected Nazi war criminals and collaborators. Still, the vast majority of such documents are classified, and are likely to remain so for the foreseeable future.

With access to the records of RCMP Special Branch so restricted, is it possible to adequately research immigration screening during the 1940s and 1950s? The answer is yes, although extensive and systematic consultation of other records is required. Perhaps the best source in this regard is the record of the proceedings of the Commission of Inquiry on War Criminals, over which Justice Jules Deschenes presided in 1985–6. Part of the Royal Commissions record group (RG 33) at the National Archives, the Deschenes materials include transcripts of witness evidence and numerous documents. At present, there are considerable restrictions on the release of these materials. One way around the problem is by consulting the papers of the late Senator Paul Yuzyk (MG 32 C 67), which contain the commission's complete public record.

The Deschenes Commission materials are quite useful for determining RCMP intentions, but they give little indication as to the manner in which these intentions were translated into action in the field. To some extent, the gap between intentions and outcomes can be bridged by individual cases reported in other collections. The papers of Prime Ministers Mackenzie King (MG 26 J) and Louis St Laurent (MG 26 L), to cite but two examples, are replete with dossiers on persons who sought admission to Canada from Europe during the postwar period. Many of these cases are well documented and thus provide insight into RCMP screening practices.

A fairly complete picture of the size, intent, and modus operandi of Canada's immigration-screening apparatus can be obtained by consulting the records of other government departments. The records of Immigration Branch (RG 76) and the Department of Citizenship and Immigration (RG 26), for example, include extensive documentation on screening. Immigration screening is also dealt with in some detail in the correspondence of the Department of External Affairs (RG 25), although External's unwavering pro-immigration stance tended to skew its reporting on RCMP screening operations. Since the postwar refugee movement consisted mainly of labourers destined for employment in Canadian agriculture and primary industries, it is not surprising that documents on screening can also be found in the records of the Department of Labour (RG 27). Finally, cabinet and Privy Council records (RG 2) are essential for understanding Ottawa's intentions with respect to immigration-screening policy, although they contain few insights into the conduct of screening operations in the field.

Documentation on immigration screening is not confined to the records of government departments. Also useful are the official papers of senior bureaucrats responsible for the development and implementation of Canada's immigration policy. The papers of Hugh Keenleyside (MG 31 E 102), the deputy minister responsible for immigration between 1947 and 1950, are noteworthy in this regard. So are the papers of Laurent Beaudry (MG 30 E 151), who was an official at External Affairs during the 1940s. Different in content, but of equal importance, are the records of the main immigration lobby groups. The papers of Canadian Lutheran World Relief (MG 28 V 120) and the North American Baptist Immigration and Colonization Society (MG 28 V 18), for example, both of which include extensive correspondence with government departments and the Canadian Christian Council for Resettlement of Refugees (CCCRR), show the immigration-screening apparatus in action, particularly in cases involving Volksdeutsche and German nationals.

Despite the availability of a wide range of archival sources, no serious scholarly work on postwar immigration screening was undertaken until the 1980s. At that time, two major studies appeared. Prepared concurrently with the public hearings of the Deschenes Commission, each was characterized by allegations that a succession of governments were either indifferent to or complicit in the admission to Canada of Nazi war criminals and collaborators. Each attempted to link the failures of the system of immigration screening to a particular cast of mind on the part of RCMP and Immigration Branch officials. And each, in its own way, was flawed.

The first and by far the most important study was prepared for the Deschenes Commission by Alti Rodal, a historian employed by the federal government. Titled 'Nazi War Criminals in Canada: The Historical and Policy Setting from the 1940s to the Present,' Rodal's lengthy report accused postwar governments of negligence in permitting the admission to Canada of Nazi war criminals and collaborators. At its core, the report was informed by a cast-of-mind argument. Citing the bias of Canadian bureaucrats against Jewish would-be immigrants during the 1930s, Rodal posited a link between their attitudes and the government's handling of immigration screening after 1945. 'It seems reasonable to assume,' she opined, 'that a lack of empathy for the victims may have contributed to a lack of interest in seeking out the perpetrators of the crimes from amongst persons deemed to be highly attractive and desirable immigrants' (p. 117). According to Rodal, this indifference to the suffering inflicted on the Jews manifested itself in two ways. First, the danger of Nazi infiltration of the immigration stream was underestimated, with the result that prior Nazi affiliations were not adequately reflected in Canada's immigration-screening criteria. Second, there was constant pressure to relax those criteria that had anything to do with a prospective immigrant's activities during the Second World War.

In addition to her indictment of official Ottawa for its alleged lack of interest in the war criminal and collaborationist pasts of prospective immigrants, Rodal was also unsparing in her criticism of the government's immigration-screening apparatus. Canadian visa application forms, she claimed, were wholly inadequate to the task of screening for war criminal or collaborationist background. An additional problem was the fact that most of the RCMP officers assigned to screening duty overseas were insufficiently trained and poorly motivated. Finally, by involving certain lobby groups in the actual processing of immigrants, Ottawa, according to Rodal, allowed its immigration-screening operations to be influenced, distorted, and, ultimately, compromised.

In conducting the research for her report, Rodal was given virtually unfettered access to records at the National Archives, including those in the CSIS record group. She also had the assistance of a team of researchers. Despite this, key sources were omitted or subjected to only the most cursory examination. For example, the National Archives contains extensive materials on the screening to which members of the Polish 2nd Corps were subjected in 1946. These were missed altogether. Rodal was scathing in her criticism of the inadequacy of the Canadian visa application forms, yet she and her team failed to consult files in the Immigration Branch (RG 76) record group that would have provided for a more balanced view. Rodal suggested that immigration lobby organizations like CCCRR influenced immigration screening negatively, yet she apparently made no attempt to conduct a systematic review of their papers. None of these omissions are fatal by themselves, of course. Yet they do call into question Rodal's conclusions on significant points of interpretation.

Indeed, more serious than any shortcomings in the research supporting Rodal's report were problems in interpretation. This was particularly true with respect to its analysis of Canada's immigration-
screening procedures. By any standards of measurement, the report
betrays only a superficial understanding of the procedures employed by
Canadian immigration authorities during the 1940s and 1950s. For
example, Rodal characterized the visa application forms in use at the
time as inadequate (in the process ignoring the security-friendly forms
employed at the Paris and Stockholm offices), yet she did not even consider the possibility that their main flaw – namely, the lack of space for
a detailed accounting of residency and employment information –
might be overcome by other routine RCMP practices, such as interviews and security checks. She lamented the relaxation of the Second
World War–related screening criteria, yet made no attempt to determine what impact, if any, it would have had on Canada's ability to prevent the admission of Nazi war criminals and collaborators. Finally,
she was dubious about the effectiveness of refugee screening, yet failed
to pick up on important redundancies within the combined International Refugee Organization – Canadian operations, such as the use of
IRO's security-friendly application and registration forms by Canadian
immigration authorities.

Another attempt to assess Canadian immigration screening during
the postwar era was Reg Whitaker's *Double Standard: The Secret History of Canadian Immigration*. Published the same year (1987) as the
Rodal report was released to the public, Whitaker's study employed a
far narrower range of sources than Rodal's. Thus, the usefulness of his
study was limited to its analysis of government intentions. In this
regard, Whitaker's thesis was a simple one. Any lapses with respect to
Nazi infiltration of the immigration stream, he suggested, were the
result of Ottawa's overriding concern with preventing the admission of
communists and communist sympathizers.

Like Rodal's study, *Double Standard* was informed by a cast-of-
mind argument. In Whitaker's view, the relaxation of Second World
War–related screening criteria was a direct consequence of Canada's
adoption of Cold War policies. This is a major point of interpretation,
yet it is one for which the direct evidence is surprisingly thin. Apart
from repeated references to the Cold War context within which immi-

gration screening was carried out, Whitaker offered little to support his contention that Canadian immigration officials were obsessed with communist infiltration. Moreover, this emphasis on alleged ideological biases within the system of immigration screening led to some serious errors, such as Whitaker's contention that the admission of members the 14th SS Division was a result of Cold War imperatives, a contention openly contradicted by the archival record.

Notes

Introduction

1 The report, titled 'Nazi War Criminals in Canada: The Historical and Policy Setting from the 1940s to the Present,' was prepared by Alti Rodal for the Deschenes Commission of Inquiry on War Criminals in 1986. Criticisms of various parts of the report can be found throughout this book as well as in the appendix.

2 Statistics on postwar immigration to Canada can be found in 'Canadian Immigra-

tion: An Outline of Developments in the Post-War Period,' November 1957, NA, V.J. Kaye Papers, vol. 13, file 1, and 'Notes on the Canadian Family Tree,' 1955, NA, RG 25, vol. 2786, file 633–40.

3 For the purposes of this book, the term 'war criminal' refers to any enemy or Allied national who perpetrated crimes against Allied soldiers or civilians during the Second World War. The term 'collaborator,' on the other hand, refers to any Allied national who assisted the Germans in maintaining the occupation of conquered territories. Thus, while a western European national who took a job as a clerk at the local German Army headquarters might be considered by some to have been a traitor, such action does not, in my view, rise to the level of betrayal of one's country. The definition posited here requires a more active role, and is therefore limited to persons who enforced German rule in an official capacity, for example as civil administrators, auxiliary police, or volunteers in the German armed forces.

4 The figure of 150,000 is cited in 'Immigration to Canada Showing Displaced Persons by Racial Origin, from April 1947 to November 30, 1951,' undated [January 1952], NA, RG 26, vol. 140, file 3-40-4, part 1.

5 Owing to a bureaucratic policy that called for the destruction of most Canadian immigration files after a period of two years, there is no way of ascertaining with precision the percentage of the total pool of rejected would-be immigrants that suspected Nazis and collaborators constituted. On the policy of destroying files, see Commission of Inquiry on War Criminals, *Report* (Ottawa, 1986), 202. It is possible to make an educated guess, however. We know that between 1947 and 1956, approximately 23,500 prospective immigrants were rejected on security grounds. See Commissioner L.H. Nicholson to L. Fortier, 25 January 1956, NA, RG 26, vol. 166, file 3-25-11, part 2. We know too that during the fiscal year 1950–1, about four-fifths of such rejections were for Nazi affiliations. See C.E.S. Smith to Deputy Minister of Citizenship and Immigration, 18 May 1951, NA, RG 76, vol. 957, file SF-S-1, part 2. Since about half of the 1950–1 rejections included persons in categories that by the early 1950s were no longer automatically barred from admission – such as former members of the Nazi Party or the regular German armed forces – I settled on 45 per cent as a more reasonable figure of Nazi sympathizers among total rejections for the period 1950–6.

During the period 1946–50, the situation was somewhat more complicated. Owing to the blanket prohibition on members of the SS and the more restrictive policy toward members of the regular German armed forces then in place, there would have been a higher rejection rate in these categories. On the other hand, the number of persons who would have been rejected because of Nazi Party membership would have been much lower given the highly restrictive policy toward the admission of German nationals during the first few years after the war. Of course, the lower Nazi Party figures would have been offset by the higher rejection rate for persons of enemy (i.e., German) nationality, which remained grounds for security rejection until the summer of 1948. See Superintendent G.B. McClellan to Major J.A. Wright, 26 July 1948, ibid., vol. 800, file 547–1, part 1. The rate of rejections for collaborators was also likely to have been higher. Taking all of this into account, I determined that approximately 80 per cent of total rejections for the period 1946–50 were Nazi sympathizers. Averaging the two periods suggests that 62.5 per cent of total rejections were Nazi sympathizers – that is, 15,000 of 24,000 rejections.

6 Flaws in Canada's immigration-screening system were acknowledged both by the bureaucrats who designed it and the immigration and security officers who enforced it. For some examples, see *Memoirs of Hugh L. Keenleyside* (Toronto, 1982), 2: 300–1; cross-examination of Albert L. Greening, Deschenes Commission, NA, P. Yuzyk Papers, vol. 63, file/vol. 8, p. 1053, and examination of George O'Leary, ibid., file/vol. 6, pp. 730–1; cross-examinations of Clifford W. Harvison, 27 April 1966, Spence Commission, NA, RG 33, series 96, vol. 1, transcripts file, part 3, pp. 234–6, and George B. McClellan, 28 April 1966, ibid., part 4, pp. 259– 60 and 265–6.

7 Compare the immigration statistics in Department of Mines and Resources memorandum, 5 September 1945, NA, RG 25, vol. 4164, file 939–40, part 1, with those cited in 'Canadian Immigration: An Outline of Developments in the Post-War Period,' November 1957, NA, Kaye Papers, vol. 13, file 1.

8 For arguments that Canadian officials were obsessed with Communist infiltration of the immigration stream, see Reg Whitaker, *Double Standard: The Secret History of Canadian Immigration* (Toronto, 1987), 103, and Freda Hawkins, *Canada and Immigration: Public Policy and Public Concern*, 2nd ed. (Montreal, 1988), 282.

9 Even before the end of hostilities in Europe, Ottawa had been informed that Allied war crimes investigators were focusing their attention on 'members of the S.S., Gestapo, Waffen S.S., S.A., [Nazi] Party officials, Vlassov Cossacks and certain police categories.' See Dominion Affairs to External Affairs, 1 March 1945, NA, RG 25, vol. 5706, file 7–R(s). During the immediate postwar period, the attention of Canadians could not help but have been riveted on the war crimes issue. First, there was the trial in December 1945 of SS Brigadier General Kurt Meyer, who was accused of having ordered the murder of Canadian prisoners of war in Normandy. For more on the Meyer trial, see Howard Margolian, *Conduct Unbecoming: The Story of the Murder of Canadian Prisoners of War in Normandy* (Toronto, 1998), chap. 16. Second, throughout most of 1946, Canadian newspapers carried frequent reports on the trial of the major Nazi war criminals before an international military tribunal at Nuremberg, Germany.

1: Escape

1 On the fate of the Volksdeutsche toward the end of the war, see Valdis O. Lumans, *Himmler's Auxiliaries: The Volksdeutsche Mittelstelle and the German National Minorities of Europe, 1933–1945* (Chapel Hill, 1993), 250–61, and Michael R. Marrus, *The Unwanted: European Refugees in the Twentieth Century* (New York, 1985), 297 and 325–7. The estimate of 8 million includes only those Volksdeutsche who made their way to western Germany. See E. Reid to the Church of England in Canada, 18 December 1948, NA, RG 26, vol. 115, file 3-24-20, part 1. Another 4.5 million fled to eastern Germany. For statistics on Volksdeutsche flight from eastern Europe and the Soviet Union, see Gerhard Reichling, 'Fluchtvertriebung der Deutsche,' in *Fluchtlinge und Vortriebene in der westdeutsche Geschichte* (Hildesheim, 1987), 46–68.
2 Marrus, *The Unwanted*, 299 and 309, and Louise Holborn, *The International Refugee Organization, A Specialized Agency of the United Nations: Its History and Work, 1946–1952* (London, 1956), 20.
3 Marrus, *The Unwanted*, 299 and 315–16.
4 Gerald E. Dirks, *Canada's Refugee Policy: Indifference or Opportunism?* (Montreal, 1977), 100.
5 Holborn, *International Refugee Organization*, 22. For more on the troubled history of IGCR, see Martin Gilbert, *The Holocaust: A History of the Jews of Europe during the Second World War* (New York, 1985), 64; Irving Abella and Harold Troper, *None Is Too Many* (Toronto, 1982), 32; and Alti Rodal, 'Nazi War Criminals in Canada: The Historical and Policy Setting from the 1940s to the Present' (Commission of Inquiry on War Criminals, Ottawa, 1986), 67–8. See also Dominion Affairs to External Affairs, 8 January 1946, NA, RG 25, vol. 3672, file 5127-40C, part 2.
6 Holborn, *International Refugee Organization*, 17.
7 On UNRRA's problems, see Marrus, *The Unwanted*, 320–3, and Allied Commission Report, 16 July 1946, AN, IRO records, AJ 43/79.
8 On the dissemination of anti-repatriation propaganda among Ukrainian refugees, see Confidential Paper, 3 January 1946, NA, RG 25, vol. 2103, file AR 405/1/4/4, part 1. For similar activities among Yugoslav expatriates, see Dominion Affairs to External Affairs, 5 February 1947, ibid., vol. 3673, file 5127-40C, part 9. British occupation authorities complained that the representative of a Ukrainian-Canadian group was engaging in such propaganda. See Control Commission for Germany to (British) Foreign Office, 5 March 1946, ibid., vol. 3747, file 6980-GR-40, part 1. At one point the anti-repatriation fervour became so intense that the U.S. military governor in Germany offered to have agitators physically segregated from the rest of the refugee population. See UNRRA cable, 19 May 1947, appended to dispatch from H. Wrong to External Affairs, 24 June 1947, NA, RG 26, vol. 147, file 3-43-1.

9 Marrus, *The Unwanted*, 316 and 323–4.

10 For the hardening of the Allied position on repatriation, see ibid., 317, and Yuri Boshyk, 'Repatriation and Resistance: Ukrainian Refugees and Displaced Persons in Occupied Germany and Austria, 1945–1948,' in *Refugees in the Age of Total War*, ed. Anna C. Bramwell (London, 1988), 206. Canada had no say in these developments. As part of the British army of occupation, Canadian forces were obligated to adhere to the new policy. See 'The Problem of Refugees in Germany,' 15 April 1946, NA, RG 25, vol. 3672, file 5127-40C, part 2.

11 The estimate of several hundred thousand collaborators was based on RCMP reports. See Assistant Commissioner H.A.R. Gagnon to L. Beaudry, 16 May 1946, NA, RG 25, vol. 5788, file 233(s), part 2.

12 Marrus, *The Unwanted*, 314. Knowing what was in store for them if they returned to the Soviet Union, the Cossacks begged their British captors to grant them asylum. Their pleas fell on deaf ears. Amid heart-rending scenes, the Cossacks were forcibly repatriated during the summer of 1945. See Martin Gilbert, *The Day the War Ended: VE-Day 1945 in Europe and around the World* (London, 1995), 271–2 and 369.

13 'Displaced Persons in Europe,' 20 February 1946, NA, RG 25, vol. 3798, file 8296-40.

14 Holborn, *International Refugee Organization*, 38–9.

15 'Yugoslav Proposal re War Criminals, Quislings and Traitors,' undated, NA, RG 25, vol. 1053, file 6-5-0.

16 Some contemporary observers were of the view that Soviet-bloc countries had painted all refugees with the collaborationist brush so as to embarrass the western Allies into resuming mass repatriation. For example, see P.T. Molson to High Commissioner, 30 March 1946, ibid., vol. 2103, file AR 405/1/4/4, part 1.

17 The various elements of the deal are described in a session of UNRRA Council, 29 March 1946, and N.A. Robertson to G. Turgeon, 4 April 1946, NA, RG 76, vol. 443, file 673931, part 11, reel C-10320; UNRRA Order No. 40G, 11 August 1946, AN, IRO records, AJ 43/578; and Holborn, *International Refugee Organization*, 207.

18 Report by (UN) Special Committee on Refugees and Displaced Persons, June 1946, NA, RG 25, vol. 3640, file 4060-40, part 8.

19 For a contemporary assessment of the deal, see 'The Refugee Problem,' 4 September 1946, ibid., vol. 2105, file AR 405/1/4/27, part 1.

20 Rodal, 'Nazi War Criminals,' 90.

21 'Yugoslav Proposal re War Criminals, Quislings and Traitors,' undated, NA, RG 25, vol. 1053, file 6-5-0.

22 See Questionnaire for Displaced Persons (used by U.S. 3rd Army Headquarters),

undated, AO, G.R.B. Panchuk Papers, series C, box 17, file Screening Question-naires – U.S.

23 PCIRO Administrative Order No. 60, 16 December 1947, AN, IRO records, AJ 43/ 1038.

24 On the UNRRA forms, which varied from region to region, see petition to U.S. Army Headquarters (Frankfurt), 4 February 1947, HI, box 12. Unfortunately, no facsimile has been found.

25 'Yugoslav Proposal re War Criminals, Quislings and Traitors,' undated, NA, RG 25, vol. 1053, file 6-5-0.

26 'Note Concerning Screening Procedure in UNRRA DP Camps,' 14 February 1947, ibid., vol. 4164, file 939-40, part 2. In her report for the Deschenes Commission of Inquiry on War Criminals, Alti Rodal contended that Allied military authorities screened only former members of the German armed forces, not civilian refugees, for collaboration or war crimes. See 'Nazi War Criminals,' 92. Her interpretation appears to be based on too narrow a reading of the documents pertaining to UNRRA screening procedures. While I agree that the documents describe screen-ing responsibilities as having been split between UNRRA and Allied military authorities, I believe they also show that the division of labour was along investiga-tive lines, not between civilian and military refugees. If, as Rodal seems to suggest, there was to be only partial screening for civilian refugees, then there would have been no reason for the regional UNRRA screening boards to send the civil ques-tionnaires on to the appropriate military authorities. Yet this was done as a matter of course. Finally, prior to being considered for emigration, a UNRRA-assisted ref-ugee had to adduce proof that he had been screened both civilly and for security. See Intergovernmental Committee on Refugees (IGCR) Personal Data form, undated, NA, RG 27, vol. 3036, file 70, which required the UNRRA director to attest to the fact that the prospective immigrant was screened by military authorities (the date had to be provided) and that his questionnaire had established his status as a displaced person.

27 For complaints about rushed or half-hearted military screening, see report to (UNRRA) Council, 8 July 1946, NA, RG 25, vol. 2153, file UNRRA, part 5; 'Memorandum on the Problem of the European Refugees,' 19 February 1947, NA, ibid., vol. 3673, file 5127-40C, part 9; and UNRRA report, 14 April 1947, NA, RG 76, vol. 443, file 673931, part 13, reel C-10320.

28 For example, see Ethel Ostry, 'After the Holocaust: My Work with the UNRRA,' 152–3, NA, E. Ostry Papers, and memorandum to R.G. Riddell, 7 February 1946, NA, RG 25, vol. 3798, file 8296-40.

29 Captured German records included the files of the Einwandererzentralstelle, or Immigrant Central Office, which processed Volksdeutsche applications for German citizenship during the war. These and other Nazi records have been housed at the

Document Centre in Berlin (BDC) since the Nuremberg Trials. The repository was under American military administration until 1994, when it reverted to the control of Germany's archival administration. The BDC is now referred to as Bundesarchiv-Aussenstelle Zehlendorf, or the Zehlendorf branch of the German Federal Archives.

30 On the problems with Italian records, see minutes of meeting on security problems held on 28 February 1952, NA, RG 76, vol. 800, file 547-1, part 2.

31 Even if access had been granted, it is not clear that the captured records would have been of immediate assistance. During my tenure with the Crimes against Humanity and War Crimes Section of the Department of Justice of Canada, I had numerous opportunities to review German records housed in archives in eastern Europe and the former Soviet Union. These records, classified as 'trophy documents' by Soviet authorities, usually were placed in archives in the regions where they had been abandoned by or confiscated from the Germans. Central archival administrations sometimes did not know what was in these regional repositories. Thus, while lists or even identity papers of indigenous auxiliaries might be extant, an investigator would have to have reasonably detailed biographical information on a suspected collaborator and some knowledge of the history of the collaborator's unit before the appropriate checks could be done.

In the aftermath of the Second World War, tens of thousands of persons suspected of collaboration were investigated and tried in eastern Europe and the former Soviet Union. Like the captured German documents, the record of these 'trials' constituted an important source of information on collaborators who may have escaped to the West. Indeed, it was from these proceedings that Soviet authorities compiled lists of persons wanted for collaboration. However, the lists were a work in progress. Most of the postwar trials took place from the late 1940s on. Thus, even if UNRRA or Allied military investigators had been granted some degree of access to these records in 1946, it is likely that they would have been of only marginal assistance.

32 Rodal, 'Nazi War Criminals,' 30, 96, and 387.

33 Holborn, *International Refugee Organization*, 181 n.1 and 208.

34 'Yugoslav Proposal re War Criminals, Quislings and Traitors,' undated, NA, RG 25, vol. 1053, file 6-5-0.

35 See (British) Armed Forces Headquarters to War Office, 27 January 1947, PRO, FO371/66601. I am indebted to Julian Hendy of Yorkshire, UK, for providing me with a copy of this document. See also Dominion Affairs to External Affairs, 5 February 1947, NA, RG 25, vol. 3673, file 5127-40C, part 9.

36 N.A. Robertson to External Affairs, 15 March 1947, NA, RG 25, vol. 2105, file AR 405/1/4/27, part 2, and Robertson to External Affairs, 25 April 1947, NA, RG 26, vol. 147, file 3-43-1.

37 On Maclean's experiences in Yugoslavia, see Mark Aarons and John Loftus, *Ratlines: How the Vatican's Nazi Networks Betrayed Western Intelligence to the Soviets* (London, 1991), 205.

38 A petition sent to the Canadian government in the aftermath of the Maclean mission cited a figure of 130 Yugoslav DPs imprisoned by British authorities on suspicion of collaboration. See Serbian National Shield Society of Canada to Prime Minister Mackenzie King, 18 October 1947, NA, RG 25, vol. 3977, file 9884-40. At least a few of these individuals were tipped off and had to be apprehended after making good their escape. See Dominion Affairs to External Affairs, 14 March 1947, ibid., vol. 3673, file 5127-40C, part 9.

39 The 600,000 or so non-Jewish refugees included 310,000 Poles, 155,000 Balts, 100,000 Ukrainians, and 30,000 Yugoslavs. These figures are cited in 'The International Refugee Organization,' 1954, ibid., vol. 8118, file 5475-T-40, part 18.2.

40 Collaboration among ethnic Germans is discussed in Lumans, *Himmler's Auxiliaries*, passim. The extent of collaboration in Poland is a matter of some controversy. For example, compare Jan Tomasz Gross, *Polish Society under German Occupation: The Generalgouvernement, 1939–1944* (Princeton, NJ, 1979) with Richard C. Lukas, *The Forgotten Holocaust: The Poles under German Occupation, 1939–1944* (Lexington, KY, 1986). The phenomenon of collaboration in the Soviet Union has become the subject of a growing body of literature. For an overview, see Richard Breitman, 'Himmler's Police Auxiliaries in the Occupied Soviet Territories,' *Simon Wiesenthal Center Annual* 7 (1994): 23–39.

41 Despite the availability of German records, the success of screening for Volksdeutsch origins was by no means assured. See 'Visit to Refugee and Displaced Persons Camps in the British Zone of Occupation in Germany,' undated, NA, RG 76, vol. 443, file 673931, part 12, reel C-10320.

42 External Affairs to cabinet, 25 February 1947, NA, RG 2, vol. 65, file C-20-5, document nos 345–415.

43 Actually, responsibility for the care and maintenance of the refugee camps was first turned over to IGCR. See Holborn, *International Refugee Organization*, 9 and 23. However, this was a just a stop-gap measure until the new refugee organization was fully prepared to assume its duties. See IGCR memorandum, 11 April 1947, NA, RG 76, vol. 443, file 673931, part 13, reel C-10320.

44 Rodal, 'Nazi War Criminals,' 76–8, and Holborn, *International Refugee Organization*, 39 and 49–50.

45 On the differences in criteria between UNRRA and IRO, see PCIRO Eligibility Directive, 25 June 1947, AN, IRO records, AJ 43/1054.

46 On IRO rules regarding repatriation, see Constitution of the International Refugee Organization, 1946, NA, L.S. St Laurent Papers, vol. 225, file I-17.

47 There were also practical considerations for keeping Germans ineligible for IRO

assistance. Had all Germans who claimed refugee status actually been granted eligibility, IRO would have been confronted with a second refugee crisis. Between 1945 and the early 1970s, more than eight million displaced Germans were absorbed into the population of western Germany. On these refugees, see Marrus, *The Unwanted*, 330–1.

48 On IRO's criteria for rendering assistance to Volksdeutsche, see PCIRO Eligibility Directive, 25 June 1947, AN, IRO records, AJ 43/1054; R. Innes to PCIRO, 2 September 1947, ibid., AJ 43/639; Constitution of the International Refugee Organization, 1946, NA, St Laurent Papers, vol. 225, file I-17; T.O.F. Herzer to W.A. Tucker, 27 April 1947, NA, Canadian Lutheran World Relief Papers, reel H-1391; 'Volksdeutsche,' 24 July 1947, NA, RG 76, vol. 655, file B41075, part 1, reel C-10592; 'Volksdeutsche in Austria,' undated [January 1948], ibid., vol. 443, file 673931, part 16, reel C-10321; report by Interdepartmental Committee on Immigration, undated, ibid., part 18; and resolution passed by IRO General Council, 24 September 1948, NA, RG 25, vol. 3688, file 5475-T-40, part 9.

49 Lumans, *Himmler's Auxiliaries*, 211–16.

50 On IRO's change of heart regarding the Mennonites, see M. Cohen to J.H. Allard, 23 June 1949, M.D. Lane to Allard, 17 August 1949, and Cohen to Allard, 3 October 1949, NA, RG 26, vol. 122, file 3-24-4, part 1; minutes of Immigration-Labour Committee meetings held on 30 August and 8 November 1949, ibid., vol. 72, file 11/1/49-8/6/50, part 3. See also J.J. Thiessen, C.F. Klassen, and W.T. Snyder to H.L. Keenleyside and A.L. Jolliffe, 9 August 1949, Commissioner of Immigration to P.W. Bird, 25 August 1949, and Jolliffe to Klassen, 31 August 1949, NA, RG 76, vol. 855, file 544-22, part 1.

51 IRO criteria for Nazi war criminals and collaborators can be found in 'War Criminals, Quislings and Traitors,' 10 June 1947, AN, IRO records, AJ 43/1039; PCIRO Eligibility Directive,' 25 June 1947, ibid., AJ 43/1054; (IRO) Form CM/2, 2 July 1949, ibid., AJ 43/863; and Constitution of the International Refugee Organization, 1946, NA, St Laurent Papers, vol. 225, file I-17.

52 On the recruitment of ethnic Germans from Romania, see Higher SS and Police Leader Russia-South to SS and Police Leader in Stalino, 19 June 1943, MHA, collection HSSPf Ru-Süd, file 22/3. On the recruitment of ethnic Germans from other Balkan states, see orders issued by Reich Leader of SS and Police, 3 and 5 November 1943, ibid., collection Stabskompanie der Waffen-SS beim Flugmotorwerk Reichshof, file 2. On Lithuanians, see order issued by Reich Leader of the SS and Police, 3 July 1943, NARA, RG 242, series T-580, reel 71, no frame numbers. On the recruitment of Ukrainians, see H. Himmler to SS Brigadier-General Wächter, 28 March 1943, ibid., series T-175, reel 74, frames 2592484–5; minutes of conference held in Lemberg [Lviv] on 12 April 1943, ibid., frames 2592467–74; SS Brigadier General Berger to Himmler, 16 April 1943, ibid., frames 2592462–4; and SS

Main Office to Himmler, 3 June 1943, ibid., 2592444–6. On the recruitment of Byelorussians, see orders issued by White Ruthenian Central Council, undated [1944], and orders issued by Reich Leader of SS and Police to White Ruthenian Central Council, undated [1945], BNA, collection 383, shelf list 1, files 2 and 11a. On the recruitment of Estonians, see directive issued by SS High Command, 29 September 1942, NARA, RG 242, series T-175, reel 127, frames 2652928–30; Reich Leader of SS and Police to General Commissar (Reval), 8 April 1943, ibid., series T-580, reel 71, no frame numbers; event report, 31 March 1944, ibid., series T-354, reel 120, frame 2754142; draft order, April 1944, ibid., series T-175, reel 22, frame 2527855; and Order No. 431, 1 January 1945, *Verordnungsblatt der Waffen-SS*, ibid., series T-611, reel 6, no frame number. On the recruitment of Latvians, see Reich Leader of SS and Police to SS Lieutenant-General Jeckeln and SS Major-Generals Jüttner, Berger, and Wolff, 30 January 1943, ibid., series T-175, reel 22, frame 2527882; Jeckeln to Reich Leader of SS and Police, 19 February 1943, ibid., frame 2527868; and Dr Drechsler to Berger, 12 October 1943, ibid., reel 71, frame 2588951.

53 On the history of the various Waffen-SS units raised in German-occupied Europe, see Samuel W. Mitcham, *Hitler's Legions: The German Army Order of Battle in World War II* (London, 1985), 446–71.

54 International Refugee Organization, *Manual for Eligibility Officers* (Geneva, n.d. [1948]), 54–5, Documents in Evidence in the Matter of Revocation of Citizenship between the Minister of Citizenship and Immigration and Wasily Bogutin.

55 In the case of the Estonians, there was general agreement that conscription had not been invoked until 30 January 1944. No such consensus existed for Latvian members of the Waffen-SS. Initially, IRO officials settled on 23 November 1943 as the cut-off date. However, owing to the discovery of new information, the date was pushed back to 15 April 1943. Even this date did not satisfy everyone, and so the case of the Latvian SS would remain a matter of controversy. See PCIRO Eligibility Division to PCIRO Area V Director, 20 September 1948, and P. Jacobsen to IRO Eligibility Officers, 7 May 1951, AN, IRO records, AJ 43/978.

56 See minutes of meeting of IRO Eligibility Review Board, 10 November 1948, ibid., AJ 43/79, and extract of report made to IRO's Executive Committee on 28 March 1949, quoted in memorandum from M.R. Thomas to J.H. Allard, 2 May 1950, NA, RG 76, vol. 31, file 682, part 6, reel C-4690.

57 On the stringency with which the conscript/volunteer criterion was applied, see report from Review Board to Director General, September 1948, AN, IRO records, AJ 43/457.

58 For different versions of the form, see (PCIRO) Application for Assistance, undated, ibid., AJ 43/1054; Application for IRO Assistance, 22 February 1948, ibid., AJ 43/866; and Form CM/1, 6 November 1951, ibid., AJ 43/863. The CM/1

is also described in Instructions for Completing the Application Form for Assistance from PCIRO, 25 June 1947, ibid., AJ 43/1054, and PCIRO Administrative Order No. 60, 16 December 1947, ibid., AJ 43/1038.

59 O. Cormier to Commissioner of Immigration, 22 June 1948, NA, RG 26, vol. 122, file 3-32-6.

60 W.H. Tuck to Chief IRO Eligibility Officer, 12 April 1949, AN, IRO records, AJ 43/978.

61 Holborn, *International Refugee Organization*, 208–9.

62 On IRO methods of screening for war criminal or collaborationist background, see 'War Criminals, Quislings and Traitors,' 10 June 1947, AN, IRO records, AJ 43/1039, and 'Control Centre, Munich Area 7, Werner Caserne, Block A,' 31 October 1950, ibid., AJ 43/863. The policy of blacklisting is described in Decision Procedure, undated [July 1947], ibid., AJ/1038.

63 P.T. Molson to High Commissioner, undated, NA, RG 76, vol. 443, file 673931, part 12, reel C-10320.

64 Summary of PCIRO Information Bulletin No. 23, 12 July 1948, ibid., part 18, reel C-10321.

65 See the examples cited in Annex 'A,' undated, appended to memorandum from Lieutenant-Colonel J.A.K. Rutherford to Security Panel, 30 March 1948, NA, RG 2, vol. 251, file S-100-D, Security Panel Document SP-24.

66 For complaints about the coaching of refugees, a practice in which IRO eligibility officers sometimes engaged, see D. Segat to A. Bedo, 13 December 1948, AN, IRO records, AJ 43/978.

67 For examples, see S. Wiesenthal to A. Bedo, 20 October 1948, ibid., AJ 43/457 and (UN) Press Release, 1 March 1949, NA, RG 76, vol. 443, file 673931, part 19, reel C-10321. There were also allegations that the administration of some IRO camps had been infiltrated by communists. For example, see L.D. Wilgress to L.B. Pearson, 14 May 1948, NA, RG 26, vol. 169, file 3-32-1, part 1.

68 On the limitations of sources available in the West, see O. Cormier to Commissioner of Immigration, 22 June 1948, NA, RG 76, vol. 662, file B83052, part 1, reel C-10598; 'War Criminals, Quislings and Traitors,' 10 June 1947, AN, IRO records, AJ 43/1039; and A. Rucker to R. Innes, 17 November 1949 ibid., AJ 43/645.

69 Thus, I am somewhat more sanguine about the effectiveness of IRO screening than Alti Rodal. Rodal's view can be found in 'Nazi War Criminals,' 94–102. In comparing our respective analyses, readers should be aware that Rodal relied almost exclusively on the manual for IRO eligibility officers. See the notes in ibid., 498–9. While the manual is an important source, it is by no means the only one that touches on the issue of IRO screening. As my notes reveal, a more complete picture can be gleaned from IRO records kept at the Archives nationales in Paris and from Canadian government records housed at the National Archives in Ottawa.

70 On IRO's success in screening out Volksdeutsche, see the statistics reported in 'Notes on the Canadian Close Relatives Scheme,' 2 September 1947, AN, IRO records, AJ 43/639.
71 Minutes of cabinet meeting held on 10 September 1946, NA, RG 2, vol. 2638, reel T-2364, frames 1573–4.
72 John W. Holmes, *The Shaping of Peace: Canada and the Search for World Order, 1943–1957* (Toronto, 1979), 1: 95.

2: Fortress Canada

1 See the statistics reported in Department of Manpower and Immigration, *Highlights from the Green Paper on Immigration and Population* (Ottawa, 1975), 32.
2 W.E. Harris to cabinet, 21 February 1952, NA, RG 2, vol. 212, file C-20-5.
3 Gerald E. Dirks, *Canada's Refugee Policy: Indifference or Opportunism?* (Montreal, 1977), 24–6 and 50–3, and Franca Iacovetta, *Such Hardworking People: Italian Immigrants in Postwar Toronto* (Montreal, 1992), 23–4.
4 W.E. Harris to cabinet, 21 February 1952, NA, RG 2, vol. 212, file C-20-5.
5 PC 695, 21 March 1931, NA, L. Beaudry Papers, vol. 6, file 114.
6 Department of Mines and Resources memorandum, 5 September 1945, NA, RG 25, vol. 4164, file 939-40, part 1.
7 See the statistics reported in 'Canadian Immigration: An Outline of Developments in the Post-War Period,' November 1957, NA, V.J. Kaye Papers, vol. 13, file 1.
8 Post-1929 immigration statistics can be found in Department of Mines and Resources memorandum, 5 September 1945, NA, RG 25, vol. 4164, file 939-40, part 1.
9 Within days of Ottawa's declaration of war on Germany, an order-in-council was enacted that prohibited the admission of enemy aliens and residents of any territory occupied by the enemy. See PC 2653, 14 September 1939, NA, Beaudry Papers, vol. 6, file 114. Though conceived as a means of protecting the country from infiltration by enemy agents, the order-in-council effectively barred any European nationals from admission to Canada if their country was under German occupation.
10 Department of Mines and Resources memorandum, 5 September 1945, NA, RG 25, vol. 4164, file 939-40, part 1.
11 For example, see R.G. Robertson to J. McKenna, 22 December 1945, NA, W.L.M. King Papers, series J2, vol. 399, file D-22-E, and Robertson to G. Lawreniuk, 8 January 1946, ibid., file D-22-8.
12 A.L. Jolliffe to External Affairs, 10 November 1945, NA, RG 25, vol. 3672, file 5127-40C, part 1.
13 Ibid., and Immigration Branch to External Affairs, 23 April 1946, ibid., vol. 3798, file 8296-40.

14 Minister of Mines and Resources to cabinet, 5 September 1945, ibid., vol. 4164, file 939-40, part 1.

15 Minutes of cabinet meetings held on 17 and 25 October 1945, NA, RG 2, vol. 2637, reel T-2364, frames 728 and 737–9, and A.D.P. Heeney to J.A. Glen, 25 October 1945, ibid., vol. 63, file C-20-2, part 2.

16 On the admission of the 3,500 aliens, see 'The Canadian National Committee on Refugees,' 7 February 1946, NA, Canadian National Committee on Refugees Papers, vol. 4, file 41. On the handling of their case, see Alti Rodal, 'Nazi War Criminals in Canada: The Historical and Policy Setting from the 1940s to the Present' (Commission of Inquiry on War Criminals, Ottawa, 1986), 136–7; Irving Abella and Harold Troper, *None Is Too Many* (Toronto, 1982), 201–2; and minutes of cabinet meeting held on 25 October 1945, NA, RG 2, vol. 2637, reel T-2364, frames 737–9.

17 For example, in autumn 1945 twenty-five MPs sent a telegram to Prime Minister King on behalf of Ukrainian refugees. See N.A. Robertson to Prime Minister, 12 December 1945, NA, King Papers, series J4, vol. 336, reel H-1523, frame C231874.

18 For an example of the use of this tactic, see travel application submitted by Ukrainian Canadian Committee, 30 October 1945, External Affairs to High Commissioner, 19 February 1946, V.J. Kaye to Citizenship Branch, 23 September 1946, 'A Canadian Relief Mission to Europe for Direct Aid to Ukrainian Refugees, Displaced Persons and Victims of War,' 11 September 1946, B. Panchuk to Director of Citizenship Branch, 27 November 1946, High Commissioner to External Affairs, 13 December 1946, and N.A. Robertson to L.B. Pearson, 7 January 1946 [*sic*; should read 1947], NA, RG 25, vol. 3747, file 6980-GR-40, part 1. See also Robertson to J.W. Arsenych, 1 February 1946, NA, King Papers, series J1, vol. 413, reel C-9176, frames 372862–3.

19 Dirks, *Canada's Refugee Policy*, 72–4, 134, and 137.

20 For an example of the lobbying efforts of an individual company, see C.P. Tuck to C. Hayward, 28 February 1946, Hayward to Tuck, 7 March and 3 December 1946, Tuck to Canadian National Committee on Refugees, 5 December 1946, Hayward to Tuck, 10 December 1946, Canada Cabinets and Furniture Limited to A.L. Jolliffe, 17 June 1947, and Canada Cabinets and Furniture Limited to H.L. Keenleyside, 2 December 1947, NA, Canadian National Committee on Refugees Papers, vol. 5, file 2.

21 Dirks, *Canada's Refugee Policy*, 128, and Iacovetta, *Such Hardworking People*, 24. For examples of corporate lobbying, see British Columbia Interior Vegetable Marketing Board to Prime Minister, 12 January 1946, and Canadian Chamber of Commerce to Prime Minister, 4 September 1946, NA, King Papers, series J2, vol. 428, file I-20, part 1.

22 See report by Standing Committee on Immigration and Labour, undated, NA, A. Roebuck Papers, vol. 4, file 4-1.

23 Abella and Troper, *None Is Too Many*, 228–9.

24 N.A. Robertson to Director of Immigration, 6 February 1946, NA, RG 25, vol. 2084, file AR 16/20.

25 The committee's recommendations can be found in minutes of meeting of Interdepartmental Committee on Immigration Policy held on 4 March 1946, NA, RG 76, vol. 443, file 673931, part 10, reel C-10320; minutes of meeting of Cabinet Committee on Immigration Policy held on 21 March 1946, NA, RG 25, vol. 4165, file 939-B-40, part 1; minutes of meeting of Interdepartmental Committee on Immigration Policy held on 28 March 1946, NA, RG 27, vol. 3041, file 125; report issued by Interdepartmental Committee on Immigration Policy, 4 April 1946, NA, RG 2, vol. 82, file I-50-M, part 1; N.A. Robertson to J.G. Turgeon, 4 April 1946, NA, King Papers, Series J4, vol. 415, file 3996; and minutes of meeting of Interdepartmental Committee on Refugee Policy held on 16 July 1946, NA, RG 25, vol. 4164, file 939-40, part 1.

26 In 1946, 71,719 immigrants were admitted to Canada, a substantial increase over the roughly 23,000 who were admitted the previous year. However, the number of European refugees in this group was negligible. In 1947, immigration actually declined slightly, totalling just over 64,000. Less than 8,000 of them were European refugees. For statistics on postwar immigration to Canada, see W.E. Harris to cabinet, 21 February 1952, NA, RG 2, vol. 212, file C-20-5, and Department of Mines and Resources memorandum, 5 September 1945, NA, RG 25, vol. 4164, file 939-40, part 1. For a year-by-year accounting of the number of European refugees admitted to Canada (and other countries), beginning in 1947, see Louise Holborn, *The International Refugee Organization, A Specialized Agency of the United Nations: Its History and Work, 1946–1952* (London, 1956), 442.

27 On Britain's 'Distressed Relatives Scheme,' see extract from Hansard, 13 November 1945, appended to note by H.W. Emerson, 17 December 1945, NA, RG 25, vol. 2112, file AR 408/1, part 5; Emerson to High Commissioner, 14 January 1946, V. Massey to External Affairs, 21 March 1946, and 'Note on the Operation of the "Distressed Relatives" Scheme,' 20 August 1946, ibid., vol. 2084, file AR 16/20.

28 The amendment can be found in PC 2071, 28 May 1946, NA, RG 2, vol. 1940, file 3434G. See also circular by Canadian Military Mission (Berlin), 17 August 1946, NA, RG 76, vol. 31, file 682, part 5, reel C-4689.

29 PC 2070, 28 May 1946, NA, RG 2, vol. 1940, file 3434G.

30 On the IRO's travel documents, see Holborn, *International Refugee Organization*, 322–3. For a facsimile, see IRO Certificate of Identity, undated, appended to memorandum from O. Cormier to Canadian visa offices, 1 March 1949, NA, RG 76, vol. 902, file 569-22-1, part 1. On the LTD, see J.R. Robillard to A.J. Andrew, 3 August

1951, ibid., vol. 978, file 5420-1-551. Unlike IRO's travel document, which consisted of a long sheet, the Allies' Temporary Travel Document looked like a regular passport. See Temporary Travel Document in lieu of passport, undated, NA, RG 25, vol. 3674, file 5127-D-40, part 1.

31 E. Reid to Director of Immigration, 3 August 1946, NA, RG 76, vol. 31, file 682, part 5, reel C-4689.

32 M. Pope to External Affairs, 28 February 1947, ibid.

33 Canadian Military Mission (Berlin) to External Affairs, 17 July 1946, NA, RG 25, vol. 3673, file 5127-40C, and External Affairs to Canadian Military Mission (Berlin), 5 September 1946, NA, RG 76, vol. 31, file 682, part 5, reel C-4689.

34 Canadian Military Mission (Berlin) to External Affairs, 17 July 1946, and S.M. Scott to External Affairs, 19 August 1946, NA, RG 76, vol. 31, file 682, part 5, reel C-4689.

35 The next major amendment to the regulations was PC 371, 30 January 1947, NA, RG 2, vol. 1963, file 3565G.

36 On the shortage of shipping, see minutes of cabinet meeting held on 28 November 1945, ibid., vol. 2637, reel T-2364, frames 817–18; Canadian Embassy (Athens) to External Affairs, 20 March 1946, NA, RG 25, vol. 3672, file 5127-40C, part 2; note for H. Wrong, 2 October 1946, ibid., vol. 3673, file 5127-40C, part 7; N.A. Robertson to L.B. Pearson, 24 December 1945, ibid., vol. 3798, file 8296-40; High Commissioner to External Affairs, 25 March 1947, Robertson to External Affairs, 19 March 1947, and External Affairs to High Commissioner, 2 May 1947, ibid., vol. 4164, file 939-40, part 2; C.D. Howe to H.L. Keenleyside, 29 August 1947, NA, RG 76, vol. 651, file B29300, part 3, reel C-10589. See also R.G. Robertson to J. McKenna, 22 December 1945, NA, King Papers, series J2, vol. 399, file D-22-E, and G.J. Matte to Mrs P. Foster, 28 May 1946, ibid., vol. 428, file I-20-D.

37 Prior to the Second World War, Canada maintained immigration offices in Rotterdam, Paris, and Antwerp. The office in Holland was closed in 1932, while the French and Belgian offices were shut down following Germany's invasion of Poland in September 1939. See External Affairs to Canadian Embassy (Paris), 7 June 1946, NA, RG 25, vol. 3673, file 5127-40C, part 6. As late as June 1946, Ottawa had not set a deadline for the reopening of Canadian immigration offices in Europe. See A.D.P. Heeney to J.A. Glen, 25 October 1945, NA, RG 2, vol. 63, file C-20-2, part 2; minutes of meeting on immigration matters held on 6 February 1946, NA, Beaudry Papers, vol. 6, file 114; and E. Reid to Director of Immigration, 3 August 1946, NA, RG 76, vol. 31, file 682, part 5, reel C-4689.

38 N.A. Robertson to Lieutenant-General M. Pope, 6 July 1946, NA, RG 25, vol. 3673, file 5127-40C, part 6.

39 Minutes of meeting of Interdepartmental Committee on Immigration Policy held on 9 August 1946, NA, RG 27, vol. 3041, file 125.

40 Dirks, *Canada's Refugee Policy*, 149.

41 It took a long time for the immigration bureaucracy to recover from Depression-era budget cuts. In the interim, other departments vied with Immigration Branch for control over Canada's immigration policy. On the jurisdictional squabbles that characterized the relationship between External Affairs and the Department of Labour, see H.L. Keenleyside to Minister of Mines and Resources, 16 August 1948, NA, H.L. Keenleyside Papers, vol. 19, file Immigration 1938–85; minutes of meeting of Cabinet Committee on Immigration Policy held on 8 December 1947, NA, RG 2, vol. 82, file I-50-M, part 1; J. Colley to 'Colonel Bob,' 15 March 1947, NA, RG 25, vol. 2113, file AR 408/4, part 2; Keenleyside to Minister of Mines and Resources, 18 March 1949, NA, RG 26, vol. 126, file 3-33-12, part 1; Director of Immigration Branch to Deputy Minister of Citizenship and Immigration, 22 November 1952, ibid., vol. 127, file 3-33-13; A. MacNamara to Keenleyside, 23 October 1947, V.C. Phelan to O. Cormier, 8 May 1948, Minister of Labour to C. Gibson, 4 November 1949, NA, RG 27, vol. 276, file 1-26-1-2, part 1; Staff Memorandum No. 3, 3 July 1951, and L. Fortier to A.H. Brown, 19 November 1953, ibid., part 2; Immigration Branch to Deputy Minister of Mines and Resources, 3 February 1948, and Keenleyside to MacNamara, 5 February 1948, NA, RG 76, vol. 652, file B29300, part 6, reel C-10590. On the differing views of External and Immigration, see Colley to 'Colonel Bob,' 15 March 1947, NA, RG 25, vol. 2113, file AR 408/4, part 2; G. Vanier to External Affairs, 27 March 1947, ibid., vol. 3310, file 9323-40, part 1; C.E.S. Smith to Fortier, 12 October 1950, NA, RG 26, vol. 127, file 3-33-13; and Director of Immigration Branch to Deputy Minister of Citizenship and Immigration, 28 November 1950, NA, RG 76, vol. 31, file 682, part 6, reel C-4690.

42 John W. Holmes, *The Shaping of Peace: Canada and the Search for World Order, 1943–1957* (Toronto, 1979), 1: 96.

43 In her report for the Commission of Inquiry on War Criminals, Alti Rodal asserted that racism, not cynicism or an abundance of caution, was the prime motivating factor in the bureaucrats' reluctance to relax Canada's immigration restrictions. See 'Nazi War Criminals,' 106. There is no doubt that, once large-scale immigration was resumed, it was based, at least in part, on ethnic preferences. See Department of Mines and Resources memorandum, 5 September 1945, NA, RG 25, vol. 4164, file 939-40, part 1; L. Fortier to External Affairs, February 1955, NA, RG 6, vol. 129, file 14-7-6; and J.B. Thom to J.S. McGowan, 24 January 1956, NA, RG 30, vol. 8319, file 3133-1. Yet that does not explain why the bureaucrats would have been reluctant to resume immigration in the first place.

44 In reality, two of the immigration bureaucrats were from the West Coast. One was Robertson, who was born there. The other was Hugh L. Keenleyside. Though born in Toronto, Keenleyside grew up in Vancouver, his family having moved there

before his first birthday. See *Memoirs of Hugh L. Keenleyside* (Toronto, 1981), 1: 16 and 40.

45 PC 703, 29 January 1941, NA, RG 32, vol. 1126, file N.A. Robertson, part 1.

46 Though Robertson's appointment as high commissioner did not formally take effect until 17 September 1946, he had in fact been functioning in that capacity since late August. See PC 3732, 4 September 1946, ibid.

47 On Robertson's career at External Affairs and in the Privy Council Office, see J.L. Granatstein, *A Man of Influence: Norman A. Robertson and Canadian Statecraft, 1929–68* (Toronto, 1981), passim.

48 See the assessment of Robertson's views in Maurice Pope diary, entry for 30 October 1945, NA, M. Pope Papers, vol. 2, file 1945, and Granatstein, *Man of Influence*, 272–3 n.

49 Robertson's concerns over the direction in which Canada's immigration policy seemed to be heading can be found in Dominion Affairs to External Affairs, 23 January 1947, NA, RG 25, vol. 2113, file AR 408/5, and N.A. Robertson to L.B. Pearson, 26 January 1948, ibid., vol. 2105, file AR 405/1/4/27, part 3.

50 Granatstein, *Man of Influence*, 82–6, 158–67, and 180.

51 On Keenleyside's career at External Affairs, see his curriculum vitae, undated, External Affairs to Governor General in Council, 8 November 1944, and notice issued by Canadian Information Service, 12 September 1946, NA, RG 32, vol. 822, file H.L. Keenleyside, parts 1 and 2.

52 PC 174, 14 January 1947, NA, King Papers, series J1, vol. 425, reel C-11038, frame 386196.

53 Abella and Troper, *None Is Too Many*, 240.

54 Keenleyside's participation in the Committee on Orientals in British Columbia is noted in his curriculum vitae, undated, NA, RG 32, vol. 822, file H.L. Keenleyside, part 1. On his attempts to moderate government policy toward the Japanese, see Granatstein, *Man of Influence*, 103, 158, 159 n., and 167, and Patricia E. Roy, J.L. Granatstein, Masako Iino; and Hiroko Takamura, *Mutual Hostages: Canadians and Japanese during the Second World War* (Toronto, 1990), 43–4 and 81–3.

55 H.L. Keenleyside to L. Beaudry, 15 May 1947, NA, King Papers, series J1, vol. 425, reel C-11038, frames 386210–11.

56 For Keenleyside's tough stand on enemy aliens, see H.L. Keenleyside to F.P. Varcoe, 29 May 1947, Keenleyside to C. Gibson, 31 May 1947, Keenleyside to L.B. Pearson, 23 June 1947, Varcoe to Deputy Minister of Mines and Resources, 3 June 1947, Keenleyside to Varcoe, 27 October 1947, and Varcoe to Deputy Minister of Mines and Resources, 30 October 1947, NA, RG 26, vol. 151, file 3-32-11.

57 L. Fortier to Director of Immigration, 31 December 1948, NA, RG 76, vol. 443, file 673931, part 19, reel C-10321. Keenleyside's advice was heeded. See minutes of

cabinet meeting held on 29 September 1948, NA, RG 2, vol. 2642, reel T-2365, frames 1755–60.

58 See H.L. Keenleyside to External Affairs, 11 August 1949, NA, RG 25, vol. 3674, file 5127-C-40, part 2; Keenleyside to R.W. Mayhew, 2 September 1948, and memorandum by Keenleyside, 4 November 1949, NA, RG 26, vol. 126, file 3-33-10, parts 1 and 2; Keenleyside to A. MacNamara, 15 July 1949, NA, RG 27, vol. 287, file 1-26-38, part 3.

59 See H.L. Keenleyside to Minister of Mines and Resources, 7 April 1949, NA, RG 2, vol. 166, file I-50-10.

60 In his administrative diary, General Pope expressed admiration for Robertson's attitude toward Europe's refugees, describing it as 'tolerant and humane.' His own views on the subject were coloured by a personal bias against Immigration Branch. 'These damned Immigration people,' he wrote in the autumn of 1945, had raised objections to the admission of his foreign-born wife and eldest son. See Maurice Pope diary, entry for 30 October 1945, NA, Pope Papers, vol. 2, file 1945.

61 On Pope's role in drafting the Defence of Canada Regulations, see J.L. Granatstein, *The Generals: The Canadian Army's Senior Commanders in the Second World War* (Toronto, 1993), 211–12; *Soldiers and Politicians: The Memoirs of Lt.-Gen. Maurice A. Pope* (Toronto, 1962), 129; and handwritten notes by G.R.B. Panchuk, 1947, AO, G.R.B. Panchuk Papers, series C, box 15, correspondence file January–March 1947.

62 S.M. Scott to E.H. Coleman, 10 June 1942, NA, RG 32, vol. 472, file S.M. Scott, part 1.

63 On Jolliffe's career, see ibid., vol. 139, file A.L. Jolliffe, parts 1 and 2.

64 On Blair, see Abella and Troper, *None Is Too Many*, 7–10 and passim.

65 A.L. Jolliffe to Colonel W.W. Murray, 4 July 1946, NA, RG 32, vol. 139, file A.L. Jolliffe, part 2.

66 On Smith's career, see ibid., vol. 635, file C.E.S. Smith, parts 1 and 2.

67 On Fortier's career, see 'The National Advisory Council on Manpower,' February 1951, NA, RG 27, vol. 679, file 30-2-3-1, and J-4 Unit to Civil Service Commission, 18 February 1950, NA, RG 32, vol. 813, file L. Fortier.

68 On Benoit's career, see NA, RG 32, vol. 1111, file G.R. Benoit, and Benoit, to Director of Immigration Branch, 13 September 1951, NA, RG 76, vol. 800, file 547-1, part 2.

69 Minutes of meeting of Interdepartmental Committee on Immigration Policy held on 9 August 1946, NA, RG 27, vol. 3041, file 125.

70 On Cormier and Bird, see NA, RG 32, vol. 601, file O. Cormier, parts 1–3, and vol. 419, file P.W. Bird, parts 1 and 2. Cormier's reputation for toughness could be a double-edged sword. During his posting in Lisbon, Portugal, in 1943–4, what some historians have referred to as his 'fetish for detail' effectively prevented all but a

handful of Jewish refugees from admission to Canada. On Cormier's treatment of the refugees, see Abella and Troper, *None Is Too Many*, 157 and 164–8.

71 A summary of events from the time of Gouzenko's defection can be found in J.L. Granatstein and Robert Bothwell, eds., *The Gouzenko Transcripts: The Evidence Presented to the Kellock–Taschereau Royal Commission of 1946* (Toronto, 1982), 1–11.

72 J.L. Granatstein and David Stafford, *Spy Wars: Espionage and Canada from Gouzenko to Glasnost* (Toronto, 1990), 63.

73 On the genesis of the government's new security advisory panel, see Acting Lieutenant-Commander J.W.C. Barclay to Cabinet Defence Committee, 4 May 1946, NA, RG 2, vol. 103, file S-100-D; E.W.T. Gill to Halliday, 20 May 1946, and A.D.P. Heeney to Air Marshal R. Leckie, 23 May 1946, ibid., vol. 63, file C-20-2, part 1; minutes of cabinet meeting held on 22 May 1946, ibid., vol. 2638, reel T-2364, frames 1233 and 1238; and Acting Director of Immigration to Deputy Minister of Citizenship and Immigration, 25 November 1963, NA, RG 26, vol. 164, file 3-18-17, part 2. See also Granatstein and Bothwell, *Gouzenko*, 18–19, and Granatstein, *Man of Influence*, 157.

74 Granatstein, *Man of Influence*, 181.

75 Memorandum on visa control, 9 April 1946, NA, RG 25, vol. 4164, file 939-40, part 1, and minutes of meeting held in the East Block, Room 123, on 26 April 1946, ibid., vol. 5788, file 233(s), part 2.

76 The genesis of the decision can be found in minutes of Security Panel meetings held on 24 June, 8 July, and 19 August 1946, NA, RG 2, vol. 251, file S-100-M; Annex 'A,' undated, appended to memorandum from Lieutenant-Colonel J.A.K. Rutherford to Security Panel, 30 March 1948, ibid., file S-100-D, Security Panel Document SP-24; J.A. Glen to cabinet, 15 October 1946, ibid., vol. 83, file I-50-2; A.D.P. Heeney to N.A. Robertson, undated, ibid.; minutes of cabinet meeting held on 29 October 1946, ibid., vol. 2639, reel T-2364, frames 1700–2; memorandum by A.L. Jolliffe, 5 July 1946, NA, RG 76, vol. 957, file SF-S-1, part 1; and Security Panel to Glen, 23 August 1946, ibid., vol. 800, file 547-1, part 1.

77 Commissioner S.T. Wood to Staff Sergeant W.W. Hinton, 23 October 1946, NA, RG 76, vol. 800, file 547-1, part 1.

78 Alti Rodal took this position in her report for the Deschenes Commission of Inquiry on War Criminals. In the wake of the Gouzenko affair, according to Rodal, 'concern about the possibility that Nazis and Nazi sympathizers might enter Canada was soon overtaken by apprehension about the possible infiltration of Communist agents.' See 'Nazi War Criminals,' 177.

79 For example, Canada cooperated with U.S. efforts to exclude from the western hemisphere Germans deemed 'obnoxious' or 'dangerous to ... security' by virtue of their having adhered to an enemy government or to the principles thereof during the

war. As part of this cooperation, Canadian immigration authorities and the RCMP were supplied with a list of 'dangerous enemy aliens' compiled in Washington. See W.J. Gallman to O.C. Harvey, 26 June 1946, J.M. Troutbeck to Gallman, 30 August 1946, S.A. Goulborn to P.T. Molson, 9 September 1946, Molson to External Affairs, 23 September 1946, minute by H.R. Horne, 25 September 1946, Molson to External Affairs, 25 September 1946, and External Affairs to High Commissioner, 8 October 1946, NA, RG 25, vol. 2087, file AR 22/13.

80 PC 2653, 14 September 1939, NA, Beaudry Papers, vol. 6, file 114.

81 PC 3547, 21 May 1941, NA, RG 2, vol. 1717, file 2342G.

82 Memorandum from Commissioner of Immigration to F. Blair, 15 March 1941, NA, RG 32, vol. 601, file O. Cormier, part 3.

83 Minutes of cabinet meeting held on 17 October 1945, NA, RG 2, vol. 2637, reel T-2364, frame 728.

84 PC 1373, 9 April 1946, ibid., vol. 1934, file 3411G.

85 Within a year, cabinet conceded that the 'opposition to an enemy government' clause in PC 1373 had actually perpetuated the ban on enemy aliens. See J.D. McFarlane to Immigration Inspector-in-Charge (Toronto), 25 April 1947, NA, RG 76, vol. 811, file 551-1, part 3, and memorandum for Council, 21 May 1947, NA, L.S. St Laurent Papers, vol. 225, file I-17. The reader should note that this view differs sharply from that of Alti Rodal, who implied that PC 1373 made it easier for enemy aliens to gain admission to Canada. See 'Nazi War Criminals,' 176. On this point, Rodal's analysis is untenable. The 'opposition to an enemy government' requirement severely limited the number of so-called enemy aliens who would have been admissible. After all, the only people in a position to prove their opposition to Nazi rule would have those who had suffered punishment as a result, such as political prisoners or concentration camp inmates. Jews also might have been able to argue that their treatment as pariahs during the era of the Third Reich had automatically rendered them opponents of the Nazi regime. It is difficult to imagine any other categories of opponents who could have either made or proven such claims.

86 For the problems encountered by Germans in this regard and the strictness with which Canadian immigration officials applied the enemy-alien provision, see M. Pope to External Affairs, 30 December 1946, NA, RG 25, vol. 3673, file 5127-40C, part 8; H.L. Keenleyside to S. Garson, 1 February 1949, and Deputy Minister of Mines and Resources to C. Gibson, 8 August 1949, NA, RG 26, vol. 151, file 3-32-11.

87 A.L. Jolliffe to External Affairs, 14 August 1946, NA, RG 76, vol. 31, file 682, part 5, reel C-4689.

88 Immigration Act, R.S. 1927, Section 3, pp. 2069–71, and Section 41, pp. 2084–5.

89 On the problems with implementing the Allies' early denazification efforts, see Tom Bower, *Blind Eye to Murder: Britain, America and the Purging of Nazi Germany – A Pledge Betrayed* (London, 1981), 161–3.

90 For a facsimile of the questionnaire used in the British zone of occupation, see Military Government of Germany Fragebogen, undated [revised 1 January 1946], NA, R. Funke Papers, vol. 2, file 48.

91 See Allied Control Council Directive No. 24, 12 January 1946, in *Documents on Germany under Occupation, 1945–54*, ed. Beate Ruhm von Oppen (London, 1955), 102–7.

92 Minutes of meeting on immigration matters held on 6 February 1946, NA, Beaudry Papers, vol. 6, file 114.

93 Biographical information on Jesionek and a summary of the assistance he rendered to Canadian war crimes prosecutors can be found in Howard Margolian, *Conduct Unbecoming: The Story of the Murder of Canadian Prisoners of War in Normandy* (Toronto, 1998), 146–50 and 163–4.

94 J.W. Holmes to G.G. Congdon, 8 January 1946, NA, RG 25, vol. 2090, file AR 25/3, part 1.

95 Lieutenant-Colonel B.J.S. Macdonald to High Commissioner, 24 January 1946, NA, RG 24, vol. 12839, file 67/Kurt Meyer/2/2.

96 On the rejection of Jesionek's application, see G.G. Congdon to J.W. Holmes, 23 January 1946, NA, RG 25, vol. 2090, file AR 25/3, part 1, and Holmes to Lieutenant-Colonel B.J.S. Macdonald, 30 January 1946, NA, RG 24, vol. 12839, file 67/Kurt Meyer/2/2. The idea of admitting Jesionek temporarily as a non-immigrant, with his application for permanent admission to be reviewed later, was based on waivers that were being granted to Polish nationals with relatives in Canada. See External Affairs to High Commissioner, 17 September 1945, NA, RG 25, vol. 2090, file AR 25/3, part 1, and External Affairs memorandum, 18 September 1945, NA, Beaudry Papers, vol. 6, file 114.

97 G.G. Crean to E.W.T. Gill, 23 July 1946, NA, RG 2, vol. 249, file I-50.

98 On the interdepartmental debate over the proposed amendment, see External Affairs note, 26 June 1946, NA, RG 76, vol. 957, file SF-S-1, part 1; R.G. Robertson to P. Martin, ibid., vol. 811, file 551-1, part 2; minutes of cabinet meeting held on 5 August 1946, NA, RG 2, vol. 2638, reel T-2364, frame 1475; J.R. Baldwin to J.A. Glen, 6 August 1946, NA, RG 26, vol. 100, file 3-18-1, part 1; minutes of Security Panel meeting held on 19 August 1946, NA, RG 2, vol. 251, file S-100-M; and Annex 'A,' undated, appended to memorandum from Lieutenant-Colonel J.A.K. Rutherford to Security Panel, 30 March 1948, ibid., file S-100-D, Security Panel Document SP-24. A similar amendment was proposed two years later. It too was rejected, this time on legal grounds. See minutes of cabinet meeting held on 19 February 1948, ibid., vol. 2641, reel T-2365, frames 1150–1, and Commissioner

S.T. Wood to A. MacNamara, 23 February 1948, NA, R.G. Robertson Papers, vol. 1, file 6.

99 Security Panel to J.A. Glen, 23 August 1946, NA, RG 76, vol. 800, file 547-1, part 1, and A.D.P. Heeney to N.A. Robertson, undated, NA, RG 2, vol. 83, file I-50-2.

100 See minutes of cabinet meeting held on 29 October 1946, NA, RG 2, vol. 2639, reel T-2364, frames 1700–2.

101 Critics of Canada's postwar system of immigration screening have suggested that the failure to include an explicit ban in the Immigration Act made it easier for Nazi war criminals and collaborators to gain admission to Canada. In her study for the Deschenes Commission of Inquiry on War Criminals, Alti Rodal suggested the absence of such a ban was harmful, noting that it 'permitted considerable flexibility in changing, re-interpreting and in using wide discretion in applying criteria in individual cases in the following years.' See 'Nazi War Criminals,' 179. The attorney David Matas took the argument a step farther, suggesting that categories such as 'enemy aliens,' 'Nazis,' and 'members of the German military' were poor substitutes for a ban on war criminals and collaborators. See Matas, *Justice Delayed: Nazi War Criminals in Canada* (Toronto, 1987), 26. In my view, neither argument can be sustained. The flexibility offered by 'departmental administrative action' need not, as Rodal implied, have facilitated the entry of ex-Nazis into Canada. It could just as easily have led to more stringency in screening for war criminal or collaborationist background. That certainly was what occurred when the RCMP began screening prospective immigrants of German nationality. See Deputy Minister of Mines and Resources to C. Gibson, 8 August 1949, NA, RG 26, vol. 151, file 3-32-11. As we shall see, such stringency was true for RCMP screening generally. As for Matas's contention, it misses the point completely. If a prospective immigrant were going to lie about his activities during the Second World War, the precise wording of the Immigration Act would have no bearing on the ability of Canadian immigration authorities to detect the lie. Indeed, a specific term like 'war criminal' might be easier to evade than one or more general categories like 'Nazi,' 'Fascist,' 'member of the SS,' or 'concentration camp guard,' all of which, presumably, would leave the visa seeker with less room to obfuscate. Better still would have been a simple requirement to divulge all wartime activities. The duty of candour implied in a general instruction such as 'recount your activities during the period 1939–45' would have been much higher than in the more subjective 'war criminal' or 'collaborator' categories.

102 'The Nazi Party, Its Formations and Affiliated Organizations,' undated [summer 1946], appended to letter from Superintendent L.H. Nicholson to A.L. Jolliffe, 25 July 1946, NA, RG 76, vol. 800, file 547-1, part 1. In informing Staff Sergeant W.W. Hinton of his duties, RCMP Commissioner S.T. Wood ordered that 'in deciding what factors render a potential immigrant undesirable you will be guided

by the verbal instructions given at this headquarters.' See Wood to Hinton, 23 October 1946, ibid. No record of these instructions has been found. However, it is possible to make certain inferences as to their content. From the outset of their immigration-screening operations, the RCMP conducted checks at the Document Centre in Berlin (BDC, now called the Bundesarchiv-Aussenstelle Zehlendorf), the repository of an enormous amount of Nazi-era documentation, including records of membership in the Nazi Party and affiliated organizations. On the RCMP's early use of the BDC, see R. Innes to Brigadier M. Lush, 24 February 1947, NA, RG 25, vol. 2113, file AR 408/4, part 1.

103 See E. Reid to H. Wrong, 2 October 1946, NA, RG 25, vol. 3673, file 5127-40C, part 7. It was not until late in 1947 that a permanent Canadian immigration mission was set up in Germany. On the reasons for the delay, see Commissioner of Immigration to A.L. Jolliffe, 27 June 1947, NA, RG 76, vol. 31, file 682, part 5, reel C-4690; Maurice Pope diary, entry for 24 July 1947, NA, Pope Papers, vol. 2 file 1947; Jolliffe to H.L. Keenleyside, 24 July 1947, NA, RG 27, vol. 3029, file Interdepartmental Committee on Immigration-Labour Correspondence; report to Keenleyside, 24 July 1947, and External Affairs to High Commissioner, 20 August 1947, NA, RG 25, vol. 2113, file AR 408/4, part 2; 'Entry to Canada of Persons Now Residing in Germany and Austria,' 17 September 1947, ibid., vol. 3673, file 5127-40C, part 10; G.D. Mallory to J.H. Warren, 22 December 1947, ibid., vol. 3896, file 9294-R-40, part 1; memorandum by J.A. MacKinnon, 8 August 1947, NA, RG 2, vol. 66, file C-20-5, document nos 416–520; and minutes of cabinet meeting held on 14 August 1947, ibid., vol. 2640, reel T-2365, frames 735 and 742.

3: Test Cases

1 External Affairs to High Commissioner, 19 October 1946, NA, RG 25, vol. 2113, file AR 408/4, part 1, and minutes of cabinet meetings held on 15 and 29 October 1946, NA, RG 2, vol. 2639, reel T-2364, frames 1674–5 and 1700–2.

2 IGCR memorandum, 11 April 1947, NA, RG 76, vol. 443, file 673931, part 13, reel C-10320.

3 External Affairs to High Commissioner, 19 October 1946, and 'Text of an Announcement Made by the Prime Minister of Canada,' 7 November 1946, NA, RG 25, vol. 2113, file AR 408/4, part 1.

4 'Mennonites in Germany,' 26 November 1946, and Canadian Military Mission (Berlin) to P.T. Molson, 27 November 1946, ibid.

5 Maurice Pope diary, entry for 17 May 1946, NA, M. Pope Papers, vol. 2, file 1946, and A.L. Jolliffe to External Affairs, 20 July 1946, NA, RG 25, vol. 3673, file 5127-40C, part 6.

6 'Mennonites in Germany,' 26 November 1946, NA, RG 25, vol. 2113, file AR 408/ 4, part 1.

7 S.M. Scott to External Affairs, 30 December 1946, NA, RG 2, vol. 83, file I-50-2.

8 This is conceded in the definitive history of the Mennonites in Canada. See T.D. Regehr, *Mennonites in Canada, 1939–1970: A People Transformed*, vol. 3 of *Mennonites in Canada* (Toronto, 1996), 90. See also Regehr, 'Of Dutch or German Ancestry? Mennonite Refugees, MCC, and the International Refugee Organization,' *Journal of Mennonite Studies* (1995): 14–15.

9 Valdis O. Lumans, *Himmler's Auxiliaries: The Volksdeutsche Mittelstelle and the German National Minorities of Europe, 1933–1945* (Chapel Hill, NC, 1993), 186.

10 Canadian Military Mission (Berlin) to P.T. Molson, 6 December 1946, NA, RG 25, vol. 2113, file AR 408/4, part 1.

11 On the strict criteria applied to the first close relatives movement, see S.M. Scott to External Affairs, 30 December 1946, NA, RG 2, vol. 83, file I-50-2, and R.G. Riddell to N.A. Robertson, 2 April 1947, NA, RG 25, vol. 3913, file 9408-40, part 1. Of the 725 refugees who constituted the first close relatives movement, only five were Mennonites. See 'Statistical Breakdown of First Movement by USAT *General Stewart*, 24th July 1947,' appended to letter from K.J.W. Lane to J.P. Sigvaldason, 30 August 1947, ibid., vol. 2113, file AR 408/4, part 2.

12 The following description of the arrival of the 2,900 Polish immigrants was pieced together from Lieutenant-Colonel W.J. McLaughlin to Department of Labour, RCMP, Adjutant-General's Office, and other agencies, 16 October 1946, NA, RG 27, vol. 3032, file 7, and memorandum by McLaughlin, 21 October 1946, ibid., file 18; draft order for the movement of Polish veterans from the United Kingdom to Canada, 30 October 1946, ibid., vol. 626, file 23-7-2-1, part 1; and Immigration Branch Inspector in Charge to Atlantic District Superintendent, 27 November 1946, NA, RG 76, vol. 649, file A85451, part 2, reel C-10588.

13 The following sketch of the history of the Polish 2nd Corps was drawn from Lt-General W. Anders, *An Army in Exile: The Story of the Second Polish Corps*, reprint ed. (Nashville, TN, 1981), passim.

14 For a summary of the diplomatic manoeuvring involving Britain, the Soviet Union, and the Polish government-in-exile that led to this decision, see Richard C. Lukas, *The Forgotten Holocaust: The Poles under German Occupation, 1939–1944* (Lexington, KY, 1986), 45–6.

15 On the reasons for Moscow's change of heart, see ibid., 131–3.

16 Anders, *Army in Exile*, 181.

17 The estimate of the 2nd Corps' strength is contained in dispatch from F. Hudd to External Affairs, 20 June 1946, NA, RG 25, vol. 2089, file AR 25/1, part 5.

18 When it became known that members of the Polish 2nd Corps would be granted admission to Canada, some groups protested, alleging that Anders and many of his

soldiers were of fascist political orientation, if not outright Nazi collaborators. See *Edmonton Journal*, 24 August 1946, P.A. Gardner to Mackenzie King, 1 September 1946, and A. Johnson to Prime Minister King, 20 November 1946, NA, RG 76, vol. 648, file A85451, part 1, reel C-10587. See also the telegrams in NA, W.L.M. King Papers, series J2, vol. 429, file I-50-2, part 2. Though such charges were based less on solid evidence than on a dislike for Anders's politics (see V. Massey to External Affairs, 1 February 1946, NA, RG 25, vol. 2089, file AR 25/1, part 5), they ought to have been taken seriously. According to a former U.S. Nazi-hunter who had connections within the American intelligence community, Byelorussian collaborators managed to infiltrate the ranks of the Polish 2nd Corps during the final weeks of the war. See John Loftus, *The Belarus Secret: The Nazi Connection in America* (New York, 1982), 41–50. See also Loftus and Mark Aarons, *Ratlines: How the Vatican's Nazi Networks Betrayed Western Intelligence to the Soviets* (London, 1991), 204. Parenthetically, it is strange that Alti Rodal, who was highly critical of the Canadian government for its alleged carelessness in screening immigrants for war criminal or collaborationist background, would have missed the Anders–Byelorussian connection. After all, Loftus's book on Byelorussian collaborators had been published a few years prior to the release of her report. Indeed, she cited it in a note on the admission to Canada of alleged Byelorussian collaborators. On her failure to take account of the Anders–Byelorussian connection and its implications for the admission to Canada of suspected collaborators, see 'Nazi War Criminals in Canada: The Historical and Policy Setting from the 1940s to the Present' (Commission of Inquiry on War Criminals, Ottawa, 1986), 142–3. On evidence that the report's author was acquainted with Loftus's book, see ibid., 441 and 551 n.70.

19 On the growth of the guerrilla threat in Byelorussia and its persistence, even in the face of massive German anti-partisan operations, see Alexander Dallin, *German Rule in Russia 1941–45: A Study of Occupation Policies*, reprint ed. (New York, 1980), 209–10; report prepared by Commander of (German) Armed Forces East, 12 July 1942, ZSt, miscellaneous collection, file 70; and Commander of Security Police in Latvia to heads of departments and other subordinate agencies, 2 April 1943, SRA-Vitebsk, collection 2831, shelflist 1, file 1.

20 The Führer had expressed this view to his generals prior to the invasion of the Soviet Union. See war diary of High Command of (German) Armed Forces, entry for 3 March 1941, *Kriegstagebuch des Oberkommandos der Wehrmacht (Wehrmachtsführungstab)*, ed. Percy Ernst Schramm, vol. I/1 (Munich, 1982), 341.

21 See Reich Leader of SS and Police to SS Main Office, 7 October 1941, NARA, RG 242, series T-580, reel 7, no frame numbers, and 'Applications by Ukrainians and Balts to Join the German Armed Forces,' 23 February 1942, ibid., series T-175, reel 99, frame 7131517.

22 On the evolution of German policy toward approval of the idea of a Byelorussian home-defence force, see Loftus, *The Belarus Secret*, 32–3. On the force's subordination to the SS and German police, see orders issued by Byelorussian Central Council, undated [1944], BNA, collection 383, shelflist 1, file 2.

23 On the planned mobilization of Byelorussian manpower, see Higher SS and Police Leader for Russia-Centre and Byelorussia to subordinate units and agencies, 23 February 1944, NARA, RG 242, series T-175, reel 7, no frame number, and Byelorussian Central Council to SS Main Office, 30 October 1944, BNA, collection 383, shelflist 1, file 2/2. On the integration of officers and NCOs from the Byelorussian OD, see Loftus, *The Belarus Secret*, 34–6.

24 For references to the participation of the OD in the Holocaust in Byelorussia, see (Security Police) Event Report No. 70, 1 September 1941, NARA, RG 242, series T-175, reel 233, frames 2722148–53. For estimates both of the prewar Jewish population in Byelorussia and of the number of Jews annihilated there during the German occupation, see Raul Hilberg, *The Destruction of the European Jews*, rev. ed. (New York, 1985), 1: 291, and Lucy S. Dawidowicz, *The War against the Jews, 1933–1945* (New York, 1981), 544.

25 Eight different auxiliary police units, four of them Ukrainian, three Byelorussian, and one Cossack, formed the nucleus of the 30th SS Division. See Hans-Joachim Neufeldt, Jürgen Huck, and Georg Tessin, *Zur Geschichte der Ordnungspolizei, 1936–1945*, part 2 of *Die Stäbe und Truppeneinheiten der Ordnungspolizei* (Koblenz, 1957), 104–5.

26 Loftus, *The Belarus Secret*, 39–40, and Samuel W. Mitcham, *Hitler's Legions: The German Army Order of Battle, World War II* (London, 1985), 467.

27 Reich Leader of SS and Police to Byelorussian Central Council, undated [1945], BNA, collection 383, shelflist 1, file 11a.

28 On the establishment and brief combat career of the Byelorussian SS brigade, see Notice No. 431, 15 January 1945, *Verordnungsblatt der Waffen-SS*, VI/2, NARA, RG 242, series T-611, reel 6, no frame number, and Loftus, *The Belarus Secret*, 41.

29 Anders, *Army in Exile*, 276–9 and 288–9.

30 Loftus, *The Belarus Secret*, 41–50.

31 D.V. Le Pan to External Affairs, 8 June 1945, NA, RG 25, vol. 3672, file 5127-40, part 1; J.W. Holmes to External Affairs, 25 October 1945, 'Memorandum on the Present State of Anglo-Polish Relations,' undated, ibid., vol. 2089, file AR 25/1, part 4, and Dominion Affairs to External Affairs, 19 March 1946, ibid., vol. 5756, file 58(s).

32 J.W. Holmes to External Affairs, 25 October 1945, and 'Memorandum on the Present State of Anglo-Polish Relations,' undated, ibid., vol. 2089, file AR 25/1, part 4.

33 Dominion Affairs to External Affairs, 20 December 1945, and Dominion Affairs to External Affairs, 26 February 1946, ibid., vol. 5756, file 58-F(s).

34 'The Polish Emigration,' undated [1954], ibid., vol. 8378, file 1019-40, part 2.2.

35 According to General Anders, only 14,200 out of the 2nd Corps' 112,000 men volunteered for repatriation. See Anders, *Army in Exile*, 287.

36 On London's request for assistance in resettling the Poles and the tepid international response, see Dominion Affairs to External Affairs, 19 March 1946, NA, RG 25, vol. 5756, file 58-F(s); High Commissioner to External Affairs, 24 April 1946, ibid., vol. 3672, file 5127-40C, part 2; and High Commissioner to External Affairs, 4 May 1946, ibid., vol. 2089, file AR 25/1, part 5. See also Dominions Office note, 16 March 1946, and letter from D.G. Brock to H.H. Eggers, 23 March 1946, NA, Dominions Office and Commonwealth Relations Office Records, vol. 1207, file WF 307/127, reel B-5240.

37 On the Polish Resettlement Corps, see 'The Polish Emigration,' undated [1954], NA, RG 25, vol. 8378, file 1019-40, part 2.2; copy of Hansard, 22 May 1946, ibid., vol. 5756, file 58-F(s); and Keith Sword, 'The Absorption of Poles into Civilian Employment in Britain, 1945–50,' in *Refugees in the Age of Total War*, ed. Anna C. Bramwell (London, 1988), 236–50.

38 For example, see R.G. Robertson to Peter Kruk, 2 August 1945, NA, King Papers, series J2, vol. 399, file D-22-6; Bernice Bukowska to Mackenzie King, 1 September 1945 and 28 February 1946, ibid., vol. 429, file I-20-2, part 2; and G.J. Matte to John Bailey, 23 May 1946, ibid. See also D.V. Le Pan to External Affairs, 12 August 1946, ibid., series J1, vol. 405, reel C-9171, frame 366265.

39 On this exception to the immigration regulations, see External Affairs memorandum, 18 September 1945, NA, L. Beaudry Papers, vol. 6, file 114.

40 Minutes of meeting of Interdepartmental Committee on Immigration Policy held on 26 March 1946, and R.F. Clarke to B.G. Sullivan, 27 March 1946, NA, RG 27, vol. 3041, file 125.

41 A.D.P. Heeney to Vice-Admiral J.C. Jones, 21 December 1945, NA, RG 2, vol. 63, file C-20-2, part 2.

42 For example, see E. Poole to the Prime Minister, 12 January 1946, NA, King Papers, series J2, vol. 428, file I-20, part 1, and S. Graham to A.L. Jolliffe, 8 February 1946, NA, RG 27, vol. 3041, file 125.

43 A.D.P. Heeney to J.A. Glen, 21 December 1945, NA, RG 2, vol. 63, file C-20-2, part 2.

44 A.D.P. Heeney to N.A. Robertson, 15 February 1946, ibid., and External Affairs to cabinet, 6 February 1946, ibid., vol. 65, file C-20-5, document nos 134–229.

45 A.D.P. Heeney to N.A. Robertson, 6 April 1946, ibid., vol. 63, file C-20-2, part 2.

46 N.A. Robertson to Prime Minister, 9 May 1946, NA, RG 25, vol. 3401, 621-PF-40C, part 1.

47 External Affairs to Minister of Labour, 14 May 1946, ibid.

48 'Replacement of Prisoners of War by Demobilized Polish Soldiers,' 24 May 1946,
   ibid., and A.D.P. Heeney to H. Mitchell, 23 May 1946, NA, RG 2, vol. 63, file C-
   20-2, part 2.
49 On the respective 'suitability' and security concerns of the two departments, see
   A.L. Jolliffe to file, 24 May 1946, and Deputy Minister of Labour and Director of
   Immigration to Messrs H. Mitchell and J.A. Glen, 24 May 1946, NA, RG 27, vol.
   626, file 23-7-2-1, part 1. See also External Affairs to High Commissioner, 31 May
   1946, NA, RG 76, vol. 648, file A85451, part 1, reel C-10587.
50 A.D.P. Heeney to H. Wrong, 30 May 1946, NA, RG 2, vol. 63, file C-20-2, part 2,
   and External Affairs to High Commissioner, 1 June 1946, NA, RG 25, vol. 3401,
   file 621-PF-40C, part 1.
51 High Commissioner to External Affairs, 24 May 1946, NA, RG 25, vol. 3401, file
   621-PF-40C, part 1.
52 High Commissioner to External Affairs, 12 November 1946, ibid., vol. 2084, file
   AR 16/20.
53 High Commissioner to External Affairs, 5 June 1946, ibid., vol. 2090, file AR 25/3,
   part 1.
54 High Commissioner to External Affairs, 4 May and 10 July 1946, ibid., vol. 3673,
   file 5127-40C, part 6.
55 Dominion Affairs to External Affairs, 5 June 1946, NA, King Papers, series J1, vol.
   413, reel C-9176, frame 372936.
56 Several individuals were expelled for these reasons. For examples, see External
   Affairs to Minister of Mines and Resources, 11 February 1949, and External
   Affairs to Department of Citizenship and Immigration, 15 May 1952, NA, RG 76,
   vol. 750, file 514-15, part 1.
57 On the elements of the plan to bring the demobilized Polish soldiers to Canada, see
   External Affairs to High Commissioner, 1 June 1946, minutes of meeting of Interdepartmental Committee regarding Polish soldiers who are or will be demobilized
   held on 18 June 1946, High Commissioner to External Affairs, 10 July 1946, memorandum for R.G. Riddell, 11 July 1946, agenda for meeting of Interdepartmental
   Committee regarding Polish soldiers who are or will be demobilized, 12 July 1946,
   minutes of meeting of Interdepartmental Committee regarding Polish soldiers who
   are or will be demobilized held on 12 July 1946, and note regarding meeting held at
   the Dominions Office on 10 July 1946, NA, RG 25, vol. 3401, file 621-PF-40C,
   part 1. See also Minister of Labour to Colonel R. Kennedy, 24 July 1946, NA, RG
   27, vol. 3032, file 19.
58 For the announcement of Ranger's appointment, see A.D.P. Heeney to H. Mitchell,
   30 May 1946, NA, RG 2, vol. 63, file C-20-2, part 2. On Ranger's career, both in
   and out of government, see 'The National Advisory Council on Manpower,' February 1951, NA, RG 27, vol. 679, file 30-2-3-1.

59 Note on meeting of Interdepartmental Committee regarding the admission to Canada of Polish veterans held on 12 July 1946, NA, RG 25, vol. 3401, file 621-PF-40C, part 1.

60 On the various appointments, see Deputy Minister of Labour to External Affairs, 6 August 1946, External Affairs to High Commissioner, 9 August 1946, and Department of Labour News Release, 17 August 1946, ibid. See also Acting Minister of Labour to A.D.P. Heeney, 12 December 1946, NA, RG 27, vol. 3033, file 27, and A. MacNamara to A.L. Jolliffe, 6 August 1946, NA, RG 76, vol. 648, file A85451, part 1, reel C-10587.

61 See Deputy Minister of Labour and Director of Immigration to H. Mitchell and J.A. Glen, 24 May 1946, NA, RG 27, vol. 626, file 23-7-2-1, part 1. An official with Canada's High Commission in London noted that the only way not to arouse public opposition to the 2nd Corps movement was to ensure that it was 'hedged with safeguards.' See memorandum by D.V. Le Pan, undated [July 1946], NA, RG 25, vol. 2090, file AR 25/3, part 1.

62 The quoted passage is from PC 3112, 23 July 1946, NA, RG 25, vol. 3401, file 621-PF-40C, part 1.

63 On the various security arrangements, see A. MacNamara to N.A. Robertson, 24 July 1946, External Affairs to High Commissioner, 29 July 1946, High Commissioner to External Affairs, 31 July 1946, and minutes of meeting held at Canada House on 19 August 1946, ibid. See also minutes of meeting held at Dominions Office on 10 July 1946, ibid., vol. 2090, file AR 25/3, part 1, and Canmilitary to Defensor, 3 August 1946, ibid., part 2.

64 The following screening procedures are described in 'Report of Activities of Canadian Polish Movement Unit,' 26 November 1946, NA, RG 76, vol. 649, file A85451, part 2, reel C-10588.

65 On the mandatory document check, see minutes of the conference held at the Deputy Adjutant-General's office on 9 September 1946, NA, RG 27, vol. 3032, file 18, and draft order for the movement of Polish veterans from the United Kingdom to Canada, 30 October 1946, ibid., vol. 626, file 23-7-2-1, part 1.

66 According to Norman Robertson, 'our screens are made with different types of mesh, and probably it was the finest through which the Anders Poles had to pass.' Quoted from dispatch from Robertson to L.B. Pearson, 26 January 1948, NA, RG 25, vol. 2105, file AR 405/1/4/27, part 3.

67 A.L. Jolliffe to R. Ranger, 9 August 1946, NA, RG 76, vol. 648, file A85451, part 1, reel C-10587.

68 Immigration Act, R.S. 1927, Section 3, pp. 2069–71, and Section 41, pp. 2084–5.

69 For the instructions on interpreting PC 3112, see External Affairs to High Commissioner, 19 September 1946, NA, RG 25, vol. 3401, file 621-PF-40C, part 2.

70 See Application Form to Be Completed by Polish Veterans to Accept, under Direc-

tion, Farm Employment in Canada for a Period of Two Years, undated, appended to minutes of meeting of Interdepartmental Committee regarding Polish soldiers who are or will be demobilized held on 12 July 1946, ibid. The same question, incidentally, appeared on the longer form that the applicant's Canadian sponsor was required to fill out. See Questionnaire to Be Completed by Polish Veterans Prepared to Accept Farm Employment in Canada for a Period of Two Years, undated, NA, RG 76, vol. 648, file A85451, part 1, reel C-10587.

71 See memorandum concerning some members of the Anders Army, undated [September 1946], NA, RG 25, vol. 3401, file 621-PF-40C, part 2.

72 For the type of information contained in a typical file, see dispatch from K.P. Kirkwood to External Affairs, 29 April 1949, ibid., vol. 3402, file 621-PF-40C, part 5.

73 Commissioner of Immigration to F.W. Cotsworth, 19 August 1946, NA, RG 76, vol. 648, file A85451, part 1, reel C-10587, and High Commissioner to External Affairs, 9 September 1946, NA, RG 27, vol. 3021, file Polish veterans correspondence, part 2.

74 Applications were withdrawn from approximately 2,500 men who either were married or had insufficient agricultural experience. See High Commissioner to External Affairs, 9 September 1946, NA, RG 25, vol. 3401, file 621-PF-40C, part 2.

75 See Canmilitary to Major General E.G. Weeks, 3 August 1946, NA, RG 27, vol. 626, file 23-7-3. To some extent, the lack of British screening was a non-issue. As has been noted above, the documentation upon which screening of the Polish soldiers would rely consisted of their British Army personnel files. As long the Canadians were granted access to the files, there was no real need for the British to carry out screening in advance.

76 High Commissioner to External Affairs, 9 September 1946, ibid., vol. 3021, file Polish veterans correspondence, part 2.

77 According to the final report of the Canadian mission, the number of applicants processed per day varied from 85 to 185. See 'Report of Activities of Canadian Polish Movement Unit,' 26 November 1946, NA, RG 76, vol. 649, file A85451, part 2, reel C-10588.

78 Report by Staff Sergeant K. Shakespeare, 4 January 1947, appended to memorandum from A.W. Parsons to External Affairs, 17 January 1947, NA, RG 25, vol. 3402, file 621-PF-40C, part 3.

79 The tolerance of Shakespeare and Stevenson for any hint of German affiliation was quite low. For example, those of Anders's men who had been permitted to complete high school during the occupation were viewed with suspicion by the Mounties, their assumption being that such preferential treatment would have been accorded only to those Poles who had somehow curried favour with the German authorities. See ibid. and Martin Thornton, 'Domestic and International Dimensions of Canadian Foreign Policy, 1943–1948: The Resettlement in Can-

ada of Ex-Servicemen of the Second Polish Corps' (PhD diss., University of London, 1989), 253.

80 K. Shakespeare and J.A. Stevenson to H.R. Hare, undated [September 1946], NA, RG 27, vol. 3040, file 106, and High Commissioner to External Affairs, 9 September 1946, NA, RG 25, vol. 3401, file 621-PF-40C, part 2.

81 Memorandum concerning members of the Anders Army, undated [September 1946], NA, RG 25, vol. 3401, file 621-PF-40C, part 2.

82 On discovery of the Poles' ineligibility and the Canadian mission's initial reaction, see 'Bunny' [H.R. Hare] to 'George' [George V. Haythorne], 12 September 1946, and High Commissioner to External Affairs, 19 September 1946, ibid. See also H.R. Hare to 'Bill' [William Rutherford], undated [September 1946], NA, RG 27, vol. 626, file 23-7-4.

83 External Affairs to High Commissioner, 11 September 1946, NA, RG 25, vol. 3401, file 621-PF-40C, part 2.

84 External Affairs to High Commissioner, 19 and 20 September 1946, NA, RG 76, vol. 648, file A85451, part 1, reel C-10587.

85 On the reaction of the Poles, see High Commissioner to External Affairs, 18 September 1946, and External Affairs to High Commissioner, 19 September 1946, NA, RG 25, vol. 3401, file 621-PF-40C, part 2; 'Bunny' to 'George,' 20 and 25 September 1946, NA, RG 27, vol. 626, file 23-7-4; and High Commissioner to External Affairs, 1 October 1946, NA, RG 76, vol. 648, file A85451, part 1, reel C-10587.

86 'Bunny' to 'George,' 17 September 1946, NA, RG 25, vol. 3401, file 621-PF-40C, part 2.

87 High Commissioner to External Affairs, 21 September 1946, ibid.

88 Memorandum [from N.A. Robertson] to External Affairs, 23 September 1946, ibid.

89 Memorandum for E. Reid, 27 September 1946, ibid.

90 External Affairs to High Commissioner, 28 September 1946, ibid.

91 Minutes of meeting of Interdepartmental Committee regarding Polish soldiers who are or will be demobilized held on 12 October 1946, NA, RG 76, vol. 648, file A85451, part 1, reel C-10587.

92 (British) Armed Forces Headquarters to War Office, 20 October 1946, NA, RG 25, vol. 2090, file AR 25/3, part 2.

93 H.R. Horne to War Office, 23 October 1946, ibid., and H.R. Hare to A. MacNamara, 19 March 1947, NA, RG 27, vol. 3033, file 28.

94 Minutes of conference regarding arrival of ex-members of the Polish armed forces held on 21 October 1946, NA, RG 27, vol. 3032, file 18.

95 The problem with the papers of the three men is reported in High Commissioner to External Affairs, 10 January 1947, and H.R. Hare to R. Ranger, 16 January 1947, ibid., vol. 626, file 23-7-2-1, part 2.

96 The leaked excerpts were from 'Report of Activities of Canadian Polish Move-

ment Unit,' 26 November 1946, NA, RG 76, vol. 649, file A85451, part 2, reel C-10588.

97 See clipping from *Montreal Standard*, undated [May 1947], NA, RG 27, vol. 3032, file 21.

98 'Statement to the House of Commons by Minister of Labour Humphrey Mitchell,' 5 May 1947, ibid., vol. 626, file 23-7-8, part 1.

99 The effectiveness of the screening done by the Canadian selection teams in Italy is a legitimate subject for debate. After the arrival in Canada of the first contingent of Poles, the Department of Labour conceded that the personnel files on which the Canadian mission had relied were 'incomplete.' See Acting Minister of Labour to A.D.P. Heeney, 12 December 1946, NA, RG 2, vol. 94, file P-65-1, correspondence – Poland, 1945–49. But it is wrong to leave the impression, as Alti Rodal did in her report for the Commission of Inquiry on War Criminals, that the Polish veterans were not subjected to security screening. Based solely on the recollections of an immigration officer who had not participated in the Canadian mission to Italy, Rodal's assessment simply does not stand up to scrutiny. As the notes for this chapter reveal, the National Archives in Ottawa houses abundant documentation on the admission of Polish veterans to Canada in the autumn of 1946. The screening procedures and criteria employed by the Canadian selection teams are described therein in considerable detail. How Rodal could have missed such basic source materials, especially in view of the liberal archival access granted to the Deschenes Commission, is a mystery. For her handling of the 2nd Corps movement, see 'Nazi War Criminals,' 141–3 and the notes on 503–4. On the erroneous claim by a Canadian immigration official that the Poles had not been screened, see examination and cross-examination of Joseph R. Robillard, Deschenes Commission, NA, P. Yuzyk Papers, vol. 63, file/vol. 11, pp. 1264 and 1304.

100 Report by Staff Sergeant K. Shakespeare, 4 January 1947, appended to memorandum from A.W. Parsons to External Affairs, 17 January 1947, NA, RG 25, vol. 3402, file 621-PF-40C, part 3.

101 The British government's request is reported in High Commissioner to External Affairs, 7 February 1947, ibid., vol. 5756, file 58(s). Canada's response is reported in A.D.P. Heeney to J.A. Glen, 1 May 1947, NA, RG 26, vol. 100, file 3-18-1.

102 Screening procedures for the final contingent are described in H.R. Hare to A. MacNamara, 19 March 1947, NA, RG 27, vol. 628, file 23-7-21, part 1; memorandum by Commissioner of Immigration, 12 April 1947, NA, RG 76, vol. 648, file A85451, part 3, reel C-10588; High Commissioner to External Affairs, 16 April 1947, NA, RG 26, vol. 129, file 3-33-26; and 'Report of Canadian Mission to Select Polish Veterans in the British Isles, April to June, 1947,' 29 October 1947, NA, G.V. Haythorne Papers, vol. 3, file 12.

The rate of rejections in the summer 1947 movement was 39 per cent (1,066 rejected out of a total of 2,717 applicants). In the autumn 1946 movement, the rejection rate was 35 per cent (1,600 rejected out of a total of 4,500 applicants).

103 See PC 4233, 22 September 1948, NA, RG 2, vol. 2021, file 3858G.

104 See draft Press Release, undated [September 1948], NA, L.S. St Laurent Papers, vol. 237, file Jacques Bernonville.

105 What follows is only a sketch of the de Bernonville affair. The case is dealt with at length in Alti Rodal's report for the Commission of Inquiry on War Criminals. See 'Nazi War Criminals,' 343–65. In general, her treatment of the case accords with the documentary evidence, and thus the story need not be repeated at length.

106 On de Bernonville's wartime activities, see note issued by Welfare Officer of the Waffen-SS, 15 March 1944, NA, RG 76, vol. 1098, file SF-D-2, part 4; précis of External Affairs papers relating to de Bernonville, undated [February 1948], ibid., part 2; and notes of investigation conducted by French intelligence, undated [1949], ibid.

107 On de Bernonville's first year in Canada, see Alfred Plourde 'To Whom It May Concern,' 12 January 1948, and certificate issued by Franco-Canadian Milk Products Co. Ltd, 6 January 1948, ibid., part 1. See also Yves Lavertu, *The Bernonville Affair: A French War Criminal in Post-WWII Quebec*, trans. George Tombs (Montreal, 1994), 28.

108 On de Bernonville's discovery and his reaction, see Acting Immigration Inspector in Charge to Atlantic District Superintendent, 4 February 1948, NA, RG 76, vol. 1097, file ED1-321, part 1; J.H. McDonald to L.J. McGinnis, 13 January 1948, and J. de Bernonville to Commissioner of Immigration, 15 January 1948, ibid., vol. 1098, file SF-D-2, part 1.

109 Transcript of Board of Inquiry held in Immigration Building at Montreal on 30 January 1948, 2 February 1948, ibid., and J.A. MacKinnon 'To Whom It May Concern,' 22 September 1948, ibid., vol. 1097, file ED1-321, part 1.

110 L.B. Pearson to Department of Mines and Resources, 9 August 1948, and French Ambassador to L.S. St Laurent, 23 August 1948, ibid., vol. 1098, file SF-D-2, part 1.

111 Immigration Inspector in Charge to Atlantic District Superintendent, 7 September 1948, ibid., part 2; F.P. Varcoe to Director of Immigration, 12 October 1948, ibid., part 3; H.L. Keenleyside to C.E.S. Smith, 19 October 1948, ibid.; and Superior Court (Montreal) judgment, 21 February 1949, ibid., part 4.

112 According to an analysis prepared by the Department of Citizenship and Immigration, the government received 558 letters and petitions, signed by 2,019 individuals, regarding the de Bernonville case. Of these, 543 were for de Bernonville, only 15 against. See 'Representations of Record on Behalf of or Against Jacques de Bernonville,' 13 December 1950, ibid., part 6. For sample letters of support, see J. Thibodeau to L.S. St Laurent, 11 September 1948, ibid.,

part 2, and P. Hamel to St Laurent, 21 September 1948, NA, St Laurent Papers, vol. 43, file D-12-d. Public opinion on the case became so inflamed that Immigration Branch was compelled to plot an entire public relations strategy. See I. Baird to Department of Mines and Resources, 10 September 1948, NA, RG 76, vol. 1098, file SF-D-2, part 2.

113 On the rejection of de Bernonville's last appeal, see minutes of cabinet meeting held on 8 February 1951, NA, RG 2, vol. 2647, reel T-2367, frames 615–16, and P. Asselin to J. de Bernonville, 19 March 1951, NA, St Laurent Papers, vol. 115, file I-20-f, part 4. On de Bernonville's departure from Canada, see Director of Immigration to file, 17 August 1951, NA, RG 76, vol. 1098, file SF-D-2, part 6, and Superior Court (Montreal) judgment, 18 October 1951, ibid., part 7.

114 Minutes of cabinet meeting held on 1 September 1948, NA, RG 2, vol. 2642, reel T-2365, frames 1694 and 1702–4; A.D.P. Heeney to J.A. MacKinnon, 3 September 1948, NA, RG 76, vol. 947, file SF-C-1, part 1; and External Affairs to High Commissioner, 18 October 1948, NA, RG 25, vol. 2122, file AR 1179/1.

115 On Canada's position with respect to the lesser French collaborators, see L.B. Pearson to External Affairs, 28 August 1948, NA, King Papers, series J4, vol. 272, reel H-1473, frame C187565; minutes of cabinet meeting held on 1 September 1948, NA, RG 2, vol. 2642, reel T-2365, frames 1694 and 1702–4; A.D.P. Heeney to J.A. MacKinnon, 3 September 1948, NA, RG 76, vol. 947, file SF-C-1, part 1; and Pearson to Prime Minister, undated [September 1948], NA, St Laurent Papers, vol. 43, file D-12-d.

116 PC 4233, 22 September 1948, NA, RG 2, vol. 2021, file 3858G.

117 On the problem of forged French identity papers, see Constable F. de Miffonis to RCMP Special Branch, 30 September 1948, NA, RG 76, vol. 106, file 18040, part 2, reel C-4679.

118 On the lax screening at the Canada–U.S. border, see memorandum on visa control, 9 April 1946, NA, RG 25, vol. 4164, file 939-40, part 1.

119 On the government's response to the problem of false French identity papers, see memorandum for Minister of Mines and Resources and Secretary of State for External Affairs, 28 October 1948, NA, RG 26, vol. 167, file 3-25-11-12, part 1, and L. Fortier to A.J. Desjardins, 27 December 1948, ibid., vol. 126, file 3-33-12, part 1. See also minutes of cabinet meeting held on 8 December 1948, NA, vol. 2642, reel T-2366, frames 63 and 67. On the government's response to the problem of French citizens using U.S. visas to gain admission to Canada, see A.L. Jolliffe to Deputy Minister of Mines and Resources, 16 March 1949, NA, RG 26, vol. 126, file 3-33-12, part 1, and Fortier to F.P. Varcoe, 6 October 1950, NA, RG 76, vol. 513, file 800070, part 2, reel C-10611.

120 A. MacNamara to J.A. Glen, 9 December 1946, NA, RG 27, vol. 275, file 1-26-1, part 1.

121 Dominion Affairs to External Affairs, 23 January 1947, NA, RG 25, vol. 2113, file AR 408/5.

4: The Door Ajar

1 On the pressure exerted by the sugar-beet growers, see J. Colley to 'Colonel Bob,' 15 March 1947, NA, RG 25, vol. 2113, file 408/4, part 2; minutes of meeting of Cabinet Committee on Immigration Policy held on 3 March 1947, NA, RG 26, vol. 100, file 3-18-1, part 1; T.G. Wood to Colley, 19 March 1947, H.L. Keenleyside to A.L. Jolliffe, 2 April 1947, Wood to Senator W.A. Buchanan, 26 June 1947, Buchanan to Keenleyside, 5 July 1947, and Keenleyside to Buchanan, 7 July 1947, ibid., vol. 144, file 3-41-10, part 1; W. Davidson to G. Haythorne, 16 February 1947, and J.A. Glen to A. MacNamara, 6 March 1947, NA, RG 27, vol. 279, file 1-26-10-2, part 1. On the lobbying by the metal-mining association, see J.V. Argyle to S.H. McLaren, 16 July 1947, and V.C. Wasbrough to interdepartmental committee on immigration, 14 July 1947, ibid., vol. 3021, file Canadian Metal Mining Association submission re immigrant labour. On the efforts of the fur industry to acquire refugee labour, see N. Genser to Keenleyside, 1 December 1947, Keenleyside to Genser, 5 December 1947, MacNamara to Keenleyside, 5 February 1948, Mac-Namara to Genser, 5 February 1948, and summary of meeting held with representatives of Canadian fur industry on 18 February 1948, NA, RG 26, vol. 144, file 3-41-9. For corporate lobbying in general, see W.W. Dawson to MacNamara, ibid., vol. 90, file 3-1-4, part 1; E. Poole to Prime Minister, 12 January 1946, and Canadian Chamber of Commerce to Prime Minister, 4 September 1946, NA, W.L.M. King Papers, series J2, vol. 428, file I-20, part 1.
2 For example, see C. Hayward to A. Brayley, 29 October 1947, NA, Canadian National Committee on Refugees Papers, vol. 4, file 42, and Record of Proceedings of the Third Meeting of the Canadian Council of Churches, 13–15 November 1946, NA, Canadian Council of Churches Papers, vol. 1, file Annual Meetings 1944–7.
3 On the activities of the Canadian Baltic Immigrant Aid Society, see H.L. Keenleyside to Baron C. Hahn, 2 October 1947, NA, RG 26, vol. 126, file 3-33-10, part 1, and minutes of meeting of directors of Canadian Baltic Immigrant Aid Society held on 22 March 1948, NA, Canadian Baltic Immigrant Aid Society Papers, vol. 1, file Minutes and Agenda 1948, 1950–3. On the efforts of the Lithuanian Minister in Washington, see P. Zadeikis to L.B. Pearson, 6 March 1946, and External Affairs to Canadian Ambassador (Washington), 29 April 1946, NA, RG 25, vol. 3672, file 5127-40C, part 2.
4 On the Ukrainian-Canadian Committee (UCC), the main Ukrainian lobby group, see N.A. Robertson to J.W. Arsenych, 1 February 1946, NA, King Papers, series J1, vol. 413, reel C-9176, frames 372862–3; External Affairs to High Commissioner,

19 February 1946, Control Commission for Germany to (British) Foreign Office, 5 March 1946, V.J. Kaye to Director of Citizenship Branch, 23 September 1946, 'A Canadian Relief Mission to Europe for Direct Aid to Ukrainian Refugees, Displaced Persons and Victims of War,' 11 September 1946, B. Panchuk to Director of Citizenship Branch, 27 November 1946, High Commissioner to External Affairs, 13 December 1946, External Affairs to High Commissioner, 21 December 1946, and Robertson to L.B. Pearson, 7 January 1946 [sic; should read 1947], NA, RG 25, vol. 3747, file 6980-GR-40, part 1. On the lobbying activities of other Ukrainian organizations, see Ukrainian Evangelical Alliance of North America to Prime Minister Mackenzie King, undated [August 1947], ibid., vol. 4019, file 10268-40, part 1, and Canadian Relief Mission for Ukrainian Refugees to PCIRO, 12 September 1947, NA, RG 76, vol. 856, file 554-33.

5 For lobbying on behalf of displaced Germans, see Assistant District Superintendent to Immigration Inspector in Charge, 15 September 1947, report by S.B. Sigurdson, 24 September 1947, and Inspector A.W. Parsons to Commissioner of Immigration, 13 December 1947, NA, RG 76, vol. 31, file 682, part 5, reel C-4690; Mrs W.P. Clement to Minister of Mines and Resources, 11 November 1948, NA, RG 26, vol. 116, file 3-24-34, part 1; and J. Oberhoffner to L.S. St Laurent, 18 May 1949, ibid., vol. 151, file 3-32-11.

6 For more on the establishment of the CCCRR, see Angelika Sauer, 'A Matter of Domestic Policy? Canadian Immigration Policy and the Admission of Germans, 1945–50,' *Canadian Historical Review* 74, 2 (June 1993): 243–7.

7 For various complaints from the German immigration lobby regarding this problem, see F. Hudd to P.T. Molson, 29 October 1947, NA, RG 25, vol. 2094, file AR 36/1; External Affairs to High Commissioner, 2 April 1947, High Commissioner to External Affairs, 8 April 1947, External Affairs to High Commissioner, 22 April 1947, memorandum by R. Innes, 12 May 1947, J.P. Sigvaldason to N.A. Robertson, 12 May 1947, External Affairs to High Commissioner, 17 May 1947, and Dominion Affairs to External Affairs, 20 May 1947, NA, RG 25, vol. 2113, file AR 408/4, part 1; Dominion Affairs to External Affairs, 3 June 1947, ibid., part 2; H.H. Erdman to Molson, 20 January 1948, ibid., file AR 408/5; note for R.G. Riddell, 31 March 1947, ibid., vol. 3673, file 5127-40C, part 9; IRO Resolution, 24 September 1948, ibid., vol. 3688, file 5475-T-40, part 9; Delegation of German-Canadian Associations to J.A. MacKinnon, 11 December 1948, NA, RG 26, vol. 116, file 3-24-34, part 1; Evangelical Lutheran Emigration Mission to Immigration Branch, 25 April 1946, Director of Immigration to file, 7 May 1947, and A.L. Jolliffe to Reverend Hennig, 11 June 1946, NA, RG 76, vol. 31, file 682, part 5, reel C-4689; 'Visit to Refugee and DP Camps in the British Zone of Occupation in Germany,' undated, ibid., vol. 443, file 673931, part 12, reel C-10320; Director of Immigration to External Affairs, 30 May 1947, ibid., part 14; 'Volksdeutsche in Austria,'

undated [January 1948], ibid., part 16, reel C-10321; 'Inter-Departmental Committee on Immigration, Volksdeutsche,' undated [1948], ibid., part 18; External Affairs to High Commissioner, 23 April 1947, ibid., vol. 655, file B41075, part 1, reel C-10592; J. Colley to C. Hayward, 11 August 1947, NA, Canadian National Committee on Refugee Papers, vol. 5, file 17; P. Gibson to Hayward, 10 September 1947, ibid., file 14; report on meeting held in St Peter's Lutheran Church in Winnipeg on 9 February 1946, NA, Canadian Lutheran World Relief Papers, reel H-1391; R. Innes to PCIRO, 2 September 1947, and W. Duncan to Colley, 3 May 1948, AN, IRO records, AJ 43/639.

8 See 'List of delegates and the organizations they represent which are to meet in the Prime Minister's office on 7 February 1947,' NA, King Papers, series J1, vol. 424, reel C-11038, frames 385022–3.

9 For a statement to this effect, see Canadian Council of Churches General Secretary to Immigration Branch, 15 November 1949, NA, RG 76, vol. 650, file B8727, part 1, reel C-10588.

10 For the intentions of CCCRR in this regard, see Reverend H.H. Erdman to A.L. Jolliffe, 24 June 1947, and External Affairs to High Commissioner, 27 June 1947, NA, RG 25, vol. 2113, file AR 408/4, part 2; 'Entry to Canada of Persons Now Living in Germany and Austria,' undated [1947], NA, RG 76, vol. 31, file 682, part 5, reel C-4690; Director of Immigration to External Affairs, 30 May 1947, ibid., vol. 443, file 673931, part 14, reel C-10320; summary of CCCRR meeting held on 23 June 1947, Jolliffe to Deputy Minister of Mines and Resources, 25 June 1947, and 'Volksdeutsche,' 24 July 1947, ibid., vol. 655, file B41075, part 1, reel C-10592; Maurice Pope diary, entry for 6 August 1947, NA, M. Pope Papers, vol. 2, file 1947; and S. Gifford to M. Cohen, 15 July 1947, AN, IRO records, AJ 43/639.

11 The negotiations between Ottawa and CCCRR that led to official recognition can be followed in External Affairs to High Commissioner, 28 November 1947, NA, RG 25, vol. 2113, file AR 408/4, part 3; minutes of meeting of Cabinet Committee on Immigration Policy held on 7 November 1947, NA, RG 27, vol. 3028, file Cabinet Committee on Immigration Policy; memorandum by A.L. Jolliffe, 4 November 1947, and Director of Immigration to file, 10 November 1947, NA, RG 76, vol. 856, file 554-33; 'Entry to Canada of Persons Now Residing in Germany and Austria,' 17 September 1947, ibid., vol. 31, file 682, part 5, reel C-4690; Jolliffe to External Affairs, 15 October 1947, Canadian Military Mission (Berlin) to External Affairs, 15 October 1947, CCCRR to J.A. Glen, 24 October 1947, and Jolliffe to T.O.F. Herzer, 22 November 1947 ibid., vol. 655, file B41075, part 1, reel C-10592.

12 External Affairs to High Commissioner, 28 November 1947, NA, RG 25, vol. 2113, file AR 408/4, part 3; Lieutenant-General M. Pope to Major-General G.P. Hays,

20 December 1947, and Pope to Brigadier A.G. Kenchington, 19 December 1947, ibid., vol. 3674, file 5127-C-40, part 1.

13 T.O.F. Herzer to J.A. Glen, 14 January 1948, NA, RG 30, vol. 8367, file 3300-C-31.

14 On the government's decision to bail out CCCRR, see minutes of cabinet meetings held on 4 March and 25 August 1948, NA, RG 2, vols 2641 and 2642, reel T-2365, frames 1209, 1687, and 1689–90; J.A. Glen to cabinet, 23 February 1948, H.L. Keenleyside to A.D.P. Heeney, 16 August 1948, and Keenleyside to Treasury Board, 26 April 1949, NA, RG 26, vol. 104, file 3-24-1, part 1; Heeney to Glen, 5 March 1948, NA, C.D. Howe Papers, vol. 5, file S-8-1.

15 A.L. Jolliffe to Deputy Minister of Mines and Resources, 6 February 1948, NA, RG 26, vol. 104, file 3-24-1, part 1.

16 On CCCRR's acquisition of the Mühlenberg camp, see F. Hudd to P.T. Molson, 29 October 1947, NA, RG 25, vol. 2094, file AR 36/1; 'Entry to Canada of Persons Now Residing in Germany and Austria,' 17 September 1947, NA, RG 76, vol. 31, file 682, part 5, reel C-4690; H.H. Erdman to A.L. Jolliffe, 10 August 1947, ibid., vol. 655, file B41075, part 1, reel C-10592; T.O.F. Herzer to External Affairs, 7 September 1948, ibid., part 2; and C.F. Klassen, Reverend N. Warnke, and Erdman to CCCRR Executive Committee, 3 October 1947, NA, North American Baptist Immigration and Colonization Society Papers, series A, vol. 1, file 13. The camp was moved to Bremen in June 1949. See P.W. Bird to Overseas Commissioner, 23 July 1949, NA, RG 76, vol. 655, file B41075, part 3, reel C-10592.

17 T.O.F. Herzer to External Affairs, 7 September 1948, NA, RG 76, vol. 655, file B41075, part 2, reel C-10592.

18 On the expansion of the close relatives category, see minutes of cabinet meetings held on 23 and 29 January, 23 April, and 1 May 1947, NA, RG 2, vols 2639 and 2640, reel T-2365, frames 138–9, 162, 165–6, 439, and 476–7; minutes of Cabinet Committee on Immigration Policy meeting held on 23 April 1947, ibid., vol. 82, file I-50-M; PC 371, 30 January 1947, ibid., vol. 1963, file 3565G; and PC 1734, 1 May 1947, ibid., vol. 1972, file 3612G.

19 On the expansion of the occupational categories, see minutes of cabinet meetings held on 23 and 29 January 1947, ibid., vol. 2639, reel T-2365, frames 138–9, 162, and 165–6, and PC 371, 30 January 1947, ibid., vol. 1963, file 3565G.

20 The full text of Croll's address can be found in *Official Report of Debates: House of Commons* (Ottawa, 1947), 2: 1001–6.

21 See Mackenzie King diary, entry for 17 March 1947, NA, King Papers, series J13, microfiche no. 239, p. 222, and *Memoirs of Hugh L. Keenleyside* (Toronto, 1982), 2: 297.

22 'Statement by the Prime Minister to the House of Commons,' 1 May 1947, NA, King Papers, series J5, vol. 80, file January–August 1947.

23 *Memoirs of Hugh L. Keenleyside*, 2: 297.

24 Mackenzie King diary, entry for 1 May 1947, NA, King Papers, series J13, micro-fiche no. 241, p. 396.

25 See the complaints registered in High Commissioner to External Affairs, 25 March 1947, N.A. Robertson to External Affairs, 19 March 1947, and External Affairs to High Commissioner, 2 May 1947, NA, RG 25, vol. 4164, file 939-40, part 2.

26 For a detailed account of the meeting, see J. Colley to 'Colonel Bob,' 15 March 1947, ibid., vol. 2113, file AR 408/4, part 2.

27 C.D. Howe to H.L. Keenleyside, 29 August 1947, NA, RG 26, vol. 100, file 3-18-1, part 1.

28 On Howe's meeting with IRO officials, see R. Innes to IRO Department of Reset-tlement, 4 August 1947, AN, IRO records, AJ 43/622, and Howe to J. Colley, 13 September 1947, RG 76, vol. 651, file B29300, part 3, reel C-10589. On his inter-vention in the shipping problem, see C.W. Jackson to file, 9 September 1947, ibid., and 'Entry to Canada of Persons Now Residing in Germany and Austria,' 17 September 1947, ibid., vol. 31, file 682, part 5, reel C-4690.

29 The quoted passage is from J. Colley to 'Colonel Bob,' 15 March 1947, NA, RG 25, vol. 2113, file AR 408/4, part 2.

30 C. Hayward to P. Gibson, 29 October 1947, NA, Canadian National Committee on Refugees Papers, vol. 5, file 14.

31 H.L. Keenleyside to cabinet, 3 September 1948, NA, RG 25, vol. 4165, file 939-B-40, part 1.

32 H.L. Keenleyside to L. Beaudry, 15 May 1947, NA, King Papers, series J1, vol. 425, reel C-11038, frames 386210–11.

33 Minister of Mines and Resources to Governor General in Council, 20 May 1947, and minutes of meeting of Cabinet Committee on Immigration Policy held on 27 May 1947, NA, RG 26, vol. 100, file 3-18-1, part 1; memorandum from C.D. Howe and R. Ranger to cabinet, 2 June 1947, NA, RG 2, vol. 66, file C-20-5, Cabinet Document nos 466 and 467; minutes of cabinet meeting held on 5 June 1947, ibid., vol. 2640, reel T-2365, frames 582–3; and PC 2180, 6 June 1947, ibid., vol. 1975, file 3632G.

34 On Glen, see Irving Abella and Harold Troper, *None Is Too Many* (Toronto, 1982), 240.

35 C.D. Howe and H.L. Keenleyside to cabinet, 4 July 1947, NA, RG 26, vol. 100, file 3-18-1, part 1.

36 See A.D.P. Heeney to C.D. Howe, 11 July 1947, ibid.; minutes of cabinet meeting held on 10 July 1947, NA, RG 2, vol. 2640, reel T-2365, frames 693–4; and PC 2856, 18 July 1947, ibid., vol. 1978, file 3653G.

37 On the admission of various occupational groups as a result of amendments to PC 2180, see minutes of cabinet meetings held on 25 August, 1 October 1947, 21 April

1948, 28 July 1948, and 29 September 1948, ibid., vol. 2640 and 2642, reel T-2365, frames 756–7, 810–11, 1354–7, 1650, and 1755–60; PCs 3926, 1009, 1628, 3371, and 3721, 1 October 1947, 9 March 1948, 22 April 1948, 28 July 1948, and 5 October 1948, ibid., vols 1985, 2002, 2007, 2017, and 2022, files 3683G, 3760G, 3786G, 3834G, and 3861G; A.D.P. Heeney to H. Mitchell, 6 October 1947, ibid., vol. 64, file C-20-2, part 2; Mitchell to J.A. Glen, 6 October 1947, and Glen to Mitchell, 18 October 1947, NA, RG 27, vol. 279, file 1-26-10-1, part 1. On the admission of Volksdeutsche, see H.L. Keenleyside to Cabinet Committee on Immigration Policy, 1 September 1948, NA, RG 26, vol. 100, file 3-18-1, part 2, and 'Immigration to Canada Showing Displaced Persons by Racial Origin, from April 1947 to November 30, 1951,' undated [January 1952], ibid., vol. 140, file 3-40-4, part 1.

38 On the processing of prospective immigrants under the relatives program, see External Affairs to High Commissioner, 19 October 1946, NA, RG 25, vol. 2113, file AR 408/4, part 1; External Affairs to CBC International Service, 3 April 1947, ibid., vol. 3673, file 5127-40C, part 9; 'The International Refugee Organization,' undated [1954], ibid., vol. 8118, file 5475-T-40, part 18.2; Brigadier M.S. Lush to Messrs E.M. Shirk and Rickford and Capitaine le Vernoy, 13 January 1947, External Affairs to Canadian Military Mission (Berlin), 27 January 1947, and R. Innes to Brigadier Lush and General Wood, 24 February 1947, NA, RG 76, vol. 443, file 673931, part 12, reel C-10320; 'Notes on the Canadian Close Relatives Scheme,' 2 September 1947, AN, IRO records, AJ 43/639; and summary of meeting between R. Innes and O. Cormier held on 7 November 1947, ibid., AJ 43/622.

39 The joint Canadian–IRO procedures for the labour-selection program are described in detail in 'The International Refugee Organization,' undated [1954], NA, RG 25, vol. 8118, file 5475-T-40, part 18.2. On their development, see minutes of cabinet meeting held on 27 March 1947, NA, RG 2, vol. 2640, reel T-2365, frames 365–7; Director of Immigration to A. MacNamara, 19 December 1947, NA, RG 26, vol. 72, file 8/4/47–16/12/47; memorandum for Cabinet Committee on Immigration Policy, 10 April 1948, NA, RG 27, vol. 3029, file Department of Labour memoranda to cabinet; G.G. Congdon to K. Feldmanis, 28 February 1948, NA, RG 76, vol. 824, file 552-1-582; MacNamara to A.L. Jolliffe, 11 February 1947, Jolliffe to file, 25 February 1947, MacNamara to Jolliffe, 25 February 1947, Jolliffe to file, 28 February 1947, J.R. Baldwin to MacNamara, 11 March 1947, J.A. Glen to cabinet, undated [March 1947], and MacNamara to Jolliffe, 17 March 1947, ibid., vol. 651, file B29300, part 1, reel C-10589; Immigration Branch to External Affairs, 6 December 1947, ibid., reel C-10590. For the manner in which these procedures were implemented, see the early movement of lumbermen, reported in Immigration Branch to Deputy Minister of Mines and Resources 15 May 1947, Jolliffe to External Affairs, 15 May 1947, High Commissioner to External Affairs, 16 May 1947,

External Affairs to High Commissioner, 17 May 1947, minutes of meeting of Immigration-Labour Committee held on 11 June 1947, Jolliffe to A. MacNamara, 21 June 1947, and O. Cormier to Commissioner of Immigration, 5 August 1947, ibid., part 1, reel C-10589.

40 Statistics on the immigration destinations of IRO-sponsored refugees can be found in Louise Holborn, *The International Refugee Organization, A Specialized Agency of the United Nations: Its History and Work, 1946–1952* (London, 1956), 442. The numbers of IRO-eligible and ineligible refugees who made their way to Canada between 1947 and 1951 are reported in 'International Refugee Organization,' undated [1952], NA, RG 25, vol. 8117, file 5475-T-40, part 17.2, and 'Immigration to Canada Showing Displaced Persons by Racial Origin, from April 1947 to November 30, 1951,' undated [January 1952], NA, RG 26, vol. 140, file 3-40-4, part 1.

5: No Safe Haven, 1947–1951

1 See 'Entry to Canada of Persons Now Living in Germany and Austria,' undated [1947], NA, RG 76, vol. 31, file 682, part 5, reel C-4690, and Dominion Affairs to External Affairs, 3 April 1948, NA, RG 25, vol. 2107, file AR 405/1/16/4.

2 Maurice Pope diary, entry for 24 July 1947, NA, M. Pope Papers, vol. 2, file 1947.

3 The problems plaguing Canada's immigration teams in Europe were elaborated in Jolliffe's report to Ottawa. See Jolliffe to H.L. Keenleyside, 24 July 1947, NA, RG 27, vol. 3029, file Interdepartmental Committee on Immigration-Labour Correspondence.

4 Jolliffe's recommendations can be found in ibid.

5 On the process whereby Jolliffe's recommendations were approved, see Acting Minister of Mines and Resources to cabinet, 8 August 1947, NA, RG 2, vol. 66, file C-20-5, document nos 416–520; minutes of cabinet meeting held on 14 August 1947, ibid., vol. 2640, reel T-2365, frames 735 and 742; and External Affairs to High Commissioner, 20 August 1947, NA, RG 25, vol. 2113, file AR 408/4, part 2. It should be noted that Jolliffe's mission and cabinet's implementation of all of his recommendations are powerful arguments against Alti Ròdal's assertion that 'strengthening Canada's own security screening facilities had low priority.' For her questionable assertion, see 'Nazi War Criminals in Canada: The Historical and Policy Setting from the 1940s to the Present' (Commission of Inquiry on War Criminals, Ottawa, 1986), 183.

6 List of Personnel (Karlsruhe), 8 October 1948, appended to note from L. Fortier to file, 8 October 1948, NA, RG 26, vol. 91, file 3-2-5. The figure of seventy-one included twenty-six permanent secretarial and house-cleaning staff.

7 On the expansion of Canada's contingent of immigration personnel overseas, see

'Entry to Canada of Persons Now Residing in Germany and Austria,' 17 September 1947, NA, RG 25, vol. 3673, file 5127-40C, part 10; L. Fortier to External Affairs, 9 November 1948, ibid., vol. 3674, file 5127-C-40, part 2; A.L. Jolliffe to External Affairs, 15 March 1949, ibid., vol. 6245, file 9323-D-2-40, part 1; Commissioner S.T. Wood to H.L. Keenleyside, 8 November 1947, NA, RG 26, vol. 166, file 3-25-11, part 1; minutes of meeting of Immigration–Labour Committee held on 1 December 1947, ibid., vol. 72, file 8/4/47–16/12/47; memorandum to cabinet, 8 August 1947; memorandum for Cabinet Committee on Immigration Policy, 3 September 1948, ibid., vol. 91, file 3-2-6; distribution of Canadian immigration offices as of 1 July 1949, list of Canadian immigration staff in Europe, undated, appended to memorandum from Fortier to External Affairs, 2 February 1951, and Fortier to External Affairs, 20 February 1951, ibid., file 3-2-5; RCMP Commissioner to External Affairs, 29 October 1948, and G.G. Congdon to Associate Commissioner of Immigration, 10 December 1948, NA, RG 76, vol. 957, file SF-S-1, part 1.

8 The date of the move from Heidelberg to Karlsruhe is uncertain. But it appears to have been carried out between mid-March and mid-June 1948. The change in address of Canada's immigration mission in Germany can be found by comparing the letterhead on the correspondence from J.D. McFarlane to A.L. Jolliffe, 17 March 1948, NA, RG 76, vol. 818, file 552-1-513, with that on the memorandum from O. Cormier to all visa officers, 17 June 1948, ibid., vol. 652, file B29300, part 7, reel C-10590.

9 On the reductions in the immigration budget, see W.E. Harris to cabinet, 21 February 1952, NA, RG 2, vol. 212, file C-20-5. On the deputy minister's recommendations and their implementation by the government, see H.L. Keenleyside to Minister of Mines and Resources, 14 August 1948, NA, H.L. Keenleyside Papers, vol. 19, file Immigration 1938–85; minutes of cabinet meeting held on 29 September 1948, NA, RG 2, vol. 2642, reel T-2365, frames 1755–60; memorandum from Keenleyside to Minister of Mines and Resources, 18 March 1949, ibid., vol. 249, file I-50, part 1; memorandum for Cabinet Committee on Immigration Policy, 3 September 1948, Immigration Branch memorandum, 26 February 1949, and Immigration Branch to Deputy Minister of Citizenship and Immigration, 2 March 1950, NA, RG 26, vol. 91, file 3-2-6; and C.E.S. Smith to Deputy Minister of Citizenship and Immigration, 9 November 1951, NA, RG 76, vol. 31, file 682, part 7, reel C-4690.

10 L. Fortier to External Affairs, 20 February 1951, NA, RG 26, vol. 91, file 3-2-5.

11 Memorandum for Council, 21 May 1947, NA, L.S. St Laurent Papers, vol. 225, file I-17, and H.L. Keenleyside to S. Garson, 1 February 1949, NA, RG 26, vol. 151, file 3-32-11.

12 C.P. Stacey and Barbara M. Wilson, *The Half-Million: The Canadians in Britain, 1939–1946* (Toronto, 1987), 138 and 140.

13 'Entry to Canada of Persons Now Living in Germany and Austria,' undated [1947], NA, RG 76, vol. 31, file 682, part 5, reel C-4690.

14 Minutes of meeting held at Department of Mines and Resources on 22 May 1947, NA, RG 25, vol. 6251, file 9504-40, part 1.

15 The consequences of Ottawa's normalization of relations with its former enemies are described in minutes of cabinet meetings held on 31 July and 10 October 1947, NA, RG 2, vol. 2640, reel T-2365, frames 723, 818, and 821–3; PC 2908, 31 July 1947, ibid., vol. 1979, file 3656G; and A.L. Jolliffe to External Affairs, 17 December 1947, NA, RG 25, vol. 3674, file 5127-C-40, part 1. For examples of how the change in status worked in practice, see the case of four Romanians recounted in J.W. Pickersgill to H.L. Keenleyside, 17 March 1947, memorandum from Director of Immigration to Deputy Minister of Mines and Resources, 19 March 1947, Keenleyside to Pickersgill, 20 March 1947, and Keenleyside to R.G. Robertson, 2 February 1948, NA, W.L.M. King Papers, series J2, vol. 428, file I-20-D, and the case of an Italian family recounted in W.J.F. Pratt to G. Sylvestre, 19 March 1948, and A.L. Jolliffe to L.S. St Laurent, 20 and 26 May 1948, NA, St Laurent Papers, vol. 13, file 70.

16 N.A. Robertson to Lieutenant-General M. Pope, 6 July 1946, NA, RG 25, vol. 3673, file 5127-40C, part 6, and F.B. Cotsworth to J.P. Sigvaldason, 27 November 1947, ibid., vol. 2113, file AR 408/4, part 3.

17 See C. Monk to T.O.F. Herzer, 17 November 1948, ibid., vol. 6248, file 9408-A-40, part 1, and 'Report on All Cases Handled by CCCRR up to November 13th, 1948,' NA, RG 76, vol. 655, file B41075, part 2, reel C-10592.

18 The quoted passage is from T.O.F. Herzer to A.L. Jolliffe, 8 November 1948, NA, RG 76, vol. 655, file B41075, reel C-10592.

19 On the high rate of rejection for Volksdeutsche applicants, see L.G. Chance to Canadian Military Mission (Berlin), 22 November 1949, Canadian Military Mission (Berlin) to External Affairs, 25 November and 13 December 1949, External Affairs to Canadian Military Mission (Berlin), 20 December 1949, T.O.F. Herzer to A.L. Jolliffe, 2 January 1950, J.J. Chenard to Canadian Military Mission (Berlin), 17 January 1950, and Herzer to Prime Minister L.S. St Laurent, 20 September 1949, NA, RG 25, vol. 3914, file 9408-40, part 2; P.W. Bird to Immigration Branch, 23 March 1950, NA, RG 76, vol. 445, file 673931, part 22, reel C-10322; report on visa refusals, 14 October 1949, ibid., vol. 653, file B29300, part 13, reel C-10591; Director of Immigration to Deputy Minister of Mines and Resources, 18 January 1950, and Herzer to C. Gibson, 20 September 1949, ibid., vol. 655, file B41075, parts 3 and 4, reel C-10592.

20 For some examples, see CCCRR to W.E. Harris, 2 February 1950, NA, RG 26, vol. 104, file 3-24-1, part 1; C.F. Klassen, Reverend N. Warnke, and Reverend H.H. Erdman to CCCRR Executive Committee, 3 October 1947, and minutes of

CCCRR meeting held on 17 December 1949, NA, North American Baptist Immigration and Colonization Society Papers, series A, vol. 1, file 13; CCCRR to Prime Minister L.S. St Laurent, 20 December 1949, ibid., file 14; minutes of CLWR executive meeting held on 3 September 1949, and minutes of meeting of CLWR officers held on 28 January 1950, NA, Canadian Lutheran World Relief Papers, reel H-1390.

There is no question that many Volksdeutsche had German citizenship conferred on them without prior consultation. This was particularly true in German-occupied Poland. Of the almost 2.75 million Volksdeutsche who were registered on the German Ethnic List (DVL), approximately 1.7 million, or 62 per cent, had been automatically designated as citizens of the Reich or German nationals. The remainder could acquire German citizenship only by individual application. An additional 800,000 arrived from German-occupied (but not formally annexed) eastern Poland, the Baltic states, and Romania. Of these, more than half were resettled in either the annexed Polish territories or in Germany proper. In their cases, naturalization was not automatic. Rather, they underwent a process of racial examination and selection carried out by the SS Race and Resettlement Main Office (RuSHA). On the basis of this assessment, they were classified as either suitable for immediate naturalization or as possibly suitable. Those in the second category, who constituted the vast majority, were eligible for German citizenship, but they would have to apply individually. See J. Noakes and G. Pridham, eds., *Foreign Policy, War, and Racial Extermination: A Documentary Reader*, vol. 3, *Nazism, 1919–1945* (Exeter, UK, 1988), 942–50; Martin Broszat, *Nationalsozialistische Polenpolitik, 1939–1945* (Stuttgart, 1961), 98–100 and 121–5; and Robert F. Koehl, *RKFDV: German Resettlement and Population Policy, 1933–1945: A History of the Reich Commission for the Strengthening of Germandom* (Cambridge, MA, 1957), 100–7. For the criteria used by Canadian security officers in determining the citizenship of Volksdeutsche, see E.J. Bye to P.W. Bird, undated [1949], appended to memorandum from Bird to Acting Commissioner of Immigration, 22 November 1949, NA, RG 76, vol. 876, file 560-2-551.

21 On the results of IRO's investigation of Mennonite claims of involuntary naturalization, see M. Cohen to H. Allard, 23 July 1949, NA, RG 25, vol. 6248, file 9408-A-40, part 1, and M.D. Lane to Allard, 17 August 1949, NA, RG 76, vol. 855, file 544-22, part 1. On the results of Canada's consultations with IRO, see Commissioner of Immigration to Canadian Government Immigration Mission (Karlsruhe), 25 August 1949, ibid.; minutes of meeting of Immigration–Labour Committee held on 30 August 1949, NA, RG 26, vol 72, file 11/1/49–8/6/50, part 3; Inspector in Charge to Central District Superintendent, 22 September 1949, P.W. Bird to Commissioner of Immigration, 17 October 1949, and J.G. Keil to T.O.F. Herzer, 7 November 1949, NA, RG 76, vol. 655, file B41075, part 3, reel C-10592; A.C.A. Kaarsberg to Combined Travel Board, 28 November 1949, ibid., part 4. See also

A.L. Jolliffe to External Affairs, 10 November 1949, NA, RG 25, vol. 3914, file 9408-40, part 2. The quote about 'inaccurate and specious' representations can be found in Jolliffe to C.F. Klassen, 31 August 1949, NA, RG 26, vol. 122, file 3-32-4, part 1.

22 On the German lobby's change in strategy, see J.G. Keil to Reverend C.L. Monk, 26 July 1949, S.W. Herman to Reverend Monk, 5 August 1949, and 'Labour Scheme,' undated, NA, Canadian Lutheran World Relief Papers, reel H-1393. On Ottawa's refusal to countenance significant changes to the regulations governing German immigration, see R. Ranger to Cabinet Committee on Immigration Policy, 26 April 1949, NA, RG 2, vol. 127, file I-50-D; H.L. Keenleyside to Minister of Mines and Resources, 7 April 1949, and N.A. Robertson to Prime Minister, 29 April 1949, ibid, vol. 166, file I-50-10; minutes of cabinet meeting held on 4 April 1949, ibid., vol. 2643, reel T-2366, frames 450–1; L.G. Chance to External Affairs, 1 March 1949, and Consular Division to External Affairs, 25 May 1949, NA, RG 25, vol. 6248, file 9408-A-40, part 1; Robertson to C. Gibson, 6 April 1949, NA, RG 26, vol. 151, file 3-32-11; Immigration Branch to F. Kaeble, 12 May 1949, NA, RG 76, vol. 31, file 682, part 5, reel C-4690; and Robertson to Prime Minister, 7 April 1949, NA, St Laurent Papers, vol. 56, file I-20-33.

23 On the first steps in the relaxation of the ban on German nationals, see N.A. Robertson to C. Gibson, 15 September 1949, NA, RG 2, vol. 124, file C-20-2, part 2; Gibson to cabinet, undated [September 1949], ibid., file C-20-5, document nos 1020–75; minutes of cabinet meetings held on 3 May and 13 September 1949, ibid., vols 2643 and 2644, reel T-2366, frames 534–5, 771, and 777–9; L.G. Chance to External Affairs, 12 July 1949, and Chance to MacDermot, 5 August 1949, NA, RG 25, vol. 6248, file 9408-A-40, part 1; Gibson to H.L. Keenleyside, 28 April 1949, memorandum to cabinet, 30 April 1949, and Deputy Minister of Mines and Resources to Gibson, 8 August 1949, NA, RG 26, vol. 151, file 3-32-11.

24 This was confirmed by an examination of lists, which include biographical sketches, of the German nationals for whom the regulations were waived. See PCs 5766, 6286, and 6379, November–December 1949, NA, RG 2, vols 2059, 2061, and 2062. See also PCs 103, 334, 488, 625, 770, 883, 1423, 1509, and 1602, January–March 1950, ibid., vols 2064, 2065–8, and 2070–1. For total admissions under the waivers, see J.D. McFarlane to Superintendent of European Emigration, 27 September 1949, McFarlane to External Affairs, 29 September 1949, and P.W. Bird to McFarlane, 14 October 1949, NA, RG 76, vol. 31, file 682, part 5, reel C-4690.

25 This was confirmed by comparing the names of those male German nationals of military age for whom the regulations were waived against the UN's lists of known or suspected war criminals. The lists can be found in NA, RG 25, vol. 2608. They were also compared against the Department of Justice of Canada's current list of suspected war criminals and collaborators.

26 The case of O. W—— is summarized in PC 103, 10 January 1950, NA, RG 2, vol. 2064, file 4081G.

27 W.E. Harris to cabinet, 18 August 1950, ibid., vol. 137, file C-20-5, document nos 191–250. By the beginning of 1951, IRO was able to supply only half of Canada's immigrant-labour requirements. See memorandum for Departmental Advisory Committee on Immigration, undated [March 1951], NA, RG 26, vol. 73, binder no. 1.

28 On the evolution of the government's thinking on the issuance of visitor's visas to German businessmen, see N.A. Robertson to C. Gibson, 27 December 1949, NA, RG 2, vol. 124, file C-20-2, part 2; Gibson and L.B. Pearson to cabinet, 7 December 1949, ibid., file C-20-5, document nos 1076–150; Robertson to W.E. Harris, 10 February 1950, ibid., vol. 136, file C-20-2, part 2; Harris to cabinet, 1 February 1950, ibid., vol. 137, file C-20-5, document nos 1–90; H.F. Clark to L.G. Chance, 25 February 1949, and Official Circular No. 68 to all immigration officers, 20 January 1950, NA, RG 25, vol. 6248, file 9408-A-40, part 1; A.J. Hicks to External Affairs, 6 April 1949, Overseas Commissioner to Canadian Government Immigration Mission (Karlsruhe), 29 July 1949, B.O. Siverts to Canadian Consulate (Frankfurt am Main), 20 July 1949, J.D. McFarlane to Canadian Government Immigration Mission (Karlsruhe), 7 September 1949, B.J. Bachand to P.W. Bird, 12 September 1949, and Bird to Commissioner of Immigration, 17 September 1949, NA, RG 76, vol. 31, file 682, part 5, reel C-4690. On the rescinding of the prohibition against naturalized Volksdeutsche, see minutes of cabinet meetings held on 25 and 28 March 1950, NA, RG 2, vol. 2645, reel T-2366, frames 1381–2, 1386, and 1388, and PC 1606, 28 March 1950, ibid., vol. 2071, file 4128G. On the decision to remove German nationals from the class of inadmissible enemy aliens, see Robertson to Harris, 5 September 1950, ibid., vol. 136, file C-20-2, part 2; Harris to cabinet, 18 August 1950, ibid., vol. 137, file C-20-5, document nos 191–250; minutes of cabinet meeting held on 1 September 1950, ibid., vol. 2646, reel T-2367, frames 134 and 138; and PC 4364, 14 September 1950, NA, RG 27, vol. 275, file 1-26-1, part 5.

29 The state of war between Canada and Germany was not formally terminated until the summer of 1951. See cabinet decision, 10 July 1951, NA, RG 2, vol. 208, file W-22-5-G, part 6. The signing of the peace treaty was concurrent with the ending of the state of war between Germany and both the United Kingdom and France. The United States did not sign a treaty with the German government until October 1951.

30 See L. Fortier to External Affairs, 12 September 1950, NA, RG 76, vol. 31, file 682, part 6, reel C-4690. What cabinet's decision had done, in effect, was to render German nationals admissible under PC 2856 of 9 June 1950, which, in addition to providing much freer access to prospective American, British, and

French immigrants, also contained a clause that allowed for the admission of any other national provided the individual was 'a suitable immigrant having regard to the climatic, social, educational, industrial, labour, or other conditions or requirements of Canada; and [was] not undesirable owing to his [or her] peculiar customs, habits, modes of life, methods of holding property, or because of his [or her] probable inability to become readily adapted and integrated into the life of a Canadian community and to assume the duties of Canadian citizenship within a reasonable time after his [or her] entry.' See PC 2856, 9 June 1950, NA, RG 2, vol. 2078, file 4171G, and examination of Maurice H. Brush, Deschenes Commission, NA, P. Yuzyk Papers, vol. 63, file/vol. 2, pp. 219–21. On the tough screening regime to which German nationals continued to be subjected, see J.R. Robillard to A.J. Andrew, 3 August 1951, and notes of meeting held at Wahnerheide on 16 August 1951, NA, RG 76, vol. 978, file 5420-1-551.

31 On the adoption of the 'Austria as victim' thesis by Canada's wartime allies, see Robert H. Keyserlingk, *Austria in World War II: An Anglo-American Dilemma* (Montreal, 1988), 185–91.

32 L.S. St Laurent to J.A. Glen, 13 February 1948, and Glen to St Laurent, 16 February 1948, NA, RG 26, vol. 151, file 3-32-11; and Canadian Government Immigration Mission (Salzburg) to A.L. Jolliffe, 17 March 1948, NA, RG 76, vol. 818, file 552-1-513, part 1.

33 Some 150,000 Austrians volunteered for service in the SS, while another 800,000 were conscripted into the regular German armed forces. See Radomír Luza, *Austro-German Relations in the Anschluss Era* (Princeton, NJ, 1975), 352.

34 On the deliberations with respect to Austrians who had served in the regular German armed forces, see H.L. Keenleyside to L.B. Pearson, 4 June 1948, L.G. Chance to Keenleyside, 14 October 1948, and Keenleyside to E. Reid, 27 October 1948, NA, RG 26, vol. 151, file 3-32-11. See also Assistant Commissioner to Superintendents for Pacific, Western, Eastern, and Atlantic Districts, 27 October 1948, NA, RG 76, vol. 866, file 555-61.

35 Peter R. Black, *Ernst Kaltenbrunner: Ideological Soldier of the Third Reich* (Princeton, NJ, 1984), 82–3 and 283.

36 Official Circular No. 72 to all visa and immigration officers, 20 May 1950, NA, RG 25, vol. 6248, file 9408-A-40, part 1.

37 On the high esteem in which prospective Baltic immigrants were held, see M. Pope to External Affairs, 30 July 1946, J.W. Holmes to H. Wrong, 29 August 1946, note to file, 24 September 1946, and Wrong to J.L. Ilsley, 27 September 1946, ibid., vol. 3674, file 5127-C-40, part 1.

38 L.G. Chance to Department of Mines and Resources, 5 August 1947, ibid., vol. 3673, file 5127-40C, part 10.

39 For example, see O. Cormier to Commissioner of Immigration, 5 August 1947, NA, RG 76, vol. 651, file 29300, part 2, reel C-10589.

40 For External's view, see L.G. Chance to Department of Mines and Resources, 5 August 1947, and Chance to External Affairs, 16 October 1947, NA, RG 25, vol. 3673, file 5127-40C, part 10. For the Immigration Branch view, see Maurice Pope diary, entry for 7 August 1947, NA, Pope Papers, vol. 2, file 1947.

41 On Howe's intervention, see R. Innes to IRO Department of Resettlement, 4 August 1947, AN, IRO records, AJ 43/622; Immigration Branch to O. Cormier, 11 August 1947, NA, RG 76, vol. 443, file 673931, part 15, reel C-10321; Acting High Commissioner to External Affairs, 2 August 1947, NA, RG 26, vol. 121, file 3-32-2; and Immigration Branch to C.W. Jackson, 12 August 1947, ibid., vol. 151, file 3-32-11.

42 On the hard line the RCMP took toward members of the German armed forces, see H.G. Dehn to PCIRO Headquarters, 23 December 1947, AN, IRO records, AJ 43/793; PCIRO Resettlement Division to IRO Eligibility Branch, 6 January 1948, ibid., AJ 43/622; M. Hacking to K.J.W. Lane, 21 January 1948, ibid.; and G.G. Congdon to Acting Superintendent, 5 February 1948, NA, RG 76, vol. 443, file 673931, part 15, reel C-10320.

43 See Rodal, 'Nazi War Criminals,' 235.

44 The director of immigration's recommendation is in A.L. Jolliffe to RCMP Commissioner, 14 April 1948, AN, IRO records, AJ 43/622. The RCMP's response is quoted in Rodal, 'Nazi War Criminals,' 236.

45 On the removal of service in the German armed forces as an automatic bar to admission, see N.A. Robertson to W.E. Harris, 6 April 1950, NA, RG 2, vol. 136, file C-20-2, part 2; minutes of cabinet meeting held on 5 April 1950, ibid., vol. 2645, reel T-2366, frames 1409, 1414–15, and 1417; External Affairs note, 11 April 1950, NA, RG 25, vol. 3914, file 9408-40, part 2; Official Circular No. 72 to all visa and immigration officers, 20 May 1950, ibid., vol. 6248, file 9408-A-40, part 1; and L. Fortier to C.E.S. Smith, 20 April 1950, NA, RG 76, vol. 947, file SF-C-1, part 1.

46 Immigration Act, R.S. 1927, Section 3, pp. 2069–71, and Section 41, pp. 2084–5.

47 The quoted passage is from Commissioner S.T. Wood to H.L. Keenleyside, 10 May 1948, NA, RG 26, vol. 164, file 3-18-17, part 1.

48 In April 1948, after a fact-finding trip, Associate Commissioner of Immigration Laval Fortier castigated the RCMP for its inability to deal effectively with the threat of communist infiltration via the immigration route. So concerned was Fortier that he called for a 'total reorganization of our security screening and a total change of the officers now employed on the security work.' See Fortier to A.L. Jolliffe, 22 April 1948, ibid. Fortier's outburst was sparked by two developments. First, less than a month earlier, the Security Panel had received a report outlining

serious irregularities in IRO-administered refugee camps. Of particular concern was evidence that the organization was facilitating the movement of subversive elements out of Europe. While some of the immigrants were 'high ranking Nazis,' the real problem, the report had noted, was with communists. According to the report, 'I.R.O. in some camps is ... infiltrated by Communists[,] and Communist sympathy, if not membership, seems to be an important qualification if the D.P. hopes to be selected for movement abroad.' See Annex 'A,' undated, appended to memorandum from Lieutenant-Colonel J.A.K. Rutherford to Security Panel, 30 March 1948, NA, RG 2, vol. 251, file S-100-D, Security Panel Document SP-24. See also memorandum from G.G. Crean to L. Chance, 6 April 1948, NA, RG 25, vol. 5788, file 233(s), part 2.

The second development was the concurrent failure of the RCMP to screen out known communists from among American visa seekers. Two cases in particular stood out. The first involved Reid Robinson, an official with a communist-dominated labour union in the United States who was granted a visitor's visa despite his record of prior subversive activity in Canada. See minutes of meeting of cabinet Committee on Immigration Policy held on 25 February 1948, NA, RG 2, vol. 249, file I-50-M, and minutes of cabinet meeting held on 19 February 1948, ibid., vol. 2641, reel T-2365, frames 1150–1. The other case involved two members of the communist-dominated Croatian Fraternal Union of America, whose applications for visitor's visas initially raised no alarm bells. Indeed, it was only as a result of a tip from the Vancouver Board of Trade that they were stopped at the border. See H.L. Keenleyside to E.W.T. Gill, 29 May 1948, and Director of Immigration Branch to Deputy Minister of Mines and Resources, 23 May 1949 [sic; should read 1948], NA, RG 26, vol. 169, file 3-32-1, part 1. Beyond the failure of the screening apparatus, what may have provoked Fortier's ire was the RCMP's view that the government's policy of trying to exclude known or suspected communists could not withstand a court challenge. See Commissioner S.T. Wood to A. MacNamara, 23 February 1948, NA, R.G. Robertson Papers, vol. 1, file 6. For an opposing view, see minutes of cabinet meeting held on 14 May 1948, NA, RG 2, vol. 2642, reel T-2365, frames 1427–8.

On the changes made to the system of immigration screening as a result of the bureaucratic warfare between the police and immigration officials, see memorandum from H.M. Jones to Minister of Citizenship and Immigration, 3 June 1963, NA, RG 26, vol. 164, file 3-18-17, part 2; J. George to Constable F. de Miffonis, 27 July 1948, ibid., vol. 166, file 3-25-11, part 1; Wood to Jolliffe, 3 and 8 July 1948, and Superintendent G.B. McClellan to Major J.A. Wright, 26 July 1948, NA, RG 76, vol. 800, file 547-1, part 1; minutes of meeting on security problems held on 28 February 1952, ibid., part 2; and McClellan to Fortier, 3 February 1949, ibid., vol. 957, file SF-S-1, part 1. With respect to the changes called for in the administrative subordination of the RCMP, it should be noted that, prior to 1948, security officers assigned to a Canadian immigration mission abroad did not come under the jurisdiction of the immigration officer in charge. See O. Cormier to A. Wright-Harvey, 1 May 1947, ibid., vol. 443, file 673931, part 14, reel C-10320. The orders to the RCMP regarding the compilation of a list of screening criteria can be found in letter from Wright to McClellan, 7 July 1948, quoted in Decision in the Matter of Revocation of Citizenship between the Minister of Citizenship and Immigration and Johann Dueck, 21 December 1998, p. 110 (hereafter cited as Dueck Decision).

49 On the RCMP's practice of non-disclosure, see minutes of cabinet meeting held on 5 March 1947, NA, RG 2, vol. 2639, reel T-2365, frame 268; minutes of meeting held at Department of Mines and Resources on 22 May 1947, NA, RG 25, vol. 6251, file 9504-40, part 1; and A.L. Jolliffe to file, 29 May 1947, NA, RG 76, vol. 800, file 547-1, part 1.

50 This can be deduced from two facts. First, cabinet and the prime minister took the unusual step of vetting the RCMP's immigration-screening criteria. Second, the criteria, once approved, were made the subject of a cabinet directive. See 'Rejection of Immigrants on Security Grounds,' 28 October 1949, NA, RG 76, vol. 947, file SF-C-1, part 1; memorandum for cabinet, 22 August 1949, ibid., vol. 957, file SF-S-1, part 1; minutes of cabinet meeting held on 24 August 1949, NA, RG 2, vol. 2644, reel T-2366, frame 737; and N.A. Robertson to Prime Minister, 21 September 1949, ibid., vol. 252, file S-100-1, part 2.

51 The RCMP's response to the charges levelled by the immigration bureaucrats can be found in Commissioner S.T. Wood to H.L. Keenleyside, 10 May 1948, NA, RG 26, vol. 164, file 3-18-17, part 1. On the extent of the Mounties' capitulation, see 'Duties and Responsibilities of Security Officers Attached to the Canadian Immigration Mission in Occupied Countries,' 12 July 1948, NA, RG 76, vol. 800, file 547-1, part 1.

52 N.A. Robertson to Prime Minister, 21 September 1949, NA, RG 2, vol. 252, file S-100-1, part 2. It is of interest to note that the quoted passage is almost identical to the instructions issued by RCMP headquarters to its security officers overseas some three years earlier. See Commissioner S.T. Wood to Staff Sergeant W.W. Hinton, 23 October 1946, NA, RG 76, vol. 800, file 547-1, part 1.

53 The complete list of rejection criteria can be found in 'Screening of Applicants for Admission to Canada,' 20 November 1948, appended to letter from Commissioner S.T. Wood to A.L. Jolliffe, 27 November 1948, NA, RG 25, vol. 5788, file 233(s), part 2.

54 Reg Whitaker, *Double Standard: The Secret History of Canadian Immigration* (Toronto, 1987), 123.

55 E.J. Garland to External Affairs, 20 September 1949, NA, RG 25, vol. 3674, file 5127-C-40, part 2.

56 The quoted passages are from Superintendent G.B. McClellan to N.A. Robertson, 24 January 1952, NA, RG 2, vol. 235, file S-100-5.

57 Minutes of meeting on immigration matters held on 6 February 1946, NA, L. Beaudry Papers, vol. 6, file 114.

58 Minutes of meeting of Cabinet Committee on Immigration Policy held on 26 September 1947, NA, RG 27, vol. 3028, file Cabinet Committee on Immigration Policy; minutes of cabinet meeting held on 9 October 1947, NA, RG 2, vol. 2640, reel T-2365, frames 818 and 821–3; A.L. Jolliffe to External Affairs, 17 December 1947, NA, RG 25, vol. 3674, file 5127-C-40, part 1; L.G. Chance to heads of Canadian missions abroad, 8 January 1948, ibid., vol. 4165, file 939-B-40, part 1; memorandum from Director of Immigration to file, 13 December 1947, Circular No. 181 from W.J. Bambrick to all [Eastern District] immigration inspectors, 17 December 1947, Instructions No. 43 from H.U. McCrum to [Atlantic District] immigration inspectors-in-charge, 13 January 1948, and Circular No. 96B from District Superintendent to [Atlantic District] immigration officers, 26 May 1948, NA, RG 76, vol. 866, file 555-61; memorandum from L. Fortier to file, 7 February 1949, ibid., vol. 957, file SF-S-1, part 1.

59 See Annex 'A,' undated, to memorandum from Lieutenant-Colonel J.A.K. Rutherford to Security Panel, 30 March 1948, NA, RG 2, vol. 251, file S-100-D, Security Panel Document SP-24; N.A. Robertson to Prime Minister, 21 September 1949, ibid., vol. 252, file S-100-1, part 2; External Affairs to High Commissioner, 21 July 1949, NA, RG 25, vol. 2122, file AR 1179/1; Immigration Branch Circular No. 72, 20 May 1950, ibid., vol. 6248, file 9408-A-40, part 1; Deputy Minister of Citizenship and Immigration to Minister of Citizenship and Immigration, 9 June 1950, NA, RG 26, vol. 166, file 3-25-11, part 1; draft memorandum from Robertson to Prime Minister, 16 September 1949, NA, RG 26, vol. 164, file 3-18-17, part 1; H.M. Jones to Minister of Citizenship and Immigration, 3 June 1963, ibid., part 2; 'Screening of Applicants for Admission to Canada,' 20 November 1948, NA, RG 76, vol. 957, file SF-S-1, part 1; Inspector R.A.S. MacNeil to Commissioner of Immigration, 2 June 1950, and G.R. Benoit to MacNeil, 12 June 1950, ibid., vol. 31, file 682, part 6, reel C-4690; examination of George O'Leary, Deschenes Commission, NA, Yuzyk Papers, vol. 63, file/vol. 5, p. 646.

In her report to the Deschenes Commission of Inquiry on War Criminals, Alti Rodal contended that, 'prior to 1951, there were no specific security screening guidelines for persons who may have collaborated with the Nazis in the occupied territories and who were no longer residing in those territories, other than those who served in the German armed forces.' See 'Nazi War Criminals,' 256. Her interpretation was based on a literal reading of the screening criteria agreed to by Immigration Branch and the RCMP early in 1949. According to the written guidelines, collaborators 'presently residing in previously occupied territory' were deemed inadmissible to Canada on security grounds. See 'Screening of Applicants for Admission to Canada,' 20 November 1948, NA, RG 76, vol. 957, file SF-S-1, part 1. On its face, the phrasing appeared not to exclude former collaborators who were living in Germany as refugees. There is no evidence, however, that this distinction ever found its way into Canadian screening practice. On the contrary, persons suspected of collaboration who were *not* living in previously occupied territory were routinely dropped from the rolls of prospective immigrants. For example, see C.P. Henry to E.M. Shirk, 4 April 1947, ibid., vol. 443, file 673931, part 13, reel C-10320; R.G. Riddell to Robertson, 2 April 1947, NA, RG 25, vol. 3913, file 9408-40, part 1; and Inspector MacNeil to J. George, 2 November 1948, ibid., vol. 5798, file 267(s), part 1. Nonetheless, in recognition of its potential for confusion, and after being assured that the RCMP considered it meaningless, Ottawa excised the offending passage from the criteria in September 1949. See Robertson to Prime Minister, 21 September 1949, NA, RG 2, vol. 252, file S-100-1, part 2, in which he drew a line through the words 'presently residing in previously occupied territory' in the same ink as his signature. The passage had been left in an earlier version. See draft memorandum from Robertson to Prime Minister, 16 September 1949, NA, RG 26, vol. 164, file 3-18-17, part 1. Assurances that the RCMP had been ignoring the passage were contained in the memorandum from E.W.T. Gill to Robertson, 22 September 1949, NA, RG 2, vol. 166, file I-50-10.

There is no simple explanation for how and why such unhelpful wording found its way into the RCMP's 20 November 1948 list of grounds for rejection. But there are clues in the extant documentation. Not long after the resumption of mass immigration from Europe, Ottawa realized that the RCMP's London office could not handle the growing number of requests for security checks. Accordingly, screening was decentralized. Starting in November 1947, only applications from eastern European nationals and non-nationals of the countries of western Europe would be checked through the Mounties' London office. Everyone else would be screened locally. See decisions reached at a meeting held in the office of Deputy Minister of Mines and Resources on 2 October 1947, and A.L. Jolliffe to Acting Commissioner of Immigration, 10 October 1947, NA, RG 76, vol. 800, file 547-1, part 1; and Commissioner of Immigration to External Affairs, 29 October 1948, ibid., vol. 957, file SF-S-1, part 1. By definition, most of the cases dealt with by London could not have involved collaborators, at least not persons who had collaborated with the Germans in the countries from which they were attempting to emigrate. This lack of experience with collaborators was confirmed in the London office's first draft of the list of grounds for rejection, which did not include a prohibition on collaborators. See Major J.A. Wright to RCMP Commissioner, 11 August 1948, quoted in Dueck Decision, 21 December 1998, p. 111. It was also what prompted RCMP Special Branch to remind London that the list ought to include a prohibition on 'collaborators presently residing in previously occupied territory,' in other words, collaborators from eastern Europe still living in the countries in which their collaboration had taken place. See Inspector A.W. Parsons to Wright, 23 September 1948, quoted in ibid. pp. 112–13. Why Special Branch limited the correction in this way is unclear. Perhaps RCMP headquarters was confident that all other collaborators were being screened out as a matter of routine in Germany and Austria, and thus limited its concern to its London operation.

60 L. Fortier to E.F. Gaskell, 23 May 1951, NA, RG 76, vol. 957, file SF-S-1, part 2; minutes of Security Panel meeting held on 15 May 1952, NA, RG 2, vol. 232, file S-100-1-M; and H.M. Jones to Minister of Citizenship and Immigration, 3 June 1963, NA, RG 26, vol. 164, file 3-18-17, part 2. In fact, the decision to remove Nazi Party membership as an automatic bar to admission was made late in 1950. See Fortier to T.O.F. Herzer, 18 November 1950, ibid., vol. 104, file 3-24-1, part 1. However, owing to a delay in informing Canada's overseas immigration teams, the new policy did not come into effect for several weeks. See Immigration Branch to P.T. Baldwin, 1 December 1950, NA, RG 76, vol. 856, file 555-3, part 1; T.R. Burns to J.D. McFarlane, 27 December 1950, ibid., vol. 800, file 547-1, part 1; and McFarlane to District Superintendents of Immigration, 3 January 1951, ibid., part 2.

61 In 1952, Ottawa decided that collaborators who had been convicted of lesser offences, served their time, and been released from prison, ought not automatically to be denied consideration as immigrants. On the relaxation of the criteria for these so-called minor collaborators, most of whom were from western Europe, see L. Fortier to N.A. Robertson, 19 March 1952, NA, RG 2, vol. 235, file S-100-5; P.M. Dwyer to Security Panel, 30 April 1952, ibid., vol. 232, file S-100-1-D, Security Panel Document SP-119; minutes of Security Panel meeting held on 15 May 1952, ibid., file S-100-1-M; T.P. Malone to C.E.S. Smith, 26 February 1957, NA, RG 25, file 8541, file 11687-40, part 3.1; Fortier to Superintendent G.B. McClellan, 15 December 1951, and Chief of Operations to Director of Immigration Branch, 12 May 1952, NA, RG 26, vol. 166, file 3-25-11, part 1; Security Panel Document SP-198, 8 April 1959, and J.M. Bella to Fortier, 14 September 1959, ibid., vol. 153, file 1-18-7, part 2; Fortier to Minister of Citizenship and Immigration, 19 October 1959, and Fortier to Cabinet Committee on Immigration, 9 November 1959, ibid., vol. 164, file 3-18-17, part 2; H.M. Jones to Minister of Citizenship and Immigration, 3 June 1963, ibid.; Commissioner L.H. Nicholson to Fortier, 14 May 1951, NA, RG 26, vol. 166, file 3-25-11, part 1; Fortier to file, 3 May 1951, NA, RG 76, vol. 800, file 547-1, part 2; Fortier to E.F. Gaskell, 23 May 1951, Fortier to Nicholson, 26 November 1951, G. de T. Glazebrook to R.G. Robertson, 29 November 1951, Baldwin to Fortier, 10 December 1951, W. Hickman to Baldwin, 23 January 1952, McClellan to Robertson, 24 January 1952, Baldwin to Director of Immigra-

tion, 4 March 1952, and Acting Director of Immigration to Minister of Citizenship and Immigration, 4 March 1952, ibid., vol. 957, file SF-S-1, part 2; and memorandum by Cabinet Committee on Immigration, 9 November 1959, ibid., vol. 959, file SF-S-23, part 2.

62 On the process whereby the blanket prohibition against Waffen-SS volunteers was eroded, see G.H. Ashley to RCMP Special Branch, 9 March 1955, NA, RG 26, vol. 167, file 3-25-11-13, part 1; C.E.S. Smith to Deputy Minister of Citizenship and Immigration, 30 May 1955, ibid., vol. 127, file 3-33-13; Smith to Commissioner L.H. Nicholson, 24 February 1956, ibid., vol. 166, file 3-25-11, part 2; J.R. Robillard to Operations Division, 23 March 1955, NA, RG 76, vol. 801, file 547-5-551, part 1; Vice-Consul (Bonn) to Legal Division, 10 January 1956, and Canadian Government Immigration Mission (Karlsruhe) to Operations Division, 16 January 1956, ibid., vol. 821, file 552-1-551; Operations Division to all posts abroad, 21 March 1955, Robillard to C.S.A. Ritchie, 22 April 1955, Ritchie to L. Fortier, 20 May 1955, Nicholson to Fortier, 28 June 1955, Smith to Deputy Minister of Citizenship and Immigration, 15 November 1955, Fortier to Minister of Citizenship and Immigration, 16 November 1955, and Fortier to Nicholson, 9 December 1955, ibid., vol. 957, file SF-S-1, part 3; Robillard to Ritchie, 7 June 1955, ibid., vol. 978, file 5420-1-551. See also examination of George O'Leary, Deschenes Commission, NA, Yuzyk Papers, vol. 63, file/vol. 5, pp. 710 and 722.

63 The cabinet directive describing the criteria was addressed to 'all government departments and agencies *concerned*' (italics added). See 'Rejection of Immigrants on Security Grounds,' 28 October 1949, NA, RG 76, vol. 947, file SF-C-1, part 1. On the limited distribution of the criteria, see Superintendent G.B. McClellan to L. Fortier, 3 February 1949, ibid., vol. 957, file SF-S-1, part 1.

64 On the rules for the exchange of information between the RCMP and Immigration Branch, see G.B. McClellan to Major J.A. Wright, 26 July 1948, ibid., vol. 800, file 547-1, part 1; McClellan to L. Fortier, 3 February 1949, and Fortier to Commissioner of Immigration, 7 February 1949, ibid., vol. 957, file SF-S-1, part 1. For evidence that the RCMP's rejection criteria were kept from immigration officers in the field, see H.M. Jones to Minister of Citizenship and Immigration, 3 June 1963, RG 26, vol. 164, file 3-18-17, part 2. The quoted passage is from 'The Immigration Act,' undated, NA, Jewish Labour Committee of Canada Papers, vol. 16, file 16-15. Prior to the enactment of the new Immigration Act in 1952, persons suspected of Nazi affiliation were rejected because they did not 'fulfil, meet or comply with the conditions and requirements of any regulations which for the time being are in force and applicable to such persons under the Act.' Quoted from Immigration Act, R.S.C. 1927, Section 3, p. 2070. For examples of how the RCMP's rejection criteria were translated into the relevant provisions of the Immigration Act, see 'Report of Visas Refused – 1000 Mennonite Families,' 14 October 1949, NA, RG 76, vol.

653, file B29300, part 13, reel C-10591; 'Cases Rejected – Lutheran Labour Scheme,' undated [1950], NA, Canadian Lutheran World Relief Papers, reel H-1400; T.O.F. Herzer to W.E. Harris, 17 April 1951, NA, North American Baptist Immigration and Colonization Society Papers, series A, vol. 1, file 14; Herzer to Fortier, 21 April 1951, NA, RG 26, vol. 104, file 3-24-1, part 1; CCCRR Weekly Progress Report Nos 13 and 21, 7 December 1948 and 30 May 1949, NA, RG 30, vol. 8367, file 3300-C-31A; and 'CCCRR – Bremen – Processing January 1, 1952–December 31, 1952,' Canadian Lutheran World Relief Papers, reel H-1398.

65 See Allied Control Council Directive No. 24, 12 January 1946, in *Documents on Germany under Occupation, 1945–54*, ed. Beate Ruhm von Oppen (London, 1955), 102–7.

66 'The Nazi Party, Its Formations and Affiliated Organizations,' undated [summer 1946], appended to letter from Superintendent L.H. Nicholson to A.L. Jolliffe, 25 July 1946, NA, RG 76, vol. 800, file 547-1, part 1.

67 Quoted from Allied Control Council Directive No. 38, 14 October 1946, NARA, RG 260, series 3, vol. 3.

68 Examination of William H. Kelly, Deschenes Commission, NA, Yuzyk Papers, vol. 63, file/vol. 7, pp. 899–900 and 913–14.

69 The RCMP tended to look askance at promotions, particularly when they appeared to have been garnered in rapid succession. See cross-examination of William H. Kelly, ibid., pp. 937–8.

70 This did not preclude others within the immigration bureaucracy from making use of the directives. One such case was the movement of a few dozen German scientists to Canada during the late 1940s. At the time, the Canadian military mission in Berlin was instructed to process a small number of German scientists and technicians who were to be granted limited-term visas to Canada. Applicants were screened three times – first by one of two special British panels, second by the RCMP, and lastly by Allied occupation authorities – this in order to obtain exit permits. See High Commissioner to External Affairs, 9 November 1946, NA, King Papers, series J1, vol. 413, reel C-9176, frames 373076–7; N.A. Robertson to External Affairs, 27 November 1946, and memorandum to Privy Council Committee on Scientific and Industrial Research, 21 April 1947, NA, RG 2, vol. 102, file R-100-1; PC 2047, 29 May 1947, ibid., vol. 1974, file 3628G; G. Dubé to G.D. Mallory, 5 July 1947, NA, RG 25, vol. 3896, file 9294-R-40, part 1; and J. Léger to External Affairs, 21 June 1947, ibid., vol. 7900, file 7-DC(s). Results of the screening were referred to the Canadian mission. See L. Reid to Léger, 12 September 1947, and Léger to External Affairs, 4 November 1947, ibid., vol. 2086, file AR 22/5, part 2; U.S. Information Service to Office of Military Government, 4 April 1947, appended to dispatch from Lieutenant-General M. Pope to External Affairs, 16 April 1947, ibid., vol. 3895, file 9294-40; A.D.P. Heeney to C.D. Howe, 11 July

1947, NA, RG 26, vol. 100, file 3-18-1; and Heeney to H. Mitchell, 12 July 1947, NA, RG 27, vol. 278, file 1-26-4, part 1. A critical element in the screening of the scientists was completion of the lengthy questionnaire that was the cornerstone of the Allies' denazification procedures under Control Council Directive Nos 24 and 38. Applicants seeking Canadian visas as scientific or technical immigrants had to fill out such a questionnaire, even if they had already done so. For example, see (completed) Military Government of Germany Fragebogen, 31 December 1947, NA, R. Funke Papers, vol. 2, file 48, on which it is revealed that the German national in question had completed the same questionnaire the previous year.

Once the enemy-alien status of German nationals had been revoked, use of the directive by Immigration Branch, particularly in cases of Nazi Party membership, appears to have become commonplace. See P.W. Bird to Acting Director of Immigration, 27 September 1950, NA, RG 76, vol. 31, file 682, part 6, reel C-4690; P.T. Molson to Consular Division, 7 October 1950, and G. de T. Glazebrook to Consular Division, 17 October 1950, NA, RG 25, vol. 3914, file 9408-40, part 2; Heeney to L. Fortier, 25 October 1950, NA, RG 26, vol. 166, file 3-25-11, part 1. For instructions on the use of Allied directives to assess cases of so-called minor collaborators, see W. Hickman to P.T. Baldwin, 23 January 1952, and Baldwin to Deputy Minister of Citizenship and Immigration, 4 March 1952, NA, RG 76, vol. 957, file SF-S-1, part 2.

71 See 'Reasons for Rejection,' undated, appended to memorandum from W.H. Kelly to RCMP Special Branch, 21 January 1953, NA, RG 146, Public Document.

72 On the new division of labour between Immigration Branch and the RCMP, see Superintendent G.B. McClellan to L. Fortier, 3 February 1949, and memorandum from Fortier to file, 7 February 1949, NA, RG 76, vol. 957, file SF-S-1, part 1; Deputy Minister of Citizenship and Immigration to Minister of Citizenship and Immigration, 9 June 1950, NA, RG 26, vol. 166, file 3-25-11, part 1. On the inability of immigration officers in the field to overturn security rejections, see Director of Immigration to Acting Commissioner of Immigration, 10 October 1947, NA, RG 76, vol. 800, file 547-1, part 1.

73 Ottawa's interest in a sponsor's economic circumstances was spelled out in Immigration Branch Instruction No. 1, 29 March 1947, NA, RG 76, vol. 800, file 547-1, part 1. Subsequently, a section that required the sponsor to list all financial assets and property was added to the IMM-55. See Application for Admission of Nominated Immigrants, undated [1954], ibid., accession 86–87/112, box 1, file IMM.O.S.16 to IMM.446, and examination of George O'Leary, Deschenes Commission, NA, Yuzyk Papers, vol. 63, file/vol. 5, p. 635.

74 See IMM-55, undated [1946], appended to memorandum from C.E.S. Smith to Commissioner of European Emigration, 2 November 1946, NA, RG 76, vol. 811, file 551-1, part 1. The earliest version of the form that I was able to find dates from

the summer of 1946. See (completed) IMM-55, 16 August 1946, ibid., vol. 8, file A89909. Somewhat different in its layout than subsequent IMM-55s, this version may have been surplus paperwork to be used until the supply had been exhausted. See Commissioner of Immigration to R.N. Munroe, 18 June 1946, ibid., vol. 811, file 551-1, part 2.

75 For facsimiles of the UK form, see IMM-362, undated [1948], appended to letter from Inspector in Charge to Commissioner of Immigration, 8 January 1949, NA, RG 76, vol. 757, file 517-36-417, and IMM-362, undated, ibid., file 517-36-419, part 1. No copy of the Paris office's IMM-362 has been found. However, reference to its use in Paris was made by the local Canadian immigration officer. See A.J. Desjardins to Commissioner of Immigration, 19 August 1949, ibid., vol. 844, file 553-80-550.

76 Originally intended as a report on prospective homesteaders and farm labourers, the IMM-359 seems to have been superceded by the IMM-357. See Report on Agriculturalist Desirous of Proceeding to ... (Province), undated, appended to Instruction to Canadian Visa Officers No. 3, 29 July 1947, NA, RG 25, vol. 3900, file 9323-N-40, part 1. On the use of the IMM-359 as an all-purpose form at Stockholm, see F. Palmer to External Affairs, 10 June 1948, ibid., vol. 3674, file 5127-C-40, part 1; L. Fortier to External Affairs, 24 September 1948, ibid., part 2; and External Affairs to Director of Immigration, 19 August 1948, NA, RG 27, vol. 287, file 1-26-38, part 1.

77 G.G. Congdon to Associate Commissioner of Immigration, 10 December 1948, NA, RG 76, vol. 957, file SF-S-1, part 1.

78 For the form used at Brussels, see Application for Immigration Visa, undated [1949], appended to memorandum from C. Lauzière to Commissioner of Immigration, 25 May 1949, ibid., vol. 758, file 517-36-432, part 1.

79 See Application for Immigration Visa, undated, appended to letter from G. Wallace to Associate Commissioner of Immigration, 5 January 1949, ibid., vol. 759, file 517-36-434, part 1.

80 See C.E.S. Smith to J.S. McGowan, 23 May 1950, ibid., vol. 31, file 682, reel C-4690.

81 For a facsimile of the IMM-357, see Questionnaire, undated, appended to Immigration Branch Instruction No. 3, 29 July 1947, NA, RG 25, vol. 3900, file 9323-N-40, part 1.

82 For a facsimile, see CCCRR Form ML-10, undated, NA, Canadian Lutheran World Relief Papers, reel H-1400. Eventually, CCCRR developed forms for various bulk-labour problems. For example, see Fragebogen – Single Farm Workers, undated [1952], and Fragebogen – Domestic(s), undated [1952], NA, North American Baptist Immigration and Colonization Society Papers, vol. 5, file 58. These questionnaires, which required the prospective immigrant to include a curriculum vitae,

were submitted to CCCRR along with the completed visa application form.
CCCRR then forwarded both forms to the Canadian security officer for clearance.
See memorandum from G.M. Berkefeld to Reverend C.L. Monk, 7 May 1953, ibid.

83 On the practice of having visa application forms printed locally, see G.R. Benoit to
all Canadian immigration offices in Europe, 1 March 1951, NA, RG 76, vol. 804,
file 548-10, part 2, and J.R. Robillard to Director of Immigration Branch, 20 April
1951, ibid., vol. 805, file 548-10, part 3.

84 On the introduction of the IMM-OS.8, see Immigration Branch working instructions, 28 June 1950, NA, RG 27, vol. 275, file 1-26-1, part 5; memorandum from
O. Cormier to Director of Immigration, 15 July 1950, NA, RG 76, vol. 811, file
551-1, part 5; and Immigration Branch Directive No. 69, 15 December 1950, ibid.,
vol. 804, file 548-10, part 2. For a facsimile of the first OS.8, see IMM-OS.8,
undated [1950], appended to memorandum from G.R. Benoit to all Canadian
immigration offices in Europe, 1 March 1951, ibid., vol. 804, file 548-10, part 2.

85 For example, see IMM-362, undated, NA, RG 76, vol. 757, file 517-36-419, part 1,
and Application for Immigration Visa, undated [1949], appended to memorandum
from C. Lauzière to Commissioner of Immigration, 25 May 1949, ibid., vol. 758,
file 517-36-432, part 1.

86 See IMM-55, undated [1946], appended to memorandum from C.E.S. Smith to
Commissioner of European Emigration, 2 November 1946, ibid., vol. 811, file 551-
1, part 1.

87 See IMM-362, undated [1948], appended to letter from Inspector in Charge to
Commissioner of Immigration, 8 January 1949, ibid., vol. 757, file 517-36-417.

88 For example, see IMM-OS.8 and Employment Information form, undated [1951],
appended to memorandum from J.R. Robillard to Director of Immigration, 20
April 1951, ibid., vol. 805, file 548-10, part 3; IMM-OS.8 and Employment Information form, undated [October 1952], ibid., vol. 758, file 517-36-432, part 1;
IMM-OS.8 and Employment Information form, undated [1952], appended to memorandum from G.R. Benoit to Director of Immigration, 22 December 1952, NA,
RG 26, vol. 138, file 3-38-6; IMM-OS.8, April 1953, appended to memorandum
from Acting Chief of Canadian Immigration Mission (Karlsruhe), 21 July 1953,
NA, RG 76, vol. 807, file 548-11, part 2; and IMM-OS.8, April 1953, appended to
letter from C.V. Holm to Director of Immigration, 25 July 1953, ibid. See also the
facsimile of the OS.8 reproduced in the Transmundial Travel Service pamphlet
titled 'Auswandern – leicht gemacht! Kanada – Tor der Welt, Blick in die Zukunft –
auch für Dich!' undated [1952], NA, K. von Cardinal Papers, vol. 5, file German
Immigration – History.

89 On the form in use by the Paris office, see Questionnaire ou Demande de Visa Tem-
poraire ou d'Immigration, undated [1949], appended to letter from A.J. Desjardins
to Overseas Service Commissioner, 19 August 1949, NA, RG 76, vol. 844, file

553-80-550. Prior to this, the Paris office used a form that required applicants to account for their previous residences, but not their previous jobs. See Questionnaire, undated, appended to letter from Desjardins to Commissioner of Immigration, 24 August 1948, ibid., vol. 811, file 551-1, part 4. Shortly after Ottawa unveiled the OS.8, the Paris office amended it by adding a special residency and employment section. See Renseignements sur vos residences et emplois antérieurs depuis 1939, undated, appended to memorandum from O. Cormier to Director of Immigration, 8 January 1951, ibid., vol. 804, file 548-10, part 2. On the forms in use by the Stockholm office, see (completed) OS.8, Employment Information form, and Settlement Service Report, undated [1950], ibid., and Form No. 29, undated, appended to memorandum from Officer in Charge (Stockholm) to Chief of Operations Division, 5 August 1952, ibid., vol. 761, file 517-36-440, part 1. The Stockholm office also instructed prospective immigrants to provide 'your occupation and as much of your history as possible.' See instructions titled 'Emigration to Canada,' undated, appended to memorandum from J.M. Ihme to Acting Superintendent of Immigration, 13 September 1950, ibid.

90 See Canadian Commercial Corporation Information Form, undated, appended to memorandum from L. Fortier to file, 3 May 1951, ibid., vol. 800, file 547-1, part 2.

91 See CCCRR Form ML-10, undated, NA, Canadian Lutheran World Relief Papers, reel H-1400. A similar form was used by the German-Baptist immigrant-aid society. See (completed) Baptist World Alliance Immigration Form, undated [1951], NA, North American Baptist Immigration and Colonization Society Papers, vol. 1, file 20.

92 For the case of an ethnic German whose application for a Canadian visa was rejected as a result of the information he provided on his ML-10 form, see curriculum vitae of A. S——, undated, appended to note from (German) Foreign Office to J.R. Robillard, 16 May 1953, NA, RG 76, vol. 801, file 547-5-551, part 1.

93 See Questionnaire, undated, appended to Immigration Branch Instruction No. 3, 29 July 1947, NA, RG 25, vol. 3900, file 9323-N-40, part 1.

94 Immigration Branch Circular 96A, 7 June 1949, NA, RG 76, vol. 804, file 548-10, part 1.

95 Quoted from memorandum from Inspector W.H. Kelly to RCMP Special Branch, 9 January 1953, NA, RG 146, Public Document. When such information was not provided with the initial application, Canadian immigration authorities typically asked for it. See B.N. Munroe to C.E.S. Smith, 3 February 1948, NA, RG 76, vol. 811, file 551-1, part 3, and Smith to G. Sylvestre, 5 March 1948, NA, St Laurent Papers, vol. 13, file 70-1.

96 Inspector K.W.N. Hall to Director of Immigration, 26 April 1952, NA, RG 76, vol. 800, file 547-1, part 2. At diplomatic missions where there was no immigration officer, the application was forwarded to Immigration Branch, which passed it on to

the RCMP for security checks. See memorandum from Consular Division to G. de T. Glazebrook, 15 October 1952, NA, RG 25, vol. 6178, file 232-AE-40, part 1.

97 P.T. Baldwin to F.B. Cotsworth, 7 October 1950, NA, RG 76, vol. 804, file 548-10, part 1, and testimony of Roger St-Vincent, cited in Decision in the Matter of Revocation of Citizenship between the Minister of Citizenship and Immigration and Peteris Vitols, 23 September 1998, p. 81 (hereafter cited as Vitols Decision). Another means whereby Canadian immigration authorities attempted to elicit employment and residency information was by requiring applicants to provide a curriculum vitae. The archives are replete with examples of this practice. For a case in point, see W. Morin to W.J.F. Pratt, 15 April 1947, and curriculum vitae, undated, appended to letter from Acting Private Secretary to W.J.F. Pratt, 6 August 1947, NA, St Laurent Papers, vol. 13, file 70.

In her report for the Commission of Inquiry on War Criminals, Alti Rodal asserted that 'no provision was made in any of the [immigration] application forms before 1953 for information with regard to military service or POW standing, or even for a record of employment during the war years.' She further asserted that 'this omission ... indicates the very low priority attached to eliciting Nazi or collaborationist background for immigration purposes during this period.' See Rodal, 'Nazi War Criminals,' 195. The Deschenes Commission repeated this assertion in its own report. See Commission, *Report*, 1: 200. It is clear that neither Rodal nor the commissioners were aware of the existence of the Paris and Stockholm forms. Nor were they aware, apparently, that it was the RCMP's practice to attempt to elicit a detailed accounting of residency and employment information as a prelude to conducting Stage B inquiries. Thus, an applicant who filled out the pre-1954 form had as strong a duty of candour to report his wartime activities as an applicant who filled out the post-1954 form. Conversely, if a prospective immigrant were going to lie about or attempt to hide his activities during the Second World War, the post-1954 form would have been no more effective at deterring such misrepresentation than the pre-1954 form.

98 During the initial phase of the refugee movement, Canadian immigration authorities referred to the IGCR registration form, which required, among other things, an applicant's current and original nationality as well an accounting of prior residences and jobs. See M.S. Lush to Messrs Shirk and Rickford and Capitaine le Vernoy, 13 January 1947, R. Innes to Brigadier Lush and General Wood, 24 February 1947, and Innes to Lush, 24 February 1947, NA, RG 25, vol. 2113, file AR 408/4, part 1. For a facsimile, see Intergovernmental Committee on Refugees Registration Record, undated, appended to memorandum from C.E.S. Smith to E. O'Connor, 9 July 1947, NA, RG 76, vol. 651, file B29300, part 2, reel C-10589. Subsequently, reference was made to the IRO's resettlement registration form. For evidence that the latter was presented to the immigrant-processing missions of all countries,

including Canada, see International Refugee Organization, *Operational Manual* (Geneva, 1950), part B.6.05, Documents in Evidence in the Matter of Revocation of Citizenship between the Minister of Citizenship and Immigration and Wasily Bogutin; testimony of Andrew C.A. Kaarsberg, quoted in Decision in the Matter of Revocation of Citizenship between the Minister of Citizenship and Immigration and Serge Kisluk, 7 June 1999, pp. 56–7; and IRO Resettlement Registration Form, undated, AN, IRO records, AJ 43/863. The form, which contained space for the visa-issuing country to record the results of its labour, security, medical, and civil examinations, required that the applicant account for all jobs and residences over the previous twelve years. For IRO-assisted refugees who applied for visas outside Germany, Canadian authorities seem to have relied on the organization's CM/1 application form. See L. Fortier to A.A. Ewen, 22 July 1949, NA, RG 76, vol. 445, file 673931, part 20, reel C-10321. For evidence that the form was included in each IRO file seen by Canadian authorities, see L.W. Lloyd to D.A. Reid, 26 September 1951, ibid., vol. 860, file 555-50, in which it was reported that the IRO branch office in Hull, Quebec, had in its possession 100,000 files 'uniform in substance, each comprising identical documentation, including the IRO Resettlement Registration Form, IRO Resettlement Examination Form, Application for IRO Assistance, and Canadian Declaration Form.'

99 High Commissioner to External Affairs, 4 August 1948, NA, RG 25, vol. 6178, file 232-L-40, part 1; 'Security Screening of Immigrants – Present Problems,' 29 March 1949, NA, RG 2, vol. 251, file S-100-D, Security Panel Document SP-40; and (draft) memorandum by Commissioner S.T. Wood, undated [November 1949], NA, Keenleyside Papers, vol. 19, file Immigration 1939–1985. For an example of this practice, see the case of a prospective immigrant recounted in A. Kuznecov to Minister of Justice, 27 September 1948, and C.K. Grey to RCMP Commissioner, 7 October 1948, NA, St Laurent Papers, vol. 13, file 70-2. At the 1998 civil proceedings against a suspected Nazi collaborator, a witness for the respondent conceded that, prior to coming to Canada from a refugee camp in Germany in February 1949, he was asked by Canadian immigration authorities 'what he had done from year to year.' See Vitols Decision, 23 September 1998, p. 80.

100 See examination of Albert L. Greening, Deschenes Commission, NA, Yuzyk Papers, vol. 63, file/vol. 8, pp. 1002 and 1014–15; examination of Joseph R. Robillard, ibid., file/vol. 11, pp. 1275 and 1283; and cross-examination of John McCordick, ibid., file/vol. 20, pp. 2502–4. See also G.R.B. Panchuk to R. Innes, 1 December 1947, AN, IRO records, AJ 43/622; Panchuk to A.J. Desjardins, 19 January 1948, NA, RG 76, vol. 856, file 544-33; N.A. Robertson to External Affairs, 4 August 1948, NA, RG 25, vol. 6178, file 232-L-40, part 1; J.R. Robillard to Commissioner of Immigration, 3 June 1949, NA, RG 76, vol. 818, file 552-1-513; Immigration Branch Circular 96A, 7 June 1949, ibid., vol. 804, file 548-

10, part 1; and W. Herke to W. Sturhahn, 23 June 1950, NA, Canadian Lutheran
World Relief Papers, reel H-1398.

101 See Acting Superintendent to Commissioner of Immigration, 9 April 1948, NA,
RG 76, vol. 647, file A70063, part 1, reel C-10587; 'Duties and Responsibilities
of Security Officers Attached to the Canadian Immigration Mission in Occupied
Countries,' 12 July 1948, ibid., vol. 800, file 547-1, part 1; and Acting Head of
Organization and Methods to Immigration Branch, 30 August 1961, ibid., vol.
895, file 569-1, part 9. See also examination of Albert L. Greening, Deschenes
Commission, NA, Yuzyk Papers, vol. 63, file/vol. 8, pp. 998–9, and examination
of John McCordick, ibid., file/vol. 20, pp. 2486–7.

102 See E.D. Fulton to cabinet, 10 May 1958, NA, RG 76, vol. 948, file SF-C-1-1,
part 2. For an example, see Commissioner L.H. Nicholson to L. Fortier,
25 November 1954, ibid., vol. 978, file 5420-1-551.

103 As late as June 1950, rejected applications were marked 'not clear for security.'
Use of the 'Stage B' terminology appears to have started the following month.
Compare the memorandum from Deputy Minister of Citizenship and Immigration
to Minister of Citizenship and Immigration, 9 June 1950, NA, RG 26, vol. 166,
file 3-25-11, part 1, with the memorandum from Eastern District Superintendent
to Commissioner of Immigration, 18 July 1950, NA, RG 76, vol. 800, file 547-1,
part 1.

104 On the practice of blacklisting, see O. Cormier to all medical, labour, security, and
immigration officers, 1 May 1948, NA, RG 76, vol. 652, file B29300, part 6, reel
C-10590; 'Security Screening of Immigrants – Present Problems,' 29 March
1949, NA, RG 2, vol. 251, file S-100-D, Security Panel Document SP-40; minutes
of meeting on security problems held on 28 February 1952, Commissioner L.H.
Nicholson to L. Fortier, 4 March 1952, and Inspector K.W.N. Hall to Director of
Immigration, 24 March 1952, NA, RG 76, vol. 800, file 547-1, part 2; T.R. Burns
to Chief of Operations, 19 January 1954, and Canadian Government Immigration
Mission (Karlsruhe) to Acting Chief of Operations, 30 July 1956, ibid., vol. 762,
file 517-44, part 1; Consular Circular No. 1/55, 6 January 1955, ibid., vol. 784,
file 541-17, part 1.

105 On the agencies with which the RCMP cooperated, see dispatch from Canadian
Military Mission (Berlin) to External Affairs, 21 May 1948, report from Office of
Director of Intelligence (Office of U.S. Military Government) to Canadian Military Mission (Berlin), 16 July 1948, and High Commissioner to External Affairs,
4 August 1948, NA, RG 25, vol. 6178, file 232-L-40, part 1; P.W. Bird to Acting
Director of Immigration, 27 September 1950, NA, RG 26, vol. 104, file 3-24-1,
part 1; Commissioner C.W. Harvison to G.F. Davidson, 7 November 1960, ibid.,
vol. 164, file 3-18-17, part 2; Superintendent G.B. McClellan to L. Fortier,
23 March 1949, NA, RG 76, vol. 957, file SF-S-1, part 1; J.R. Robillard to A.J.

Andrew, 3 August 1951, and notes of meeting held at Wahnerheide on 16 August
1951, ibid., vol. 978, file 5420-1-551; R. Norfolk to O. Cormier, 1 November
1948, ibid., vol. 443, file 673931, part 18, reel C-10321; and Staff Memorandum
No. 13, 10 May 1954, ibid., vol. 812, file 551-1, part 7. See also examination of
George O'Leary, Deschenes Commission, NA, Yuzyk Papers, vol. 63, file/vol. 5,
pp. 655–6; examination of William H. Kelly, ibid., file/vol. 7, pp. 901–2; examination of Albert L. Greening, ibid., file/vol. 8, pp. 1006–10; and examination of
Joseph R. Robillard, ibid., file/vol. 11, p. 1273. For an example of the consultation
process, see J.W. O'Brien to Canadian Ambassador (Paris), 5 May 1948, M. Pope
to External Affairs, 21 May and 12 June 1948, External Affairs to Canadian
Military Mission (Berlin), 18 June 1948, O'Brien to High Commissioner,
12 July 1948, and O'Brien to A. Hlynka, 29 July 1948, NA, RG 25, vol. 6178,
file 232-L-40, part 1.

106 For examples of consultations with European police forces, see memorandum
from A.J. Hicks to Defence Liaison 2 Division, 17 April 1958, NA, RG 25, vol.
4326, file 12248-40, part 1; minutes of meeting regarding security problems held
on 28 February 1952, NA, RG 76, vol. 800, file 547-1, part 2; Officer in Charge
(Copenhagen) to Director of Immigration, 6 April 1955, ibid., vol. 805, file 548-
10, part 7; G.H. Ashley to RCMP Special Branch, 27 November 1953, ibid., vol.
977, file 5420-1-550, part 1; L.S. Grayson to RCMP Special Branch, 17 February
1955, ibid., vol. 979, file 5420-1-636, part 1; Constable F. de Miffonis to RCMP
Special Branch, 30 September 1948, ibid., vol. 106, file 18040, part 2, reel C-
4679; and draft memorandum by Commissioner S.T. Wood, undated [November
1949], NA, Keenleyside Papers, vol. 19, file Immigration 1939–1985.

107 This is confirmed in minutes of Security Panel meeting held on 11 March 1952,
NA, RG 2, vol. 232, file S-100-1-M; R. Innes to Brigadier M.S. Lush and General
Wood, 24 February 1947, NA, RG 25, vol. 2113, file AR 408/4, part 1; Lieutenant-General M. Pope to External Affairs, 16 April 1947, ibid., vol. 3895, file
9294-40; D.W. Jackson to G.D. Mallory, 16 May 1947, ibid., vol. 3896, file 9294-
AE-40; A.L. Jolliffe to External Affairs, 10 November 1949, External Affairs to
Canadian Military Mission (Berlin), 11 November 1949, Canadian Military Mission (Berlin) to External Affairs, 12 November 1949, and K. Rosenow to Canadian Military Mission (Berlin), 18 November 1949, ibid., vol. 3914, file 9408-40,
part 2; Annex 'A,' undated, appended to dispatch from Canadian Consulate
(Frankfurt am Main) to External Affairs, 5 September 1951, ibid., vol. 6245, file
9323-D-2-40, part 1; and Inspector K.W.N. Hall to Director of Immigration,
24 March 1952, NA, RG 76, vol. 800, file 547-1, part 2.

In her report for the Commission of Inquiry on War Criminals, Alti Rodal
claimed that Canadian security officers did not carry out their own checks at the
Berlin Document Centre (BDC, now called the Bundesarchiv-Aussenstelle

Zehlendorf), the repository of an enormous amount of Nazi-era documentation, but only through British military intelligence. Her assertion was based on a document in which Ottawa refused an RCMP officer's suggestion that a Canadian official be stationed there permanently. See 'Nazi War Criminals,' 190 and 510 n.38. This is a red herring. After all, security officers did not have to be on site to conduct checks. The results of such checks were reliable, regardless of whether they were obtained by mail, telephone, or in person. For a case where an individual was rejected on the basis of information received from the BDC over the phone, see H.W. Meybaum to Dr T.O.F. Herzer, 12 February 1951, NA, Canadian Lutheran World Relief Papers, reel H-1392. For evidence that Canadian security officers were conducting checks at the BDC from the outset of their screening operations, see Innes to Brigadier Lush, 24 February 1947, NA, RG 25, vol. 2113, file AR 408/4, part 1. For evidence that a BDC check was automatic in cases of prospective immigrants of German ethnic origin, see Canadian Military Mission (Berlin) to External Affairs, 24 January 1950, ibid., vol. 3914, file 9408-40, part 2.

108 See O. Cormier to Superintendent of Immigration, 10 September 1948, NA, RG 76, vol. 662, file B83052, part 1, reel C-10598; I.R. Stirling to Acting Director of Immigration, 18 October 1950, ibid., vol. 654, file B29300, part 15, reel C-10591; and 'The Problem of Refugees in Europe,' 27 December 1955, NA, V.J. Kaye Papers, vol. 12, file 17.

109 See Canadian Military Mission (Berlin) to External Affairs, 12 June 1948, NA, RG 25, vol. 6178, file 232-L-40, part 1; L. Fortier to Minister of Citizenship and Immigration, 8 March 1955, NA, RG 26, vol. 127, file 3-33-13; Commissioner L.H. Nicholson to Fortier, 7 March 1958, ibid., vol. 166, file 3-25-11, part 3; and examination of William H. Kelly, Deschenes Commission, NA, Yuzyk Papers, vol. 63, file/vol. 7, pp. 901–2.

110 See L. Fortier to A. MacNamara, 12 March 1951, NA, RG 26, vol. 145, file 3-41-15, part 1; G.M. Berkefeld to Reverend C.L. Monk, 5 December 1951, NA, Canadian Lutheran World Relief Papers, reel H-1400; minutes of meeting between Reverend W. Sturhahn and G.M. Berkefeld held at Bremen on 4 November 1953, NA, North American Baptist Immigration and Colonization Society Papers, vol. 1, file 6; memorandum from Officer in Charge (Copenhagen) to Director of Immigration, 4 June 1957, NA, RG 76, vol. 811, file 551-1, part 8; and Acting Chief of Operations Division to Dr W.H. Frost, 2 April 1958, ibid., vol. 895, file 569-1, part 8. See also testimony of Roger St-Vincent, cited in Decision in the Matter of Revocation of Citizenship between the Minister of Citizenship and Immigration and Vladimir Katriuk, 29 January 1999, p. 74.

111 See Annex 'A,' undated, appended to memorandum from Lieutenant-Colonel J.A.K. Rutherford to Security Panel, 30 March 1948, NA, RG 2, vol. 251, file S-100-D, Security Panel Document SP-24; E.W.T. Gill to N.A. Robertson, 22 Sep-

tember 1949, ibid., vol. 166, file I-50-10; Inspector R.A.S. MacNeil to J. George,
2 November 1948, NA, RG 25, vol. 5798, file 267(s), part 1; and G.J. Matte to
J.B. Laidlaw, 1 December 1948, NA, St Laurent Papers, vol. 56, file I-20-5-S.

112 Ottawa changed its policy in an effort to bring its screening procedures in line
with those of IRO. Though the organization regarded the blood-group tattoo as a
means of identifying former SS men, discovery of such a tattoo did not, under
IRO rules, render them ineligible for its assistance. See extract from IRO Provisional Order No. 42, 31 December 1947, quoted in memorandum from R. Innes to
L. Fortier, 24 April 1950, NA, RG 76, vol. 31, file 682, part 6, reel C-4690, and D.
Segat to IRO Eligibility Officers, 31 August 1948, AN, IRO records, AJ 43/979.
The determining factor, as was noted in Chapter 1, was whether the refugee's service in the Waffen-SS had been conscripted or voluntary. See PCIRO Eligibility
Division to PCIRO Director, 20 September 1948, ibid., AJ 43/978. After receiving
complaints that its overseas security officers were rejecting prospective immigrants on the basis of the tattoo alone, without recourse to any questioning regarding the nature of the applicant's service, Ottawa relented. According to new
instructions issued in the spring of 1948, Canadian security officers could admit a
non-German former member of the Waffen-SS if he could demonstrate to their
satisfaction that his service had been compulsory. On IRO's complaints and the
Canadian reaction, see PCIRO Resettlement Division to IRO Eligibility Branch,
6 January 1948, and A.L. Jolliffe to RCMP Commissioner, 14 April 1948, ibid.,
AJ 43/622; G.G. Congdon to Acting Superintendent, 5 May 1948, NA, RG 76,
vol. 443, file 673931, part 15, reel C-10321. On the continuing use of the blood-
group tattoo as a means of detecting membership in the Waffen-SS, see 'Screening of Applicants for Admission to Canada,' 20 November 1948, ibid., vol. 957,
file SF-S-1, part 1; N.A. Robertson to Prime Minister, 21 September 1949, NA,
RG 2, vol. 252, file S-100-1, part 2; Deputy Minister of Citizenship and Immigration to Minister of Citizenship and Immigration, 9 June 1950, NA, RG 26, vol.
166, file 3-25-11, part 1; Security Panel Document SP-198, 8 April 1959, ibid.,
vol. 153, file 1-18-7, part 2; and H.M. Jones to Minister of Citizenship and Immigration, 3 June 1963, ibid., vol. 164, file 3-18-17, part 2.

113 Report by M.J.M. Lasalle, 28 February 1948, NA, RG 29, vol. 3084, file 854-3-1,
part 1. In fact, there is only one recorded case of SS men with blood-group tattoos
or scars resulting from their removal having evaded detection by Canadian immigration authorities overseas. In September 1947, IRO informed the Canadian government that a small number of men aboard the vessel *General Stewart*, which
had just departed from Bremerhaven, Germany, with a contingent of 831 refugees
destined for placement with various lumber companies in Ontario, had suspicious
marks that had not been detected when they were examined overseas. On arrival at
Halifax, the suspects were subjected to physical examination. Twenty were found

to have small scars on their left arms at or near the spot where members of the SS typically were tattooed. Under questioning, most of the men admitted having had their blood group tattooed on their arms, but denied ever having served in the German armed forces. Uncertain as to whether the men had been granted visas despite their apparent SS affiliation, the authorities on the scene in Halifax submitted their names to RCMP headquarters for further investigation, and, in the meantime, allowed them to disembark and proceed to their destinations. For reasons unknown, the RCMP did not pursue the matter. On this incident, see J. Colley to G.G. Congdon, 9 September 1947, O. Cormier to Immigration Branch, 10 September 1947, Director of Immigration to RCMP Commissioner, 10 September, Corporal W.J. Lawrence to RCMP Headquarters (Nova Scotia), 16 September 1947, A.S. Christie to Atlantic District Superintendent, 19 September 1947, list of [marked] individuals [on the *General Stewart*], undated [September 1947], A. MacNamara to A.L. Jolliffe, 26 September 1947, and Inspector A.W. Parsons to Commissioner of Immigration, 26 September 1947, NA, RG 76, vol. 651, file B29300, parts 2 and 3, reel C-10589. Despite the government's efforts to keep this embarrassing incident under wraps, it was publicized almost immediately by Joe Salsberg, a communist member of the Ontario legislature who happened to be in Europe on a fact-finding tour at the time. On Salsberg's report, see cross-examination of Joseph R. Robillard, Deschenes Commission, NA, Yuzyk Papers, vol. 63, file/vol. 11, pp. 1343–4, and Irving Abella and Harold Troper, *None Is Too Many* (Toronto, 1982), 254.

114 For a facsimile of the TTD application form, see Application for a Temporary Travel Document, undated, NA, RG 25, vol. 3674, file 5127-D-40, part 1. For a facsimile of the TTD itself, see Temporary Travel Document in Lieu of Passport, undated, appended to note from G.G. Congdon to External Affairs, 30 September 1947, ibid. On the establishment and mandate of the CTB, see 'Tripartite Agreement Concerning Travel into and out of Occupied German Territory,' undated, and Appendix 'A,' undated, appended to Combined Travel Security Board instructions, 7 September 1946, ibid. For a facsimile of the IRO travel document, see IRO Certificate of Identity, undated, appended to memorandum from O. Cormier to Canadian visa officers in Europe, 1 March 1949, NA, RG 76, vol. 902, file 569-22-1, part 1. On the LTD, see J.R. Robillard to A.J. Andrew, 3 August 1951, ibid., vol. 978, file 5420-1-551, and 'The International Refugee Organization,' undated [1952], NA, RG 25, vol. 8118, file 5475-T-40, part 18.2. For a facsimile of the ML-101, see CCCRR Certificate of Identity for the Purpose of Emigration to Canada, undated, NA, RG 76, vol. 902, file 569-22-1, part 1. As of 1 July 1950, exit permits were no longer required by persons leaving the British zone of Germany. See (British) Passport Control Department Circular No. V/70, 18 July 1950, NA, RG 25, vol. 3914, file 9408-40, part 1.

115 On exit-permit procedures, see F.B. Buckingham to Regional Resettlement Officers at Hannover, Kiel, and Düsseldorf, 9 September 1947, NA, RG 25, vol. 3674, file 5127-D-40, part 1; Combined Travel Security Board instructions, 7 September 1946, ibid.; V.C. Phelan to A. MacNamara, 28 April 1948, NA, RG 27, vol. 279, file 1-26-10-1, part 1; Phelan to MacNamara, 21 May 1948, ibid., file 1-26-10-2, part 1; J.R. Robillard to Commissioner of Overseas Service, 3 June 1949, NA, RG 76, vol. 801, file 547-5-513; and E. Reid to Director of Immigration, 3 August 1946, ibid., vol. 31, file 682, part 5, reel C-4689. In her report for the Commission of Inquiry on War Criminals, Alti Rodal underestimates the significance for immigration screening of the requirement to obtain a travel document and exit permit. See 'Nazi War Criminals,' 139. As the preceding discussion has demonstrated, the requirement constituted a major hurdle to a prospective immigrant's departure from Germany.

116 On the change in British procedures, see L.G. Chance to Canadian Military Mission (Berlin), 22 November 1949, Canadian Military Mission (Berlin) to External Affairs, 25 November and 13 December 1949, External Affairs to Canadian Military Mission (Berlin), 20 December 1949, T.O.F. Herzer to A.L. Jolliffe, 2 January 1950, and J.J. Chenard to Canadian Military Mission (Berlin), 17 January 1950, NA, RG 25, vol. 3914, file 9408-40, part 2; E.J. Bye to A.C.A. Kaarsberg, 6 December 1949, Director of Immigration to Deputy Minister of Mines and Resources, 18 January 1950, J.G. Keil to Reverend C.L. Monk, 2 March 1950, Jolliffe to Deputy Minister of Citizenship and Immigration, 11 March 1950, and P.W. Bird to Acting Director of Immigration, 1 May 1950, NA, RG 76, vol. 655, file B41075, part 4, reel C-10592; Bird to Acting Director of Immigration, 23 March 1950, ibid., vol. 445, file 673931, part 22, reel C-10322; CCCRR to W. Harris, 2 February 1950, NA, Canadian Lutheran World Relief Papers, reel H-1400; T.O.F. Herzer to Minister of Citizenship and Immigration, 15 March 1950, ibid., reel H-1399; and O. Bachmann to Combined Travel Board (Herford), undated, ibid., reel H-1392.

117 On the Canadian practice of reviewing the results of British screening, see R.S. Staveley to PW and DP Division (Lemgo), 11 November 1948, H.F. Clark to J.W. O'Brien, 24 November 1948, O'Brien to Director of Immigration, 25 November 1948, O. Cormier to Brigadier Staveley, 27 December 1948, and A.L. Jolliffe to External Affairs, 3 February 1949, NA, RG 25, vol. 3674, file 5127-D-40, part 2. See also P.W. Bird to Acting Director of Immigration, 1 May 1950, NA, RG 76, vol. 655, file B41075, part 4, reel C-10592, and Bird to Acting Director of Immigration, 21 September 1950, ibid., vol. 843, file 553-75, part 1. It should be noted that the foregoing correspondence effectively refutes Alti Rodal's assertion that 'Canadian screening officers accepted Temporary Travel Documents (TTDs) issued by the Combined Travel Board (CTB), usually without checking official

German sources in order to determine whether German naturalization had been received.' For her erroneous assertion, made without reference (indeed, in opposition) to the documentary evidence, see 'Nazi War Criminals,' 204.

118 These problems were reported in Annex 'A,' undated, appended to memorandum from Lieutenant-Colonel J.A.K. Rutherford to Security Panel, 30 March 1948, NA, RG 2, vol. 251, file S-100-D, Security Panel Document SP-24. For specific instances of such IRO misrepresentation, see report by J.M. Knowles, undated [February 1950], P.W. Bird to Director of Immigration, 10 February 1950, F.B. Cotsworth to Canadian Government Immigration Mission, 13 February 1950, C.E.S. Smith to External Affairs, 24 February 1950, Smith to RCMP Commissioner, 24 February 1950, and Acting Director of Immigration to Bird, 9 March 1950, NA, RG 76, vol. 445, file 673931, part 22, reel C-10322.

119 Citing a Security Panel report on the problem, Alti Rodal suggested that reapplication, particularly for bulk-labour schemes, could take place within days of an initial rejection, thereby vitiating the effect of any blacklist. See 'Nazi War Criminals,' 199, and 'Security Screening of Immigrants – Present Problems,' 29 March 1949, NA, RG 2, vol. 251, file S-100-D, Security Panel Document SP-40. This no doubt happened on occasion, but Canadian bulk-labour schemes typically took weeks to organize. Thus, the chance that a rejected applicant could reapply before his name had been blacklisted was relatively low. For the case of an inadmissible applicant who was caught twice within the space of five months trying to apply for admission to Canada under farm-labour schemes, see A.L. Jolliffe to H. Allard, 11 August 1949, NA, RG 76, vol. 445, file 673931, part 21, reel C-10321. For a similar case, see J.M. Knowles to Canadian Immigration Mission (Karlsruhe), 15 September 1949, and P.W. Bird to Superintendent of Emigration, 20 September 1949, ibid., part 20. For a contemporary report that demonstrated the overall effectiveness of blacklisting, see J.R. Robillard to Chief of Operations, 28 May 1954, ibid., vol. 801, file 547-5-551, part 1.

120 Swiss, French, and Italian forgeries seem to have been quite prevalent. See L. Clark to L. Beaudry, 12 April 1946, and Beaudry to Clark, 18 April 1946, NA, RG 25, vol. 3361, file 11-EMJ-40C; Constable F. de Miffonis to RCMP Special Branch, 30 September 1948, and C.E.S. Smith to RCMP Commissioner, 14 October 1948, NA, RG 76, vol. 106, file 18040, part 2, reel C-4769; L.B. Pearson to J.A. MacKinnon, 15 October 1948, ibid., vol. 107, file 18040, part 3, reel C-4770; and minutes of meeting on security problems held on 28 February 1952, ibid., vol. 800, file 547-1, part 2.

121 On the Karlsruhe case, see statement by ———, 18 December 1951, RCMP report, 29 December 1951; note to file, 2 January 1952, RCMP report, 28 January 1952, and Lookout No. 66, undated [1952], NA, RG 76, vol. 721, file 540-6-551, part 1; J.R. Robillard to Canadian Ambassador (Bonn), 9 September 1952,

and Chief of Admissions to Director of Immigration, 4 November 1953, ibid., part 2.

122 For an early indication that the backlog was becoming a serious problem, see E.W.T. Gill to cabinet, 4 February 1947, NA, King Papers, series J4, vol. 420, file January–March 1947. The growth of the backlog, which reached twenty thousand uncleared cases by the end of 1949, can be followed in Annex 'A,' undated, appended to memorandum from Lieutenant-Colonel J.A.K. Rutherford to Security Panel, 30 March 1948, NA, RG 2, vol. 251, file S-100-D, Security Panel Document SP-24; L. Fortier to Commissioner of Immigration, 20 June 1949, NA, RG 76, vol. 800, file 547-1, part 1; draft memorandum, undated [August 1949], ibid., vol. 957, file SF-S-1, part 1; and minutes of Security Panel meeting held on 19 September 1949, NA, RG 2, vol. 251, file S-100-M.

123 For Ottawa's initial attempts to deal with the backlog, see A.L. Jolliffe to RCMP Commissioner, 14 December 1946, Director of Immigration to F.B. Cotsworth, 3 January 1947, Jolliffe to file, 24 January 1947, and Jolliffe to J.A. Glen, 27 January 1947, NA, RG 76, vol. 800, file 547-1, part 1. On the decision to refer the matter to the Security Panel, see minutes of cabinet meeting held on 29 January 1947, NA, RG 2, vol. 2639, reel T-2365, frames 162 and 165–6, and A.D.P. Heeney to Glen, 31 January 1947, NA, RG 76, vol. 947, file SF-C-1, part 1.

124 Minutes of Security Panel meeting held on 30 January 1947, NA, RG 2, vol. 251, file S-100-M.

125 See Commissioner S.T. Wood to A.L. Jolliffe, 27 January 1947, NA, RG 76, vol. 800, file 547-1, part 1.

126 E.W.T. Gill to cabinet, 4 February 1947, NA, King Papers, series J4, vol. 420, file January–March 1947.

127 More than two years later, an Immigration Branch official lamented the continued backlog of uncleared cases, ascribing it to the 'abandoning of [RCMP] Commissioner Wood's original idea of spot-checking in favour of complete clearance of all cases.' See A.W. Baskerville to L. Fortier, 8 June 1949, NA, RG 76, vol. 800, file 547-1, part 1. It should be noted that the aforementioned document effectively refutes Alti Rodal's suggestion that the Security Panel's recommendation meant 'an undetermined number of immigrants during this period could therefore have entered Canada without any security screening.' For her highly questionable inference, which removed the panel's recommendation from its historical context, see 'Nazi War Criminals,' 183.

Despite evidence to the contrary, the perception persists that a spot-check system of immigration screening was implemented as a result of the panel's decision. For example, in 1998 counsel for an alleged war criminal convinced a Federal Court judge that less than 20 per cent of all refugees who emigrated to Canada from Europe during the early postwar period had been screened. See Dueck Decision, 21 December 1948, pp. 93–4. The percentage was arrived at by comparing an Immigration-Labour Committee figure of 8,728 refugees admitted to Canada between 1946 and 1 April 1948 with an RCMP report that only 1,611 refugees had been screened during the same period. See table titled 'Group Movements,' 8 April 1948, appended to memorandum from R. Ranger to cabinet, 10 April 1948, NA, RG 26, vol. 100, file 3-18-1, part 2, and Annex 'A,' undated, appended to memorandum from Lieutenant-Colonel J.A.K. Rutherford to Security Panel, 30 March 1948, NA, RG 2, vol. 251, file S-100-D. (In fact, the number of refugees admitted during this period was 13,201, Dueck's counsel having neglected the 4,473 admitted under the close relative scheme. See table titled 'Immigration to Canada, Showing Displaced Persons by Groups, from April 1947 to March 15, 1948,' appended to minutes of Immigration-Labour Committee meeting held on 1 June 1948, NA, RG 26, vol. 72, file Immigration-Labour Committee Meetings, part 2.) This was a classic case of comparing apples with oranges. The figure of 1,611 screened refugees, which included 272 who were rejected, clearly did not refer to the totality of RCMP screening. After all, almost one hundred refugees were screened out of a single bulk-labour movement on security grounds in July 1947. See O. Cormier to Commissioner of Immigration, 12 and 15 July 1947, NA, RG 76, vol. 651, file B29300, part 2, reel C-10589. Another three hundred were rejected on security grounds at one refugee camp during the latter half of 1947. See H.G. Dehn to PCIRO, 23 December 1947, AN, IRO records, AJ 43/973. Those two examples alone exceeded the number of 272 rejections reported by the RCMP. If the figure of 272 was incomplete, then, by extension, so too was the total of 1,611 refugees screened. In all likelihood, the figures reported by the RCMP reflected only cases dealt with by the Mounties' liaison office in London, and not those handled by screening teams in the field. On the limited categories of prospective immigrants for which the RCMP's London office was responsible, see Immigration Branch Instruction No. 1, 29 March 1947, NA, RG 76, vol. 800, file 547-1, part 1, and Immigration Branch Instruction No. 3, 29 July 1947, RG 25, vol. 3900, file 9323-N-40, part 1.

128 For cabinet's decision with respect to the backlog, see A.D.P. Heeney to J.A. Glen, 7 February 1947, NA, RG 2, vol. 63, file C-20-2, part 2; minutes of cabinet meeting held on 5 February 1947, ibid., vol. 2639, reel T-2365, frames 184–6; Immigration Branch Instruction No. 3, 29 July 1947, NA, RG 25, vol. 3900, file 9323-N-40, part 1; A.L. Jolliffe to Commissioner S.T. Wood, 17 February 1947, Immigration Branch Instruction No. 1, 29 March 1947, and Jolliffe to Acting Commissioner of Immigration, 10 October 1947, NA, RG 76, vol. 800, file 547-1, part 1.

129 See Superintendent G.B. McClellan to RCMP Commissioner, 26 September 1950, NA, RG 146, Public Document, and Operations Memorandum No. 3,

16 March 1962, NA, RG 6, vol. 129, file 14-3-8. Owing to the virtual impossibility of conducting security checks behind the Iron Curtain, the fourteen-day procedure was dropped for refugee women and children from eastern Europe by the summer of 1949. See McClellan to L. Fortier, 19 July 1949, NA, RG 76, vol. 800, file 547-1, part 1.

130 Inspector A.W. Parsons to Director of Immigration, 13 November 1947, and L. Fortier to Overseas Commissioner for European Emigration, 20 June 1947, NA, RG 76, vol. 800, file 547-1, part 1; 'Security Screening of Immigrants – Present Problems,' 29 March 1949, NA, RG 2, vol. 251, file S-100-D, Security Panel Document SP-40; and minutes of Security Panel meeting held on 5 April 1949, ibid., file S-100-M.

131 This case is reported in Annex 'A,' undated, appended to memorandum from Lieutenant-Colonel J.A.K. Rutherford to Security Panel, 30 March 1948, NA, RG 2, vol. 251, file S-100-D, Security Panel Document SP-24.

132 On this problem, see Superintendent G.B. McClellan to RCMP Commissioner, 26 September 1950, NA, RG 146, Public Document.

133 On the problem of rushed clearances in general, see examination of William H. Kelly, Deschenes Commission, NA, Yuzyk Papers, vol. 63, file/vol. 7, pp. 906–7. On spot checking four hundred farm labourers from Germany, see P.W. Bird to Acting Director of Immigration Branch, 8 September 1950, NA, RG 76, vol. 843, file 553-75, part 1. On the problem with the Italian farm workers' clearances, see L. Fortier to A. MacNamara, 19 December 1952, NA, RG 26, vol. 132, file 3-35-2, part 2. On the German engineer, see G.R. Benoit to Director of Immigration, 13 September 1951, Superintendent of Immigration (Eastern District) to Director of Immigration, 30 November 1951, W.E. Harris to C.D. Howe, 10 December 1951, and Benoit to Director of Immigration, 28 November 1952, NA, RG 76, vol. 800, file 547-1, part 2. See also M.F. Gregg to B. Claxton, 14 February 1952, NA, RG 2, vol. 232, file S-100-1-D, Security Panel Document SP-117. The case of the German engineer focused Ottawa's attention on the larger problem of screening immigrants who were slated for employment in sensitive positions in defence plants. On the government's handling of the issue, see Fortier to N.A. Robertson, 25 February 1952, NA, RG 76, vol. 800, file 547-1, part 2, and minutes of Security Panel meeting held on 11 March 1952, NA, RG 2, vol. 232, file S-100-1-M.

To be fair, Canadian authorities tried to ensure that priority clearance did not mean sloppy screening. For the case of two hundred Latvian miners who were prevented from boarding a ship bound for Canada because of questions about their clearance, see A. MacNamara to R.N. Bryson, 2 February 1951, and Bryson to MacNamara, 19 March 1951, NA, RG 27, vol. 290, file 1-26-56-3.

134 On this problem, see Commissioner S.T. Wood to H.L. Keenleyside, 8 November 1947, NA, RG 26, vol. 166, file 3-25-11, part 1; Methods and Procedures Section

to Immigration Branch, 24 September 1957, NA, RG 76, vol. 808, file 548-12-
153; and P.H. Irwin to B. Godbout, 22 June 1965, ibid., vol. 809, file 548-16, part
1. For an admission that the training of Canadian immigration teams stationed in
Europe during the 1950s had left much to be desired, see examination of Albert L.
Greening, Deschenes Commission, NA, Yuzyk Papers, vol. 63, file/vol. 8, p. 991.

135 This estimate of Einsatzgruppen victims can be found in Helmut Krausnick and
Hans-Heinrich Wilhelm, *Die Truppe des Weltanschauungskrieges: Die Einsatzgruppen der Sicherheitspolizei und des SD, 1938–1942* (Stuttgart, 1981), 621.

136 The omission of the Schutzmannschaften and the incorrect description of the Einsatzgruppen can be found in Allied Control Council Directive No. 38, 14 October
1946, NARA, RG 260, series 3, vol. 3.

137 See cross-examination of John McCordick, Deschenes Commission, NA, Yuzyk
Papers, vol. 63, file/vol. 20, p. 2502. For specific cases of misrepresentation on
application forms and in interviews, see cross-examination of Albert L. Greening,
ibid., file/vol. 8, p. 1052; T.O.F. Herzer to Messrs N.J. Warnke and J.G. Keil,
8 May 1950, Warnke to Herzer, 15 May 1950, and Herzer to Warnke and Keil,
27 May 1950, NA, Canadian Lutheran World Relief Papers, reel H-1398; H.
Streuber to Herzer, 25 May 1951, NA, North American Baptist Immigration and
Colonization Society Papers, series B3, vol. 5, file 58.

138 For an official acknowledgment of this problem, see minutes of Security Panel
meeting held on 5 April 1949, NA, RG 2, vol. 251, file S-100-D.

139 The loss of sources in the Soviet bloc is reported in O. Cormier to Superintendent
of Immigration, 10 September 1948, NA, RG 76, vol. 662, file B83052, part 1,
reel C-10598; Department of Mines and Resources memorandum, 4 February
1949, and RCMP to Commissioner of Immigration, 10 March 1949, ibid., vol.
802, file 547-5-573, part 1; 'Security Screening of Immigrants – Present Problems,' 29 March 1949, NA, RG 2, vol. 251, file S-100-D, Security Panel Document SP-40; and draft memorandum by Commissioner S.T. Wood, undated
[1949], NA, Keenleyside Papers, vol. 19. file Immigration 1938–1985. See also
examination of Albert L. Greening, Deschenes Commission, NA, Yuzyk Papers,
vol. 63, file/vol. 8, p. 1017.

140 E. Reid to External Affairs, 23 September 1948, NA, RG 25, vol. 4165, file 939-
B-40, part 1; minutes of Security Panel meeting held on 5 April 1949, NA, RG 2,
vol. 251, file S-100-M; L. Fortier to RCMP Commissioner, 8 August 1949, and
Superintendent G.B. McClellan to Fortier, 13 August 1949, NA, RG 76, vol. 957,
file SF-S-1, part 1; E.W.T. Gill to Security Panel, 16 September 1949, NA, RG 2,
vol. 251, file S-100-D, Security Panel Document SP-51; minutes of Security Panel
meeting held on 19 September 1949, ibid., file S-100-M; N.A. Robertson to cabinet, 22 September 1949, ibid., vol. 124, file C-20-5, document nos 1020–75; minutes of cabinet meeting held on 22 September 1949, ibid., vol. 2644, reel T-2366,

frames 807 and 810–11; Robertson to C. Gibson, 26 September 1949, NA, RG 76, vol. 957, file SF-S-1, part 1; External Affairs to Canadian Legation (Prague), 12 November 1949, ibid., vol. 785, file 541-25-36; Department of Citizenship and Immigration to Canadian Government Immigration Mission (Salzburg), 9 March 1950, ibid., vol. 804, file 548-10, part 1; and IRO Director-General to Head of Canadian Delegation, 14 April 1951, NA, RG 25, vol. 8117, file 5475-T-40, part 15.2.

141 For examples of German nationals who were caught in the act of lying or with-holding information by virtue of Canadian checks at the BDC, see Inspector in Charge to Central District Superintendent, 22 September 1949, NA, RG 76, vol. 655, file B41075, part 3, reel C-10592; F.B. Cotsworth to Canadian Government Immigration Mission (Karlsruhe), 7 December 1949, ibid., vol. 31, file 682, part 5, reel C-4690; W. Herke to W. Sturhahn, 23 June 1950, NA, Canadian Lutheran World Relief Papers, reel H-1398; and H.W. Meybaum to T.O.F. Herzer, 12 February 1951, ibid., reel H-1393. For the case of a German trade delegate whose application for permanent admission was rejected on the basis of RCMP security checks, see curriculum vitae of J. ———, 28 May 1953, P.T. Baldwin to RCMP, 15 June 1953, Admissions Division to Immigration Officer in Charge (Montreal), 9 September 1953, RCMP to Director of Immigration, 7 October 1953, Appeals Sub-Committee to Minister of Citizenship and Immigration, undated [1953], and Deportation Statistics, undated, NA, RG 76, accession 81–82/198, box 9, file C-67830.

142 This summary of the Rauca case is from Sol Littman, *War Criminal on Trial: The Rauca Case* (Toronto, 1983), 115–18, and submission by Littman, Deschenes Commission, NA, Yuzyk Papers, vol. 63, file/vol. 3, pp. 386–93.

143 During my tenure with the Crimes against Humanity and War Crimes Section of the Department of Justice of Canada, I worked on the case of an eastern European national who had received a security clearance from a U.S. Army CIC unit shortly after the end of the war. This individual was subsequently able to obtain a Canadian visa by presenting the written clearance to Canadian immigration authorities. Perhaps Rauca did the same.

144 Thus, I find myself in partial agreement with York University political scientist Reg Whitaker, who speculated that Rauca was able to gain admission to Canada through the use of false documents provided by a 'friendly' government. See Whitaker, *Double Standard*, 115. In view of the stringency with which German nationals were screened for immigration purposes even after their removal from the 'enemy alien' category, it may well be that Rauca had received a security clearance from Allied occupation authorities, which he later presented to the Canadian immigration team that examined him and to the CTB. On the other hand, Rauca carried a valid German passport under his own name, so whatever

assistance he may have received from a foreign intelligence service, it was not in the form of false documents.

6: Exceptions That Proved the Rule

1 Clarence G. Lasby, *Project Paperclip: German Scientists and the Cold War* (New York, 1971), 18–19.
2 Tom Bower, *Blind Eye to Murder: Britain, America and the Purging of Nazi Germany – A Pledge Betrayed* (London, 1981), 111–13.
3 On the T-Force raids and the reaction in Moscow, see J. Léger to External Affairs, 1 August 1947, NA, RG 25, vol. 3896, file 9294-R-40, part 1; Léger to External Affairs, 14 November 1947, and draft *Financial Post* article, undated, appended to note from J.H. Warren to L.B. Pearson, 25 November 1946, NA, RG 25, vol. 7900, file 7-DC(s). On the Soviets' program of scientific exploitation, see Bower, *Blind Eye to Murder*, 112.
4 On the NRC's position with respect to the allocation of German scientists and technicians, see A.G. Shenstone to V. Massey, 16 July 1945, High Commissioner to External Affairs, 30 July 1945, and C.J. Mackenzie to H. Wrong, 1 September 1945, NA, RG 25, vol. 7900, file 7-DC(s).
5 On the United Kingdom's position regarding the scientists' political backgrounds, see Dominion Affairs to External Affairs, 18 September 1945, ibid. On the Canadian government's concern with the political implications of any attempt to acquire German scientists and technicians, see H. Wrong to C.J. Mackenzie, 14 December 1945, Mackenzie to External Affairs, 31 December 1945, and External Affairs to High Commissioner, 4 January 1946, ibid.
6 External Affairs to Acting High Commissioner, 10 September 1946, ibid.
7 N.A. Robertson to Prime Minister, 10 September 1946, NA, W.L.M. King Papers, series J4, vol. 331, reel H-1522, frame C229073.
8 See C.J. Mackenzie to C.D. Howe, 26 September 1946, NA, RG 76, vol. 649, file B6737, part 1, reel C-10588. On McMaster's request for S——, see Mackenzie to L.B. Pearson, 11 October 1946, NA, RG 25, vol. 3897, file 9294-S-40C.
9 On the survey, see A.D.P. Heeney to cabinet, 2 December 1946, NA, RG 2, vol. 65, file C-20-5, document nos 230–344, and Heeney to J.A. Glen, 5 December 1946, ibid., vol. 63, file C-20-2, part 2.
10 On External's concerns, see L.B. Pearson to R.G Riddell, 22 October 1946, and J.H. Warren to Pearson, 23 October 1946, NA, RG 25, vol. 7900, file 7-DC(s). For the government's approval of the change in policy, see minutes of cabinet meeting held on 2 October 1946, NA, RG 2, vol. 2639, reel T-2364, frame 1648.
11 On attempts by companies to recruit German scientists directly, see G.D. Mallory to A.L. Jolliffe, 6 November 1946, NA, RG 76, vol. 649, file B6737, part 1, reel C-

10588. On the requests submitted by companies through government departments, see L.B. Pearson to High Commissioner, 18 October 1946, NA, RG 25, vol. 7900, file 7-DC(s), and Jolliffe to J.A. Glen, 9 November 1946, NA, RG 2, vol. 102, file R-100-1. For an example of such a request, see G. Beavers to Major A.J.J. Macdonnell, 12 September 1946, NA, RG 25, vol. 3897, file 9294-Y-40, and J.W. Holmes to External Affairs, 21 September 1946, ibid., vol. 7900, file 7-DC(s).

12 A.L. Jolliffe to J.A. Glen, 9 November 1946, NA, RG 2, vol. 102, file R-100-1.

13 On the decision to expand the program of technician immigration, see minutes of cabinet meeting held on 12 November 1946, ibid., vol. 2639, reel T-2364, frame 1733; External Affairs note, 12 November 1946, NA, RG 25, vol. 7900, file 7-DC(s); and A.D.P. Heeney to J.A. Glen, 14 November 1946, NA, RG 26, vol. 100, file 3-18-1, part 1.

14 On the practice of reserving scientists through BIOS, see High Commissioner to External Affairs, 30 July 1945, and J.W. Holmes to External Affairs, 21 September 1946, NA, RG 25, vol. 7900, file 7-DC(s); Beavers Dental Burs to Department of Trade and Commerce, 20 October 1946, NA, RG 76, vol. 649, file B6737, part 1, reel C-10588. On the vetting of requests by the JSM, see note for Bower, 23 September 1947, NA, RG 25, vol. 2086, file AR 22/5, part 1. For some examples, see F.J. Broomfield to J. Léger, 4 September 1947, Léger to External Affairs, 6 September 1947, Léger to Broomfield, 8 September 1947, Léger to External Affairs, 9 September 1947, Broomfield to Léger, 11 September and 30 October 1947, L. Reid to Léger, 18 November 1947, Broomfield to Léger, 28 November 1947, and G.M. Bryant to Léger, 9 February 1948, ibid., part 2. See also High Commission to External Affairs, 6 January 1949, ibid., vol. 3896, file 9294-AD-40. On the rules for settling disputes over allocation, see N.A. Robertson to External Affairs, 27 November 1946, NA, RG 2, vol. 102, file R-100-1.

15 For the case of the chemist W. S——, who was requested by a Canadian company that specialized in the production of citric acid, see F.J. Broomfield to J. Léger, 17 October 1947, and Broomfield to D.V. Le Pan, 25 November 1947, NA, RG 25, vol. 2086, file AR 22/5, part 2; L. Beaudry to Canadian Embassy (Washington), 20 November 1947, Canadian Embassy (Washington) to External Affairs, 12 December 1947, Léger to External Affairs, 20 December 1947, Canadian Embassy (Washington) to External Affairs, 6 January 1948, M. Pope to General L.D. Clay, 5 February 1948, Clay to Pope, 23 February 1948, Canadian Military Mission (Berlin) to External Affairs, 8 April 1948, Canadian Military Mission (Berlin) to External Affairs, 11 May 1948, A.L. Jolliffe to External Affairs, 22 October 1948, External Affairs to High Commissioner, 23 December 1948, and High Commissioner to External Affairs, 6 January 1949, ibid., vol. 3896, file 9294-AD-40. Only a direct appeal to General Lucius D. Clay, head of the U.S. military government in Germany, resulted in S——'s release to Canada. For the case of Dr G. B——, a

microbiologist and one of Europe's foremost authorities on viral diseases, see J.J. Gryse to G.S.H. Barton, 28 July 1947, ibid., file 9294-AE-40; External Affairs to High Commission, 9 October 1947, Léger to Broomfield, 11 October 1947, and Broomfield to Léger, 17 and 24 October 1947, ibid., vol. 2086, file AR 22/5, part 2; and Broomfield to J.G.H. Halstead, 13 December 1948, ibid., part 3. Requested by the Department of Agriculture in the summer of 1947, Dr B—— was not made available to Canada for a year and a half, when the Americans were through with him. For the case of E. B——, an expert in the design and styling of costume jewellery, see G.B. Mallory to External Affairs, 4 November 1947, and B. Mairowitz to Léger, 11 June 1948, ibid.; Canadian Embassy (Washington) to External Affairs, 22 September 1948, ibid., vol. 3896, file 9294-AN-40.

16 For some examples, see Canadian Embassy (Washington) to External Affairs, 16 December 1946, ibid., vol. 7900, file 7-DC(s), and N.A. Robertson to External Affairs, 27 October 1948, ibid., vol. 2086, file AR 22/5, part 3.

17 F.J. Broomfield to J.G.H. Halstead, 18 November and 13 December 1948, and F. Hudd to B.J. Bachand, 21 December 1948, ibid., vol. 2086, file AR 22/5, part 3; Broomfield to Halstead, 31 December 1948, ibid., vol. 3896, file 9294-R-40, part 2; B.R. Hayden to External Affairs, 17 January 1949, and External Affairs to High Commission, 19 January 1949, ibid., file 9294-BJ-40; Hayden to External Affairs, 20 January 1949, ibid., file 9294-R-40, part 2; and High Commission to External Affairs, 27 January 1949, ibid., vol. 3897, file 9294-BM-40.

18 The screening conducted by the panels was based on the questionnaires filled out by the German scientists under authority of Control Council Directive Nos 24 and 36. For evidence of this, see J. Léger to External Affairs, 4 November 1947, ibid., vol. 3896, file 9294-AE-40.

19 The process was pieced together from High Commission to External Affairs, 9 November 1946, NA, King Papers, series J1, vol. 414, reel C-9176, frames 373076–7; 'Notes for the Guidance of Representatives Who Will Be Approaching Germans Accepted by the Darwin Panel and Resident in the British Zone,' undated [November 1946], and N.A. Robertson to External Affairs, 27 November 1946, NA, RG 2, vol. 102, file R-100-1; J. Léger to External Affairs, 21 June 1947, NA, RG 25, vol. 7900, file 7-DC(s); G.E. Beavers to R. Funke, 24 January 1947, Funke to Beavers, 30 January and 14 March 1947, and Beavers to Funke, 16 April 1947, NA, R. Funke Papers, vol. 1, file 14; C.E.S. Smith to Funke, 15 September 1947, ibid., vol. 2, file 49.

20 F. Hudd to B.J. Bachand, 21 December 1948, NA, RG 25, vol. 2086, file AR 22/5, part 3, and High Commission to External Affairs, 27 January 1949, ibid., vol. 3897, file 9294-BM-40.

21 N.A. Robertson to External Affairs, 27 November 1946, NA, RG 2, vol. 102, file R-100-1.

22 For examples, see J. Léger to G.M. Bryant, 23 January and 15 June 1948, T-Force Frankfurt to T-Force London, 3 October 1947, Canadian Economic Section to Bower, 6 October 1947, and telephone message from Bower, 18 December 1947, NA, RG 25, vol. 2086, file AR 22/5, part 2; R.A.D. Ford to Bryant, 22 July 1948, ibid., part 3.

23 Arrangements were made with the March Shipping Agency Limited in Montreal to provide berths for the scientists on transatlantic voyages from Hamburg to Canadian ports. See PC 2047, 29 May 1947, NA, RG 2, vol. 1974, file 3628G. As minister of reconstruction and supply, Howe was well aware of the difficulties that even the European dependants of Canadian residents were having in procuring passage. He also was in a position to do something about it, as he demonstrated as minister responsible for immigration a few months later. See C.W. Jackson to file, 9 September 1947, NA, RG 76, vol. 651, file B29300, part 3, reel C-10589, and 'Entry to Canada of Persons Now Residing in Germany and Austria,' 17 September 1947, ibid., vol. 31, file 682, part 5, reel C-4690.

24 This was confirmed to the March Shipping line when it raised concerns that authorities at its western European ports of call might attempt to remove its scientist passengers as suspected war criminals. In response, External Affairs assured the company that the scientists would all be screened and that none would be wanted 'for war crimes or anything of that nature.' See G. Dubé to G.D. Mallory, 5 July 1947, E.A. Coté to E.R. Hopkins, 10 July 1947, and Hopkins to Mallory, 17 July 1947, NA, RG 25, vol. 3896, file 9294-R-40, part 1.

25 J.H. Warren to Canadian Embassy (Washington), 10 December 1946, and Canadian Embassy (Washington) to External Affairs, 16 December 1946, ibid., vol. 7900, file 7-DC(s).

26 On the regime of screening to which the RCMP agreed, see A.L. Jolliffe to L.B. Pearson, 25 November 1946, ibid.; Jolliffe to Commissioner S.T. Wood, 16 and 25 November 1946, and RCMP Headquarters to Director of Immigration, 28 November 1946, NA, RG 76, vol. 649, file B6737, part 1, reel C-10588; RCMP Headquarters to Director of Immigration, 6 January 1947, NA, RG 2, vol. 102, file R-100-1.

27 See M.W. Mackenzie to A. MacNamara, 20 June 1947, NA, RG 27, vol. 278, file 1-26-4, part 1. Some thought was given to fingerprinting the scientists/technicians upon their entry to Canada, but this idea was dropped. See J. Leopold to Commissioner of Immigration, 30 April 1947, Commissioner of Immigration to RCMP Commissioner, 7 June 1947, and RCMP Commissioner to Commissioner of Immigration, 12 June 1947, NA, RG 76, vol. 649, file B6737, part 1, reel C-10588.

28 In her report for the Commission of Inquiry on War Criminals, Alti Rodal suggested that the screening procedures for German scientists and technicians were inadequate. Her conclusions in this regard are based on what she perceived to be Canada's 'virtually total reliance for security screening on British and American

authorities,' as well as the latter's penchant for 'cover[ing] up incriminating information about possible war criminal background.' Rodal also suggested that Canadian officials attempted to circumvent American screening. See 'Nazi War Criminals in Canada: The Historical and Policy Setting from the 1940s to the Present' (Commission of Inquiry on War Criminals, Ottawa, 1986), 331 and 340–1. Neither of these conclusions can be sustained. There was essentially no difference between the screening procedures that German scientists and technicians underwent and those applied to ordinary German nationals, except, perhaps, that there was an additional layer of screening – first the Darwin and DCOS panels, later the BAC – in the case of the scientists and technicians. Otherwise, the usual visa and exit-permit checks were applied. These included checks at the Berlin Document Centre (BDC, now called Bundesarchiv-Aussenstelle Zehlendorf), whose storehouse of personnel files from the Nazi Party and affiliated organizations would have revealed whether the scientist/technician in question had been a Nazi sympathizer. For evidence that BDC checks were carried out on the scientists/technicians, see Information Section to Office of Military Government for Germany (U.S.), 4 April 1947, appended to dispatch from Lieutenant-General M. Pope to External Affairs, 16 April 1947, NA, RG 25, vol. 3895, file 9294-40. Also, the fact that all requests for the issuance of temporary visas to the scientists/technicians, which were to be made only after the Darwin or DCOS and exit-permit procedures had been carried out, had to be submitted through the RCMP's liaison officer in London, is further proof that Canadian procedures were not fundamentally altered in the case of the German scientists/technicians. See RCMP Headquarters to Director of Immigration, 6 January 1947, NA, RG 2, vol. 102, file R-100-1. Finally, Rodal herself admitted that the RCMP were involved in screening the scientists/technicians. Citing C.D. Howe's attempts to speed up their admission in the summer of 1947, Rodal quoted one document in which it was reported that Howe was dismayed 'apparently because of delays in security investigations by the RCMP.' See 'Nazi War Criminals,' 340. In this regard, it should be noted that Howe was unable to expedite Canadian immigration-screening procedures. On his attempts to do so, see minutes of cabinet meeting held on 10 July 1947, ibid., vol. 2640, T-2365, frames 693–4; A.D.P. Heeney to Howe, 11 July 1947, NA, RG 26, vol. 122, file 3-32-6; and Heeney to H. Mitchell, 12 July 1947, NA, RG 27, vol. 278, file 1-26-4, part 1. For proof that screening procedures continued as before, see A.L. Jolliffe to External Affairs, 13 April 1948, NA, RG 25, vol. 3896, file 9294-AD-40, and Jolliffe to External Affairs, 20 April 1948, ibid., file 9294-AM-40. As to Rodal's contention that Canada tried to speed up American screening procedures, this is based on her misunderstanding of the functions of the JSM, and, later, the BAC. As described above, the JSM and BAC did not carry out screening, but rather were allocation agencies. The documentation cited by Rodal reflected an attempt by

Canadian officials to circumvent the JSM because of irregularities and unfairness in way it was allocating scientists and technicians.

29 For cases of German scientists/technicians brought to Ottawa's attention by the British government, see R.G. Riddell to Deputy Minister of Trade and Commerce, 11 April 1947, NA, RG 25, vol. 3896, file 9294-R-40, part 1, and N.A. Robertson to External Affairs, 12 March 1947, NA, RG 2, vol. 251, file R-100-1.

30 On the Anglo-American fears and Canada's response, see M.W. Mackenzie to External Affairs, 11 February 1947, NA, RG 2, vol. 102, file R-100-1; Dominion Affairs to External Affairs, 1 February 1947, NA, RG 25, vol. 7900, file 7-DC(s); and L.B. Pearson to Director of Immigration, 8 February 1947, NA, RG 76, vol. 649, file B6737, part 1, reel C-10588.

31 On Ottawa's lack of interest in the scientists recommended by the British government, see M.W. Mackenzie to R.G. Riddell, 16 April 1947, NA, RG 25, vol. 3896, file 9294-R-40, part 1. On the establishment of a card index of available German scientists, see G.D. Mallory to J.H. Warren, 14 August 1947, ibid. On the clarification of the BIOS procedures, see M. Pope to External Affairs, 28 February 1947, External Affairs to Deputy Minister of Trade and Commerce, 18 April 1947, Mackenzie to Riddell, 26 and 28 April 1947; Pope to External Affairs, 30 April 1947, Canadian Military Mission (Berlin) to External Affairs, 16 December 1947, Warren to Deputy Minister of Trade and Commerce, 17 December 1947, Pope to External Affairs, 17 December 1947, and Mallory to Warren, 22 December 1947, ibid. On Ottawa's decision to waive the regulations for a limited number of German scientists and technicians, see minutes of meeting of Interdepartmental Committee on German Scientists held on 22 April 1947, NA, RG 2, vol. 102, file R-100-1; C.D. Howe to cabinet, 20 May 1947, ibid., vol. 66, file C-20-5, document nos 416–520; minutes of cabinet meeting held on 21 May 1947, ibid., vol. 2640, reel T-2365, frames 532–3; and PC 2047, 29 May 1947, ibid., vol. 1974, file 3628G.

32 On the fortunes of the scientists who were admitted to Canada, see F.M. Hereford to A. MacNamara, 24 January 1949, NA, RG 27, vol. 278, file 1-26-4, part 1; External Affairs to Director of Immigration, 20 July 1949, NA, RG 76, vol. 31, file 682, part 5, reel C-4690; and PC 886, 23 February 1950, NA, RG 25, vol. 3896, file 9294-R-40, part 2.

33 For example, see curriculum vitae of K. V——, 17 November 1946; R. H——, 31 December 1946; F. B——, 24 October 1946; and H. S——, undated, appended to dispatch from N.A. Robertson to External Affairs, 12 March 1947, NA, RG 2, vol. 251, file R-100-1. See also G.D. Mallory to External Affairs, 1 November 1947, NA, RG 25, vol. 2086, file AR 22/5, part 2.

34 For the case of a scientist with marginal Nazi affiliations who was admitted to Canada, see J.J. Gryse to G.S.H. Barton, 28 July 1947, and B.R. Hayden to External Affairs, 5 January 1949, ibid., vol. 3896, file 9294-AE-40.

35 High Commissioner to External Affairs, 29 November 1948, ibid., vol. 2086, file AR 22/5, part 4.

36 The denunciation is in S. Davis to High Commission, 23 December 1947, ibid., part 2. For the results of the security investigation on Funke, see (completed) Military Government of Germany Fragebogen, 30 October 1945, NA, Funke Papers, vol. 1, file 22, and decree issued by NSDAP Kreisleitung (Düsseldorf), 22 May 1939, ibid., vol. 11, file 5.

37 See curriculum vitae of W. S——, undated, appended to dispatch from N.A. Robertson to External Affairs, 12 March 1947, NA, RG 2, vol. 251, file R-100-1; J.S. Duncan to M.W. Mackenzie, 22 July 1947, NA, RG 25, vol. 3896, file 9294-AM-40; and C.J. Mackenzie diary, entry for 8 December 1948, NA, C.J. Mackenzie Papers, vol. 2, diary no. 27.

38 On this case, see E. H—— to Canadian Military Mission (Berlin), 26 March 1947, appended to dispatch from Lieutenant-General M. Pope to External Affairs, 29 March 1947, NA, RG 2, vol. 251, file R-100-1, and C.J. Mackenzie to External Affairs, 17 April 1947, NA, RG 25, vol. 3897, file 9294-S-40C.

39 Minutes of informal discussion held at Canadian Legation (Stockholm) on 26 July 1948, NA, RG 25, vol. 3751, file 7198-40C.

40 H.R. Horne to L.G. Chance, 19 November 1947, ibid., vol. 3674, file 5127-C-40, part 1, and J.D. Foote to External Affairs, 3 August 1948, NA, RG 2, vol. 249, file I-50-2.

41 Karl Aun, *The Political Refugees: A History of the Estonians in Canada* (Toronto, 1985), 25.

42 For the story of the *Edith*, see 'Fishing Craft to Cross Atlantic,' *Times* (London), 23 July 1947, appended to dispatch from J.W. Holmes to E. Reid, 24 July 1947, and L.G. Chance to Director of Immigration, 7 August 1947, NA, RG 25, vol. 3674, file 5127-C-40, part 1; National Lutheran Council (U.S.) and Canadian Lutheran World Relief to A.L. Jolliffe, 24 October 1947, NA, RG 76, vol. 656, file B48329, reel C-10593.

43 T.O.F. Herzer to A.L. Jolliffe, 21 October 1947, National Lutheran Council (U.S.) and Canadian Lutheran World Relief to Jolliffe, 24 October 1947, and Jolliffe to file, 25 October 1947, NA, RG 76, vol. 656, file B48329, reel C-10593.

44 On the decision to admit the *Edith*'s passengers, see A.L. Jolliffe to RCMP Commissioner, 25 October 1947, Inspector A.W. Parsons to Commissioner of Immigration, 4 November 1947, and Jolliffe to file, 4 November 1947, ibid.; Jolliffe to H.L. Keenleyside, 6 November 1947, and J.A. Glen to Governor in Council, 6 November 1947, NA, RG 26, vol. 126, file 3-33-10, part 1; PC 4680, 19 November 1947, NA, RG 2, vol. 1991, file 3706G.

45 See the correspondence in NA, RG 76, vol. 656, file B48329, reel C-10593.

46 On the consideration given to sending an immigration team to Stockholm, see J.W.

O'Brien to Canadian Legation (Stockholm), 1 June 1948, and minutes of meeting of Immigration-Labour Committee held on 11 June 1948, NA, RG 26, vol. 72, file 6/1/48–21/12/48, part 2; External Affairs to Canadian Legation (Stockholm), 23 June 1948, and H.L. Keenleyside to J.A. MacKinnon, 2 July 1948, ibid., vol. 132, file 3-35-2, part 1.

47 On Keenleyside's meeting with representatives of the Estonians in Sweden, see minutes of meeting held at Canadian Legation (Stockholm) on 26 July 1948, NA, RG 25, vol. 3751, file 7198-40C. On his meeting with the Swedish Foreign Office official, see J.D. Foote to External Affairs, 3 August 1948, and H.L. Keenleyside to External Affairs, 15 September 1948, ibid., vol. 3674, file 5127-C-40, parts 1 and 2.

48 On the decision to admit the Estonians, see minutes of meeting of Cabinet Committee on Immigration Policy held on 9 September 1948, NA, RG 27, vol. 3028, file Cabinet Committee on Immigration Policy; J.A. MacKinnon to cabinet, 15 September 1948, ibid., vol. 287, file 1-26-38, part 2; H.L. Keenleyside to External Affairs, 15 September 1948, NA, RG 26, vol. 126, file 3-33-10, part 1; minutes of cabinet meeting held on 29 September 1948, NA, RG 2, vol. 2642, reel T-2365, frames 1755–60; and PC 3721, 5 October 1948, ibid., vol. 2022, file 3861G.

49 The team was not even dispatched to Stockholm until the end of 1948. See minutes of meeting of Immigration-Labour Committee held on 9 November 1948, NA, RG 26, vol. 72, file 6/1/48–21/12/48, part 2.

50 J.D. Foote to External Affairs, 4 November 1948, H.L. Keenleyside to E. Reid, 5 November 1948, L. Fortier to External Affairs, 12 November 1948, and L.G. Chance to External Affairs, 25 February 1949, NA, RG 25, vol. 3674, file 5127-C-40, part 2. See also Instructions to Immigration Officer in Charge, Stockholm, Sweden, undated [November 1948], NA, RG 27, vol. 287, file 1-26-38, part 2.

51 On the landing of the *Astrid*, see P.A. Bridle to External Affairs, 5 August 1948, NA, RG 25, vol. 3674, file 5127-C-40, part 1; minutes of cabinet meeting held on 25 August 1948, NA, RG 2, vol. 2642, reel T-2365, frames 1689–90; and PC 3750, 25 August 1948, ibid., vol. 2019, file 3845G. On Ottawa's leniency with regard to the continued illegal landings, see memorandum to Cabinet Committee on Immigration Policy, 1 September 1948, NA, RG 26, vol. 100, file 3-18-1, part 2; H.L. Keenleyside to R.W. Mayhew, 2 September 1948, ibid., vol. 126, file 3-33-10, part 1; minutes of cabinet meeting held on 1 September 1948, NA, RG 2, vol. 2642, reel T-2365, frames 1702–4; and PC 3963, 2 September 1948, ibid., vol. 2020, file 3849G.

52 On the hardening of the government's attitude toward the illegal landings, see memorandum for Cabinet Committee on Immigration Policy, 22 February 1949, NA, RG 26, vol. 126, file 3-33-10, part 2; A.L. Jolliffe to Cabinet Committee on Immigration Policy, 1 April 1949, NA, RG 2, vol. 127, file I-50-D; minutes of cab-

inet meeting held on 27 May 1949, ibid., vol. 2643, reel T-2365, frames 596–9; summary of cabinet meeting held on 27 May 1949, NA, RG 25, vol. 3674, file 5127-C-40, part 2; A. MacNamara to H.L. Keenleyside, 12 July 1949, and Keenleyside to MacNamara, 15 July 1949, NA, RG 27, vol. 287, file 1-26-38, part 3.

53 T.A. Stone to L.G. Chance, 25 July 1949, NA, RG 26, vol. 126, file 3-33-10, part 2.

54 H.L. Keenleyside to External Affairs, 11 August 1949, NA, RG 25, vol. 3674, file 5127-C-40, part 2. In her report for the Commission of Inquiry on War Criminals, Alti Rodal implied that Keenleyside was 'soft' on the question of Estonian immigration from Sweden. She further suggested that this may have been due, at least in part, to the fact that his son had married an Estonian woman. See 'Nazi War Criminals,' 167–8. Her implication in this regard would appear to be refuted by Keenleyside's tough stance on the illegal landings.

55 Minutes of cabinet meeting held on 31 August 1949, NA, RG 2, reel T-2365, RG 2, vol. 2644, reel T-2365, frame 746, and N.A. Robertson to C. Gibson, 26 September 1949, ibid., vol. 124, file C-20-2, part 2.

56 See L. Fortier to A.A. Ewen, 22 July 1949, NA, RG 76, vol. 445, file 673931, part 20, reel C-10321.

57 On the detention of illegally landed Estonians, see H.L. Keenleyside to C. Gibson, 28 September 1949, and Keenleyside to Deputy Minister of Mines and Resources, 4 November 1949, NA, RG 26, vol. 126, file 3-33-10, part 2; W.W. Dawson to A. MacNamara, 12 September 1949, NA, RG 27, vol. 287, file 1-26-38, part 4; N.A. Robertson to J. MacKinnon, undated [September 1949], NA, RG 76, vol. 947, file SF-C-1, part 1; 'Baltic Refugees in Sweden,' undated [August 1949], and memorandum to cabinet, 29 August 1949, ibid., file SF-C-1-1, part 1. On the discovery and deportation of security risks among the Estonians, see A.L. Jolliffe to MacNamara, 27 September and 11 and 19 October 1949, and report by G.A. Lough, 4 November 1949, NA, RG 27, vol. 287, file 1-26-38, part 4; PC 5009, 30 September 1949, NA, RG 2, vol. 2054, file 4028G; and PC 5521, 1 November 1949, ibid., vol. 2057, file 4045G. For a case that resulted in deportation, see C.E.S. Smith to RCMP Commissioner, 15 December 1948, R.A.S. MacNeil to Commissioner of Immigration, 19 January 1949, memorandum by Minister of Mines and Resources, 18 February 1949, RCMP to Commissioner of Immigration, 22 February 1949, and Smith to RCMP Commissioner, 30 September 1949, NA, RG 76, accession 81–82/198, box, 9, file C-31002.

58 On Puntilis and Laak, see submission by Sol Littman, Deschenes Commission, NA, P. Yuzyk Papers, vol. 63, file/vol. 3, pp. 393–5. Puntilis died of natural causes in 1982. Laak committed suicide in 1960 after learning that he had been named in a Soviet news agency report.

59 See W.E. Harris to S. Bronfman, 5 July 1950, NA, RG 76, vol. 656, file B53802, part 2, reel C-10593.

60 For an estimate of the number of members of the division who entered Canada, see Efraim Zuroff, *Occupation: Nazi Hunter* (Southampton, UK, 1988), 209. According to the annual report of the main Ukrainian lobby group in the United Kingdom, 659 Canadian visas were obtained in 1951, while another 228 visa applications were pending. See 'Report on Activities of the Association of Ukrainians in Great Britain, Ltd, for the Period 1st January to 31st December 1951,' NA, RG 76, vol. 656, file B53802, part 2, reel C-10593. Many of these visas likely went to the former SS men.

61 On the Third Reich's initial policy of not recruiting foreign nationals into the Waffen-SS, see Reich Leader of SS and Police to SS Main Office, 7 October 1941, NARA, RG 242, T-580, reel 7, no frame numbers, and radio message by H. Himmler, undated [May 1942], ibid., series T-175, reel 66, frames 2582816–17. Hitler's belated and reluctant agreement to the establishment of a Ukrainian SS division is reported in Himmler to SS Brigadier-General Wächter, 28 March 1943, ibid., reel 74, frames 2592484–5. For the results of the initial recruitment drive, see minutes of conference held in Lemberg [Lviv] on 12 April 1943, ibid., frames 2592467–74; SS Brigadier-General Berger to Himmler, 16 April 1943, ibid., frames 2592462–4; and SS Main Office to Himmler, 3 June 1943, ibid., frames 2592444–6. For personnel files on several Ukrainian volunteers, see MCICAPN, record group 864, files 8–18. On their reasons for enlisting, see proceedings against M. W——, ibid., file SSKR 161; P. H——, ibid., file SSKR 176; and M. K——, ibid., file SSKR 195.

62 On the name changes undergone by the division during its first year of existence, see decree issued by H. Himmler, 27 June 1944, NARA, RG 242, series T-175, reel 74, frame 2592362, and Notice No. 429, *Verordnungsblatt der Waffen-SS*, 10/1b, 30 January 1944, ibid., series T-611, reel 4, no frame number.

63 See Hans-Joachim Neufeldt, Jürgen Huck, and Georg Tessin, *Zur Geschichte der Ordnungspolizei, 1936–1945*, part 2 of *Die Stäbe und Truppeneinheiten der Ordnungspolizei* (Koblenz, 1957), 52.

64 Directive issued by H. Himmler, 5 July 1943, NARA, RG 242, T-175, reel 74, frame 2592433. Training was not confined to matters of military significance. There was also heavy emphasis on indoctrination. See Instructions for the Ideological Training of the 14th Galician SS Volunteer Division, 16 March 1944, and 'The Life-Legislative Bases of National Socialism,' 29 March 1944, SARF, series P-7021, collection 148, file 322, pp. 11–12 verso and 40–2.

65 Orders issued by H. Himmler, 24 June 1943, NARA, RG 242, T-175, reel 74, frames 2592441–2; report by Chief of Order Police, 20 July 1943, ibid., reel 9, frames 510525–6; and Himmler to various subordinate authorities, 26 October 1943, ibid., frames 510513–14.

66 Directives issued by SS High Command, 30 July and 1 October 1943, ibid., reel

108, frames 2631292–3, and ibid., series T-580, reel 89, no frame numbers.

67 Orders issued by Chief of Order Police to various subordinate authorities, 23 December 1943, ibid., series T-175, reel 9, frames 2510498–9, and directive issued by Chief of Order Police, 9 June 1944, ibid., frames 2510463–6. See also report on meeting with Dr Wächter, 8 March 1944, ibid., series T-454, reel 8, frames 2509607–11, and Neufeldt, Huck, and Tessin, *Ordnungspolizei*, 2: 52, 94, and 106.

68 Orders issued by Chief of Order Police, 9 June 1944, NARA, RG 242, series T-175, reel 9, frames 2510459–62, and orders issued by Chief of Order Police, 29 June 1944, ibid., frame 2510275. At least part of the reserve was also filled with conscripts. See (Polish) Home Army report, 5 March 1944, AAN, record group 203, file XV-14.

69 On the division's combat record, see Samuel W. Mitcham, *Hitler's Legions: The German Army Order of Battle in World War II* (London, 1985), 456, and Erich Kern, *Der Grosse Rausch: Russlandfeldzug, 1941–1945* (Göttingen, 1962), 164–5. On its redesignation as a supposedly independent Ukrainian force, see Notice No. 431, *Verordnungsblatt der Waffen-SS*, 6/2, 15 January 1945, NARA, RG 242, series T-611, reel 6, no frame number.

70 Thus, I am in disagreement with Alti Rodal, who posited a 'continuity' between the Ukrainian indigenous auxiliary police and the 14th SS, despite the fact that her own survey of the files of 218 of the division's officers revealed only twelve who had prior service in the police. See 'Nazi War Criminals,' 377. Rodal's survey was flawed, since it was limited to the division's officers. For an example of a member of an auxiliary police unit who volunteered for service in the 14th SS, see proceedings against W. M——, MCICAPN, file SOJa 18.

71 Neufeldt, Huck, and Tessin, *Ordnungspolizei*, 2: 52 and 106.

72 Estimates of the prewar Jewish population in Ukraine and of the number of Jews annihilated during the German occupation can be found in Raul Hilberg, *The Destruction of the European Jews*, rev. ed. (New York, 1985), 1: 291, and Lucy S. Dawidowicz, *The War against the Jews, 1933–1945* (New York, 1981), 544.

73 See Commission of Inquiry on War Criminals, *Report* (Ottawa, 1986), 261, which found that 'charges of war crimes against members of the Galicia Division have never been substantiated.'

74 See (Polish) Home Army situation report no. 9, 17 May 1944, in *Armia Krajowa W Dokumentach, 1939–1945* (London, 1976), 3: 447, and (Polish) Home Army situation report no. 10, 24 May 1944, ibid., 458. For allegations that the regiment and other sub-units were involved in the pacification of several villages in February and March 1944, operations that resulted in the killing of hundreds of Polish civilians, see (Polish) Home Army reports, 1, 5, and 6 March 1944, AAN, record group 203, file XV-14; Czeslaw Madajczyk, *Hitlerowski Terror Na Wsi Polskiej, 1939–1945*

(Warsaw, 1965), 90; and Jerzy Markiewicz, *Partyzancki Kraj: Zamojszczyzna 1 I 1944–15 VI 1944* (Lublin, 1980), 21 and 56–7. For reports on the regiment's participation in anti-partisan operations, see various recommendations for medals, MCICAPN, record group 864, files VIII/10 and 11.

75 John A. Armstrong, *Ukrainian Nationalism* (New York, 1963), 171.

76 For example, see interrogation of V. N———, 28 September 1945, and V. V———, 12 September 1945, Ukrainian investigative records. Some members of the Ukrainian auxiliary security police were able to obtain exemptions from front-line military service. See interrogation of B. M———, 13 March 1947, ibid.

77 Only fragments of the contemporary documentation on the 14th SS's operations in Slovakia survived the war. What little is known about the division's assistance in the suppression of the Slovak National Uprising comes from postwar trials held before the National Tribunal and various people's courts.

78 On the Heidelager camp, see orders issued by Higher SS and Police Leader to supply depots of the Waffen-SS at Heidelager, Cracow, Lemberg, Lublin, Radom, and Warsaw, 13 and 26 January and 8 March 1944, SARF, series P-7021, collection 148, file 340, pp. 3–6 verso. On the Hradischko camp, see reports on Flossenbürg concentration camp's labour details, 3 February and 5 March 1945, and Commandant of Flossenbürg to Higher SS and Police Leader for Bohemia and Moravia, 1 November and 3 December 1944, SCA, collection 110, folder 4/1–562/c, file 88.

79 For evidence that the division occasionally interfered in the running of the Heidelager camp, see Commander of the Training Battalion of the SS Volunteer Division 'Galcia' to the Commandant, 21 September 1943, MHA, collection Ausb Btl z.b.V., file 11/3. On the exchange of personnel between concentration camps and combat formations of the Waffen-SS, see George H. Stein, *The Waffen SS: Hitler's Elite Guard at War, 1939–1945* (Ithaca, NY, 1966), 261–2.

80 Memorandum by G.R.B. Panchuk, 22 January 1948, AO, G.R.B. Panchuk Papers, series E, box 27, file 5-1.

81 Christopher Simpson, *Blowback: America's Recruitment of Nazis and Its Effects on the Cold War* (New York, 1988), 180–1n.

82 Mark Aarons and John Loftus, *Ratlines: How the Vatican's Nazi Networks Betrayed Western Intelligence to the Soviets* (London, 1991), 196–8. On the pressure exerted by the Ukrainian-Canadian lobby, see M. Pope to L.B. Pearson, 28 December 1946, and N.A. Robertson to Pearson, 21 February 1947, NA, RG 25, vol. 3747, file 6980-GR-40, part 1.

83 Aarons and Loftus, *Ratlines*, 194–5.

84 Ibid. See also Brigadier F. Maclean to Minister of State, 12 February 1947, PRO, FO 371/66604, in which Maclean lamented that 'it is hard to see how the commission can hope to fulfil this portion of its task in any but the most superficial man-

ner.' I am indebted to Julian Hendy of Yorkshire, UK, for providing me with a copy
of this document.

85 'Report by Refugee Screening Commission on Ukrainians in SEP [Surrendered
Enemy Personnel] Camp No. 374, Italy,' 21 February 1947, NA, RG 25, vol. 3798,
file 8296-40. For insight into the investigation of the Ukrainians, see Questionnaire,
undated, AO, Panchuk Papers, series C, box 17, file Screening Questionnaires
(U.S.).

86 'Report by Refugee Screening Commission on Ukrainians in SEP [Surrendered
Enemy Personnel] Camp No. 374, Italy,' 21 February 1947, NA, RG 25, vol. 3798,
file 8296-40. As far as can be determined, none of Porter's recommendations were
ever followed. Still, the effort had not been a complete waste of time. Despite the
resort to the spot-check method, close to three hundred men were screened out of
the UK-bound contingent. According to contemporary reports, 7,989 of the 8,272
men at Rimini were ultimately brought from Italy to the United Kingdom. This
means that 283 were rejected. See G.R.B. Panchuk to Immigration Branch and
External Affairs, 4 August 1947, RG 76, vol. 656, file B53802, part 1, reel C-
10593.

87 On the establishment and mandate of CURB, see M.J. McLeod to G. Pifher, 21
September 1945, A.W. Arsenych to Department of War Services, 31 August 1945,
and Application for Permission to Travel to Continental Europe, 30 October 1945,
NA, RG 25, vol. 3747, file 6980-GR-40, part 1; Canadian Relief Mission for
Ukrainian Refugees to IRO, 12 September 1947, NA, RG 76, vol. 856, file
554-33.

88 G.R.B. Panchuk to Immigration Branch and External Affairs, 4 August 1947, NA,
RG 76, vol. 656, file B53802, part 1, reel C-10593; Panchuk to High Commissioner, 7 August 1947, AO, Panchuk Papers, series C, box 15, file Correspondence
with High Commissioner; Panchuk to C. Gibson, 8 October 1947, and memorandum for L.G. Chance, 9 October 1947, NA, RG 25, vol. 6178, file 232-L-40, part 1.

89 G.R.B. Panchuk to Immigration Branch and External Affairs, 4 August 1947, NA,
reel C-10593, RG 76, vol. 656, file B53802, part 1, and Panchuk to High Commissioner, 7 August 1947, AO, Panchuk Papers, series C, box 15, file Correspondence
with High Commissioner. Ottawa was not taken in by this fiction. In correspondence to the Canadian high commissioner, British authorities reported that the
Ukrainian ex-soldiers 'were members of the First Ukrainian Division of the Wehrmacht, which appears to have been formed in 1944 from the remnants of what is
believed to have been a Waffen S.S. Division which came to disaster in the Battle
of Brody.' Quoted from Commonwealth Relations Office note, undated, appended
to dispatch from E. Machtig to N.A. Robertson, 5 August 1948, NA, Dominions
Office and Commonwealth Relations Office Records, vol. 3362, file M2010/7, reel
B-6141. For evidence that the government was aware of the division's SS pedigree,

see L. Fortier to Minister of Citizenship and Immigration, 11 September 1950, NA, RG 26, vol. 151, file 3-32-11.

90 On Palij's divisional history, see G.R.B. Panchuk to Central Ukrainian Relief Bureau, 15 March 1946, AO, Panchuk Papers, series C, box 15, file Internal Correspondence. Panchuk, it should be noted, was never entirely trusted by the British government. See E. Hanson to Mr Goldberg, 19 June 1950, NA, Dominions Office and Commonwealth Relations Office Records, vol. 3362, file M 2010/7, reel B-6141, in which the British official, referring to Panchuk, lamented that 'we have had course in the past to accept anything said by this gentleman with some reserve.'

91 H.L. Keenleyside to A.L. Jolliffe, 10 October 1947, NA, RG 76, vol. 856, file 554-33.

92 Memorandum for Acting Undersecretary of State for External Affairs, 16 October 1947, NA, RG 26, vol. 151, file 3-32-11.

93 Minutes of cabinet meeting held on 10 October 1947, NA, RG 2, vol. 2640, reel T-2365, frames 821–3, and A.D.P. Heeney to J.A. Glen, 14 October 1947, ibid., vol. 64, file C-20-2, part 2.

94 To be fair, Ottawa had received a copy of Porter's report on the screening of the Ukrainians in April 1947. See 'Report by Refugee Screening Commission on Ukrainians in SEP [Surrendered Enemy Personnel] Camp No. 374, Italy,' 21 February 1947, appended to dispatch from N.A. Robertson to External Affairs, 25 April 1947, NA, RG 76, vol. 443, file 673931, part 14, reel C-10320. Copies of the report were also found among the records of the Departments of Citizenship and Immigration (NA, RG 26, vol. 147, file 3-43-1) and External Affairs (NA, RG 25, vol. 3798, file 8296-40).

95 Brigadier A.G. Kenchington to Deputy Chief of British Control Commission's Prisoners-of-War and Displaced Persons Division, 20 November 1947, appended to dispatch from M. Pope to External Affairs, 24 November 1947, NA, RG 25, vol. 6178, file 232-L-40, part 1.

96 The British report is summarized in M. Pope to External Affairs, 3 December 1947, ibid.

97 Memorandum for Cabinet Committee on Immigration Policy, 23 January 1948, NA, RG 26, vol. 100, file 3-18-1, part 2; minutes of meeting of Cabinet Committee on Immigration Policy held on 15 April 1948, NA, RG 2, vol. 82, file I-50-M, part 1; and A.L. Jolliffe to file, 17 March 1948, NA, RG 76, vol. 856, file 554-33.

98 Commissioner of Immigration to Acting Superintendent, 12 June 1948, NA, RG 76, vol. 856, file 554-33, and A.L. Jolliffe to G.R.B. Panchuk, 21 April 1948, ibid., vol. 656, file B53802, part 1, reel C-10593.

99 For example, see Reverend W. Kushnir to H.L. Keenleyside, 28 May 1948, NA, RG 26, vol. 151, file 3-32-11.

100 See Director of Immigration to Deputy Minister of Mines and Resources, 2 June 1948 (and handwritten note thereupon, 3 June 1948), ibid.

101 E.D. Kuppinger to G.R.B. Panchuk, 16 October 1947, AO, Panchuk Papers, series C, box 16, file Correspondence with U.S. Embassy, and Panchuk to T. Adams, 18 October 1947, ibid., box 15, file Home Office.

102 Commissioner of Immigration to Acting Superintendent, 12 June 1948, NA, RG 76, vol. 856, file 554-33; excerpt from Hansard, 16–22 July 1948, and F.B. Cotsworth to Captain G.D. Franklin, 12 August 1948, ibid., vol. 656, file B53802, part 1, reel C-10593.

103 See 'Announcement Regarding the Bringing to Canada of Former Members of the Ukrainian Division,' in *Ukrainian News* (Edmonton) and *New Pathway* (Winnipeg), undated [summer 1948], ibid., vol. 856, file 554-33.

104 R.N. Munroe to C.E.S. Smith, 19 October 1948, ibid.

105 G.R.B. Panchuk to G. Sylvestre, 19 January 1949, and H.L. Keenleyside to Sylvestre, 14 February 1949, NA, L.S. St Laurent Papers, vol. 56, file I-20-29-P; J.A. MacKinnon to J.R. Solomon, 17 February 1949, NA, RG 26, vol. 130, file 3-33-4; and Sylvestre to Panchuk, 18 February 1949, AO, Panchuk Papers, series C, box 17, file 1st Division Halychyna – Immigration to Canada.

106 Memorandum by G.R.B. Panchuk, 22 January 1948, AO, Panchuk Papers, series E, box 27, file 5-1, and Panchuk to A. Crapleve, 1 February 1949, ibid., box 28, file 5-1.

107 G.R.B. Panchuk to Reverend S.W. Sawchuk, 17 February 1949, ibid., box 27, file 5-1.

108 Lubomyr Y. Luciuk, *Heroes of Their Day: The Reminiscences of Bohdan Panchuk* (Toronto, 1983), 109–10.

109 On the use of addresses to determine a refugee's official status, see G.G. Congdon to Acting Commissioner of Immigration, 12 December 1947, RG 76, vol. 656, file B53802, part 1, reel C-10593.

110 See the complaints in G.R.B. Panchuk to Minister of Justice and Attorney General of Canada, 23 November 1948, NA, RG 27, vol. 3022, file General Correspondence on Immigration Policy, part 4, and J.R. Solomon to J.A. MacKinnon, 16 February 1949, NA, RG 26, vol. 130, file 3-33-34.

111 V.C. Phelan to A. MacNamara, 29 June 1948, NA, RG 27, vol. 288, file 1-26-29.

112 On London's efforts on behalf of unemployable division members and Canada's response, see memorandum for Cabinet Committee on Immigration Policy, 28 October 1948, Director of Immigration to Deputy Minister of Mines and Resources, 1 November 1948, M.H. Wershof to Keenleyside, 26 January 1949, and Keenleyside to Wershof, 1 February 1949, NA, RG 26, vol. 151, file 3-32-11. See also Dominions Office note, undated [October 1948], and P.J. Noel-Baker to

E. Bevin, 19 October 1948, NA, Dominions Office and Commonwealth Relations Office Records, vol. 3362, file M2010/7, reel B-6141.

113 On the launching of the campaign, see G.R.B. Panchuk to Ukrainian-Canadian Association, 11 January 1949, NA, RG 76, vol. 656, file B53802, part 1, reel C-10593; Panchuk to Dr M.I. Mandryka, 10 March 1949, AO, Panchuk Papers, series E, box 28, file 5-1; J.R. Solomon to J.A. MacKinnon, 16 February 1949, NA, RG 26, vol. 130, file 3-33-34; Reverend Dr B. Kushnir and J.H. Syrnick to Prime Minister L.S. St Laurent, 21 April 1949, NA, St Laurent Papers, vol. 56, file I-20-29-P; and T. Danyliw to L.B. Pearson, 23 March 1950, NA, RG 25, vol. 6178, file 232-L-40, part 1.

114 On Ottawa's decision to maintain the ban on members of the 14th SS, see A.L. Jolliffe to Cabinet Committee on Immigration Policy, 1 April 1949, NA, RG 25, vol. 4165, file 939-B-40, part 2; Jolliffe to Reverend Dr B. Kushnir, 13 May 1949, NA, RG 76, vol. 443, file 673931, part 19, reel C-10321; C. Gibson to Deputy Minister of Mines and Resources, 13 August 1949, ibid., vol. 656, file B53802, part 1, reel C-10593; H.L. Keenleyside to Gibson, 12 August 1949, and Gibson to cabinet, 16 August 1949, NA, RG 26, vol. 130, file 3-33-34; minutes of cabinet meeting held on 13 September 1949, NA, RG 2, vol. 2644, reel T-2366, frames 777–9; and N.A. Robertson to Gibson, 15 September 1949, ibid., vol. 124, file C-20-2, part 2.

115 Nor was it the result of Cold War imperatives, as was claimed in Reg Whitaker, *Double Standard: The Secret History of Canadian Immigration* (Toronto, 1987), 135.

116 The relaxation of this restriction followed on the heels of the removal of German-naturalized Volksdeutsche from the category of prohibited classes. On the lifting of the ban on Volksdeutsche who had acquired German citizenship during the war, see PC 1606, 28 March 1950, NA, RG 2, vol. 2071, file 4128G. On the relaxation of the restrictions on Volksdeutsche who had served in the German armed forces, see minutes of cabinet meeting held on 5 April 1950, ibid., vol. 2645, reel T-2366, frames 1409, 1414–15, and 1417; N.A. Robertson to W.E. Harris, 6 April 1950, ibid., vol. 136, file C-20-2, part 2; External Affairs note, 11 April 1950, NA, RG 25, vol. 3914, file 9408-40, part 2; Official Circular No. 72 to all visa and immigration officers, 20 May 1950, ibid., vol. 6248, file 9408-A-40, part 1; and L. Fortier to C.E.S. Smith, 20 April 1950, NA, RG 76, vol. 947, file SF-C-1, part 1.

117 L. Fortier to W.E. Harris, 23 March 1950, NA, RG 26, vol. 130, file 3-33-34.

118 The quoted passage is from W.E. Harris to cabinet, 4 April 1950, NA, RG 2, vol. 137, file C-20-5, document nos 91–140.

119 Minutes of cabinet meeting held on 5 April 1950, ibid., vol. 2645, reel T-2366, frames 1414–15 and 1417.

120 For the RCMP's view of the OUN, see Inspector C. Batch to 'A' Division, 13

March 1942, and Constable M. Petrowsky to RCMP Special Branch, 31 January 1950, NA, RG 146, vol. 4123, file UCC.

121 N.A. Robertson to W.E. Harris, 11 April 1950, NA, RG 26, vol. 130, file 3-33-34, and A.D.P. Heeney to RCMP Commissioner, 13 April 1950, NA, RG 25, vol. 4019, file 10268-40, part 1.

122 On the JIB's findings, see report, undated [1950], appended to memorandum from Minister of National Defence to L.B. Pearson, 17 April 1950, NA, RG 25, vol. 6178, file 232-L-40, part 1. On cabinet's call for additional investigation, see cross reference sheets, 27 April and 26 May 1950, NA, RG 2, vol. 222, file I-50-9. On the decision to admit members of the 14th SS, see minutes of cabinet meeting held on 31 May 1950, ibid., vol. 2645, reel T-2366, frames 1577 and 1580; N.A. Robertson to W.E. Harris, 3 June 1950, ibid., vol. 136, file C-20-2, part 2; and L. Fortier to C.E.S. Smith, 6 June 1950, NA, RG 76, vol. 947, file SF-C-1, part 1.

123 See J.D. McFarlane to G.R. Benoit, 13 June 1950, and Immigration Branch Directive No. 26, 18 January 1951, NA, RG 76, vol. 656, file B53802, part 2, reel C-10593.

124 The question and Harris's response can be found in *Official Report of Debates: House of Commons* (Ottawa, 1950), 4: 3696.

125 S. Bronfman to W.E. Harris, 4 July 1950, NA, RG 76, vol. 656, file B53802, part 2, reel C-10593.

126 W.E. Harris to S. Bronfman, 5 July 1950, ibid.

127 On the delay in accepting applications and the investigations conducted in the interim, see memorandum by R.N. Munroe, 10 July 1950, S. Bronfman to W.E. Harris, 12 July 1950, and Harris to Bronfman, 15 September 1950, ibid. See also A.L. Jolliffe to A.D.P. Heeney, 9 August 1950, NA, RG 26, vol. 151, file 3-32-11, and High Commissioner to External Affairs, 5 September 1950, ibid., vol. 130, file 3-33-34. On the resumption of the application process, see J.E. McKenna to RCMP Commissioner, 27 September 1950, P.T. Baldwin to RCMP Commissioner, 2 November 1950, and Inspector R.A.S. MacNeil to Commissioner of Immigration, 13 November 1950, NA, RG 76, vol. 656, file B53802, part 2, reel C-10593.

128 S. Bronfman to W.E. Harris, 25 September 1950, NA, RG 26, vol. 151, file 3-32-11.

129 Extant documents reveal that individual members of the division were denied visas as a result of Canadian screening. For some examples, see A. Zaharychuk to W.E. Harris, 11 April 1951, Deputy Minister of Citizenship and Immigration to Director of Immigration, 14 April 1951, and Harris to Zaharychuk, 24 April 1951, NA, RG 76, vol. 656, file B53802, part 2, reel C-10593. Unfortunately, the specific grounds for rejection were not reported.

7: The Diminishing Threat

1 On the winding down of the refugee movement and the arrival in Canada of the last IRO-sponsored immigrants, see minutes of cabinet meeting held on 16 July 1949, NA, RG 2, vol. 2644, reel T-2366, frames 623–4; J.S. McDonald to A.P. Bibeault and W.C. Moir, undated [summer 1951], and Director to Messrs T.P. Devlin, A.R. Milne, R.M. Pym, J.R. McIntyre, and E.J. Sauvé, 10 August 1951, NA, RG 30, vol. 8305, file 3000-108. On the reduction of the immigration budget and its impact on spending allocated for assisted passages, see memorandum from W.E. Harris to cabinet, 9 December 1950, NA, RG 26, vol. 95, file 3-7-7, part 1, and Harris to cabinet, 21 February 1952, NA, RG 2, vol. 212, file C-20-5. Statistics on immigration to Canada during the late 1940s are available in Department of Manpower and Immigration, *Highlights from the Green Paper on Immigration and Population* (Ottawa, 1975), 42.

2 On the creation of the new Department of Citizenship and Immigration, see summary of Settlement Service conference held on 22–4 August 1950, NA, RG 26, vol. 90, file 3-1-4. On the increase in the immigration budget and the establishment of an assisted-passage fund, see Appendix 'A,' undated, appended to memorandum from W.E. Harris to cabinet, 9 December 1950, L. Fortier to C.E.S. Smith, 16 January 1951, and Harris to cabinet, 26 May 1951, ibid., vol. 95, file 3-7-7, part 1; Harris to cabinet, 21 February 1952, NA, RG 2, vol. 212, file C-20-5.

3 PC 2856, 9 June 1950, NA, RG 2, vol. 2078, file 4171G.

4 P. Delagrave to J.D. McFarlane, 24 November 1950, NA, RG 76, vol. 804, file 548-10, part 2.

5 Compare the figures in minutes of cabinet meeting held on 25 March 1950, NA, RG 2, vol. 2645, reel T-2366, frames 1380–1, with those cited in 'Immigration from Germany,' 30 June 1957, NA, RG 76, vol. 822, file 552-1-551, part 1.

6 Statistics on immigration to Canada during the 1950s can be found in *Green Paper on Immigration*, 42. On the increased demand for agricultural labour in 1956, see minutes of cabinet meeting held on 5 April 1956, NA, RG 2, vol. 5775, file 08/03/56–10/05/56.

7 From 1949 on, the number of refugees who emigrated to the United States and Australia exceeded the number who went to Canada. The trend continued even after the refugee movement. See Louise Holborn, *The International Refugee Organization, a Specialized Agency of the United Nations: Its History and Work, 1946–1952* (London, 1956), 442.

8 On the termination of the fourteen-day rule, see Superintendent G.B. McClellan to RCMP Commissioner, 26 September 1950, NA, RG 146, Public Document, and Operations Memorandum No. 3, 16 March 1962, NA, RG 6, vol. 129, file 14-3-8. By the autumn of 1949, the number of unscreened applications had reached 20,000.

See E.W.T. Gill to Security Panel, 16 September 1949, and minutes of Security Panel meeting held on 19 September 1949, NA, RG 2, vol. 251, file S-100-D. Within a year of the removal of the ban on German immigration, the backlog had exploded to 96,000. See C.E.S. Smith to Deputy Minister of Citizenship and Immigration, 9 November 1951, NA, RG 76, vol. 31, file 682, part 7, reel C-4690.

9 At a meeting between RCMP and Immigration representatives, those in attendance were told cabinet was insisting that procedures for 'facilitating' immigration screening be worked out by the responsible departments. See minutes of meeting between representatives of the RCMP and the Department of Citizenship and Immigration held on 26 February 1951, NA, RG 76, vol. 800, file 547-1, part 2.

10 For warnings in this regard, see Superintendent G.B. McClellan to RCMP Commissioner, 26 September 1950, NA, RG 146, Public Document.

11 On the new manual, see Instructions for the Guidance of Immigration and Visa Officers, vol. 2, undated [1954], NA, RG 76, vol. 935, file Immigration Binder No. 10, part 1.

12 As late as 1957, an internal Department of Citizenship and Immigration review revealed considerable differences in the conduct of Stage B procedures in Europe. See Officer in Charge (Copenhagen) to Director of Immigration, 4 June 1957, Officer in Charge (The Hague) to Acting Chief of Operations, 4 June 1957, Visa Section Attaché (Canadian Embassy, Vienna) to Acting Chief of Operations, 4 June 1957, P.E. Quinn (Cologne) to Acting Chief of Operations, 14 June 1957, and G.M. Mitchell (Brussels) to Chief of Operations, 5 July 1957, ibid., vol. 812, file 551-1, part 8.

13 On the loss of official sources in Czechoslovakia and attempts to compensate by questioning Czech expatriates residing in Germany, see G.B. McClellan to L. Fortier, 23 March 1949, ibid., vol. 862, file 555-54-531. On the difficulties of screening behind the Iron Curtain in the absence of official sources, see minutes of Security Panel meeting held on 5 April 1949, NA, RG 2, vol. 251, file S-100-M, and Fortier to Commissioner of Immigration, 20 June 1949, NA, RG 76, vol. 800, file 547-1, part 1.

14 On the adoption of the practice of delayed processing, see minutes of Security Panel meeting held on 5 April 1949, NA, RG 2, vol. 251, file S-100-M; Superintendent G.B. McClellan to L. Fortier, 8 and 13 August 1949, NA, RG 76, vol. 957, file SF-S-1, part 1; E.W.T. Gill to Security Panel, 16 September 1949, NA, RG 2, vol. 251, file S-100-D, Security Panel Document SP-51; minutes of Security Panel meeting held on 19 September 1949, ibid., file S-100-M; N.A. Robertson to cabinet, 22 September 1949, ibid., vol. 124, file C-20-5, document nos 1020–75; minutes of cabinet meeting held on 22 September 1949, ibid., vol. 2644, reel T-2366, frames 807 and 810–11; memorandum from A. MacNamara to Minister of Labour, 30 August 1949, NA, RG 27, vol. 275, file 1-26-1, part 4; and Robertson to C. Gib-

son, 26 September 1949, NA, RG 76, vol. 957, file SF-S-1, part 1.

15 For example, Sweden was hard-pressed to deal with a major influx of Poles. See L. Fortier to A.D.P. Heeney, 17 December 1951, NA, RG 25, vol. 6276, file 5127-40, part 12.1.

16 There were four Canadian visa-issuing facilities behind the Iron Curtain at this time. None were immigration offices. Rather, the Canadian embassies in Belgrade (Yugoslavia), Moscow (Soviet Union), Prague (Czechoslovakia), and Warsaw (Poland) all had visa sections. See 'Canadian Immigration Visa Offices,' undated, appended to Immigration Branch Directive No. 84, 30 March 1951, NA, RG 76, vol. 895, file 569-1, part 4.

17 On the proposal put forward by Canada's representative in Sweden, see minutes of meeting on security problems held on 28 February 1952, ibid., vol. 800, file 547-1, part 2.

18 On the decision to adopt the residency requirement, see Inspector K.W.N. Hall to Director of Immigration, 24 March 1952, C.E.S. Smith to Deputy Minister of Citizenship and Immigration, 28 March 1952, and L. Fortier to N.A. Robertson, 23 April 1952, ibid.; minutes of Security Panel meeting held on 15 May 1952, NA, RG 2, vol. 232, file S-100-1-M; memorandum from Director of Immigration to Deputy Minister of Citizenship and Immigration, 28 March 1952, and memorandum from P.M. Dwyer to Security Panel, 9 May 1952, NA, RG 26, vol. 153, file 1-18-14; Fortier to Minister of Citizenship and Immigration, 20 May 1952, ibid., vol. 132, file 3-35-2, part 2; and minutes of cabinet meeting held on 17 June 1952, NA, RG 2, vol. 2650, file 06/05/52–30/06/52.

19 Examination of William H. Kelly, Deschenes Commission, NA, P. Yuzyk Papers, vol. 63, file/vol. 7, p. 934.

20 On the Security Panel's recommendations, see draft memorandum titled 'Immigration Security Policy,' 25 February 1953, NA, RG 26, vol. 166, file 3-25-11, part 1, and L. Fortier to Minister of Citizenship and Immigration, 3 March 1953, NA, RG 76, vol. 957, file SF-S-1, part 2.

21 On the evolution of the policy of waiving screening for certain categories of close relatives from eastern Europe and the Soviet Union, see memorandum from L. Fortier to Minister of Citizenship and Immigration, 4 March 1955, memorandum from C.E.S. Smith to Deputy Minister of Citizenship and Immigration, 18 March 1955, 'Security Screening of Immigrants from Yugoslavia and from Countries behind the Iron Curtain,' undated [June 1955], L.H. Nicholson and Fortier to Security Panel, 16 June 1955, Fortier to Minister of Citizenship and Immigration, 30 June 1955, and memorandum from Director of Immigration to Deputy Minister of Citizenship and Immigration, 28 July 1955, NA, RG 26, vol. 168, file 3-25-11-29, part 1; minutes of cabinet meetings held on 11 July and 21 September 1955, NA, RG 2, vol. 2658, file 11/07/55–28/09/55; Consular Document No. 4/56, 19 January 1956, NA,

RG 76, vol. 784, file 541-17, part 1; and memorandum to Cabinet Committee on Immigration Policy, 9 November 1959, ibid., vol. 959, file SF-S-23, part 2.

22 On the problem of the lack of consistent reporting of residency and employment information, see G.M. Morrison to A. MacNamara, 26 February 1949, NA, RG 27, vol. 287, file 1-26-38-2. For the RCMP's concerns, see J.R. Robillard to Chief of Operations, 25 January 1954, NA, RG 76, vol. 807, file 548-11, part 3. On the changes to the form, see draft Questionnaire, undated [1953], appended to letter from Inspector G.H. Ashley to Director of Immigration, 18 December 1953, ibid., and examination of George O'Leary, Deschenes Commission, NA, Yuzyk Papers, vol. 63, file/vol. 5, pp. 635–6. For a facsimile of the revised form, see Application for Admission to Canada, undated [1954], appended to memorandum from Robillard to Chief of Operations, 11 September 1954, NA, RG 76, vol. 807, file 548-11, part 4. Parenthetically, it should be noted that the IMM-55 was similarly revised at this time, thereby rendering it more security-friendly. See Application for Admission of Nominated Immigrants, undated [1954], ibid., vol. 805, file 548-10, part 8.

23 In her report for the Commission of Inquiry on War Criminals, Alti Rodal asserted that 'the absence until 1953 of questions in immigration/security screening application forms, relating to the wartime military history of applicants constituted another major flaw.' Elsewhere, she employed even stronger language, asserting that 'this omission ... indicates the very low priority attached to eliciting Nazi or collaborationist background for immigration purposes during this period.' See 'Nazi War Criminals in Canada: The Historical and Policy Setting from the 1940s to the Present' (Commission of Inquiry on War Criminals, Ottawa, 1986), 281 and 195. The practice of eliciting residency and employment information prior to 1954 effectively refutes her first assertion (see Chapter 5 for more details). As to the second assertion, it may be relevant to note that the OS.8 also contained no questions about an applicant's communist affiliation. Surely Rodal would not suggest that this was proof of the low priority Canadian immigration authorities attached to eliciting communist background.

24 The problems that lengthy lists might cause were anticipated prior to the resumption of large-scale immigration from Europe. See Director of Immigration to RCMP Commissioner, 28 November 1946, NA, RG 76, vol. 800, file 547-1, part 1. Nonetheless, the RCMP did not make any changes until the backlog became unmanageable.

25 On the change in emphasis from security checks to interviews, see minutes of meeting between representatives of the RCMP and the Department of Citizenship and Immigration held on 26 February 1951, and Acting Director of Immigration to Deputy Minister of Citizenship and Immigration, 13 April 1951, ibid., part 2. On the addition of a dozen more security officers, see G.B. McClellan to C.E.S. Smith, 12 March 1951, ibid., vol. 957, file SF-S-1, part 2.

26 Superintendent G.B. McClellan to RCMP Commissioner, undated [1951], Documents in Evidence in the Matter of Revocation of Citizenship between the Minister of Citizenship and Immigration and Wasily Bogutin.

27 On this innovation, see P.E. Quinn to Officers in Charge, 27 July 1953, NA, RG 76, vol. 801, file 547-5-551, part 1; Canadian Immigration form, undated, appended to memorandum from G.R. Benoit to RCMP Commissioner, 23 February 1954, ibid., vol. 979, file 5420-1-636, part 1; Canadian Immigration form, undated, appended to memorandum from C.E.S. Smith to Deputy Minister of Citizenship and Immigration, 3 November 1955, NA, RG 26, vol. 91, file 3-2-5; Canadian Immigration form for G. B——, 15 November 1956, appended to letter from Inspector G.H. Ashley to Defence Liaison 2 Division, 6 December 1956, and G.G. Crean to Canadian Embassy (Caracus), 12 and 14 December 1956, NA, RG 25, vol. 8541, file 11687-40, part 3.1; Canadian Immigration Office (Linz) to Chief of Admissions, 24 February 1955, NA, RG 76, vol. 977, file 5420-1-513; and examination of George O'Leary, Deschenes Commission, NA, Yuzyk Papers, vol. 63, file/vol. 5, pp. 710–11.

28 See draft report prepared by Commissioner for European Emigration, undated [December 1955], NA, RG 26, vol. 166, file 3-25-11, part 2.

8: The Era of Risk Management, 1951–1956

1 'Screening of Applicants for Admission to Canada,' 20 November 1948, NA, RG 76, vol. 957, file SF-S-1, part 1.

2 Minutes of Security Panel meeting held on 27 October 1950, NA, RG 2, vol. 189, file S-100-M.

3 On the link between the war crimes issue and German participation in the defence of western Europe, see T.C. Davis to External Affairs, 11 September 1950, and Canadian Mission (Bonn) to External Affairs, 23 December 1950, NA, B. Claxton Papers, vol. 123, file Re-Arming of Germany; Frank M. Buscher, *The U.S. War Crimes Trial Program in Germany, 1946–1955* (New York, 1989), 56–82, and Buscher, 'The U.S. High Commission and German Nationalism, 1949–52,' *Central European History* 23 (March 1990), 68–9. On the trend toward leniency in American policy regarding German war criminals, see Buscher, *War Crimes*, 63–4. On the same trend in British policy, see Secretary of State for Commonwealth Relations to High Commissioner, 22 December 1951, NA, RG 24, vol. 2887, file 8959-9, part 13.

4 Buscher, *War Crimes*, 162.

5 Ibid., 118–24.

6 For the list of sanctions imposed on lesser offenders and followers, respectively, see

Allied Control Council Directive No. 38, 14 October 1946, NARA, RG 260, series 3, file 3.

7 On the work of the denazification courts, see T.O.F. Herzer to W.E. Harris, 18 September 1950, NA, North American Baptist Immigration and Colonization Society Papers, series B3, vol. 5, file 58, and P.W. Bird to Acting Director of Immigration, 27 September 1950, NA, RG 76, vol. 31, file 682, part 6, reel C-4690.

8 For a list of Nazi offices that fell into the lesser offender and follower categories, see Allied Control Council Directive No. 38, 14 October 1946, NARA, RG 260, series 3, file 3.

9 Buscher, *War Crimes*, 125–6.

10 In terms of Nazi Party membership, this argument is difficult to assess. It is hard to imagine that Volksdeutsche who joined the Nazi Party were ignorant of its program. Moreover, German naturalization, not Nazi Party membership, was a requirement for Volksdeutsche to acquire property and status. Yet undoubtedly there were reasons aplenty for joining the party. In one district of German-occupied Poland, the high level of Volksdeutsche membership seemed to have more to do with the meeting of party quotas than with genuine ideological commitment. See Dietrich Orlow, *The History of the Nazi Party, 1933–1945* (Pittsburgh, 1973), 293.

11 T.O.F. Herzer to W.E. Harris, 18 September 1950, NA, North American Baptist Immigration and Colonization Society Papers, series B3, vol. 5, file 58.

12 For example, see A.D.P. Heeney to 'Mike' [L.B. Pearson], 24 November 1952, NA, L.B. Pearson Papers, vol. 5, file A.D.P. Heeney.

13 'In view of changing world conditions,' the deputy minister of citizenship and immigration told the commissioner of the RCMP in September 1950, 'a review might advantageously be made of the bases upon which security clearance is withheld under the various categories as we now have them.' Quoted from L. Fortier to Commissioner S.T. Wood, 20 September 1950, NA, RG 26, vol. 151, file 3-32-11.

14 For External's position, see P.T. Molson to Consular Division, 7 October 1950, and G. de T. Glazebrook to Consular Division, 17 October 1950, NA, RG 25, vol. 3914, file 9408-40, part 2. See also A.D.P. Heeney to L. Fortier, 25 October 1950, NA, RG 76, vol. 856, file 555-3, part 1. For the RCMP's position, see minutes of Security Panel meeting held on 27 October 1950, NA, RG 2, vol. 189, file S-100-M, and memorandum by Superintendent G.B. McClellan, 16 November 1950, NA, RG 26, vol. 104, file 3-24-1, part 1. On the split between the Department of Citizenship and Immigration and its officers in the field, compare T.O.F. Herzer to Messrs N.J. Warnke and G.M. Berkefeld, 26 September 1950, NA, Canadian Lutheran World Relief Papers, reel H-1400, with P.W. Bird to Acting Director of Immigration Branch, 27 September 1950, NA, RG 76, vol. 31, file 682, part 6, reel C-4690.

15 L. Fortier to T.O.F. Herzer, 18 November 1950, NA, RG 26, vol. 127, file 3-33-

13, and P.M. Dwyer to Security Panel, 30 April 1952, NA, RG 2, vol. 232, file S-100-1-D, Security Panel Document SP-119. In its instructions to security officers in the field, the RCMP limited rejections to those members of the Party 'who [had] held an important rank or who were particularly active.' See 'Reasons for Rejection,' undated, appended to memorandum from W.H. Kelly to RCMP Special Branch, 21 January 1953, NA, RG 146, Public Document.

16 There were disagreements among the interested parties as to the best way to proceed with the review. See A.W. Baskerville to Commissioner of Immigration, 21 November 1950, and T.R. Burns to J.D. McFarlane, 27 December 1950, NA, RG 76, vol. 800, file 547–1, part 1; McFarlane to District Superintendents of Immigration, 3 January 1951, ibid., part 2. See also Director of Immigration to P.T. Baldwin, 1 December 1950, ibid., vol. 856, file 555-3, part 1, and T.O.F. Herzer to L. Fortier, 14 December 1950, NA, North American Baptist Immigration and Colonization Society Papers, series B3, vol. 5, file 58.

17 C.E.S. Smith to Deputy Minister of Citizenship and Immigration, 18 May 1951, NA, RG 76, vol. 957, file SF-S-1, part 2.

18 On the panel's inability to reach a consensus, see L. Fortier to E.F. Gaskell, 23 May 1951, and Acting Director of Immigration to file, 6 July 1951, ibid., part 2; Fortier to file, 9 July 1951, NA, RG 26, vol. 166, file 3-25-11, part 1. On the request to External Affairs, see G. de T. Glazebrook to R.G. Robertson, 29 November 1951, NA, RG 76, vol. 957, file SF-S-1, part 2.

19 For lists of Nazi offices that came under the major offender and offender categories, respectively, see Allied Control Council Directive No. 38, 14 October 1946, NARA, RG 260, series 3, file 3.

20 For the results of the embassy's inquiries and its subsequent recommendations, see G. de T. Glazebrook to R.G. Robertson, 29 November 1951, NA, RG 76, vol. 957, file SF-S-1, part 2.

21 Minutes of Security Panel meeting held on 15 May 1952, NA, RG 2, vol. 232, file S-100-1-M.

22 Michael H. Kater, *The Nazi Party: A Social Profile of Members and Leaders, 1919–1945* (Cambridge, MA, 1983), 158.

23 At its peak, the party's corps of functionaries was calculated at 373,000, and that was in 1934. By the end of 1942, the number had diminished to just over 242,000. See Orlow, *Nazi Party,* 93 and 408.

24 After Hitler's rise to power, the Nazi Party's membership rolls were opened to the German population at large only three times – from 30 January to 1 May 1933, 1 May 1937 to the end of 1938, and 1 May 1939 until 2 February 1942. The majority of memberships were taken out during the first two drives. See ibid., 48, 206, and 253.

25 Christopher R. Browning, *Ordinary Men: Reserve Police Battalion 101 and the Final Solution in Poland* (New York, 1993), 45–8.

26 On the rehabilitation of minor collaborators in Belgium, see minutes of meeting held at Belgian Ministry of Foreign Affairs on 12 October 1950, NA, RG 76, vol. 94, file 10159, part 3, reel C-4759; C.E.S. Smith to L. Fortier, 17 October 1950, NA, RG 26, vol. 124, file 3-35-5, part 1; and Officer in Charge (Brussels) to Chief of Admissions, 5 December 1956, NA, RG 76, vol. 800, file 547-1, part 3. On the amnesty bill passed by the Assemblé nationale in France, see message from External Affairs to Canadian Ambassador (Paris), 19 January 1950, and dispatch from Canadian Ambassador (Paris) to External Affairs, 8 February 1950, NA, RG 25, vol. 3751, file 7233-40, part 1; External Affairs to Canadian Embassy (Paris), 7 December 1950, NA, RG 76, vol. 1098, file SF-D-2, part 6.

27 On the rehabilitation of minor collaborators in Norway, see E.J. Garland to External Affairs, 20 September 1949, NA, RG 25, vol. 3674, file 5127-C-40, part 2. On the same phenomenon in the Netherlands, see P. Malone to C.E.S. Smith, 26 February 1957, ibid., vol. 8541, file 11687-40, part 3.1, and C.E.S. Smith to External Affairs, 6 March 1957, NA, RG 76, vol. 800, file 547-1, part 3. See also Visa Office (The Hague) to Chief of Operations, 30 October 1959, ibid., vol. 813, file 551-2, part 5.

28 See minutes of meeting held at Belgian Ministry of Foreign Affairs on 12 October 1950, NA, RG 76, vol. 94, file 10159, part 3, reel C-4759.

29 Beginning in 1951, the Mounties were required to submit all 'collaborator' cases to the immigration bureaucrats in Ottawa for review. They did so, but usually without providing details, thereby hampering the review process. See Commissioner L.H. Nicholson to L. Fortier, 14 May 1951, and Fortier to Nicholson, 29 November 1951, NA, RG 26, vol. 166, file 3-25-11, part 1; P.T. Baldwin to Deputy Minister of Citizenship and Immigration, 10 December 1951, and Fortier to Superintendent G.B. McClellan, 15 December 1951, NA, RG 76, vol. 801, file 547-5-551, part 1; McClellan to Fortier, 11 December 1951, ibid., vol. 957, file SF-S-1, part 2.

30 On the inability of the bureaucrats to reach a consensus, see L. Fortier to file, 3 May 1951, NA, RG 76, vol. 800, file 547-1, part 2; Fortier to file, 9 July 1951, NA, RG 26, vol. 104, file 3-24-1, part 1; Fortier to E.F. Gaskell, 23 May 1951, and G. de T. Glazebrook to R.G. Robertson, 29 November 1951, NA, RG 76, vol. 957, file SF-S-1, part 2.

31 G. de T. Glazebrook to R.G. Robertson, 29 November 1951, NA, RG 76, vol. 957, file SF-S-1, part 2.

32 For the discussions among immigration bureaucrats and the RCMP over the question of whether or not to relax the criteria for minor collaborators, see Superintendent G.B. McClellan to N.A. Robertson, 24 January 1952, P.T. Baldwin to Director of Immigration, 4 March 1952, and Acting Director of Immigration to

Deputy Minister of Citizenship and Immigration, 4 March 1952, ibid.; L. Fortier to Robertson, 19 March 1952, NA, RG 2, vol. 235, file S-100-5; and Chief of Operations to Director of Immigration, 12 May 1952, NA, RG 26, vol. 166, file 3-25-11, part 1.

33 See P.M. Dwyer to Security Panel, 30 April 1952, NA, RG 2, vol. 232, file S-100-1-D, Security Panel Document SP-119.

34 Minutes of Security Panel meeting held on 15 May 1952, ibid., file S-100-1-M. The RCMP's subsequent instructions to its officers in the field called for the rejection of collaborators 'where the investigating officer feels the circumstances of the collaboration are serious enough to warrant rejection.' See 'Reasons for Rejection,' undated, appended to memorandum from W.H. Kelly to RCMP Special Branch, 21 January 1953, NA, RG 146, Public Document.

35 See G.G. Crean to European Division, 23 October 1956, and T.P. Malone to C.E.S. Smith, 26 February 1957, RG 25, vol. 8541, file 11687-40, part 3.1.

36 Thus, I am registering my disagreement with Alti Rodal, who, in her report for the Commission of Inquiry on War Criminals, alleged that 'the relaxation of guidelines with regard to admission of ... Nazi collaborators provided open and legal entry to persons whose background made war criminality a distinct possibility.' See 'Nazi War Criminals in Canada: The Historical and Policy Setting from the 1940s to the Present' (Commission of Inquiry on War Criminals, Ottawa, 1986), 267. As the preceding discussion has demonstrated, only the most minor collaborators were being rehabilitated by western European governments, and even they were subjected to close scrutiny before being granted admission to Canada.

37 Guidelines for the screening of collaborators can be found in W. Hickman to P.T. Baldwin, 23 January 1952, and Baldwin to Deputy Minister of Citizenship and Immigration, 4 March 1952, NA, RG 76, vol. 957, file SF-S-1, part 2.

38 On the (re)launching of the CCCRR's campaign to get relief for former members of the Waffen-SS, see T.O.F. Herzer to Dr L. Meyer, 4 November 1950, NA, Canadian Lutheran World Relief Papers, reel H-1391; minutes of CCCRR meeting held on 7 December 1950, NA, North American Baptist Immigration and Colonization Society Papers, series A, vol. 1, file 13; and T.O.F. Herzer to L. Fortier, 14 December 1950, ibid., series B3, vol. 5, file 58.

39 T.O.F. Herzer to C.F. Klassen, 12 February 1951, NA, Canadian Lutheran World Relief Papers, reel H-1392, and minutes of CCCRR meeting held on 13 March 1951, ibid., reel H-1391.

40 Memorandum to Deputy Minister of Citizenship and Immigration, 19 March 1951, NA, RG 26, vol. 104, file 3-24-1, part 1.

41 On CCCRR's new evidence, see T.O.F. Herzer to W.E. Harris, 17 April 1951, NA, North American Baptist Immigration and Colonization Society Papers, series A,

vol. 1, file 14, and minutes of meeting of CLWR officers held on 24 April 1951, NA, Canadian Lutheran World Relief Papers, reel H-1390.

42 For External's position, see note from K.W. Burridge, undated, handwritten on memorandum from P.T. Baldwin to External Affairs, 7 May 1951, and European Division to Consular Division, 12 May 1951, NA, RG 25, vol. 3914, file 4908-40, part 2. For the position of the Department of Citizenship and Immigration, see L. Fortier to E.F. Gaskell, 23 May 1951, NA, RG 76, vol. 957, file SF-S-1, part 2. On the RCMP's change of heart, see C.E.S. Smith to Deputy Minister of Citizenship and Immigration, 22 June 1951, NA, 76, vol. 856, file 555-3, part 1.

43 For the Security Panel's recommendations, see Acting Director of Immigration to file, 6 July 1951, NA, RG 76, vol. 957, file SF-S-1, part 2; L. Fortier to file, 9 July 1951, NA, RG 26, vol. 166, file 3-25-11, part 1; Fortier to C.E.S. Smith, 9 July 1951, ibid., vol. 104, file 3-24-1, part 1; and W.E. Harris to T.O.F. Herzer, 11 July 1951, NA, North American Baptist Immigration and Colonization Papers, series B2, vol. 3, file 21. In her report for the Commission of Inquiry on War Criminals, Alti Rodal quoted from the instructions, then claimed that 'there was no mention of a cutoff dateline.' See 'Nazi War Criminals,' 252. This is clearly in error.

44 Bye is described as a colonel in various documents. This refers to his service as an intelligence officer in the Canadian Army during the Second World War, and is not indicative of an RCMP rank. Conversation with John Baker (External Affairs, retired), 22 October 1998.

45 E.J. Bye to G.A. Sincennes, 18 December 1951, NA, RG 76, vol. 856, file 555-3, part 1.

46 See E.J. Bye to A.C.A. Kaarsberg, 6 December 1949, ibid., vol. 655, file B41075, part 4, reel C-10592. For complaints about Bye's hard-nosed approach to screening, see H.W. Meybaum to T.O.F. Herzer, 12 February 1951, NA, Canadian Lutheran World Relief Papers, reel H-1393.

47 E.J. Bye to G.A. Sincennes, 18 December 1951, NA, RG 76, vol. 856, file 555-3, part 1.

48 From the chief RCMP security officer in Germany, the report went to the head of visa control in Europe, who, in turn, passed it on to RCMP Special Branch in Ottawa. Special Branch made the report available to the Security Panel. See Inspector W.H. Kelly to RCMP Special Branch, 12 March 1952, ibid., and Inspector K.W.N. Hall to E.F. Gaskell, 25 March 1952, NA, RG 2, vol. 235, file S-100-5.

49 Inspector W.H. Kelly to RCMP Special Branch, 12 March 1952, NA, RG 76, vol. 856, file 555-3, part 1.

50 For CCCRR's complaint and the government's response, see T.O.F. Herzer to L. Fortier, 19 April 1952, and Fortier to Director of Immigration, 21 April 1952, NA, RG 26, vol. 104, file 3-24-1, part 1.

51 On the request to Sincennes, see P.W. Bird to C.E.S. Smith, 21 April 1952, NA, RG

76, vol. 31, file 682, part 7, reel C-4690, and Smith to Deputy Minister, 26 April 1952, NA, RG 26, vol. 104, file 3-24-1, part 1.

52 G.A. Sincennes to Commissioner L.H. Nicholson, 29 April 1952, NA, RG 2, vol. 235, file S-100-5.

53 Ibid.

54 On Dwyer, see Reg Whitaker and Gary Marcuse, *Cold War Canada: The Making of a National Insecurity State, 1945–1957* (Toronto, 1994), 185; Whitaker, *Double Standard: The Secret History of Canadian Immigration* (Toronto, 1987), 118–19; J.L. Granatstein and David Stafford, *Spy Wars: Espionage and Canada from Gouzenko to Glasnost* (Toronto, 1990), 67; and Kim Philby, *My Silent War* (New York, 1968), 184–5 and 189.

55 For Dwyer's recommendations, see P.M. Dwyer to Security Panel, 30 April 1952, NA, RG 2, vol. 232, file S-100-1-D, Security Panel Document SP-119.

56 For the concerns of the Department of Citizenship and Immigration, see Chief of Operations to Director of Immigration, 12 May 1952, NA, RG 76, vol. 800, file 547-1, part 2.

57 For the Security Panel's decision, see minutes of Security Panel meeting held on 15 May 1952, NA, RG 2, vol. 232, file S-100-1-M, and L. Fortier to Director of Immigration, 30 May 1952, NA, RG 26, vol. 166, file 3-25-11, part 1.

58 Bonn's protest can be found in note from (German) Foreign Office to J.R. Robillard, 16 May 1953, NA, RG 76, vol. 856, file 555-3, part 1.

59 On the formation of the 7th SS, see Samuel Mitcham, *Hitler's Legions: The German Army Order of Battle, World War II* (London, 1985), 448–9. On its alleged crimes, see (Yugoslav) War Crimes Commission's 'Report on the Crimes Perpetrated by the 7th SS Division "Prinz Eugen" against the Peoples of Bosnia-Herzegovina between January 1943 and April 1945.' For a sanitized history of the division, see Otto Kumm, *'Vorwärts Prinz Eugen!' Geschichte der 7.SS-Freiwilligen-Division 'Prinz Eugen'* (Osnabrück, 1978).

60 For the personal histories of the two cases, see curriculum vitae of J. P—— and A. S——, undated [1953], NA, RG 76, vol. 801, file 547-5-551, part 1.

61 J.R. Robillard to Chief of Operations, 22 May 1953, ibid.

62 On the review of the two cases, see G.R. Benoit to Officer in Charge (Karlsruhe), 8 June 1953, ibid., vol. 856, file 555-3, part 1. On the results of the review, see C.E.S. Smith to P.M. Dwyer, 16 June 1953, ibid., vol. 978, file 5420-1-551. On the RCMP's change of heart with respect to P——, see J.R. Robillard to Director of Immigration, 30 October 1953, and Officer in Charge (Karlsruhe) to Chief District Superintendent (Toronto), 19 November 1953, ibid., vol. 801, file 547-5-551, part 1.

63 The reason for their opposition was that their officers in the field were rejecting all rank-and-file members of the Waffen-SS who had enlisted prior to 1 January 1944,

unless there were 'reasonable grounds' for believing that an individual had been conscripted or coerced into joining. See 'Reasons for Rejection,' undated, appended to memorandum from W.H. Kelly to RCMP Special Branch, 21 January 1953, NA, RG 146, Public Document.

64 In April 1953, cabinet approved a reorganization of the Security Panel. Henceforth, the panel would be comprised exclusively of the highest-ranking civil servants and would confine its deliberations to major policy matters. The more mundane details of security policy would be dealt with by a new body, the Security Sub-Panel, which comprised lower-ranking bureaucrats. On the reorganization, see J.W. Pickersgill to L. Fortier, 14 April 1953, NA, RG 26, vol. 153, file 1-18-14. See also Whitaker and Marcuse, *Cold War Canada*, 185.

65 On the referral of the matter to the Security Sub-Panel and the latter's response, see C.E.S. Smith to P.M. Dwyer, 16 June 1953 and Dwyer to Smith, 22 June 1953, NA, RG 76, vol. 978, file 5420-1-551.

66 See Howard Margolian, *Conduct Unbecoming: The Story of the Murder of Canadian Prisoners of War in Normandy* (Toronto, 1998), 8–9.

67 Examination of William H. Kelly, Deschenes Commission, NA, Yuzyk Papers, vol. 63, file/vol. 7, pp. 908–9.

68 On the continuation of the 1 January 1943 cut-off date and conscription requirement for non-German former members of the Waffen-SS, see J.R. Robillard to Chief of Operations, 23 March 1955, NA, RG 76, vol. 801, file 547-5-551, part 1, and Robillard to C.S.A. Ritchie, 22 April 1955, NA, RG 26, vol. 127, file 3-33-13. On the continuation of the 1 January 1944 cut-off date for German nationals, see Robillard to Ritchie, 7 June 1955, NA, RG 76, vol. 978, file 5420-1-551. On attempts by CCCRR to have the cut-off date changed, see Appendix 'A,' undated, appended to memorandum from T.O.F. Herzer to L. Fortier, 29 January 1953, NA, North American Baptist Immigration and Colonization Society Papers, series B3, vol. 5, file 59. On Ottawa's intransigence in this regard, see Reverend C.L. Monk to Reverend S.F. Friedrichson, 21 April 1955, NA, Canadian Lutheran World Relief Papers, reel H-1392.

69 For the government's 1955 immigration targets, see minutes of cabinet meeting held on 16 December 1954, NA, RG 2, vol. 2656. On the extent of the shortfall, see Department of Manpower and Immigration, *Highlights from the Green Paper on Immigration and Population* (Ottawa, 1975), 42.

70 Buscher, *War Crimes*, 71.

71 On the policies of other countries toward former members of the Waffen-SS, see Canadian Embassy (Bonn) to External Affairs, 26 August 1955, NA, RG 25, vol. 4385, file 11687-40, part 2.

72 Minutes of meeting held at Canadian Government Immigration Mission (Karlsruhe) on 4 February 1955, reproduced, in part, in examination of George

O'Leary, Deschenes Commission, NA, Yuzyk Papers, vol. 63, file/vol. 5, pp. 711–12. Robillard repeated his sentiments to his superiors in Ottawa and to Canada's ambassador in Bonn. See J.R. Robillard to Chief of Operations, 23 March 1955, NA, RG 76, vol. 801, file 547-5-551, part 1, and Robillard to C.S.A. Ritchie, 22 April 1955, NA, RG 26, vol. 127, file 3-33-13.

73 For the RCMP's expression of support for Robillard's suggestion, see Inspector G.H. Ashley to RCMP Special Branch, 9 March 1955, NA, RG 26, vol. 167, file 3-25-11-13.

74 C.S.A. Ritchie to L. Fortier, 20 May 1955, NA, RG 76, vol. 957, file SF-S-1, part 3.

75 See C.E.S. Smith to Deputy Minister of Citizenship and Immigration, 30 May 1955, NA, RG 26, vol. 127, file 3-33-13.

76 J.R. Robillard to C.S.A. Ritchie, 7 June 1955, NA, RG 76, vol. 978, file 5420-1-551.

77 The results of the meeting of the Security Sub-Panel are reported in Commissioner L.H. Nicholson to L. Fortier, 28 June 1955, ibid., vol. 957, file SF-S-1, part 3.

78 On the lack of interest by the German government, see R.A.D. Ford to Canadian Embassy (Bonn), 22 July 1955, and Canadian Embassy (Bonn) to External Affairs, 26 August 1955, NA, RG 25, vol. 4385, file 11687-40, part 2.

79 J.A. Dougan to G.G. Crean, 5 October 1955, Crean to External Affairs, 14 October 1955, G.H. Southam to External Affairs, 20 December 1955, and Crean to External Affairs, 29 December 1955, ibid.

80 On the sub-panel's decision, see L. Fortier to Commissioner L.H. Nicholson, 9 December 1955, NA, RG 76, vol. 957, file SF-S-1, part 3; C.E.S. Smith to External Affairs, 5 January 1956, NA, RG 25, vol. 4385, file 11687-40, part 2; Head of Canadian Government Immigration Mission (Karlsruhe) to Chief of Operations, 16 January 1956, NA, RG 76, vol. 821, file 552-1-551, part 1; Acting Deputy Minister of Citizenship and Immigration to Minister of Citizenship and Immigration, 2 February 1956, ibid., vol. 957, file SF-S-1, part 3; and J.R. Robillard to Fortier, 9 February 1956, ibid., vol. 859, file 555-49, part 1. On its approval by the Minister of Citizenship and Immigration, see examination of George O'Leary, Deschenes Commission, NA, Yuzyk Papers, vol. 63, file/vol. 6, p. 722.

81 For example, see memorandum from Acting Minister of Citizenship and Immigration, 2 April 1959, appended to memorandum from D.F. Wall to Security Panel, 8 April 1959, RG 25, vol. 5474, file 11687-B-40, part 1, Security Panel Document SP-198, and memorandum from R.L. Leeson to Chief of Operations, 30 October 1959, NA, RG 76, vol. 813, file 551-2, part 5.

82 See Allied Control Council Directive No. 38, 14 October 1946, NARA, RG 260, series 3, file 3.

83 C.E.S. Smith to Commissioner L.H. Nicholson, 24 February 1956, NA, RG 26, vol. 166, file 3-25-11, part 2.

84 L. Fortier to Commissioner L.H. Nicholson, 9 December 1955, and Acting Deputy

Minister of Citizenship and Immigration to Minister of Citizenship and Immigration, 2 February 1956, NA. RG 76, vol. 957, file SF-S-1, part 3; Head of Canadian Government Immigration Mission (Karlsruhe) to Chief of Operations, 16 January 1956, ibid., vol. 821, file 552-1-551, part 1.

85 This was in keeping with Allied directives. See Allied Control Council Directive No. 38, 14 October 1946, NARA, RG 260, series 3, file 3.

86 For the case described above, see (RCMP) Rejection Report, 10 December 1957, G.M. Bailey to Director of Security and Intelligence, 20 March 1963, and Inspector J.E.M. Barrette to Chief Visa Control Officer, 5 April 1963, NA, RG 146, Public Documents.

87 On the problem of the East German refugees and Canada's response, see Canadian Embassy (Bonn) to External Affairs, 2, 4, and 6 February 1953, L.D. Wilgress to Minister, 3 February and 12 March 1953, L. Fortier to Minister of Citizenship and Immigration, 9 February 1953, P.T. Baldwin to External Affairs, 7 March 1953, and External Affairs to Canadian Embassy (Bonn), 10 March 1953, NA, RG 25, vol. 6342, file 939-F-1-40, part 1. See also External Affairs to Ministers of Justice and Citizenship and Immigration, 6 February 1953, J.R. Robillard to Chief of Operations, 6 February 1953, Commissioner L.H. Nicholson to Fortier, 11 March 1953, and Commissioner Nicholson to C.S.A. Ritchie, 4 April 1953, NA, RG 26, vol. 127, file 3-33-13; minutes of cabinet meeting held on 6 February 1953, NA, RG 2, vol. 2652, file 07/01/53–26/02/53; C.M. Anderson to Reverend C.L. Monk, 5 March 1953, NA, North American Baptist Immigration and Colonization Society Papers, series B1, vol. 3, file 4, and W. Sturhahn to G.M. Berkefeld, 13 March 1953, ibid., series B3, vol. 5, file 59.

88 For Canada's response to the Hungarian refugee crisis, see minutes of cabinet meetings held on 23 and 28 November and 19 December 1956, NA, RG 2, vol. 5775, file 05/11/56–19/12/56; minutes of cabinet meetings held on 17 and 31 January 1957, ibid., vol. 1892, files 03/01/57–19/03/57; minutes of cabinet meeting held on 26 March 1957, ibid., file 26/03/57–24/06/57; and minutes of cabinet meeting held on 11 July 1957, ibid., vol. 1893, file 09/07/57–07/08/57. See also Robert H. Keyserlingk, ed., *Breaking Ground: The 1956 Hungarian Refugee Movement to Canada* (Toronto, 1993).

89 On the RCMP's attempts to screen the East German refugees, see L. Fortier to Minister of Citizenship and Immigration, 8 March 1955, RG 26, vol. 127, file 3-33-13.

9: Undiplomatic Passports

1 Unlike the rest of the book, much of this chapter is based on secondary sources. Normally, that would not be a problem. However, the authors cited herein often

relied on unattributed interviews and documents. Accordingly, I am not always in a position to vouch for the accuracy of their work. Wherever possible, therefore, I have tried to limit my reliance on such sources to providing general historical background.

2 Christopher Simpson, *Blowback: America's Recruitment of Nazis and Its Effects on the Cold War* (New York, 1988), 176–7, and Mark Aarons and John Loftus, *Ratlines: How the Vatican's Nazi Networks Betrayed Western Intelligence to the Soviets* (London, 1991), 205–6.

3 John Loftus, *The Belarus Secret: The Nazi Connection in America* (New York, 1982), 8–11.

4 For biographical material on Gehlen, see ibid., 10, and Peter Grose, *Gentleman Spy: The Life of Allen Dulles* (Boston, 1994), 312–13.

5 Grose, *Gentleman Spy*, 314.

6 Loftus, *Belarus*, 11, and Loftus and Mark Aarons, *The Secret War against the Jews: How Western Espionage Betrayed the Jewish People* (New York, 1994), 151.

7 Simpson, *Blowback*, 199 and 209–10.

8 On CIC's involvement in the Barbie case, see Alan A. Ryan, Jr, *Klaus Barbie and the United States Government: The Report, with Documentary Appendix, to the Attorney General of the United States* (Washington, 1983), 71.

9 On CIC's undeserved reputation as an accomplice in Nazi-smuggling, see Loftus and Aarons, *Secret War*, 112–17.

10 On Philby's prewar and wartime activities, see ibid., 23–4, 37, 52, and 107–8.

11 On Philby's postwar activities, see Kim Philby, *My Silent War* (New York, 1968), 142–6, and Aarons and Loftus, *Ratlines*, 217–20.

12 Loftus, *Belarus*, x–xi, and Loftus and Aarons, *Secret War*, 214.

13 On the Presidential Escapee Program and Canada's participation therein, see Canadian Embassy (Athens) to External Affairs, 11 February 1953, G.L. Warren to C.E.S. Smith, 12 February 1953, and L. Fortier to Minister of Citizenship and Immigration, 23 February 1953, NA, RG 26, vol. 110, file 3-24-11; J.R. Robillard to all visa officers, 11 June 1953, NA, RG 76, vol. 866, file 555-55.

14 Reg Whitaker, *Double Standard: The Secret History of Canadian Immigration* (Toronto, 1987), 118–19. Admittedly, the evidence is weak. In support of his assertion, Whitaker stated that the information regarding Dwyer's role in facilitating the admission of undesirables came from 'strictly confidential' sources.

15 J.L. Granatstein and David Stafford, *Spy Wars: Espionage and Canada from Gouzenko to Glasnost* (Toronto, 1990), 67.

16 Philby, *Silent War*, 189.

17 The extent to which Canadian security was compromised by USAREUR remains a mystery. Just as Kelly was about to go into detail, he was cut off by commission counsel on the grounds that publication of his testimony could harm the national

interest. The rest of his evidence was given in camera, and remains classified to this day. On the USAREUR ratline, see examination of William H. Kelly, Deschenes Commission, NA, P. Yuzyk Papers, vol. 63, file/vol. 7, pp. 922–4, and Alti Rodal, 'Nazi War Criminals in Canada: The Historical and Policy Setting from the 1940s to the Present' (Commission of Inquiry on War Criminals, Ottawa, 1986), 455–8. In view of the fact that Kelly's testimony was given in camera, it is not surprising that large portions of Rodal's discussion of USAREUR were excised prior to the release of her report under the Access to Information Act.

18 On Durcansky's coup attempt and Philby's manipulations, see Loftus and Aarons, *Ratlines*, 217–19.

19 On Philby's failure to get Durcansky into the United States, see ibid., 220–1.

20 On Durcansky's acquisition of a temporary Canadian visa, see D.B. Hicks to Director of Immigration, 15 December 1950, NA, RG 25, vol. 3776, file 7899-40, part 1.

21 On the blunders that permitted Durcansky to gain admission to Canada, see (British) Foreign Office to S.F. Rae, 9 December 1950, High Commissioner to External Affairs, 13 December 1950, and D.B. Hicks to High Commission, 2 February 1951, ibid., vol. 2123, file AR 1231/1.

22 For Durcansky's entreaties in this regard, see Dr F. Durcansky to W.L. Mackenzie King, 10 September 1946, and Durcansky and Dr S. Polakovic to L.S. St Laurent, 23 September 1947, ibid., vol. 3776, file 7899-40, part 1.

23 Loftus and Aarons, *Ratlines*, 221–2. See also Joseph M. Kirschbaum, *Slovaks in Canada* (Toronto, 1967), 217–18 n103.

24 For a brief sketch of Sidor's wartime career, see OSS report, 15 December 1944, NA, H.L. Keenleyside Papers, vol. 19, file Immigration 1938–85.

25 Loftus and Aarons, *Ratlines*, 335 n72.

26 Quoted from letter from G. Brandt to A.G. Klein, 13 September 1949, NA, Keenleyside Papers, vol. 19, file Immigration 1938–85.

27 Apostolic Delegate to Prime Minister St Laurent, 2 August 1949, ibid.

28 The prime minister's intervention on Sidor's behalf can be found in L.S. St Laurent to H.L. Keenleyside, 24 October 1949, Keenleyside to Prime Minister, 26 and 28 October 1949, St Laurent to Keenleyside, 27 October 1949, and Keenleyside to Prime Minister, 8 November 1949, ibid.

29 Draft memorandum by Commissioner S.T. Wood, undated [November 1949], ibid.

30 Quoted from PC 5765, 15 November 1949, NA, RG 2, vol. 2059, file 4053G.

31 The following narrative was compiled from documents entered as evidence at Grujicic's trial. See Corporal W.D. Fast to RCMP Special Section (Toronto), 16 February 1949, Inspector J. Leopold to Director of Criminal Investigation, 8 March 1949, Inspector K. Shakespeare to RCMP Commissioner, 17 August 1950, Marko Vrkljrsn to S. Garson, undated [1951], Milow Grabic to S. Garson, 21 February 1951, Commissioner S.T. Wood to Garson, 3 March 1951, C.E.S.

Smith to RCMP Special Branch, 22 March 1951, P.T. Baldwin to RCMP Special Branch, 14 May and 15 June 1951, Inspector Leopold to Director of Immigration, 15 May and 9 June 1951, Marko Jankovic's application for Canadian citizenship, 21 May 1957, Corporal L.J. Swift to Inspector L.R. Parent, 29 June 1961, Inspector Parent to Superintendent M.T. Laberge, 31 October 1961, note by Corporal Swift, 5 July 1961, and Assistant Commissioner W.L. Higgitt to Immigration Branch, 10 April 1969, Ruling Before the Honourable Mr Justice J. Donnelly, Ontario Court in Windsor, General Division, 12 September 1994, Schedules 1–15.

Conclusions

1 Neo-Nazis were another matter. For evidence that Canadian immigration authorities regarded them as a security threat, see minutes of Security Sub-Panel meeting held on 21 September 1953, NA, RG 26, vol. 153, file 1-18-14, and Canadian Embassy (Madrid) to External Affairs, 3 May 1957, NA, RG 25, vol. 8541, file 11687-40, part 3.1.
2 Mackenzie King diary, entry for 1 May 1947, NA, W.L.M. King Papers, series J13, microfiche no. 241, p. 396.
3 The risk was stated succinctly by the head of RCMP Special Branch after a fact-finding tour of Canadian immigration offices in Europe. According to Superintendent G.B. McClellan, 'mass immigration and good security just cannot go side by side. You can have mass immigration with mediocre security, or good security and a trickle of immigration.' Quoted from Superintendent G.B. McClellan to RCMP Commissioner, undated [1951], Documents in Evidence in the Matter of Revocation of Citizenship between the Minister of Citizenship and Immigration and Wasily Bogutin.

Selected List of Primary Sources

Canada

Archives of Ontario

G.R.B. Panchuk Papers (F 1417)

National Archives of Canada

L. Beaudry Papers (MG 30 E 151)
Canadian Baltic Immigration Aid Society Papers (MG 28 V 99)
Canadian Council of Churches Papers (MG 28 I 327)
Canadian Lutheran World Relief Papers (MG 28 V 120)
Canadian National Committee on Refugees Papers (MG 28 V 43)
Canadian National Railways Records (RG 30)
Canadian Security and Intelligence Service Records (RG 146)
K. von Cardinal Papers (MG 31 H 39)
B. Claxton Papers (MG 32 B 5)
Department of Citizenship and Immigration Records (RG 26)
Department of External Affairs Records (RG 25)
Department of Labour Records (RG 27)
Department of National Defence Records (RG 24)
Department of National Health and Welfare Records (RG 29)
Dominions Office and Commonwealth Relations Office Records (MG 42 DO 35)
R. England Papers (MG 30 C 181)
R. Funke Papers (MG 31 B 57)
G.V. Haythorne Papers (MG 31 E 23)
T.O.F. Herzer Papers (MG 30 C 108)

C.D. Howe Papers (MG 27 III B 20)
Immigration Branch Records (RG 76)
Jewish Labour Committee of Canada Papers (MG 28 V 75)
V.J. Kaye Papers (MG 31 D 69)
H.L. Keenleyside Papers (MG 31 E 102)
W.L.M. King Papers (MG 26 J)
C.J. Mackenzie Papers (MG 30 B 122)
D. Matas Papers (MG 31 E 109)
North American Baptist Immigration and Colonization Society Papers (MG 28 V 18)
E. Ostry Papers (MG 30 C 184)
L.B. Pearson Papers (MG 26 N)
M. Pope Papers (MG 27 III F 4)
Privy Council Office Records (RG 2)
Public Service Commission Records (RG 32)
R.G. Robertson Papers (MG 31 E 87)
A. Roebuck Papers (MG 30 C 68)
Royal Commission Records (RG 33)
L.S. St Laurent Papers (MG 26 L)
Secretary of State Records (RG 6)
P. Yuzyk Papers (MG 32 C 67)

United States

National Archives and Records Administration

Records of U.S. Occupation Headquarters, World War II (RG 260)
U.S. National Archives Collection of Foreign Records Seized (RG 242)

France

Archives nationales

International Refugee Organization Records

Index